PENNY CAPITALISM
A GUATEMALAN INDIAN ECONOMY

by

SOL TAX

OCTAGON BOOKS

A DIVISION OF FARRAR, STRAUS AND GIROUX

New York   1972

First published as Smithsonian Institution Institute of Social Anthropology
Publication No. 16. Washington: U. S. Government Printing Office, 1953

Reprinted 1972
by special arrangement with Sol Tax

OCTAGON BOOKS
A DIVISION OF FARRAR, STRAUS & GIROUX, INC.
19 Union Square West
New York, N. Y. 10003

LIBRARY OF CONGRESS CATALOG CARD NUMBER: 78-159254

ISBN 0-374-97785-2

Printed in U.S.A. by
NOBLE OFFSET PRINTERS, INC.
New York, N.Y. 10003

TO
ALFRED VINCENT KIDDER
WITH
AFFECTION, RESPECT, AND GRATITUDE

CONTENTS

ILLUSTRATIONS

MAPS

CHARTS

TABLES

PREFACE

The title of this book is intended to be catchy, but it should also convey in two words what the book describes: a society which is "capitalist" on a microscopic scale. There are no machines, no factories, no co-ops or corporations. Every man is his own firm and works ruggedly for himself. Money there is, in small denominations; trade there is, with what men carry on their backs; free entrepreneurs, the impersonal market place, competition—these are in the rural economy. But commerce is without credit, as production is without machines. It turns out that the difference between a poor people and a rich one is the difference between the hand and the machine, between money and credit, between the merchant and the firm; and that all these are differences between the "modern" economy and the primitive "underdeveloped" ones.

In laying bare the bones of an underdeveloped economy, this study hopes first to contribute to the understanding of what such an economy looks like. The community dealt with has only 800 people (although the regional economy of which it is part has a thousand times more); it is an insignificant place in a rural area which Guatemala thinks of as its backwoods. But it is just the "backwoods" which must be explored, for an economically undeveloped nation is undeveloped to the degree that it has backwoods. The community which this book describes is in that way typical of the thousands which must be changed.

From place to place in the world, on the other hand, such communities are very different. Each continent and each region has its own kinds, and in the end, of course, every one is unique. The culture of Mexico and Guatemala is very different from that of Pakistan or Kenya. The first advice one offers the administrator of a program is to know the place and the people and the character of the culture. In this instance a striking peculiarity is the combination of a childish, magical, or "primitive" world view with institutions reminiscent in microcosm of the Great Society. In most "primitive" societies about which anthropologists write, people behave in our terms irrationally, since they try by devices strange to us to maximize different, hence curious, satisfactions. This happens not to be the case in the part of Guatemala about which I write, where the social institutions and cosmology, strange as they may be to us, are as separated from the processes of making a living as are our own. For this reason the institutions need concern us but little in a description of the economy; for this reason also it is possible to use the same terms to describe their economy that are used to describe our own.

There is no economic theory in this book. I am simply describing the way a people live, picking out those elements to describe that I understand fit under the rubric of "economy." It might be argued that by selection of the same things to describe that economists select in writing about our society, I prejudge the similarity of Panajachel economy to our own. This really says that I am asking about Panajachel some of the same questions that are asked by economists about our own society. This is true. But the significant thing is that I am able to answer the questions; and that is because the Panajachel economy is like ours. If I tried to ask about a tribe of Australian aborigines what is its balance of payments, I should soon have to reinterpret the question so drastically that it would not be the same.

Although I purpose to describe the economy of Panajachel, and at least by inference to show why the material level of life is low, no solution is offered. A very good reason for this is that while the problem has its consequences locally, its cure involves the whole region, the whole of the larger society, and, indeed, much of the world. I have studied a cell in an organism, an example of many that are like it; but the organism consists of different kinds of cells in complex interrelation, and studies of the larger whole are essential to planning its solution. For such studies, the theory, methods, and techniques of disciplines other than anthropology are needed. I once asked Jean Learned, an economist who studied these materials on Panajachel, what she as an economist would have done differently. The considered reply was unexpected to me, yet wholly obvious. As an economist she would not have spent years in a community of 800 people without records of prices and the like. Panajachel is a place for the skills of (say) an anthropologist, not an economist. Conversely, an anthropologist is not trained to cope with the problems of a nation in the world community.

Let me not be understood to minimize the importance of study at the local level, or of the usefulness of the anthropological (cultural) point of view at all levels. But this *is* a study at the local level, and essential as it may be to understanding the whole, it is the study by an anthropologist of an anthropologically oriented problem. The economist will learn from it much about the economy of a community in Guatemala. He will also learn something about anthropologists (as he can learn more from Firth and Herskovits and others) and the way one anthropologist studies a place like Panajachel. I do not expect that he will learn any economics. Nor do I suppose my colleagues in anthropology will learn economics from me. What I offer is a conception of how one studies a primitive money economy. My own work falls short of an ideal because I had no model. Here is a pattern from which others may depart.

This book has been long in coming. A first short draft was written during the winter of 1938–39. I was encouraged by Dr. W. F. Ogburn to extend this to a full study. It was completed in June of 1943, when Dr. Ogburn was also kind enough to write a foreword. Delay of publication, first because of the war and then by desire to revise the manuscript, was fortunate, both because in the intervening years I learned much from colleagues at the University, and because the long delay permitted a fresh approach to the manuscript. I think it does not matter that the economy is described as of a period 10 years past (and indeed from a 1936 base) because if it is interesting it should be as representative of a type, relatively independent of time and place.

My original field notes on Panajachel have been microfilmed and as part of a series are available in many libraries, well enough indexed so that I think a patient reader can use them in connection with this volume. This is one of three books which I hope to write from these materials; a second describes the world view of the Indians; the third, their social institutions. Meanwhile the materials on these subjects may be studied in their original form. Whoever looks at them will note that my wife and I (later with our young daughter) lived in Panajachel on and off from the autumn of 1935 to the spring of 1941, and that Juan de Dios Rosales, an educated Panajacheleño who was a school teacher in 1936 and who became my assistant (and eventually an anthropologist in his own right) collected a great deal of the data in the earlier years. It was not until the last field season (1940–41), however, that I systematically collected much of the essential data on the economy. By then I had done much work on this book and had begun to know what I was looking for.

From 1934 to 1946 I was on the staff of the Carnegie Institution of Washington's Division of Historical Research. This work was done as part of the Division's grand plan for studying various aspects of Mayan Indian culture. How much I owe to its recently retired director, Dr. A. V. Kidder, for his patience and encouragement, I attempt to say by dedicating this book to him. From my colleague and teacher, Robert Redfield, with whom I have worked so closely both at home and in the field, I have received much more than I can acknowledge. I recall with pleasure the friends in Guatemala who helped us, and especially our Indian friends, whom we still miss; and jump without difficulty to my colleagues at the University of Chicago, who through the years teach me humility. I have said that my wife shared with me the experience in Guatemala; this book is hers, too.

SOL TAX.

THE UNIVERSITY OF CHICAGO,
May 1, 1951.

THE PLACE AND THE PEOPLE

LOCATION

Panajachel is one of three hundred fifty-odd *municipios* into which the Republic of Guatemala is divided. These *municipios*, not unlike our townships, are political subdivisions, but in the region where Panajachel is located they are also important cultural and economic units (Tax, 1937). Although they have a common basis, the Indians of each *municipio* differ in language and general culture and, since there is a tendency toward marriage within the *municipio*, in surnames and physical appearance. Not the least significant of the differences among *municipios* is in economic specialization, which may be partly, but only partly, accounted for by local variations of altitude and terrain. Since such specialization in production leads to trade, and since no *municipio* is economically self-sufficient, it is not possible to limit such a discussion as this to Panajachel (or any other *municipio*) alone; nor can it be assumed that any *municipio* is "typical" and its economy representative of all.

Panajachel is 1 of 11 *municipios* (map 1) whose lands form the circumference of Lake Atitlán which lies about 45 miles west of Guatemala City. The lake, at an altitude of some 5,100 feet, occupies an immense *caldera* formed by volcanic crustal collapse; it has been partially dammed also by volcanic growth on the south shore (McBryde, 1933, pp. 63–64; 1947). The volcanoes of Tolimán and San Pedro start abruptly from the southern shore; cliffs rise precipitously and almost uninterruptedly from the edge of the water to heights

of 1,000 feet and more. Consequently there are few natural town sites on the shore itself and only a small number even near the lake. Certain sites, therefore, assume commercial importance. The only good outlets to the rich coastal regions in the south are on either side of the volcano of Tolimán, where the ground levels off before meeting the lake, and here are found the towns of San Lucas and Atitlán, perhaps the most prosperous in this region. On the north shore two streams that flow into the lake have cut wide enough valleys, and built sufficiently broad deltas, to form natural town sites. One of these is the Panajachel River, on the banks of which is situated the town of Panajachel; the other is the Quixcap, which forms the delta called Jaibal, the site (until it was disastrously flooded three centuries ago (Vázquez, 1937, p. 171) of San Jorge, now situated far up on the cliff above. Both Panajachel and Jaibal are busy ports for the water traffic across the lake. The former, however, is much more important, because a town is nearby, because the main highway from the capital to the west passes through it, and because gasoline launches as well as canoes may be accommodated. A glance at map 1 will make this clear.

The lake towns as a group are in a particularly strategic position in this part of Guatemala, lying as they do between the warm lowlands and the cold highlands. The great region of tropical agriculture (coffee, bananas, cotton) of the Pacific slope is in a belt lying at altitudes of from three to five thousand feet. In the portion of this belt lying just south of the lake are to be found great

1

plantations and the important commercial towns of Mazatenango, Chicacao, and Patulul, whose markets are centers for distribution not only of the crops of the plantations, but of products (such as cattle, fish, and salt) coming from the coastal plain. The region above the lake, on the other hand, is that of temperate agriculture (wheat, wool, potatoes, etc.). This is the typical "Indian country," of small landholdings and of local specializations in crops and manufactures (pottery, baskets, rope, leather goods, textiles), and here such towns as Sololá and Tecpán are vital market centers for all the goods produced in the highlands. The produce of the lowlands and of the highlands is transported on the backs of Indians and exchanged in the market towns of both regions. One of the most used routes between the two is via Lake Atitlán, and the stream of Indian merchants skirting or crossing the lake is continuous. Many of them are from the lake towns themselves, especially from Atitlán; a large proportion pass through Panajachel, with which San Lucas and Atitlán share first importance in the north-south trade routes.

Panajachel, more than other lake towns, occupies a place of importance on an east-west trading axis as well. There is considerable commerce between communities such as Quezaltenango and Totonicapán in the western highlands and Guatemala City to the east. One of the two main highways passes through Panajachel, and Indians afoot with their freight, or in trucks, and no little Ladino passenger travel in busses and private cars, keep the road busy. Most of the traffic simply passes through, but some of the travelers make Panajachel an overnight stop and of course a portion of the freight has its origin or its terminus here. Panajachel is the only lake town that is thus on a major cross roads.

Nevertheless, Panajachel is commercially far less important than Sololá, some 5 miles (by road) to the north and some 1,800 feet above it. Sololá is not only the capital of the department to which all the lake towns, and some others, belong, but it has a population of 3,750 (1940)—mostly Ladinos—and is the site of one of the largest markets in the entire region (McBryde, 1933). Almost all merchants passing through Panajachel pass also through Sololá, and a large part of Panajachel business is actually transacted in Sololá. Besides, Sololá is the goal of many merchants from the north and west, and from the towns on the west shore of the lake, who never visit Panajachel at all.

GEOGRAPHY

Aside from a small alluvial area which is the site of the main portion of the plantation "San Buenaventura," the *municipio* of Panajachel is conveniently divisible into what may be called the "delta" and the "hill" (map 2). The delta is that of the Panajachel River. It is roughly triangular, the tip to the north, the base bordering the lake, and is bisected by the river. The sides of the delta are sharply defined by rocky hills which rise abruptly; the hillsides look down upon the delta area, and confine it. The delta is almost flat, sloping only slightly from north to south, a lush region of coffee groves and green vegetable gardens, all watered by an intricate network of ditches having their source in the river. The rough hills are cultivated only in patches, and cattle occasionally graze on them. Nobody lives on the hillsides, but all the length and breadth of the delta is dotted with houses. The hills are mysterious and dangerous, in native belief, inhabited by supernatural beings. In them strange things happen, especially at night and when one is alone. The hills are called the *monte*, best translated "wilds" (as well as "country"); the whole of the delta is called the *pueblo* or town.

The *monte*, of course, extends beyond the hillsides that border the town, both within and without the *municipio* of Panajachel; most of the land traversed from town to town is *monte*. But virtually all the *monte* lands owned or tilled by the Indians of Panajachel are on the hillsides overlooking the delta and the lake;[1] it is to them that reference will be made in this paper when the term "hill land" is used. The smaller delta, the site of San Buenaventura, is also part of the *municipio* of Panajachel; the plantation, which includes the whole delta and the hills above it, is owned by one family, and its Indian inhabitants are laborers brought from other communities. This, as well as several other plantations in the northern *monte* of the *municipio*, is not considered in the present study. What will concern us here is the area of the delta of the Panajachel River and its bordering hills.

---

[1] With the exception of a few pieces of land in the *municipios* of Santa Catarina and San Antonio Palapo and in San Jorge.

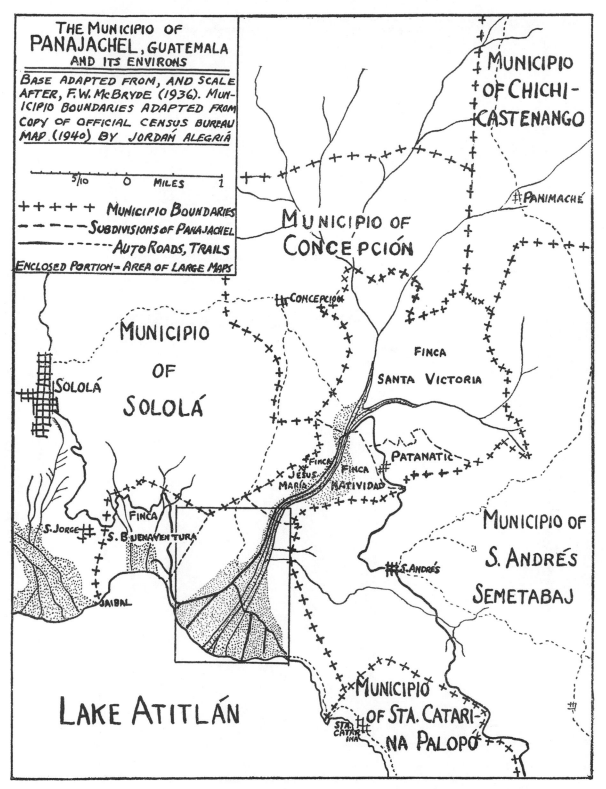

THE MUNICIPIO OF
PANAJACHEL, GUATEMALA
AND ITS ENVIRONS

BASE ADAPTED FROM, AND SCALE
AFTER, F.W. McBRYDE (1936). MUN-
ICIPIO BOUNDARIES ADAPTED FROM
COPY OF OFFICIAL CENSUS BUREAU
MAP (1940) BY JORDÁN ALEGRÍA

5/10   0   MILES   1

+ + + +   MUNICIPIO BOUNDARIES
– – – –   SUBDIVISIONS OF PANAJACHEL
– – – –   AUTO ROADS, TRAILS
ENCLOSED PORTION = AREA OF LARGE MAPS

MUNICIPIO
OF
SOLOLÁ

SOLOLÁ

MUNICIPIO
OF CHICHI-
CASTENANGO

PANIMACHÉ

MUNICIPIO OF
CONCEPCIÓN

CONCEPCION

FINCA
SANTA VICTORIA

FINCA
JESÚS
MARÍA

FINCA
NATIVIDAD

PATANATIC

S. JORGE

FINCA
S. BUENAVENTURA

S. ANDRÉS

MUNICIPIO OF
S. ANDRÉS
SEMETABAJ

JAIBAL

LAKE ATITLÁN

STA.
CATAR-
INA

MUNICIPIO
OF STA. CATARI-
NA PALOPÓ

MAP 2.—The *municipio* of Panajachel (scale=1:3,580).

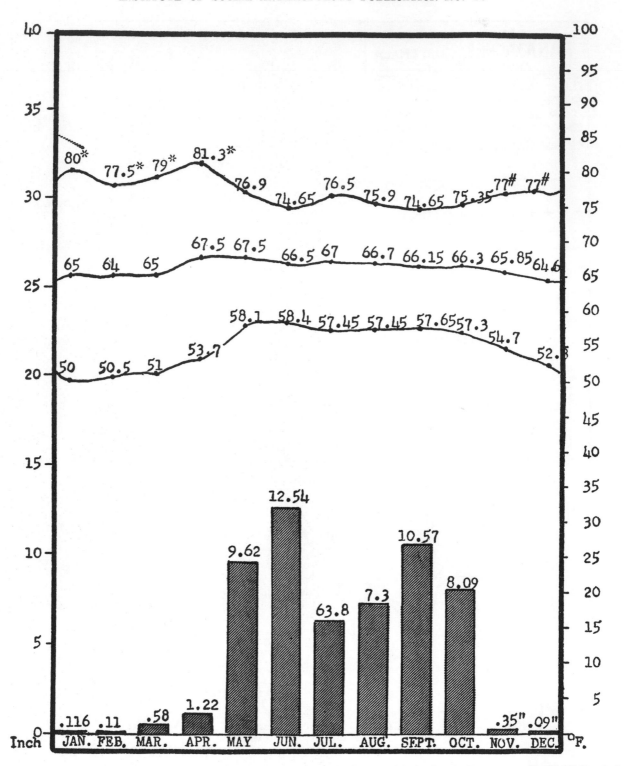

CHART 1.—Temperature and precipitation in Panajachel, 1932–36.   (Source: Mario García S., courtesy F. W. McBryde.)
*=only 1933 and 1935; #=only 1933, 1934, and 1935; and ″=only 1932, 1933, 1934, and 1935.

The Panajachel delta has an altitude above sea level of from 5,100 feet (the altitude of the lake) to about 5,200 feet. The climate is mild, the temperature rarely falling below 50° F. or rising above 80°. The mean temperature is remarkably constant throughout the year, varying only between 64° and 67.5° F. The diurnal range varies, however, with the wet and dry seasons, from about 30° in January to about 16° in June. The afternoon temperatures during the dry season are considerably warmer than during the rainy season. There is some rain in the dry season, and there are many days without rain in the rainy season; but it may be said that from the beginning of May to the end of October it rains heavily for a few hours each day, and during the remainder of the year it almost never rains.

In the rainy season outside work is often impossible for days at a time, and the Indians save many inside jobs for these months. Sickness is then much more prevalent. It is difficult to go to market and to earn wages, just when the basic breadstuff, maize, is scarcest and must be bought at high prices. The river is high and impossible to cross sometimes for days, and there is always the danger of its overrunning and destroying one's land and house.

The river, from which flow almost all the irrigation ditches, is a narrow stream in the dry season; but when it rains in the hills above, it becomes a raging brown torrent carrying rocks and branches and other debris down to the lake. At such times the stream divides into three or four channels, changing its entire course in a moment and, running along the banks, undermines and erodes the fertile soil of the edges. Each summer hundreds or even thousands of square feet of good agricultural soil are washed into the river bed.[2] Houses have been destroyed, and families, losing all their land, have been forced to borrow shelter or become laborers on the coast. How long this condition has prevailed I do not know, but the Indians have a legend to the effect that the river has been on a rampage since a deposed priest vengefully buried a figure of Christ somewhere near its source.[3]

It would be arbitrary to divide the *municipio* into urban and rural sections. The delta is inhabited; the hills are not. In the delta a small area laid out in streets contains the municipal buildings, the church, and the market place. It might be called the town, but since officially and otherwise the whole delta is so designated, it would be better to call it the town center. Over the rest of the delta the people live rather evenly dispersed, irregularly among the coffee fields and the garden plots (map 3). The town center is on the west bank of the river relatively near the apex of the delta. Most of the outlying area extends therefore to the south. The most strictly Indian portion, where most of the pure Panajachel Indians have their homes and fields, is on the other side of the river where they live almost to the exclusion of others. The town center, or west side of the river, is occupied largely by Ladinos and by Indians immigrant from other towns. It also contains such extraneous elements as hotels and country homes of wealthy Guatemalans and foreigners, for the most part along the lake shore between the river and the west edge of the delta. The Ladinos tend to live close to the town center; the wealthier, the closer. This is general Guatemalan custom, although in Panajachel the arrangement seems to be breaking down because of the development of a "gold coast" section along the lake shore.

In the immediate town center there is almost no cultivated land except the patio flower gardens. But in the remainder of the delta it may be said that the land is primarily devoted to crops, the dwellings occupying only small pieces surrounded by fields and orchards. In fact the houses are so often hidden by surrounding vegetation that a first attempt at mapping missed more than half of them.

The automobile highway from Guatemala City crosses the river from the east about a mile and a half above the town center, runs south through town and then west to the southwest corner of the delta, whence it climbs steeply to Sololá and points north and west. In the delta it is a broad and straight road, unsurfaced except for cobblestones in the center of town. The other wide roads shown

---

[2] Of a half-acre piece of land used for an experimental cornfield in 1936, for example, the river washed away in that one season at least 200 square feet.

[3] A rival story has it that when sugarcane was introduced in Panajachel, jealous canegrowers of another town (San Martín Jilotepeque) caused the river to become wild. The Maudslays visited Panajachel in 1894 and write, "There are times during the wet season when the sudden increase in the volume of water threatens the safety of the town, and we were told that not many years ago an inundation caused great damage, washing away some of the houses, and cutting off the townspeople from all outside communication" (Maudslay, 1899, p. 57). The photograph of Panajachel published by the Maudslays in 1899 shows that at the time of their visit the river had a quite different course from when McBryde photographed the delta in the early thirties. The reader is referred to McBryde's excellent photographs, published in 1947, for a general picture as well as for this comparison.

on map 3 are also used by automobiles, except that in the rainy season the river cannot usually be forded. The main footpaths are from 2 to 4 feet in width. The smaller ones, connecting the houses with one another and with the main paths and roads, accommodate only single files. Culverts for the passage of the irrigation ditches are covered over in most cases by logs and earth; but crossing the smaller paths the ditches are usually left open, to be stepped over by the pedestrian.

The irrigation ditches vary in width from 1 to 2 feet. Only the main ones are shown on map 3, but it can be seen that every part of the delta is fed by the network. The truck lands that are watered from the ditches are cultivated in small raised beds and the water flows between them when it is required. Any of the ditches can be cut off by a barrier of branches, rocks, and earth; sluice gates are not used. During the rainy season the main ditches must be watched carefully at their sources lest the water flow beyond control. During the dry season, on the other hand, there is often a shortage of water and only part of the network can be used at one time. A certain amount of cooperation is therefore required throughout the year among those who make use of the irrigation system.

The census of 1921 (Guatemala, 1924, Fourth Census, pt. 2, pp. 186–187) is the latest published census report which subdivided the populations of the *municipios* by location. (The detailed results of the 1940 census are not published.) The 1921 census subdivides the *municipio* of Panajachel as follows:

The pueblo of Panajachel, population_____ 1,041
The hamlet of Patanatic, population_____ 82
The plantations of La Dicha, Sta. Victoria, Natividad, Jesús María, and S. Felipe Bella Flcr, population_____ 257
The flour mill of S. Buenaventura, population_____ 8
The lake ports of Tzanjuyú and Monterrey, population_____ 62

Of these divisions, the only ones included in this study are the pueblo (which occupies the delta portion of map 3) and the two "lake ports," the first of which lies just beyond the southwest corner of the map and the second a short distance to the east. Both Tzanjuyú and Monterrey are sites of hotels, and at the time of this study the second was not a port at all. On the other hand, when this study was made there was another port, called Santander, still farther to the east.

Patanatic is a settlement of Indians who came two or three generations ago from the *municipio* of Totonicapán to the northwest. It may be considered a colony of Totonicapeños [4] who remain socially and economically distinct from the Indians of Panajachel. Patanatic is located in the hills north of Panajachel along the automobile highway just before it descends to the river and delta of Panajachel (map 2). The plantations Santa Victoria, Natividad, and Jesús María are to the north (map 2). La Dicha and Bella Flor are in the east delta (map 3). They are not plantations in the sense of having a permanent population of laborers. San Buenaventura, called a flour mill in the census, was at the time of this study a large and populous coffee plantation. The main portion of it is near the lake shore on a small delta just west of the Panajachel delta (map 2).

POPULATION

To the 1921 census figure of 1,041 for the "pueblo" should be added the population of the ports and the two plantations of the delta, for a total of 1,113 living in the main delta portion. Records in the municipal hall show that in the 15 years from 1921 to 1936, 365 more births were registered than deaths (table 1). The pueblo's portion of this increase would be some 288, and the 1,113 of 1921 should have increased naturally to 1,401. Such a figure takes no account of immigration or emigration; but I know no reason to believe that one outweighed the other greatly during this period. The 1940 census gave an "urban" population (probably including everything but Patanatic) of 1,871. Yet in 1936, we could account for only about 1,200 inhabitants in the delta. A careful census of the Indians revealed a few less than 800, and since only 62 Ladino families and 7 odd individuals were casually counted, it is not likely that there were more than about 400 Ladinos. Whatever the cause of the discrepancy between my figures and those inferred from official sources, for the purposes of this study the population will be taken as about 1,200.

The distinguishing characters of Ladinos and Indians, the two classes of people officially recognized in Guatemala, differ to some extent in

[4] The Spanish manner of designating inhabitants of towns will be used in this report; thus, an Atiteco is from Atitlán, an Antoñero from San Antonio Palopó, etc.

different parts of the Republic, but in general a Ladino is anybody who is not an Indian, and an Indian is defined on the basis of cultural and linguistic criteria rather than on physical features (Tax, 1937, p. 432).[5] In Panajachel the Indians are distinguishable from Ladinos because their mother tongue is Indian and their command of Spanish relatively poor, because they wear a costume distinct from that of the Ladinos (which is pretty uniform over the whole country), and because their surnames are usually of Indian rather than of Spanish origin. It is possible for an Indian to come to be considered a Ladino by both groups if he speaks Spanish like a Ladino, bears a Spanish surname, and adopts the clothing and the ways of life of the Ladinos. It must be borne in mind that since the distinction is cultural rather than physical, Indian and Ladino are not primarily thought of as race designations in the sense that Negro and White are in the United States. But there are important economic and social differences between the two classes, and each constitutes in large degree a community apart from the other. This study is concerned primarily and almost entirely with the *Indians* of Panajachel.

TABLE 1.—*Births and deaths, 1921–36, excluding stillbirths* [1]

Year	Number of births	Number of deaths	Excess of births
1921	61	24	37
1922	74	30	44
1923	58	29	29
1924	72	37	35
1925	59	32	27
1926	70	40	30
1927	66	34	32
1928	68	40	28
1929	66	31	35
1930	76	46	30
1931	58	41	17
1932	80	70	10
1933	90	42	48
1934	62	36	26
1935	79	57	22
Total	1,039	589	450

[1] Compiled from records in the Municipal Hall of Panajachel. The figures represent totals of all births and deaths registered; at the time the figures were abstracted from the records (a long task because each case is hand-written in paragraph form) we were too insufficiently acquainted to be able to distinguish registrations of local residents from those of transients; nor could we distinguish those of Patanatic and the various *fincas* from those of the town. This should have been done. Stillbirths are excluded here; in the records they are registered only as births.

Although officially the population is divided into Indian and Ladino, actually four classes of people are distinguishable in Panajachel. First there are the wealthy and educated Ladinos who participate almost completely in the culture of

modern civilization. They are relatively large landholders, government officials, and keepers of large stores. They may own automobiles and radios and they sometimes have homes in Guatemala City. They always wear good store clothes, shoes, and neckties; they normally speak a cultivated Spanish and no Indian, and are usually fairly well educated. In this class are included the few foreigners in town. Second, there are the poor Ladinos, who participate less in the culture of modern civilization and are culturally more akin to the Indians. Unlike the first group, and like the Indians, they are proletarian rather than bourgeois, working on the soil or as artisans; their clothes are countrified and they often do not wear shoes or neckties; their Spanish is that of uneducated persons, and their literacy rate is very low. Many of them speak the Indian language in addition to Spanish. The first class may be called urban, the second rural. The rural Ladinos came to Panajachel for the most part from other small towns, the urban Ladinos from the cities and larger towns. All came within the present century, the rural Ladinos generally earlier than the others. Although in cultural, social, and economic ways of life the two groups are easily distinguishable, there are cases of passage of individuals from the poor to the wealthy class. In such cases more than economic success, however, is necessary, for education and general sophistication are also prerequisites of the higher status.

The Indians are also divisible into two groups, but these groups are not thought of as relatively inferior or superior, as are the two kinds of Ladinos. First, there are the Indians of the Panajachel community who may or may not trace all of their ancestry back to Panajachel forefathers, but who consider themselves *Panajacheleños* culturally, speak the Panajachel dialect, and participate in the politico-religious organization of the community. Indians from other towns have married Panajacheleños, and their offspring have become in every social sense Panajacheleños. Indeed, there is at least one case of a family with not a drop of old Panajacheleño blood that is in every other sense a Panajacheleño family—thought of so by themselves and by the others as well.[6] Panajacheleños speak a dialect, wear a costume, and have certain beliefs and ways of life distinct from those of the Indians of other towns; they are a social and cultural unity. Secondly, there are in Panajachel a number of Indian families, originally of other towns, who do not participate, or who participate very little, in the social, political, and religious community of Panajacheleños. They wear the costumes of their own towns, and often continue the pursuit of economic specialties brought with them; their language and mentality is more like that of their blood relatives than of their present neighbors. Some of these families have lived in Panajachel only a few years; some indeed came just before the time of this study and have since left. Those that are more permanently settled tend to marry their children with Panajacheleños and thus eventually become absorbed into the local community. The allocation of particular individuals or families to one Indian group or the other is therefore to some extent arbitrary; and that is one reason why all locally resident Indians were included in this study of the economic life of the community.

The *municipios* of Guatemala (and Chiapas as well: Redfield and Villa, 1939, p. 107) are of two general kinds. In the one, the Indians live on their farms in the country and come into the town where they often set up housekeeping at intervals. In the other, they live in the town itself and repair to the surrounding countryside when necessary to till the fields (Tax, 1937, pp. 427–433). Possible explanations of the difference need not be discusse l here. A consequence of it is that in the "vacant town" *municipios* the Indians tend to lead a dual life alternating between their isolated country homes and the town, while in the "town-nucleus" *municipios* the rural territory, which is uninhabited, achieves importance only incidentally to agriculture. Unlike the Indians of Yucatan, for example, the Guatemalans of this region are not accustomed to live on their cornfields during periods of work (Redfield and Villa, 1934, p. 68); hence in town-nucleus *municipios* the men leave their town homes for no more than a day at a time to work in their cornfields.

It is apparent from the description already given that Panajachel is a variety of town-nucleus *municipios*. The Indians live in a restricted area, and their cornfields are outside this area. It is true that they do not live in a compact town, that their homes are dispersed outside of the town center, and that orchards and gardens lie around their houses; but the whole delta is considered the "town," the Indians have but one home, and their cornfields, to which they go to work a day at a time, lie outside. The allocation of Panajachel to one town type or the other is not in itself important; but it is well to remember that Panajachel and the other *municipios* of the lake differ in this fundamental ecological respect—with whatever economic and social consequences are involved—from most of the other *municipios* of the region.

THE INDIAN COMMUNITY

In the portion of Panajachel under discussion there lived, in 1936, an Indian community of 780 persons. This figure does not include Indians for the most part from other towns who lived as servants in hotels or the homes of Ladinos or as laborers on the plantations. It does include Indians from other towns who lived as domestics and hired hands in the homes of local Indians. It does not include three families, part Indian, who, in all respects but ancestry, are Ladino. Of the 780 individuals, 688 might be called "Panajacheleños," having at least some Panajachel blood or family connections, and entering into the religious and political life of the local Indian community. The remainder, 92 in number, were "foreign" Indians with no Panajachel family connections. Included among the Panajacheleños were additional foreign Indians, 8 men and 28 women, married to Panajacheleños,[7] having thereby become part of the traditional community. The remainder of 652 "ultra-pure" and part-blood Panajacheleños does not represent the total of the species in the wider region, however. Considerable numbers have migrated from Panajachel to other towns, to the capital, and to the coast plantations and have lost their connections with the local community. The genealogies collected uncovered 46 such who are still remembered (and some of whom occasionally return) but there must be more.

Table 2 classifies the 780 Indians of this study by sex and age. The figures on age, data for which were not collected with sufficient completeness or accuracy to be used, are based on the

---

[7] One man and three women were not married to Panajacheleños, but related in other ways.

assumption that the age distribution for the Indians of 1936 was the same as that given in the 1921 census (Guatemala, 1924, Fourth Census, pt. 1, pp. 303–305) for the whole population of the *municipio*. Table 3, based on an analysis of the census made in 1936 and taking into consideration the age distribution shown in table 2, reclassifies the population, adding a distinction between "Panajacheleño" and "Foreign" Indians.

TABLE 2.—*Indian population by sex and age* [1]

Age group	Percentage in 1921 census		Number of Indians, 1936			
	Male	Female	Total	Male	Female	Sex unknown
Under 7	18	20	147	67	74	[2] 6
7–14	17	12	112	66	46	
14–18	10	8	70	39	31	
19–40	37	40	300	145	155	
40–60	17	14	120	65	55	
Over 60	2	6	31	8	23	
Total	101	100	780	390	384	6

[1] The census of 1921 (p. 186) divides the 1,145 Indians of the whole *municipio* into 563 males and 582 females. The preponderance of males uncovered by my 1936 census is probably the result of errors. I think that when sex was doubtful, informants tended to assume the child was male. Or the error (if such there is) resulted from a careless misunderstanding: in some cases when I was told that there were two *hijos* in the house—and the names were not given me—I may have put them down as male children when in fact one was a female. In most cases I found out the names of people, but with infants it was often difficult and I let the matter drop; I should not have.

[2] All cases in which information on sex is lacking fall into the infant class; all are probably under 2 years of age. It would be possible from municipal birth records to determine the exact age of most of the Indians. This long and laborious task was not attempted, although the method is obviously superior and more exact than the indirect one employed.

TABLE 3.—*Population by age, sex, and class*

	Total				"Infants" under 4 years			"Children" 4–15 years		"Adults' " over 15	
	Total	Male	Female	Unknown	Male	Female	Unknown	Male	Female	Male	Female
Panajacheleño	688	351	331	6	49	36	6	75	55	227	240
Foreign [1]	92	39	53		6	9		5	12	28	32
Total	780	390	384	6	55	45	6	80	67	255	272

[1] Including foreign domestics in Panajachel households, but not foreign Indians married into them.

The 780 Indians lived, in 1936, in 157 households; of these, 134 were Panajacheleño and 23 foreign. The average number of persons per household was, therefore, 4.9, the Panajacheleños averaging 5.1 and the foreign Indians, 4.0. Table 4 shows the actual distribution of households by size. (The reason that 4 households are shown to contain half-persons is that there were two bigamous men who divided their time between two households each. For many purposes below

these dual households are combined, and the total number considered to be 132 rather than 134.) The foreign Indians live for the most part on the side of town west of the river; 21 of the 23 foreign households, containing 79 of the 86 foreign Indians, were located on the west side in 1936; and, besides, 21 of the 36 foreigners married into Panajacheleño families lived west. In 1940 there were no foreign families on the east side: one of the two had left Panajachel, and the other had moved to the other side.

The households of the foreign Indians, who are cut off from their relatives, contain for the most part simple families (parents and children); but the composition of Panajacheleño households varies greatly. Only 83 of them were counted as "simple," and that number includes 17 in which there were step-relatives and half-siblings. Of the remainder, 36 may be considered natural extensions of simple families, containing in addition married children and/or their offspring. Finally, there were 15 households which included additional relatives, most often the siblings of the parents.

There is some tendency in the families toward patrilocality: for every case in which there was a son-in-law living in the household, there were two cases in which there was a daughter-in-law instead or in addition. But all such cases together numbered but 27. Most young people set up independent establishments soon after marriage.

TABLE 4.—*Distribution of Indians by households* [1]

Number of persons	Number of households		
	Total	Panajacheleños [2]	Foreign Indians
1	1	1	
1½	1	1	
2	14	8	6
3	33	28	5
3½	1	1	
4	25	20	5
5	24	19	5
6	24	23	1
7	11	11	
7½	2	2	
8	11	10	1
9	5	5	
10	3	3	
11	2	2	
Total	157	134	23

[1] This table is based on a household census, checked and rechecked in a number of ways. It is probably not 100-percent accurate because during the months that elapsed in the gathering of the data, changes were continuously occurring (births, deaths, changes of residence with marriage, etc.) and it is difficult to know whether the picture is correct for any point of time. The attempt was to get all of the data as of May 1, 1936, but since the last doubt was not resolved until 18 months after that, it is obvious that it may not have succeeded.

[2] Not counting foreign servants as members of the households.

There was in 1936 only one household in which an unrelated person, a man, lived with the family; but there were four families with domestics and hired hands, all of them foreign Indians in the service of Panajacheleños.

Although there are evidences that in generations past there was some kind of kinship or local unit consisting of more than one household, today the household is the only functioning social entity within the community. True, familial relations that cut across households in bilateral kinship lines are recognized by formal visiting and gift giving, as are also god-parental relationships; but they do not crystallize into social segments. The only effective social segment is the individual household, whatever its constitution. That this is so can be most clearly seen in the light of the politico-religious organization.

Like the other *municipos* of Guatemala, all of which are from the point of view of the central government the smallest important administrative units, Panajachel has a series of governmental officials, some appointed and some theoretically elected. Generations back, before there were Ladinos, all officials (except a Secretary) were Indians, as they still are in other pure-Indian towns. Before 1935, when a new system was invoked, all were chosen from and by the local populace. After the Ladinos came, they were given certain of the highest offices; but the Indians continued to fill all offices unofficially from their own ranks. After 1935, when some of the offices were abolished and others became appointive from above and outside the community, the Indians continued to name a complete roster of officials; but then fewer of them were officially recognized.[8] It was still possible, however, to speak of Indian officialdom as consisting of a first *alcalde*, second *alcalde*, first and second *regidores*, first and second *regidores ayudantes*, first and second *auxiliar*, first, second, third, and fourth *mayores*, and 24 ungraded *alguaciles*. There were, thus, 36 civil offices to be filled.

At the same time, there are a series of religious offices in the Indian organization, none of which is officially recognized. These are connected with the church (of which there is no resident priest) and the cult of the saints. There are the first and second *fiscales*, first and second *sacristanes*,

cofrades of each of four *cofradías*, and two or three graded *mayordomos* of each *cofradía*, for a total of religious officials of about 16 (in 1936, 15). The 2 classes, civil and religious, are only partially separable, however. In the system of succession in the hierarchy the Indians alternate between the 2, and all offices are graded in a single hierarchy.

The Indian officials, at least insofar as the Indians have anything to say, are neither elected nor, strictly speaking, appointed. The elders (*principales*, who have passed through the succession) and the higher officials together choose the new officials each year; but since a person is not eligible to serve in an office until he has served in a lower one and since he is not obliged to accept an office unless he has had a period of rest after his previous service, the choice is limited, and often automatic. Holding office entails pecuniary disadvantage, and when there is doubt as to who should get one, a poorer man can avoid it more easily than a richer man.

What the system finally amounts to is that almost every man (together with his wife) gradually moves up through the series of offices, but in any one year a man does not take an office unless it is his turn. The point of the relationship between the family organization and the politico-religious system is that "turns" are taken not by individuals or blood-kin groups, but by households. There are some 52 offices to be filled annually, nearly all of them every year, and 132 Panajachel households from which to fill them; no household normally has more than 1 officeholder at a time, and after a person finishes his term no other member of his household is expected to serve for at least another year.

In the same manner, contributions of money for fiestas and of labor on public works come from whole households, not individuals (i. e., a household, no matter the size, might be asked to contribute one man-day of labor to repair irrigation ditches).

The household is therefore the primary social unit. By definition it is also an economic unit, since it includes those who live under one roof, or in one compound, and have a common kitchen. But there is lacking in both the native ideology and in family practice any complete economic community. Each member of the family tends to own property and to keep track of his own earnings and contributions for common needs. Never-

---

[8] In 1944, with the revolution, the legal system changed again in the pre-1935 direction.

theless, no other segments of society even approach the households in social and economic solidarity. In the household the members may be economic individualists, but they do cooperate on a noncash basis, while between even such close relatives as father and son or two brothers who live in different households, there is practically no common enterprise on a basis different from that between unrelated persons. In making this study, it was striking to find in how many ways the data had to be gathered by households rather than individuals on the one hand or family or neighborhood groups on the other. Thus, in discussing marketing it was useless to try to determine which individuals went to certain towns regularly, but it was easy to find out which households were regularly represented by one or another individual in a given town. Likewise, in land ownership it was not difficult to discover which lots were owned and worked by a certain household; but it would have required more time than we were able to give to determine which persons of the family actually owned each one.

THE WAY OF LIFE

When a tourist comes to Panajachel, the road takes him past the little town center where, surrounding a small square park, he sees the ruins of the sixteenth-century church and the drab adobe town hall, library, and jail. Driving over the cobblestones he finds the road lined for a few blocks with whitewashed adobe houses, most of which present to him a small store front and grilled windows under a red tile roof. Then for a kilometer he is out in the country, the houses spaced far apart along the road, coffee groves and open fields and garden patches between them. He arrives shortly at one of the hotels near the lake shore, from which he has a view of the broad expanse of water and the striking twin volcanoes that dwarf it. Perhaps after a trip across the lake to Atitlán, San Pedro, or San Antonio, and perhaps a stroll through the countryside near the hotel, he leaves the hotel to continue on his way. He will remember the lake, certainly. If questioned he may recall that he did go through a little town called Panajachel when en route to his hotel, but that there was nothing there to attract attention. Indeed, there was not. But in most cases the tourist has not seen Panajachel.

Nor have more than a few of the Indians seen the tourist, at least as more than a passing cloud of dust. The Indians live away from the highway, most of them on the other side of the river. They live in little thatched houses hidden in coffee groves. The tourist has seen, for the most part, the Ladino and Gold Coast sections. Along the roads he has seen more Indians from other towns than Indians of Panajachel. The latter he would probably not have recognized anyway, since, unlike Indians of such towns as Chichicastenango that wear unique costumes, there is little to distinguish them.

Yet the Panajacheleños are distinguished from all other Indians in details of costume, as well as in language, institutions, customs, and beliefs. Their economic base is different and many of the techniques in which they are proficient are foreign to inhabitants of neighboring towns. Differ as they may from each other, the norm of behavior in the community undoubtedly differs in greater or less degree from the norms of behavior of each of the other surrounding *municipios*. That is the way of this region of Guatemala, and Panajachel is not the only community different from the others; for each *municipio* tends to have its own cultural variant, and its own economic specialties. Panajachel is no doubt less colorful than some other communities; but its sociology and culture and certainly its economy is no less interesting.

Panajacheleños are almost exclusively agricultural. The women weave part of the clothing worn; the men build the houses and make a few things like tool hafts for their own use; the women cook raw materials into most of the food that is consumed; but that is as far as industrial technology goes, and none of its products are sold outside the community. All household utensils—pottery, grinding stones, baskets, gourds, china, and so on—and practically all household furnishings such as tables and chairs and mats, must be brought in from other towns. So must many articles of wearing apparel, such as material for skirts and cloaks, hats, sandals, blankets, and carrying bags, as well as cotton and thread for weaving the other things. So must most of the essential foodstuffs: the greater part of the corn, all lime, salt, and spices, most of the chile, and most of the meat. To buy all these essentials the Indians go to market, either in neighboring Sololá or in the local town center. To get the money they depend upon the sale of agricultural produce that is unimportant in their own diet and grown almost solely for the market. Onions and garlic, a number of fruits, and coffee[9] are the chief commodities produced for sale. To produce them consumes the great preponderance of the Indians' productive time, and to take them to market consumes much of the remainder.

Corn is the first essential of life to the Indian as a consumer; he thinks often in terms of his tortillas and his beans which are, in a way, his bread and butter. But his life as a producer and in business is oriented toward onions, garlic, and the other products of his truck farming. It is to them, and the prices they bring, that his fortune is tied.

The Indian is perhaps above all else an entrepreneur, a business man, always looking for new means of turning a penny. If he has land enough to earn a good living by agriculture as such, he is on the lookout for new and better seeds, fertilizer, ways of planting; and always new markets. If his land is not sufficient, he begs and borrows land where he can, often paying a rental price that is, for him, high. If he must, he works as a day laborer for another. But he would rather strike a bargain of some kind; perhaps he can buy the harvest of some fruit trees to gather and sell, or buy up onion seed to take to Mixco or the capital. Even adolescent boys and girls make deals when they can, perhaps renting a piece of land and working it on their own; and young children are alert to small opportunities.

Yet, although money is that which everybody tries to get more of, it is not of highest value in the culture. It alone does not bring the highest respect, although it is, among other things, a means of quickly ascending the scale of offices to become a respected *principal*. The richest man in town is also the first *principal*, and possibly the most highly respected person; but he also happens to be good and kind and religious and wise. The next-to-richest man is probably one of the most disliked, and he happens to be irritable and tactless—and suspected, as well, of having killed off, by sorcery, most of his relatives for their share of the inheritance. People seem

to be respected for their personal virtues (as evaluated by the community): industry, friendliness and amiability, willingness to share in communal duties; and in a town as small as Panajachel such virtues cannot be long simulated. Yet it cannot be gainsaid that wealth is at the least an obvious evidence of industry, and its reward.

Nor is business exempted from the ordinary rules of decent behavior. People frankly try to make a living, and to get rich, but not at the expense of their self-respect; they do not ordinarily try to cheat; a debt, unless it is secured, seems to be a moral burden; they do not, when sober, beg; when they ask a favor they bring a gift, and when they do a favor they do not ordinarily accept payment for it; when they receive a gift they return a gift. Loss of face is probably worse for most people than loss of money; a man may stay in the house for days at a time because he is ashamed to face his townsmen.

This is a study of the economy of a group of people who by our standards live in the most primitive condition. Their houses have no floors or windows and are filled with smoke from the open fire. They are often in rags. Their diet has few luxuries, and hardly a person is fatter than thin. A newborn baby's chance for life is something less than good, and with medical care at a minimum, life is always precarious. A few dollars' capital can, with hard work and good fortune, be run up into what is, according to local standards, a tidy nest egg. But the accumulation of years can disappear with one prolonged sickness, or one spell of drinking, or the acceptance of a public office at an inopportune time. With good luck and hard work a poor family can in a generation become a rich family; but the largest fortune can as quickly be frittered away.

The community as a whole is not poor. At least it is able to indulge in luxuries beyond the needs of food, clothing, and shelter. It supports a rather elaborate ritual organization requiring the expenditure not only of time but of money, especially for liquor. It allows people to go to festivals and to markets even when these serve no commercial needs. It sustains a no-work-in-the-fields Sabbath and a number of holidays. It permits its youth their fashion fripperies. All this in the face of perfect knowledge that time is money and so, definitely, is a penny.

---

[9] Which is important in the diet; the Indians frequently sell their entire crop, however, and buy coffee grown elsewhere, at retail.

But the Indians work for such luxuries. Rich and poor, men, women, and children, bend over the soil or under their burdens from morning to night; and when it is too dark to work they go to sleep. There is ordinarily no fireside hour, no roistering in the evening. If there is any fun in workaday life, it must be in the work itself. Or perhaps the Indians derive satisfactions from the well of inner life that is a heritage of their culture. For while in their ways and means of getting along with nature and with each other they are not so different from ourselves, their view of the world about them—the sun and the earth, the heart and the soul, plants and animals, God and the Devil, butchers and bakers, life and death—is not only different from ours, and naive and picturesque, but is a coherent whole that may well be as satisfying as it is self-explanatory.

If the Indians are on the whole a cheerful lot,

however, it is neither because they are satisfied nor because the course of life runs smooth. Ambition, a desire for the security and prestige that more land will allow, seems to be a generous current flowing through Indian life. Worry, with both health and fortune so tenuous, can never be long absent. But beyond the recurring major griefs and sorrows, perhaps the most persistent obstacles to peace of mind are the continued vexations of social life: fear, envy, fear of envy; rumors, slander, gossip, fear of gossip; quarrels; insults; faithlessness; ridicule; enemies. Passions are close to the surface and continually running over into words that feed them. Within the family, between lovers, among neighbors—any day some little thing may send one scurrying to the courthouse for redress and revenge.

The community is rich enough to support that, too.

TECHNOLOGY AND ECONOMY

THE KIND OF ECONOMY

The Indians of Panajachel, and the people among whom they live and with whom they do almost all of their business, are part of what may be characterized as *a money economy organized in single households as both consumption and production units, with a strongly developed market which tends to be perfectly competitive.*

Although as consumers the Indians enter, in minor ways, into the world economy of firms—for many years, for example, they purchased matches manufactured by a monopoly granted the Krueger interests—their production is accomplished quite strictly on a "household" rather than a "firm" basis.[10] The producing unit is the simple family;

there are no factories, no estates, no cooperatives. But because of the regional specialization of labor, it is also very strongly a market economy. In many, if not most, communities, a large proportion of what is consumed has to be purchased. The chief products of Panajachel, for example, are onions, garlic, and fruit produced almost entirely for sale, while the staples of the diet—corn, beans, peppers, salt, meat, bread—and the clothing or the materials from which it is made, and almost all tools and utensils, must be purchased.

All business is done on a money basis; barter almost does not exist. Moreover, almost all of it is done on a cash basis. It is possible to borrow money, at interest, in various ways; but although lending may sometimes become a business (and Ladinos may earn part of their living from the proceeds) credit institutions are undeveloped. A person borrows money because he needs it for some consumption rather than business purpose; Indian merchants work almost exclusively on the basis of funds actually accumulated and saved.

[10] Following a suggestion of my colleague Bert F. Hoselitz (to whom I am much indebted for advice on this section), I am using the terminology of Oscar Lange (1945–46, pp. 19–32) who distinguishes as "units of economic decision" *households*, whose decisions by definition have the objective of satisfying consumption wants of the unit, from *firms*, whose objects are money profits, and says that "The economic organization that leaves production to firms is called capitalism." By this definition the title of this book appears to be a misnomer. However, Lange goes on to point out not only that firms have "nonrational" ends but that households may be "rational" in maximizing the magnitude of utility, as I believe that those of Panajachel tend to do, and he adds (p. 31) that there seems "to be some difference between households operating in the capitalist economy and households of the domestic economy of pre-capitalist societies. The dominance of business enterprises with a tangible and quantified magnitude (money profit) as their objective has created a mental habit of considering all kinds of decisions as a pursuit of a single objective, expressed as a magnitude. Some authors call this mental habit the 'capitalist spirit.' It spreads beyond the specific decisions of business enterprises and affects the mode of operation of other units, including households. Under the influence of the mental habit

mentioned, households are encouraged to order their preferences along a scale; i. e., to maximize utility. In capitalist society, therefore, the decisions of households are more likely to conform to the deductions derived from the postulate of rationality than in societies which preceded the rise of modern capitalism." I think it will appear in this description that the economy of Panajachel (which is a market rather than a domestic economy of isolated units of decision) has these characteristics of the capitalist society. Whether Lange would prefer to call Panajachel households "firms" or to accept an intermediate class of what I call "penny capitalism" I do not know.

The idea of borrowing money either to buy merchandise for resale, or to rent land and hire agricultural labor, is virtually nonexistent.

In the regional economy, market places are exceedingly important. There are stores owned by Ladinos, but most transactions of both Ladinos and Indians occur in established outdoor market places. Occasional peddlers distribute their wares to homes, some merchants buy produce at the establishments where they are produced, but such practices are exceptional to the more general pattern. And in any case, it is in the market place where a number of buyers and a number of sellers meet that prices for all tend to be set.[11]

In the market place, frequently the central plaza of the town, vendors spread their wares and buyers come to purchase them. Almost every town has its market day once or twice a week; the larger towns have them daily. The people who have produce to sell know where and when the markets are held, and they make their choice of markets in accordance with their particular circumstances. They know that if they go to a farther market, they will—other factors being equal—get better prices for their goods, which are worth more the farther from their source they are, but they may prefer to spend less time in travel and get a smaller price. Or the men may go to far markets with large quantities while the women go to sell in the local markets. Likewise, the purchasers of goods make a choice of markets according to what they want to buy and how much time they are willing to spend to get it more cheaply and closer to its source. Everybody in the region I have studied knows that Tecpán is the place to buy lime, that bananas are cheaper in Atitlán, that pitch pine and pigs are cheaper in Chichicastenango. If one wants a few ounces of lime for the weekly cooking of corn, he will not go to Tecpán for it. But if he wants a hundred pounds for the building of a house, it may pay him to take the journey. Nobody will normally take a day's trip to Chichicastenango for a few cents' worth of pitch pine, but if a person wants to buy a little pig or two for fattening, it will pay him to go there.

This basic knowledge about markets is known even to a child, and it is consistently acted upon when conditions permit.

[11] McBryde (1933) describes the Sololá market particularly and (1947) the market system of the entire region.

People arrive at market at 9 or 10 in the morning and take their usual places, generally arranged so that vendors of the same product sit one next to the other. The vendor unloads his wares, arranges them on a mat or table in front of him, and waits for the customers. A prospective buyer comes up and looks over his tomatoes, for example, touching them at will. He asks how much they are. "Two cents a pound." The buyer offers a cent a pound, and the merchant shakes his head. The buyer passes on, presumably to look for tomatoes elsewhere. He does not return. The same happens with several other prospective customers. The tomatoes are not selling at 2 cents a pound. Perhaps one of the buyers, when that price is mentioned, remarks that he is asking too much, that others are selling tomatoes for less. Even if this does not happen, the vendor after an hour may notice that he is selling no tomatoes at his price. Another customer comes. "How much are the tomatoes?" "Two cents." "One cent," says the buyer. "No; my bottom price is 1½ cents." The customer takes some at that price. The next customer perhaps counters the 2 cents proposal with an offer of 1½ cents. "Take them," says the merchant.

Sometimes a merchant finds that he is the only one who happens to be selling tomatoes in this particular market this particular day. Seeing this, he perhaps asks 4 cents a pound. He soon finds, let us say, that despite his fortunate position, people prefer to do without than to pay more than 2 cents a pound. And eventually his price comes down to that. Or he may unluckily discover that everybody has the intention of selling tomatoes in this market this day; and our merchant who may have bought these tomatoes the day before in a market near the tomato-producing area for a cent a pound, may find himself unloading at half that price. Tomatoes are highly perishable, so the factor of chance is important. With respect to nonperishable items, however, there is still fluctuation in price with the supply and demand of the particular time and place, since if supply is short people will pay a little more to get what they want when they want it, while if supply is long a merchant will reduce his price at least to the point where the loss will be no greater than the value of the time spent in repeating a trip to market. Generally speaking, however, and particularly with respect to less perishable items, prices are established over longer periods of time in all of the market places together; hence there tends to be a competitive market. The price itself of course varies with the product, the season, the distance of the market from the center of its production, and so on. Beyond such accidental factors as the toughness and business acumen of the merchant and upon his immediate financial and other circumstances (a sick child at home may cause a vendor who needs money quickly to accept a lower price and possibly depress the whole market) prices are fixed in accord with the usual ways of the market.

This is so even when recourse is not had to the common, open market place. In Panajachel, where merchants come to the farm and bargain for beds of onions even before they are harvested, the farmer calculates his chances of getting more by harvesting the onions, taking them to market, and so selling them at wholesale or retail. In doing so he calculates the value of his time; and in doing so, both he and the buyer also use their knowledge of what market prices are apt to be when the onions are taken to town. Since there are several merchants going the rounds, and since there are many onion growers, here again competition enters the picture. The price is established in a particular case in terms of the various factors that enter in; and that price in the particular case influences what may be called the market price.

Since most of the people in the region are illiterate it may be questioned whether they are capable of the mental bookkeeping that is involved if we are to call them economically wise. Are they able to figure their costs of production with some accuracy? I think that in most cases the answer is unequivocally in the affirmative. In Panajachel where I laboriously calculated costs of production I had frequent occasion to remark the accuracy of the estimates given by the Indian producers themselves. They know when they are doing well and when they are doing poorly. My favorite example is the woman weaver with whom I spent some days calculating the costs of various garments. She wove her garments for the use of her family, and never—as far as I know—made a practice of selling her textiles. Yet when I finished my silent paper calculations, taking into consideration the value of her time as well as of the materials, she could tell me almost to the half-

penny what the result should be; and if I did not have it, I—not she—was wrong.

This rather impressionistic description suggests that the regional market [12]—whether thought of in a general or abstract sense, or as the market place—may be characterized as perfectly competitive insofar as it tends to be (a) atomistic, (b) open, (c) free, and (d) based on "rational" behavior.

(a) It is atomistic, of course, in that the buyers and sellers are small (no one of them able significantly to affect the market) and act independently of one another. Characteristically, a number of small vendors of identical merchandise—standard bunches of onions, or peanuts sold by the pound, for examples—sit side by side in the market place, competing for the money of a large number of equally small and independent buyers who appear during the space of a few hours to purchase the same merchandise either for consumption or for resale. Likewise, an employer is able to choose among a number of potential workers, independent of one another; and each worker characteristically has a choice of employers none of whom is so large as to affect the wage rates substantially more than the others.

(b) It is open in that there is no barrier to new competitors entering or old ones leaving the market. I have never heard even a suggestion of an attitude that vendors or classes of vendors ought to be excluded from a market, much less any organized effort to do so.

(c) The market is relatively very free in that prices are set by the interplay of supply and demand with almost no authoritarian regulation. I detect three kinds of "interferences" to the "free play" of the forces of supply and demand. The first, which hardly needs discussion, is that of the wider world economy. Since the local economy is not autonomous, events in the world (wars, depressions, etc., and the less startling economic changes) influence local prices, which are not, then, determined wholly by the free play of local buyers and sellers.

The second class of interferences are those caused by Government intervention. Leaving aside the monetary system, to changes in which the regional economy must adjust, the more

[12] Here defined as any given areal and temporal space in which a given commodity is sold for a fixed set of prices; "the market" includes all institutionally recognized exchange relations.

important of these interferences, such as import and export taxes, have few direct effects on the regional economy, since the goods entering the local economy are with few exceptions not only domestic but even regional. Such revenue-producing taxes of the National Government as stamps and stamped paper for legal documents, and those on real estate, affect the regional economy very slightly. Taxes on tobacco and liquors, and the governmental controls on their manufacture and sale are of greater importance. It is difficult to say, however, whether people would drink or smoke substantially more if the price were lower. License fees, and market taxes, although not very large, affect merchants and certain producers and of course prices. Almost all taxes are levied solely for the purpose of raising revenue; once Panajachel levied no market tax on vendors of a scarce item (pitch pine) to encourage an increase in the supply; this may be more common than I know. Except as sumptuary taxes (liquor, tobacco) may have a moral element in their motivation, I know of no other such use of the power to tax.

There is occasional interference with the price mechanism. Once during the period of this study the Government controlled the price, and to some degree the distribution, of corn when an extraordinarily short supply produced a crisis. The case emphasizes the rarity of such interference. On the other hand, the Government has always had laws respecting both land and labor. The former, regulating the distribution of public lands, etc., have had virtually no effect on the regional economy; but the labor laws, always in effect discriminatory against Indians, who by one means or other have been forced to go to plantations to work, have influenced the local economy. In the thirties there were minimum wage laws, and similar pieces of social legislation that in fact had little if any effect.[13] Similarly, there have always been mechanisms to supply labor on the roads and in other public works; males are subject to head taxes that may be worked out or paid in cash. Finally, the Government enforces weights-and-measures regulations (which in terms of economic theory need not be thought of as hindrances to free competition).

---

[13] Since these data were gathered from 1936 to 1941, no account is taken of changes that may well have occurred since the revolution of 1944, after which social legislation became much more important.

The third class of interferences are those which customs, institutions, and beliefs impose on the "free play" of supply and demand. These are, I think, remarkably few and unimportant. There are a few beliefs that perhaps impede the most efficient production, such as that lumber and corn are to be cut and harvested only in certain phases of the moon. There are some sentiments impeding the most economic allocation of time and resources; for example, in Panajachel it is felt that every housewife should have chickens, even if they do not "pay." There are social considerations that prevent land, for example, from being treated absolutely as a commodity, though in Panajachel it is nearly that. But on the whole, one is hard put to find clear examples of any "cultural" interferences with economic behavior; even those just mentioned are equivocal. The difficulty here is the methodological one of having to document a negative statement. As one examines the materials contained in this monograph, it becomes clear that "cultural interference" is largely absent; but there is a possible exaggeration involved in the very bookkeeping method that is employed. All I am able to say is that in working out the economy of Panajachel I rarely came across anything not quickly reducible to economic terms. Customs, beliefs, sentiments, and institutions seem, where they are not divorced from, to be rather *affected by*, than affecting, economic behavior.

(d) The last paragraph drifts toward discussion of the fourth criterion of a competitive market—the assumption of "rational" behavior on the part of its participants. Rationality implies (1) consistent behavior in terms of cultural values, prices, and quality, (2) indifference on the part of buyers and sellers as to their trading partners, and (3) information on the part of buyers and sellers concerning prevailing prices.

With respect to the last, it is difficult to determine how much knowledge members of the market have of what others are doing. The practice of shopping in the market place is a device to obtain information; a buyer rarely makes his purchase at the first try, and I suspect that a vendor does not begin to reduce his price until he understands that others must be doing so. More important is the fact that money values are *the* favorite topic of conversation. The typical first question is, "How much did you pay for it?"

People interestedly report news of market prices, as well as wages and business transactions in general. They seem to have knowledge of price differentials in various local markets, and calculate comparative advantages. But it would require much close study to determine the accuracy and currency of such knowledge.

With respect to the second point, there is remarkable indifference. There is no discernible tendency to attend the personality of the vendor; the buyer will accept a commodity from a stranger in the market as readily as from his own brother, from a Ladino as from an Indian. There are also few artificial distinctions, such as in advertised brands; recognized differences in quality tend to be real differences (in types of oranges, for example) that distinguish commodities.

Obviously, it is more difficult to determine "indifference" in the hiring of labor or the choice of employer; the work is often not the same, the workers and employers have different expectations of one another; and there are nonquantitative factors that necessarily confuse the picture. To say that there is indeeed indifference in the "labor market" to the degree that the "commodities" are subject to no important difference might be justified; but it seems futile as only repeating, and not applying, a theoretical concept.

The criterion of rationality which involves consistent behavior is (for me) the most difficult to apply, since rational behavior is now being defined as that behavior which a given consumer displays, provided that he is consistent. Both cultural differences and personal idiosyncrasies are permitted in the definition. On this basis the Indians of Panajachel appear as rational as any. Similarly, Lange says (1945–46, p. 30) that "a unit of economic decision is said to act rationally when its objective is the maximization of a magnitude. Firms thus act rationally by definition, while households do so only when their preferred allocations of resources among different wants can be ordered along a scale." I have already suggested that by this definition the households about which I write act rationally.

On the other hand, there is the special conception of rationality as Max Weber (1947, pp. 168–171) uses the term: economic activity is rational insofar as it involves planned distribution of services at the disposal of the economizing person (or planned acquisition of those in possession of others) in accordance with his estimate of the expected cost, thus taking into account marginal utility. In this sense also most economic behavior in the Indian economy of this region of Guatemala is generally highly "rational." The Indians may of course be wrong in their "estimates," but they weigh choices in accordance with the economic principle. Weber calls exchange "economically rationally oriented" when it concludes by compromise a struggle of interests in which either both parties have expected to obtain advantage, or in which one of the parties is compelled by economic power or need to participate. To this "rational" exchange he opposes the "customary" exchange involved in gifts among friends, chiefs, and so on— although he adds that such gift-exchange may also be rationally oriented. In this sense again the local economy is highly rational, for even gift exchange (in marriage, for example) and ceremonial disposition of goods and services are notoriously rationally oriented, with the cost carefully counted and often resulting from compromises of conflicting interests.

However, Weber also opposes to "rational" exchange those exchanges that have as their purpose not gain (the chance to make a profit in the market) but the provision of commodities for the sustenance of life. In the latter case, conditions of exchange are determined individually, and exchange is thus irrational. "Thus, for instance, household surpluses will be valued according to the individual marginal utilities of the particular household economy and may on occasion be sold very cheaply. Under certain circumstances the fortuitous desires of the moment determine to a very high degree the marginal utility of goods which are sought in exchange [p. 171]." In this sense, the economy described here cannot be very rational, since most persons are too close to a subsistence level of life, too subject to the vagaries of fortune, to avoid frequent exchanges to obtain commodities necessary to life. Indeed, only in the cases of real merchants is there much "rational" exchange in this sense. Statistically, in the economy as a whole, "rational" transactions must be in the very small minority. This is another way of saying that the economy is not "capitalist" in the sense of having business firms, for as Weber points out (pp. 171, 192) a "rational" struggle for exchange develops in its highest form in transactions for commodities which are used by or exchanged between business firms. Where units are household groups, with consumption needs, wholly rational business transactions must be few.

But even though the regional economy lacks firms, I find it hard to imagine a people more endowed with the spirit of business enterprise than the Indians (and Ladinos) that I know best. There is probably no Panajachel Indian over the age of 10 who has not calculated a way to make money with his available resources. Just as boys in our society begin to "trade" at a tender age, so the Indians early take and make opportunities for profit—"for keeps," or, put another way, in terms of advantage accepted by adult society. I know of boys 8 and 10 years of age who have set themselves up in business, buying and selling independently of their parents. Boys of 12 or 14 are apt to be pretty sophisticated traders. I doubt that I know even one man in the region who is not interested in new ways of making money, who does not have, typically, an iron or two in the fire, and who does not make his living partly as a business enterpriser. His wife is often the brains behind the business, too, and women also independently engage in business enterprises of one kind or other. It is therefore easy to go for descriptions of Panajachel to the writings of classical economists, for (as Adam Smith says; 1937, p. 421): "Every individual is continually exerting himself to find out the most advantageous employment for whatever capital he can command."

The ethic of the community seems admirably suited to such an economy. There is frank admission that wealth is good. It is money that makes possible the fulfillment of recognized duties to the community and to one's family. Indeed, money is one of the *sacra* of the Indian culture, together with such other socially valuable items as corn, fire, and the land. Before the Conquest cacao beans were used as money, and entered into mythology and ritual as well as the market place; the substitution of coins and banknotes has occurred in both realms, and money is both ordinary and a subject of esoteric belief and sacred attitude.[14]

Industry and intelligence (together with honesty) are perhaps the most valued single traits of character. In folklore it is the lazy person who gets into trouble (although in folklore he may

come out on top, Cinderella fashion) and wily tricksters are spoken of with appreciation. It is clearly recognized that luck is important in determining man's prosperity; I think there is no notion of damning a man's character simply because he is poor (perhaps the community is too small, and the people too informed about one another to permit such stereotypical thinking). But by the same token, the successful man is recognized to have had more than good fortune: he has been industrious and intelligent as well. By and large, in a simple-agricultural-small-business society, this is of course a valid diagnosis.

Honesty is highly valued. In assessing the place of this good in the economy, however, two points seem relevant. In the first place, the definition of what is honest permits sharp business practices, such as "let the buyer beware"; nobody is expected to tell the whole truth, and it would be unintelligent to do so. To recognize and repay debts (even without documents to prove them); to keep a bargain; to give full measure—all these are expected. But to be fooled is also expected. Two incidents perhaps illustrate the difference. The one is the furor that occurred in the market place one day when a buyer claimed to be short-weighted (by an outside merchant); nobody thought it was funny, and the law was called in. The other incident was funny, though it concerns short weight no less. The Indian women of neighboring Santa Catarina weave red *huipiles* that make attractive tablecloths in the eyes of Americans. In 1937 the Catarinecas were not engaged in any considerable tourist trade, but we were buying such *huipiles*. At first we paid $2.50 or $3, bargaining as is customary in such cases, and purchased quite a few. The women came with greater and greater frequency; and since they were making the cloths primarily for us, we felt an obligation to continue buying. In order to put a stop to it, we lowered our price, and began paying no more than $2. They kept coming. We lowered our price to $1.50 and eventually to $1, and still they kept coming. (How foolish we had been to pay $2.50!) Eventually, a particular friend who had not before come to sell us textiles came to offer a *huipil* she had made; she wanted $3 and would not come down in price. When we told her what we had been paying, she asked to see the textiles; a comparison showed that hers weighed at least twice as much as those we were

---

[14] To be documented with publication of material on the world view of Panajachel. Meanwhile, material is available in my microfilmed **Panajachel Field Notes,** 1950 (hereafter referred to simply as my microfilmed notes), especially pp. 550–554 and the sections on beliefs, and in many stories.

currently buying. The Catarineca women had simply kept pace with our price, and nobody could of course complain.

The second point is that honesty is not so firmly established in the culture that it can be taken for granted. That the moral sanctions in Indian culture are not such as assure honesty, even in weights and measures, is shown in the fact that buyers carefully watch the scales. It was shown more dramatically one afternoon when an Indian from nearby San Antonio came to sell onion seed. He needed money, and had 2 pounds of seed; he would sell the 2 pounds at a bargain price, and I decided to buy them both to favor him and to favor any local Indian to whom I could resell the seed at this bargain price. I was with two of my Panajachel friends when I made the purchase; and when I began to look for a scale to weigh out the seed, one of my companions said, "Oh you don't have to weigh it; if this man says there are 2 pounds, there are 2 pounds; he's a *creyente*." My friends were normal Indians (i. e., not *creyentes*); the Antoñero was a convert of the American Protestant missionaries; and the Panajacheleños recognized that a "believer" would not short-weight us. The inference is clear that the usual Indian morality, in contrast to *creyente*, offers no such guarantee.

Perhaps most significant is the fact that the supernatural sanctions that govern business dealings are essentially secular in effect, punishments that fit the crime. If one commits a sin like spitting in the fire, or complaining at having to climb a hill, the punishment is sickness; but the punishment for stealing (in the form of robbery or of business dishonesty) is rather bad luck in business affairs: stolen money just does not do one any good, and may cause poverty.

Here is an ethic, in short, that encourages individual industry, acumen, and enterprise in a struggle to gain wealth.

At the same time, the culture tends to value everything in consistent monetary terms. It is true on the one hand that money is not an end in itself; that is, miserliness is certainly not a value, and one gains prestige by devoting both time and money to duties to the community; but, on the other hand, such spending is the contrary of anonymous, and it is as carefully accounted as business transactions. Religious and social patterns do not limit the operation of the economic system (although they consume wealth and are a factor in maintaining a more equal distribution of personal wealth); rather, the pattern of ritual is in part cast after the image of a money-exchange and competitive economy. Surplus wealth is nowhere "given away"; it buys prestige and political and social power; and at each step in the process, everybody knows the cost. Wealth brings with it obligations, but they are measured and limited and involve equivalent returns.

Nor is there conflict between the kind of impersonal relations characteristic of this type of economic system and the pattern of interpersonal relations general in the society. It is perhaps a *tour de force* that a community of 800 people living in a small territory should achieve such, but it is a fact that relations among members even of the Panajacheleño community appear extraordinarily impersonal. Documentation of this assertion must await publication of material on the social-political-religious structure of the community.[15] It must suffice now to say that, for its size, the community is surprisingly "atomized"; that is, individuals tend to be separate units, each related to others with respect to a single role. Just as in our society there are many relationships (such as teacher-pupil, storekeeper-customer, physician-patient, employer-employee) binding individuals by single sets of behavior, and thoroughly scrambling the population; so in Panajachel most of the ties that bind tend rather to unite many people lightly and ephemerally than to bind a few in tightly knit groups. The family group tends to break up as the children mature; neighborhood ties mean next to nothing; the groups of political and religious officials unite individuals arbitrarily and temporarily. The social system uses individuals, or simple household groups, as its units, and—to continue a figure of speech—moves them about according to external criteria. The interpersonal relations characteristic of the free economy are, in short, to be subsumed in a class of impersonal and individualized relations more general in Panajachel society.

TECHNOLOGY

The kind of economy that I have described characterizes an entire region; the Panajachel Indian economy is like this because, of course, it

---

[15] Partially documented (Tax, 1941).

is part of the region. In matters of technology, on the other hand, there are class differences within the region. In order to understand better that practiced by the Indians of Panajachel, it is therefore necessary to make some general distinctions for the whole area.

It takes only superficial familiarity with western Guatemala to notice that there coexist three technological "layers" roughly connected with the difference between the city and the rural areas. The top layer is the thin veneer of modern industrial art; the middle layer, a very substantial one, represents European technology of the centuries before the Industrial Revolution; the bottom layer is what remains of the technology of the pre-Columbian Indians. A general problem is posed by the fact that even today, after 400 years of contact, Indian culture is still largely characterized by a pre-Conquest or "primitive" technology. Living in juxtaposition with Ladinos whose culture partakes of the middle (European, preindustrial) layer and even of items of modern technology, and entering with them into a single economy, it seems remarkable that the Indians should be so "backward." A brief discussion of the general situation will serve to introduce description of the technology of Panajachel in its relation to social and cultural differences in the community.

The top technological layer in Guatemala presents no problem. It is obviously new: an extension to this country of the modern material culture of the western industrial world. It consists of such elements as electric-light plants, telephone and telegraph and radio, the steam shovel working on the highway, and motor vehicles. To the south of the region that concerns us, there runs the railroad that connects Guatemala City and the Mexican system of railroads. In a town called Cantel there is a modern, cotton-textile mill; in another town, Amatitlán, there is a smaller woolen textile mill. On the coffee plantations there is some modern farm machinery. In the city and in the larger towns there are also corn-grinding machines operated by gasoline motors. This modern technology is clearly connected with Ladino culture—much of it with educated-Ladino culture—as well as with the city. Everything electrical, mechanical, and automotive is owned and operated by Ladinos. Even their use by Indians is minimal. The

Indians very occasionally have an electric-light bulb in the house; they sometimes send telegrams; they occasionally listen to the radio owned by a Ladino or by the Ladino community. They also buy and use such things as flashlights, hair clippers, and sewing machines, which may be said to have entered Indian culture in some degree. They do not, of course, *make* any of these things; and except for sewing machines, they do not operate mechanical devices.

In Panajachel, specifically, there are Ladinos who enjoy the fruits of modern technology. The Indians are quite typical, however, in sharing it—if at all—strictly as observers. It happens that Panajachel Indians have no sewing machines; so that full technological "participation" is confined to the using of flashlights and, in the hands of the local barber, hair clippers. They use some Cantel-spun cotton and machine-woven cotton cloth; they ride on trucks and busses; they occasionally hear radios and patronize itinerant photographers. They have not, of course, the faintest notion of how these things work. A current folk belief is that (somehow) people's heads must be chopped off to make electric light. It was seriously assumed by my friends that because I came from the United States where such things are made, I "know how" to make an airplane. An amusing incident illustrates the naïveté of Indians faced with gadgets of modern society: I had given a friend a cheap alarm clock, telling him to wind it every 24 hours. A few weeks later he reported to me a narrow escape he had had the previous afternoon; he had gone to the Sololá market, and was delayed; he suddenly remembered the clock at home and—Cinderellalike—had dropped everything and run the 5 miles to his house, just in time to wind the clock.

Analysis of Indian and Ladino participation in the "middle" technology is much more difficult. It presents, first of all, a methodological problem of the distinction between Indians and Ladinos. It will be recalled that the difference is, essentially, that Ladinos are the carriers of European culture—are Spanish-speaking, wear our type of clothes, etc., and are part of the national society, while the Indians are members of small local societies whose cultures are in large part descended from the pre-Columbian regional culture. The Ladinos tend to have more white blood, and the Indians more Indian blood; but the physical distinction gives way in importance to the cultural and linguistic one. Now it must be pointed out (Tax, 1942) that the Ladino population is recruited from the Indian communities. That is, over the course of time individual Indians learn Spanish, and become acculturated to Ladino ways, and leave their local Indian societies and come to form part of the Ladino population. In some regions of Guatemala this process has already destroyed the Indian communities; all of the people are Ladinoized and recognized by most people as Ladinos. In western Guatemala this is not the case; most Indians live in easily distinguishable Indian communities.

When I speak of Indian culture I speak of the culture of communities that are still identifiably Indian. When I say that such and such a European trait is not part of Indian culture, I mean that it does not enter into the normal life of the Indian communities. When I say—and I shall—that certain European techniques are practiced by Indians who are partly Ladinoized—who have entered European culture in some degree, it may seem that I am arguing in a circle by saying that knowledge of the European technique makes a man a Ladino. What I shall mean, however, is that such an Indian is partly Ladinoized in that he has in some degree departed not only from the practices of his local Indian culture, but he has in doing so left his local Indian society to enter in some degree Ladino society. For example, I shall point out that some Indian men make pottery on the wheel, but that they do so in shops in the towns where the Ladino wheel potters live, and that they lead lives that are in many respects like those of the Ladinos. They are not full members of typical Indian societies.

In this discussion of which traits of European technology are shared by Indians, I am therefore thinking of Indian culture and of Indians defined as participating fully in Indian culture.

What, then, are included in the technologies of the two layers that I call "primitive" and "pre-industrial European" and how are their traits now distributed in Indian and Ladino cultures?

Sixteenth-century Europe, which sent its soldiers, missionaries, and colonists to the New World, had a material culture little different from that of classical times. The chief domestic animals were horses and mules, cattle, sheep, swine, and chickens and other fowl. There was a complex of dairying—milk, butter, cheesemaking, and

so on; of leather tanning and soap and tallow-candle making; of the use of animals for draft and fertilizer. The important grains were wheat, rye, barley, and oats. Rice, of course, came in somewhere. There was a technical complex in agriculture that included beast-drawn circular threshers and round millstones, powered by water wheels. There were brewing and wine making and bread making; there were baking in an oven and frying in animal fat. There was metal working, especially in iron. Guns and gunpowder supplemented metal swords and knives as weapons of war and the chase. There were carts and plows drawn by animals. There were spinning wheels—cotton, wool, flax, and silk were woven on upright foot-power looms with continuous warps. There was also tailoring of garments and of leather shoes. There were brick baking and some masonry, and houses with windows. And so on. There is no point in extending a list that is obvious in our own culture.

Now let us note what the Indians in Guatemala had when the Spaniards arrived. Besides the dog, the only important domestic animal was the turkey, whose meat and possibly eggs were used. As in Europe there were bees, honey, and wax. The skins of wild animals were cured and used. With no beasts of burden, and no vehicles, loads were carried on the head (women) or the back, with the tumpline. The only grain was maize; there were, as in Europe, a number of vegetables such as beans and squash and chile. Corn was planted with a sharpened stick; there was no important preparation of the soil. Tools were presumably stone and wood, for although copper and bronze as well as gold were known in some parts of America, they were not used in common implements, certainly not in Guatemala. The weapons of war were stone-pointed arrows and lances. The techniques of cooking were barbecuing, toasting and baking on the griddle, and boiling in pots. Cotton was grown, and spun with the hand whorl. It was woven on the backstrap loom, one end attached to a tree or post. There was a minimum of tailoring, and the footgear consisted of a leather sole attached by leather thongs round the foot. Stone masonry was of course known, but domestic architecture probably used walls either of canes or wood or of unbaked mud bricks or daub, and without windows.

If one compares the inventory of imported

European items with the technology of the Ladino population of Guatemala, the striking fact emerges that *every item* is still an integral part of Ladino culture. New items have been added, but nothing (of the list given [16]) has been lost. Since Ladinos and their culture are important in western Guatemala, this European technology is therefore part of the regional technology that I am describing. All of these items, similarly, are known in Panajachel, and are part of the culture of at least the Ladinos of Panajachel. The question is, which of these items are also part of the Indian culture of the region, and of the Panajachel Indian technology in particular.

Complementary questions need to be asked about the survival of pre-Columbian Indian technology. With the exception that stone tools and all items specifically connected with warfare (such as the bow, shields, etc.) have utterly disappeared, every item listed in the Indian inventory is still part of the Indian culture of the region. Again, the Indians have added new items but (with small exceptions such as those noted) they have lost nothing. Therefore again, since Indian culture is ubiquitous in western Guatemala, the pre-Columbian technology is also part of the regional technology, and of that of Panajachel.

But, with one exception, every item of the pre-Columbian technology that survives in Indian culture is *also* part of the *Ladino* culture of the region. The exception is the use of the spinning whorl and the backstrap loom, confined (as far as I know) to Indian women. Indian agricultural and cooking techniques, and crops and foods, are as much part of Ladino culture as of Indian. The Indian technology is therefore general in the region; and at least the Ladinos have combined it with the old-European.

The questions reduce themselves to one: the degree to and the ways in which traits of old-European technology have entered Indian culture. Therefore, we may now check the items of the European inventory to see which have, during these four centuries, become part of the Indian technology of this region of Guatemala.

Only two European complexes are as much a part of Indian culture as they are of Ladino: chicken culture, and wool technology. The chicken is more important than the aboriginal turkey; it enters importantly into ritual and social life as well as economic. True, Indians do not eat much chicken or many eggs, but only because of their poverty, for these are salable luxury goods eaten by the Indians chiefly on special occasions.

Wool technology in the higher highlands to the northwest of Panajachel is more important to Indians than to Ladinos, and is thoroughly part of Indian culture. The whole complex includes the raising of sheep (and their use in fertilizing hillsides), the shearing and washing of wool, the use of metal carders, the spinning wheel, and the footloom—all strictly European. The men of many Indian communities earn most of their livings at wool spinning and weaving, and occupy the time of the women as well in the technical processes involved.

Otherwise, domestic animals are not fully part of Indian culture. Horses and mules are used more in some regions than others, and the more Ladinoized Indians sometimes use them for packing. But in general Indians do not have pack animals, they almost never breed them, and they so rarely ride them that one can be virtually positive that any man on a horse is a Ladino. As for women—I do not recall a clearly Indian woman on a horse.

Pigs are much more common in Indian communities; but again they are on the edge of, not really part of Indian culture. Some communities breed and raise swine, and there are even Indians who know how to geld them. In other communities they are only bought to be fattened and sold again. But only rarely, that I know of, are they processed by other than Ladinos or pretty Landinoized Indians. Pig butchering is typically a Ladino trade. Nor do the Indians typically use the lard—for that matter beef is preferred to pork, too; the frying techinque is still by and large confined to Ladinas and to Indian women who have worked in Ladino homes. Indians do use the soap made of the pork fat by the pig butchers.

Cattle, similarly, have been only in small part adopted into Indian culture. Beef is commonly eaten, and if the Indians could afford to, they would eat much more. Usually they buy the meat in Ladino butcher shops, but there are Indian butchers—usually in or from towns where there are no Ladinos or where there were none

---

[16] Wine is not made—grapes are rare—but it is known; beer is brewed only in the city and largest towns. Neither the European nor the Indian "inventories" pretend to be more than exemplary.

until recently; obviously if some Indians had not learned to butcher cattle, there would have been no meat in the all-Indian communities. But the tanning of leather is as far as I know a Ladino monopoly; and although a few Indians make tallow candles, this is not a common household art. But a more important lack is the entire dairying complex. An occasional Indian owns and milks a cow, selling the milk to Ladinos; but I do not know any who makes butter or cheese. Furthermore, Indians do not normally drink milk, even when they can afford to. They do not like it.

Animals, as I have indicated, are not used to draw carts or plows. Plows are used, with oxen, by Ladinos in some parts of the country; and there is the exceptional case of northwest Guatemala—near the Mexican border—where ox-drawn plows are regularly used in Indian agriculture. I am not acquainted with the circumstances of this exception. Oxcarts are used on Ladino plantations, of course driven frequently by Indian laborers; but they are not found in the Indian communities.

In the sheep-growing regions the fields are systematically fertilized by the sheep; the Indians move their corrals periodically from place to place on the hillside. Otherwise manure is only occasionally used by Indians; of course there normally is not very much. The institutions of the stable and the barn are completely lacking in Indian culture.

Wheat is grown in some regions by Indians as well as Ladinos. I do not know how they usually thresh it—I have never lived in a wheat-growing community—but in passing I have seen horses used by Ladinos and not by Indians. Indians usually sell the grain, however; the milling of flour is a monopoly of wealthy Ladinos. In one case where wheat is grown I was told that wheat is mixed with corn and prepared in the manner of corn in the Indian kitchen.

The Indians like bread, and eat it when they can afford it and when they can buy it. It is not a part of the normal diet, but it is an important part of Indian ritual and festival life. Baking is not a domestic art, however, any more than among the Ladinos. Except in some all-Indian communities, the bakers, furthermore, are almost always Ladinos.

Very few Indians drink bottled beer from the city. The favorite beverage of both Ladinos and Indians is the hard liquor made in licensed distilleries. The making of liquor is not confined to the Ladinos and their distilleries, however. Indian bootleggers are not uncommon. Furthermore, nobody can say that distilled liquor, a European import, is not thoroughly integrated into Indian culture.

Metals have entered Indian culture in the form chiefly of tools, particularly the steel hoe and machete. In some other parts of Guatemala iron tools are made by Ladino blacksmiths (I have never heard of an Indian smith) but most of the tools are imported from Germany, England, and Connecticut. Carpenters and masons and such also have their imported tools of metal. Enamelware utensils are occasionally used. Tinware is also common. Imported sheet tin is elaborated into cups and kerosene lamps by Ladino tinsmiths in the city and elsewhere; if there is an Indian community somewhere that specializes in the trade, I do not know it, and there are no tinsmiths among the Indians of the region I write about. Gasoline tins find many uses among Indians. During Holy Week they buy canned fish. Metal money is of course also used; I trust that no Indians make it!

The footloom, with one major exception, is distinctly part of Ladino, and not of Indian culture. The Indian women use the backstrap loom exclusively with the strange exception of one Indian town in which there are shops of Indian weavers, both men and women, using the footloom. The major exception is in the wool processing that I have mentioned. In a whole large region of western Guatemala, the European techniques of carding, spinning—on the wheel—and weaving woolen cloth and blankets, is definitely part of the culture of the Indian communities. Unlike the Ladinoized Indians who weave cotton textiles on footlooms, these wool weavers are clearly not Ladinoized. Nor is the spinning wheel used by other than the wool weavers.

I shall return to this later.

Tailoring, curiously, has also not entered Indian culture except with woolen goods. In the same areas where woolen cloth is made there are Indians who are tailors to fashion the cloth into Indian garments.

On the other hand, there are no Indian shoemakers; nor have shoes ever become part of Indian culture. However, built-up sandals—*hua-raches*, as they are called in Mexico—are becoming popular among the more Ladinoized Indians, and they seem to be primarily neither a Ladino nor an Indian manufacture but are made chiefly by Ladinoized Indians, who also make such items as leather belts and coin purses and saddles, which are otherwise made by Ladinos.

I shall go no further in this rather tedious inventory, because I want to discuss some of the cases in more detail and point out their implications.

Obviously, some of the cases involve matters of taste, like the Indian food complex that has been little affected by the Europeans. I shall not discuss why rice or bread have not replaced tortillas and tamales. I assume that one cannot go much beyond saying that it is a matter of preference that goes back through the generations. Certainly nobody but a nutritionist could raise the question of the relative *efficiency* of diets. The same applies to another example. Indian houses, at least in large regions of Guatemala, do not have windows. When I asked the Indians why not, they took the view that they did not want people to look in. This again approaches a question of taste, and only an expert in hygiene might debate that of relative efficiency.

What we can more profitably explore are those culture elements in which a prima facie case for difference in value can be made. Clearly, there is no question as to why, everywhere in the world, a rifle replaces the bow, or metal tools replace stone tools. They do their jobs better. Some techniques and things are clearly dominant over others. Among the Indians of Guatemala, the pack-animal stage, and the wagon stage, were skipped over. However, an increasing number of Indians are now riding on busses and trucks, simply because they know that the round trip from Sololá or Panajachel to the Guatemala City market that takes them 6 days to walk can be made with double the load in only 2 days; and they earn more money, even taking into account the fare, if they ride the bus. It is more efficient.

We may take it for granted that if, on the other hand, the European culture element is *not* more efficient than the one it is to replace, it will not be adopted. However, efficiency is relative to particular cases, and cannot be judged except in the context of particular circumstances. Thus, for example, the beast of burden. It would seem

more efficient to have a mule carry the Indian's load than to have him carry it on his back. Our whole culture history seems to prove that beasts of burden are useful and we ought therefore to be surprised that they are so little a part of Indian culture. But if we examine the case, we find that its circumstances cast doubt on the efficiency of the beast in the particular instance. A man can carry 100 pounds on a long journey; a mule can carry 200 pounds. A man has to accompany the mule, and the mule is no faster than the man. If the mule were a free good, it would obviously be better to take 200 pounds than 100 pounds in the same time. Indeed, it would be better still to have a string of a dozen mules and transport 2,400 pounds in little more than the same time. In fact, it would be so advantageous that the investment in mules would soon be repaid. However, mules must eat. In a region where pasturage is good, that is no great problem. Indeed, even without much pasturage, but a plentitude of corn land, it would still be no great problem, since the mules could return to the soil, in fertilizer, much of what they take from it.

In much of western Guatemala there is not only a shortage of pasturage, however, but a shortage of land. Most Indians do not grow more than enough corn for their own use, and many grow even less and have to buy corn to make up the difference. Since corn is the major part of the human diet, and must become the major part of the mules' diet, corn must be purchased if the mules are to be fed. The more mules, the more corn that has to be bought. It turns out cheaper in most cases to hire two men to carry the extra goods than to feed one mule.[17]

It could be argued that the Indian could get out of this difficulty by buying corn when it is plentiful and storing it. But (in western Guatemala) he has no technique—neither do Ladinos—for storing corn in the grain, so that it does not rot. He successfully stores corn only on the ear;

---

[17] The question arises why Ladinos use pack mules, as they do. The answer is, first of all, that Ladinos are richer. They own land in much greater quantities than do Indians; they are the ones with surplus corn as well as some pasturage. Furthermore, corn is a less important part of their diet. They eat bread and meat and rice and vegetables and fruit; if they turn most of their corn into transport by feeding it to mules, they can buy the other foods with the profit. If an Indian tries to do this, and does make a profit, and has money to buy corn, he may find no corn on the market when he runs out of his own. And unlike the Ladino, he cannot comfortably eat anything else.

and as it happens, people never sell corn on the ear, but only in the grain.

One could then argue that the whole system might be changed. But if we do that, we only see what is involved in the question of why mules are not today important in Indian culture. Much of the whole technological system, and the economic system, that at first sight does not seem to have anything to do with mules, would have to be altered to accommodate them. The mule comes as part of one culture with which it grew up, so to speak; it is not immediately adaptable to another culture with a long history that did not take account of mules. From the point of view of an individual Indian, the mule is not efficient. And the only way mules can become part of Indian culture is for Indians to take to using them.

There are reverse cases, too, that could be cited to the same point. For example, many of the Indians of Panajachel know that it does not pay to raise chickens, and yet some of them do it. The chickens are their bank account, a way of saving in their peculiar situation. Also, for another example, they raise beans when they could buy them cheaper than it costs them to grow them; that is because they want the beans when beans cannot be surely obtained in the market. Sentiment enters into the matter, too, but the peculiar circumstances of the case are the main key to an apparent anomaly.

But questions of efficiency—even as broadly interpreted as I have been using that word—are not the only guiding factors in explaining why more European elements are not part of these Indian cultures.

Take the case of the potter's wheel. Here surely it ought to be evident that this Old World invention was a great technical advance. Pottery can be turned out quickly and well on the wheel. Let us see what has happened in Guatemala.

It is the women, not the men, who make pottery by hand. It is strictly a household art. The woman of the house, and her children, gather the clay and grind and knead and mold it in the kitchen and courtyard between kitchen chores. The men usually help to fire it, and they take it to market.[18]

Pottery in Europe is made on the wheel primarily by men, specialized artisans who work in their shops in the towns. When the Spanish colonists came to Guatemala, it may be assumed that potters were among them, and that they set up shops in the towns. What may we expect to have happened? Should the Indian women have taken to the wheel simply because the wheel had come to Guatemala? But cultural diffusion is not a process of osmosis; the Indian women would have had to learn to use the wheel. Perhaps they would have had to apprentice themselves to the Spanish potter. This was outside the culture of the Indian women, clearly; also, typically the women speak no Spanish and are shy of strangers; also the Spanish potter would doubtless never have thought to take a female apprentice—and an unlikely one, too. Besides, even were those obstacles overcome, what chance was there that the woman would have gone back to her community to ply and teach her new trade? She would have become Ladinoized and still the potter's wheel would have remained outside of Indian culture.

The alternative was for Indian men rather than women to learn the trade. This was much easier from all points of view. Of course, it happened, too, and there are Indian male potters using the wheel; at least, in the town of Totonicapán there are many of them. But they are partly Ladinoized and definitely town dwellers, outside of normal Indian communities.

With many people—the Ladino descendants of the Spaniards and of the Indians who learned the trade, plus the Indians only partly Ladinoized—making pottery on the wheel, what should have happened to the Indian women potters in competition with the more efficient professionals with their wheels? One might expect the women to give up their art as a losing battle against superior economic efficiency. They should long ago have stopped coiling pots, and then Guatemala pottery today would be like that of Europe, all made on the wheel, exemplifying the triumph of a superior technique.

But no. As it happens, the time of the women who make the pots has no economic value. They live in an area in which the ordinary field crops are dominant; in the agricultural division of labor, the women play small part. The culture grew up with men working in the fields and marketing pottery and with women doing the domestic work and molding pots. If a woman stopped making

---

[18] I am writing particularly of the Indian community of Chimente, a rural district of Totonicapán in which considerable pottery is made.

pottery, she would have nothing to do with her time. But she would not even think of that possibility. Actually, since her time has no economic value, the pots cost nothing to make, unless for some purchased materials. The family could clearly earn more money if she continued to make pots than if she stopped. The competition with wheel-made pottery is under such circumstances only theoretical. So women continue to make pottery, and in the old-fashioned way. In some places, as it happens, women's time is worth money. For example, in Panajachel they work in the onion beds. In a town across the lake— San Pablo—they help their husbands to make rope and hammocks. In both places the women are rapidly dropping the auxiliary household arts that they once practiced. Spinning was the first to go, and then weaving. In San Pablo, the women no longer weave at all; in Panajachel, fewer and fewer learn the art.

Perhaps, it may be suggested, the women who made pots should have found some more lucrative way of making their time earn money. Actually, in the place I am thinking of (Chimente, *municipio* of Totonicapán), the women do not even weave; presumably pottery drove out weaving there some generations ago, just as rope making drove out weaving in San Pablo. Some new art would have to be introduced or some old art expanded. Or the women could help in the fields as they never have. But consider again what changes are demanded simply to get wheel pottery to replace hand pottery in Guatemala.

Spinning and weaving are other interesting cases. I do not know whether the Spanish women who colonized Guatemala brought spinning wheels with them. If they did, spinning may have been an "accomplishment" like playing the piano. Whether they might have tried to teach Indian women to spin, I will not try to imagine—since, I repeat, I do not even know if they knew the art themselves. Today, nobody in Guatemala spins cotton on the wheel. Ladina women do not spin at all; the Indian women who spin use the hand whorl in a bowl. The big mill at Cantel now supplies most of the cotton thread that the weavers use, so Indian women are rapidly forgetting how to spin cotton.[19] The mill has not, however, replaced the hand loom, chiefly because it does not yet make the patterns of cloth that the women use in their garments. Besides, now there is great foreign demand for the hand-woven textiles, and for this market the mill will never be able to compete.

Foot looms, on the other hand, can and do turn out material which is used in Indian garments and which is also, incidentally, purchased by foreign lovers of native arts and crafts. Indeed, Indian women have almost universally stopped weaving material for their skirts because they prefer to buy that of the foot looms. The blouses of the women have more individuality from town to town, so it will take longer for the foot looms to supply the small individual demands, if they ever do. More likely what will happen is that the Indian women will give up their distinctive local blouses and wear the more generalized types that are made on foot looms, just as with the skirts. This will probably happen, however—as in the cases mentioned—only if and when and where other occupations for women give their time more value than it has at their looms. And this may never happen, now that foreigners are buying their textiles.

The foot looms, like the potter's wheels, are in the hands primarily of Ladino artisans in shops in the towns. As in the case of pottery, some Ladinoized Indian men have learned the art. The same explanations that are used to explain why Indian women do not replace their backstrap looms with foot looms obviously applies here as well.[20] Not only culture traits, but entire economic complexes come into competition.

The case of the Indian adoption of the European wool complex mentioned above confirms this thesis. There is no question of the Ladinoization of these wool-working Indians. They are rural dwellers and as much part of Indian societies as any in Guatemala. But it should be recalled that the Indians keep the sheep; sheer, wash, and card the wool—all in the European manner—as well as spin it on the wheel and weave it on the foot loom. Obviously, we are here dealing with an entire complex of European origin. In the manner that one would expect, it has diffused to the Indians in

---

[19] Unlike the case of pottery, the efficiency of the mill has its expected effect for two reasons—first, because raw cotton in the highlands is not a free good, but has to be bought; and second and more important, all women who spin can also weave, so with cheap thread from the mill, they simply spend more time at their looms.

[20] I cannot explain the exceptional case of the women of San Pedro Sacatepequez (Dept. of San Marcos), where Indian women work at foot looms in the shops. This is an extraordinary town, the only one I know that is a Spanish-type town in every respect except that it is populated exclusively by Indians. Perhaps if one studied the place he would discover that in some sense all of the Indians have become Ladinoized; and that might explain the anomaly of the women foot-loom operators.

its entirety, except that many of the designs are typically Indian. This complex was not called upon to replace anything in the culture. Wool was something new. Not only new but obviously, in that cold mountainous country, something very desirable. The men and the women both took something that gave them a source of income; the women do the washing and carding and the men the spinning—wheel spinning, learned from Ladino artisans—and the foot-loom weaving.

The lesson to be learned is that where other things are equal, an advantageous, or more efficient, trait of technology will impose itself upon an alien culture; but that other things are not of course equal, and the particular circumstances, economic and social, override the element of abstract or objective differential in efficiency. The further lesson to be learned, I think, is that the phenomena of diffusion and culture contact are to be understood only in the very intimate terms that are afforded by intimate contact with the situations in which the actual people are involved.

It need not surprise, therefore, that history and circumstance have supplied the Indians of Pana-jachel with its own peculiar roster of technological traits. This roster is amply inventoried in the course of this monograph. Here need be made only a general statement to show the sense in which Panajachel has a "primitive" (even though not pre-Columbian) technology.

Panajachel is outside the highland sheep-raising area; therefore, nothing of the entire wool complex (except the wearing of woolen garments woven elsewhere) is present. Likewise, pasture could hardly be scarcer than in Panajachel; and there is a shortage of corn even for human consumption. So horses and mules are little used; no domestic animals except fowl are fully part of local technology, although pigs are fattened, a few head of cattle are kept and the cows are milked, and there are a few sheep.

On the other hand, the culture of vegetables of European origin is the chief commercial enterprise. The fruit and vegetables grown in the Lake region were introduced soon after the Conquest; whether the irrigation technique that makes possible the year-round gardening characteristic of Panajachel was introduced from abroad, or was adapted from old Indian ideas to the new crops, is impossible to say. The technology involved (given the idea of taking water off the river by means of a network of ditches) is simple and nonspecific and could have been an invention suggested by local geography, here or elsewhere in western Guatemala.

It would be reckless to say that European technology is entirely absent in Panajachel; but it is clear, at the same time, that the technology of Panajachel is on the whole "primitive" or pre-Columbian. Panajacheleños use the products of animal husbandry (leather, soap, candles, lard, meat) but do not make them. A few metal-tool types (hoes, axes, machetes, etc.) are used, but none are manufactured; carpentry and masonry, with their specialized tools are not specialties typical of Panajachel. I doubt if there is a screw-driver, even, in any Indian's tool chest. There are no smiths. Plows are not used; the wheel is not used (not one Indian family has a cart or wheelbarrow or anything of the sort—even a pulley). Pottery is not made at all, so there is no question of the potter's wheel. Spinning (what little there is) and weaving are done in old Indian fashion; and only sewing and embroidering (with the needle—there are no machines) are perhaps European additions to textile arts.

Except that the relatively recent coffee culture has been taken over as a complex which happens to include a hand-turned rotary cylinder to remove the pulp from the bean, agriculture is accomplished by means of hand techniques entirely. Skill is important, but is confined to skill in the use primarily of the hands, aided only by simple tools like the hoe and the tin pan used in sprinkling the gardens. The Indians are skillful in preparing and fertilizing neat gardens, in planting, trans-planting, watering, and obtaining the seed. Garden culture is careful and very intensive; but it is strictly "hand" work.

If the Indian technology of the region as a whole is "primitive," that of Panajachel happens to be particularly so.

TECHNOLOGY AND ECONOMY

As we all know, it has been a popular theory that the free functioning of the system of economy that permits each individual to pursue his own interest in competition with other individuals is the system that in the long run produces the greatest wealth in the community.[21] Mercan-

---

[21] Adam Smith (1937, pp. 11–15) argues that self-interest lies behind the division of labor which is mainly responsible for the wealth. It is not clear to me how he relates division of labor to technological progress. His

tilism was assailed because it interfered with free trade and free competition and hence slowed the accumulation of the nation's wealth; and frequently any governmental planning is deplored because our high standard of living is claimed to be the result of the rugged individualism of free competition and the free functioning of the laws of supply and demand.

In the light of that theory—that it is the free-competitive economic system that makes for the production of wealth and the high standard of living—there may occur to the reader a simple question. Why is it that this region of Guatemala, which has so close an approach to the ideally free competitive economy—where rugged individualism is not bothered by governmental red tape or by labor unions or trusts—why is it, then, that the region is so poor and the standard of living so abysmally low? Here, where there should be wealth, the day-labor rate of pay is 10 to 15 cents a day. The people, entering the second third of the twentieth century, live without medical aid or drugs, in dirt-floored huts with hardly any furniture, the light only of the fire that smokes up the room, or of a pitch-pine torch or a little tin kerosene lamp; the mortality rate is high; the diet is meager and most people cannot afford more than a half-pound of meat a week. The chickens or oranges that they grow they eat only on special occasions because they are worth more on the market than their growers can afford to consume. Schools are almost nonexistent; the children cannot be spared from work in the fields. The freight of the country is carried up and down the steep mountain in loads on the backs of the Indian men or on the heads of the women. Life is mostly hard work, and one is apt to get sick if he worries or complains about it. And if he does get sick, and is kept from work for a few weeks and has to hire a medicine man—there go his life savings, and his land and his means of making a decent living. For one lives here with a precariously bare margin of safety, and the difference between wealth and poverty is a slim little piece of bad luck.

I do not know if the level of living among the

emphasis is on the skills of men that it improves rather than in accumulation of technical knowledge, although when he argues that water carriage made possible large scale, hence more effective, division of labor, hence (?) improved technology, an inference may be drawn that wealth comes from both improved division of labor and technology. In later chapters, Smith makes very clear his realization that technological improvements (e. g. in weaving, p. 246) bring about reduced prices and abundance.

Indians of Guatemala is one of the lowest in the world; it is difficult to compare with such places as China and India. But it is surely low enough to give meaning to the question: Why does not the fact that everybody works hard for himself alone, and seeks to maximize his own rewards, have the effect of creating wealth for all?

I suppose the answer is pretty obvious. The main reason is that the technology of the region, as described above, is inferior. It may be argued that the land is poor, that natural resources are lacking. This may be true: if there are important mineral deposits, they are not known; the land is perhaps not too rich. But clearly the use of natural resources is relative to the technology. The England of King Arthur's time had more coal in the ground than it has today. England's technological development is certainly as much cause as it is consequence of its natural resources. There may not be coal in this region of Guatemala, but there *are* streams of running water, and they *could* be harnessed for use. In these days when we seem on the verge of getting energy from atoms perhaps of some common materials, it seems futile to speak of natural resources unqualified by considerations of technical knowledge.

No—what seems to be lacking in Guatemala is the beginning of the accumulation of technical knowledge that eventually results in improvement in the material standards of life. This technical knowledge need not be indigenous; it could be diffused from without. Nor may it require "industrialization"—the area might well remain largely agricultural and still take advantage of better technology. How this might happen is illustrated by the case of motor vehicles. Although the Indians failed to adopt many items of sixteenth-century European technology, I have mentioned that contemporary Indians are taking to the use of motor-vehicle bus or truck lines that are owned and operated by Ladinos. A continuation of this trend alone (even if nothing else changes) will eventually contribute to raising the level of living in the region. I do not know how many man-hours of time are spent in carrying produce to market on foot, but it must run into the millions in the whole region. At least half of this time will be saved when it becomes common practice to ride in busses and trucks, and when these are available between all points. In consequence, either there will be more leisure—and possibly more mischief, of course—or more production, which usually means a higher level of living; or, more important still, it will make easier the education of children which, eventually—given the reasonably practical rural educational system that one can without danger forecast—will facilitate the introduction of new agricultural and industrial techniques which will in turn again raise the level of living and give new impetus to the whole process.

This is bound to happen in Guatemala; and if the social system permits the rural Indians their share of such improvement, physical conditions will surely improve. The point is, however, that the improvement will be the effect not of the economic system as such, but of improvement in tools of production and communication. It seems clear enough that no matter how successful the individuals of a society may be in pursuing their own interests, they will not increase the wealth of that society unless they have something with which to increase it.

This is doubtless not a new observation, although I have never seen or heard it expressed; but it seems to me to come out rather dramatically in the Guatemalan situation here described. I am led to observe also that it is perhaps a significant fact of our social history that modern economic theory had its beginnings in a period of increasing technological perfection. Probably no economic system could have prevented the increase in the wealth of industrial nations. Yet, because of the coincidence in time—if it was a coincidence, which it probably was not—this increase in wealth has been attributed at least in part to the effectiveness of the economic system from which, it was predicted, it would result. If the economists had been living not in Europe or America but in western Guatemala these past two hundred years, they could not have credited to free competition the glory that progress in technology has deserved. But of course if they had lived in Guatemala, they would not have been economists—they would have been very enterprising peddlers.

THE LAND

NATURAL RESOURCES

If "nature peoples" are contrasted with "city peoples," with the criterion simply the directness of the use of natural resources, Panajachel probably falls closer to the artificiality of the city than it does to nature. Although the Indians are dependent upon the vagaries of nature, live close to the elements, and are reasonably adapted to the climate, their positive direct utilization of what the wild flora and fauna offer is slight. In a statistical sense the products of the wild play virtually no part in the economy.

The Indians realize fully their dependence on the orderly processes of nature. They fear the end of the world, which may come from flood or an eclipse of the sun or moon or from a violent earthquake. But except that such fears may encourage prayer and some avoidance of sin, they hardly affect daily life. The Indians avoid lightning and sharp winds when possible. When rain or drought is untimely, and the eroding river becomes unruly and threatens the town, they call upon all of the spiritual resources available. When sickness comes, they often exhaust not only their spiritual but their material resources.

Some beliefs about nature materially affect everyday life. For example, the physiology of plants and animals changes with the phases of the moon so that lumber is cut and corn harvested chiefly during alternate fortnights. Or, because supernatural beings are abroad at night, commerce tends to cease at nightfall. But in the main, economic procedures are dictated by practical considerations—even on our standards—alone. This is least true when the procedures concern elements old in the culture and close to the basis of life (such as corn) and most true with newer elements and those whose value is reckoned only in terms of money (such as oranges or onions). But it is a strong tendency throughout. The following discussion of the Indian adjustment to his surroundings can therefore be made largely by economic criteria; for although in Panajachel action is grounded in a matrix of presuppositions distinct from those of our culture, it is guided by what we regard as the practical.

CLIMATE

The seasonal rain is essential to cornfield agriculture and saves watering of the irrigated gardens.

But considering the occasional torrential rains that destroy land and crops, and enforce idleness, the rains are also a liability. The Indians frequently feel it as such. The rainy season is a time of sickness and of poverty with granaries exhausted just when corn is scarcest and highest and when cash income from garden and market is lowest. It is also a time of tension, and fear of the elements. It is a relief to the Indians when the short dry period in August permits them to do their outside chores (such as supplying firewood) and freely take the mountain trails. The release is greater when the rains end entirely. The corn harvest is at hand, and gardening and commerce reach their full tempo. Even so, in the rhythm of the year the first rains of May, after the windy and dusty dry season, are welcomed by the Indians and (in their words) by the thirsty earth alike.

The clothing and shelter of the Indians is reasonably well suited to the climate. The women's garments seem too heavy for comfort in the heat of the day; some have changed their costume partly for this reason. Footgear is infrequent and all are accustomed to getting their feet wet frequently. Merchants on the road wear sandals and in the rainy season carry raincapes made of palm fronds. Around town there is little formal protection against a sudden storm. While not completely weatherproof, the thatched-roof cane-and-adobe houses are substantial, and the kitchen fire helps to keep them warm. At night a light blanket often covers three or four persons, with the temperature below 50° and the fire out. An assessment of the Indian adjustment to the climate must take into account both that the people are hardened and accustomed to what they have, and that the death rate is high, especially in the rainy season.

THE RIVER

The river is less curse than blessing. The bed of the river is a wide, rocky nuisance. In the rainy season the quiet stream in the center divides into rushing torrents of brown water carrying rocks and timber from the hills above, is impassable for days at a time, and causes particular difficulty for those who live on the side opposite the town center. Worst of all, the streams at times wash away acres of the fertile soil of the river banks, including the houses of some and all of the real possessions of a few. But the river is also the source of the irrigation system basic to the garden agriculture that in large part supports the Indians. The irrigation system serves every part of the delta, and through both an appropriate technology and communal effort and control the water is very effectively utilized. When water is short and there is moonlight, many of the Indians water their gardens at night. Although people are accused of many kinds of nonsocial acts, Indians are rarely if ever charged with wasting water. The technique of watering fields requires a minimum of water. Various farmers may use the same ditch at once by filling single gutters through their fields and shutting off the egress of water while using it. Land is flooded only for special purposes; ordinarily water is simply dipped out of the gutter in a tin basin and tossed onto the garden bed.

Most families get most of their kitchen water, and do their laundry, and the women wash their hair, in the river or in the nearest large irrigation channel. (Bathing is done in the sweat bath; relatively few Indian men, and more boys, bathe in the lake.)

In the rainy season the river provides firewood washed down from the hills, and rocks for laundering and fireplace stones, sand for building, and small fish thrown out of the rushing streams.

The few springs in the hills above town might be better utilized, perhaps by following the isolated example of one family which planted a dry-season garden below such a spring.

THE LAKE

For the towns along its shores, Lake Atitlán is important not only as a source of water for personal, household, and agricultural uses (for which purposes Panajacheleños use the river instead), but also as a means of easy travel and a source of fish and crabs, and of sedge used in making a popular type of mat.

In contrast with those of the south shore, particularly Atitlán and San Pedro, the Indians of Panajachel do not regularly travel over the water, mainly because their trade routes do not often carry them to or through the towns across the lake. When Panajachel Indians do go to Atitlán or San Pedro, they go by water (when they go to San Lucas they often go by land because it is not so much more difficult); however, they rarely go to Atitlán or San Pedro, for their communications are with Sololá, Tecpán, and the east rather than with the southland; therefore they infrequently and only exceptionally use the lake for travel. None of the Indians (even those of Atitlán or San Pedro) are fond of water travel; the lake becomes suddenly rough and dangerous. Thus, for example, Pedranos often go overland to Sololá when the lake is rough, a journey of a day that is made on the water in 3 hours. Probably the major distinction between towns is that the Indians of the south shore have strong incentives to water travel because they frequently and in great numbers go to Sololá and Tecpán.

Canoes are made only by the Indians of the south shore where suitable timber is found. Canoes in Panajachel (and Santa Catarina, which has more) are all bought from canoe makers of Atitlán, San Pedro, and San Pablo. Possibly this fact influenced the establishment of trading patterns so that the Indians of the south rather than those of the north shore carry the merchandise between the highlands and the lowlands.

Distribution of the use of canoes for commercial fishing, crab fishing, and sedge gathering is like that for transport except that Santa Catarina has a great fishing, crab fishing, and matting industry. Save on general grounds of economic specialization, it is very difficult to explain why Panajachel (or San Antonio or Santa Cruz), for example, does not engage in such activities. Take fishing for example.

The lake abounds in tiny fish; one variety is about an inch long, another twice that size, and a very few weigh up to a half pound. Some parts of the lake may be better stocked than others; the Panajachel Indians claim that a generation ago there were many more fish than now in their neighborhood. In Panajachel, informants said canoes were never used in fishing; but they described four other methods once used here, all of which are still known in some villages. According to informants who claimed to remember the old state of affairs, by one method of shore fishing, in which a party of some 20 boys drove the fish into a large conical trap, each of the boys caught as much as 25 pounds of fish after 3 hours' work. If this is true, fishing was a better business (at present-day fish prices) than anything else in Panajachel. The question is, why was fishing virtually abandoned? The Indians say that the rising of the lake has destroyed the beach (the

lake *has* risen) and that there are fewer fish near Panajachel than there once were. But another reason that was mentioned is that the people are too busy with agriculture.

Or take crab fishing. The most prominent crab fishers of the lake are the Catarinecos, who in season seem to spend most of their nights with pitch-pine torches and a long baited line of tree filament that is lowered into still water. The fishing is apparently best close to the shore, and some of the favored spots are off Panajachel. Although Panajacheleños once did much crab fishing in this manner, now only two or three exceptional persons do so occasionally. Local Indians also find crabs on the beach and among the rocks near shore, and there is considerable folklore about the pursuit; but on the whole crab gathering is rare and unimportant. The excuses made for not fishing do not all hold for crab fishing; for there *are* crabs near Panajachel. In this case, at least, it is obvious that the Indians are too busy farming to spend their nights crab fishing, particularly since it requires investment in canoes and equipment. The Catarinecos specialize in fishing and crab fishing just as the Panajacheleños specialize in vegetable growing; and the immediate explanation cannot go far beyond that.

The same may be said of the sedge that grows at Panajachel as well as at other parts of the lake shore. But if a few Panajacheleños use canoes for fishing and crab fishing, not one cuts sedge, and no Panajachel Indian manufactures mats. They are made in Santa Catarina and in other towns of the south shore, the industry evidently connected with the use of canoes.

Owners of the three canoes of Panajachel were, in 1936 and 1937, a half-Ladino and two young Indians who are brothers-in-law. They used them to ferry passengers across the lake, and around the impassable river in the rainy season; they also fished a little, with hooks and nets (new techniques learned from Ladinos) and traps bought from the Catarinecos; and they crab fished occasionally. All three are more clearly entrepeneurs than remnants of a cultural tradition.

The Atitecos and to a lesser degree the Catarinecos use their canoes to hunt the waterfowl which come in the dry season, hitting the birds with stones. The Panajacheleños say they used to hunt them from the shore with slingshots, never in canoes; but few of the Indians do this now, and never commercially.

It may be concluded that as far as the economy of the Panajachel Indians is concerned, if a magic wand should cause the lake to disappear overnight, it would hardly be missed.

WILD FAUNA

There are a few large animals in the hills of the *municipio*, and in neighboring hills where Panajacheleños hunt as freely: deer, coyotes, wildcats, and "honey bears." (See Glossary.) The meat and/or skins and other parts are valued. The Indians generally do not hunt this large game, although Ladinos, who own rifles, do.

There are more smaller animals. Rabbits, skunks, opossums, and weasels are to be found both in the hills and on the delta. They are killed when possible, for they damage the crops; but except that the weasel's skin has some value, they cannot be used for anything. Porcupines, *taltuzas*, coatis, raccoons, armadillos, *tepescuintles*, and squirrels are found in the hills. They are occasionally hunted, and the meat of the last four eaten; skins of raccoons, *tepescuintles*, and squirrels and the shell of the armadillo are used or sold; the penis bone of the raccoon or coati has special uses. It may be doubted, however, whether from one year to the next more than a dozen of all of these animals are killed.

Birds are more numerous. Besides the waterfowl, 44 kinds were described as being very common. Of these, 16 are found in the delta portion, 21 in the delta and the hills as well, and 6 exclusively in the hills; one migratory species simply passes over Panajachel twice a year. Most kinds the Indians, particularly the small boys, occasionally capture or kill. One man estimated that his family killed 80 birds in a year. A bird not hunted is the carrion buzzard which is of no use dead (except in a cure for madness) and of very considerable value alive. Some birds are killed not because their parts are utilizable but because they are dangerous alive; such for example, are the grackles which prey on the cornfields, and the hawks which prey on barnyard fowl. On the other hand, Indians will not usually kill birds that are considered augurs of ill because they fear the supernatural consequences; or birds otherwise "dangerous," like one supposed to change into a snake when about to be

caught; or others, like the swallow, because they are holy. In these cases, however, the Indians also say they would have no use for the birds killed or captured. Twenty-two species are listed as edible, and said to be killed and eaten. Fifteen are specifically said not to be edible, five of these "because they feed on insects" (but so do a few edible birds), two "because they eat excrement," and one snakes; two others are birds of ill-omen, and one is connected with sickness; the swallow is not eaten because of its saintlike character. In the cases of three birds (including the buzzard and the chicken hawk) no reason was given.

A few birds have medicinal and other uses. A few are caught and caged; but if the Indians catch them they usually sell them to Ladinos, for the Indians themselves almost never keep caged birds (except pigeons) in the house.

Few Indians own guns, licensed expensively by the Government. Sticks and stones and machetes are the commonplace weapons. A few blowguns (through which pebbles are shot) are used to kill birds, but the most commonly used weapon for birds and small animals is the slingshot, and most of the men and boys are adept in its use. It is a forked branch through which a stone or large seed is hurled with the aid of rubber bands made from inner tubes and bought in the market place. Indians know but do not have hunting dogs, although they take their ordinary dogs when they hunt the larger animals. Traps are used, not to capture game for food, but to protect fields and barnyard. Thus, coyotes are caught in pitfalls with roosters and corn as bait; grackles are usually caught by tying kernels of corn to a string so that when they swallow the corn they are held fast; rats and mice and some of the larger animals that invade the cornfields are caught in a variety of deadfalls. Boys catch songbirds to sell to Ladinos by smearing on the branches of trees a sticky substance made from bird lime which holds the birds fast.

Relatively few snakes (probably not poisonous) are to be found in the neighborhood. The Indians do not mind killing them, but the meat is not eaten; or other parts used. The several varieties of lizards found locally are not used and are usually avoided as poisonous. Frogs and toads are also for the most part avoided.

Insects are abundant, but except for bee culture and the use of insects in certain remedies, the

Indians do not utilize them in a practical way. Such smaller forms of animal life as worms and grubs and weevils are, in their relations to the Indians, only detrimental.

WILD FLORA

Much more important in Indian life than the fauna are the three hundred trees and plants, most wild, some semicultivated, described as growing in Panajachel. I have information on uses of about 200 of these. In the discussion which follows, they are divided roughly into classes such as trees, bushes, herbs, etc.

Although trees are often planted in particular places, either for shade or fences, they are almost never cared for. Since the same may be said in some degree of fruit trees, it is not easy (or important) to distinguish the wild from the cultivated, especially since shade trees in coffee fields serve a purpose clearly commercial.

At least 10 different trees furnish posts and poles for building, the hardwoods *guachipilín* and oak preferred. Oak is said to be the best firewood, but almost all are equally common. Fruit trees, especially those standing at crossroads, are felled supposedly only at the risk of one's life, and hence are rarely used in building, and only the branches are commonly used in the fire. Some woods are not used for firewood for reasons that may not be sound: *jiote* (madrone) wood when burned gives a sickness of the same Spanish name, which is the word for mange; *guachipilín* is too hard to split; to burn wood of trees that yield fruit in the rainy season causes the fruit to be wormy. But since the Indians normally cut and gather all the firewood they need, and rarely if ever import any, it must be supposed that their reasoning, if false, is not economically harmful.

The uses of trees in agriculture are many. *Ilamo*, eucalyptus, and silk-oak trees (as well as bananas) are planted for shade in the coffee fields; rotted leaves of the coffee bushes are the most common fertilizer in the vegetable gardens; willow, *ilamo*, and silk-oak branches and certain large leaves such as banana are used to cover newly planted seeds to shade them while they germinate; and willow is planted along the river edge to prevent erosion, and around springs to keep them from drying up. From *guachipilín* and oak, *taxisco*, avocado, and citrus come the hafts of iron tools as well as wedges, stakes,

harvesting nails, and mortars. Cudgels (commonly coral and citrus branches) may be chosen poorly because a hardwood supposedly becomes soft and a softwood hard in dealing with supernatural beings. Fences are made from *jocote* (Spanish plum) and the very thorny *coyol* branches; but small trees (especially madrone, coral, yucca, and *amate*), supposed never to die, are often planted for the purpose. Fiesta decorations for houses, streets, and saints come mostly from local trees—pine (needles, branches), cypress (branches), silk-oak (flowers), citrus fruits (flowers, leaves, fruit), *coyol* (branches), and *pacaya* (leaves)—and plants. Parts of trees are also used as children's toys (e. g., soapseed and *paterna* seeds, acorns, coral flowers, castor leaves) and to make toys (e. g., guava wood for horns, and citrus-fruit branches for slingshots).

Trees furnish very little of the Indians' food. Salable fruit is usually sold and varieties not interesting enough to be marketable are usually left to rot. Although aware that certain branches, flowers, seeds, and fruit of local trees are used in cooking elsewhere, Panajachel Indians make almost no use of them. On the other hand, many parts of trees are used in the preparation of medicines; for examples may be mentioned pine pitch; "buzzard tree," nance, and coral bark; madrone bark and gum; *amate* "milk"; guave, eucalyptus, and *nogal* leaves; citrus-fruit leaves, juice, and skins; and avocado and *anona* seeds.

The following miscellany, finally, will give an idea of the variety of uses of parts of trees. Yucca leaves and *capulin* bark are substitutes for leather, and the fibers of the first are used for tying; a soap is taken from the soapseed tree; pine pitch is used to repair canoes; *tuna*-leaf gum is mixed with the lime to make whitewash stick; thorny *tuna* leaves are placed in paths to keep people and animals out; the oil of cross-sapodilla seeds is used as a hairdress by some men; silk-oak gum is used as paste in kite making; *taxisco* branches are used as hangers in the house; the *toronja* is used ceremonially as a candle holder; coral seeds are used by diviners; and so on.

Yet, certainly, the Indians do not make full use of their trees. For example, the *cajete* tree is used in other places to make boxes; but the Panajacheleños do not know how. Nor do the local Indians engage in lumbering; they use the lumber undressed for their houses, and if they need boards or beams they must buy them from other Indians. Nor is there a carpenter or a cabinetmaker among the Panajacheleños.

Much the same can be said of other plants. The partial inventory that follows indicates their diverse uses; yet the Indians know that other peoples utilize them in ways that they do not. For example, a half-dozen varieties of tree filaments are known and substituted for rope in tying and binding, and in the case of one kind the leaves and flowers are used medicinally. But the Indians of Santa Catarina make special use (as crab-fishing lines) of one variety found in Panajachel.

Other examples are a small plant that grows along the irrigation ditches in Panajachel, not used locally, but gathered by Santa Catarina Indians who take it home to feed to their barnyard fowl; laurel leaves, not eaten here but known to be used in cooking by Ladinos and by Indians of Tecpán and Patzún; a plant called "white soap," used by Sololá Indians for soap, and even sold by them in the markets, but not used by Panajachel Indians who buy animal soap. The century plant is a good example of one not fully utilized. It grows wild, and is occasionally planted. Indians say that they used to beat out the fiber to make rope, bags, etc. (as is done in towns across the lake) but during the years of this study no Panajacheleño practiced the art. The only part of the plant used is the thorn at the end of the leaf which is used in the backstrap loom and to extract chigoes from the toes.

The flowers of two tree parasites and the leaves of two others find use in ceremonial adornment. Bird-lime fruit is used to trap birds. Several kinds of mushroom are eaten. A vine called "bird's claw" is used for tying, and its flower is made into a whistle by the children; animals browse on the leaves of another, *pega pega;* the flowers of the *choreque* are used in food; the "mouse ear" is placed under the vegetable-pear vine to induce it to produce fruit as abundantly as it does; and the leaves of five different vines are used medicinally.

Besides one cultivated fodder grass, at least three wild grasses are used primarily for fodder. Although most thatch straw is imported from towns where it is cultivated (local land is said to be too valuable for such use), three wild grasses are suitable. A grass called *sabagasta* is used by

muleteers to stuff pack-saddles. Another called "lime tea" is a common medicine. Wild canes, and a semicultivated variety (as well as cornstalks) are widely used in building the walls and roofs of the houses, such structures as granaries, furnishings like shelves and beds, for fences around the vegetable gardens, for beanstalks, and for other things requiring poles and hollow tubes. Cane leaves are used to wrap *tamales* and the sap, leaves, flowers, and stem tips of some varieties (e. g., the elder tree) are used medicinally.

Bushes like *chilca, barrejón,* and *pus* furnish fuel for the sweat bath, as do cane and smaller branches of many trees. *Tziquinay* and *sajoc* and many other bushes are used for kitchen firewood. Tamarisk-shrub wood is used for ax hafts, the branches of the "sunflower of the rocks" as bean poles, and "little broom," "sweat-bath plant," and *chichicaste* branches to beat the body while in the bath. *Chilca,* "little broom," and a plant called *queché,* make good brooms. *Chilca* branches are also used as bean poles and spits, and its leaves are used to cover young vegetable plants. Leaves of the "deer's tongue" bush are edible, those of many other medicinal.

The longest list of plants includes the smaller shrubs, flowers, and herbs. To many known by name, no use could be ascribed. Some two-thirds of the 34 plants on which I have information have medicinal but no other uses. In some cases it is the whole plant, in others the stem or leaves or both, in still others the juice or sap that is used; and of course the medicines are prepared in a number of different ways. To list the plants would be tiresome. It is noteworthy that wild plants are not of great importance in the preparation of food. Besides those mentioned above, of which the fruits are of greatest importance, I can add only 15 plants that find any place in the diet. Of these perhaps 4 are commonly used: the *chipilín* herb, purslane, amaranth, and the roots of the "mother of maize" plant, which the poor are said to use as a substitute for corn when the latter is not available. But on the whole the wild vegetable foods constitute only a negligible part of the total diet.

The other uses of the many small plants are not many. The leaves of one are burned in the sweat bath; those of another are used to wrap *tamales,* and of a third to line baskets of fruit and to protect other things. Three of the plants are good for animal grazing. One (skunk plant) is used to keep mice out of newly planted corn; another (bitter sunflower) to drive ants out of the milpa; a third (rosemary) is burned in the house to keep out evil spirits. A number of plants, especially flowers, are used in ceremonial adornment; among them are "mouth of the dragon," bougainvillea, "flower of death," "easter flower," and the red geranium. Many flowers in addition are cultivated for secular adornment, much less frequently by Indians than by Ladinos.

LAND USE

In explaining why the utilization of "wild" products is relatively slight one must remember that they are not free goods. It takes time to hunt or fish or gather. Simply, the Indian usually makes more profitable use of his time tilling the fields or marketing produce. The community lives, on the whole, well above a bare subsistence level; it does not eke out a living with what can be found in woods or water; it has an element of choice in the use to which human resources will be put; and therefore it can put market-selected food above what may be "freely" collected, and does. At the same time, the community is not so rich that it can choose less rather than more profitable employments of time.

In this competition for time, agriculture is the clear victor. The Indians have taken advantage of the alluvial plain, or "delta," and its possibilities of dry-season farming to develop a year-round intensive horticulture; and above all else in both an economic and a sentimental sense—above even the cultivation of milpa on the hillsides—this is their life.

It is with respect to land use, depending as it does so largely on local conditions, that the various towns of the region differ most greatly. The culture—in the sense of technology and consumption habits, of beliefs and customs, and of religious and political organization—follows rather closely a single pattern with but minor differences from one community to the next. But the economic base, in the sense of what the people exploit to earn their living, differs more widely. Most of what is reported here about the use of land in Panajachel is necessarily unique to Panajachel, where the topography makes special demands and affords special opportunities. The argument, however, that the Indians have achieved an adjustment to

the land that (given the technology) is highly efficient is doubtless more generally applicable. Each community of Indians has developed a *modus vivendi* relative to its peculiar conditions that may strike the observer as efficient—and there is no intention here to extol as peculiar the efficiency of the Panajachel adjustment.

To answer the question of how, and how well, the community utilizes its resources and fulfills its potentialities, it is necessary to accept the technology as a constant. The techniques of agriculture that are used by the Indians differentiate them on the one hand from hunting or gathering peoples, and on the other from societies with machinery; that is not difficult. But those techniques also differentiate Panajachel from other Indian communities; for the meticulous kind of intensive garden agriculture common here is quite different from the field agriculture practiced generally in the region. An acre of Panajachel garden land can require 33 times as much labor as an acre of ordinary milpa! The problem of the relations between land and labor must be very different in Panajachel from what they are in corn-raising communities like Chichicastenango or in communities which combine milpa agriculture with time-consuming industries like basketry, pottery, rope- or mat-making, or foot-loom weaving. The industrial communities frequently employ the time of men, women, and children as much as Panajachel, but not on the land. At the same time, the land may be just as "intensively" used, given the kind of agriculture. The situations are simply not comparable.

Since technology is evidently *not* constant—either in the world, or as between towns in Guatemala—it is evident that one cannot assess the success of a people in making use of its resources. When one says that an Iowa farmer "makes better use of the land" because he gets so many bushels of corn per acre as compared with some other place, one means that Iowa technology is more advanced. *Given* Panajachel technology, it would be difficult to argue that the Indians do not get more out of their land than the best Iowa farmers. But again such comparisons are meaningless.

HILL LAND

The area of the *municipio* of Panajachel included in this study is shown on the insert in

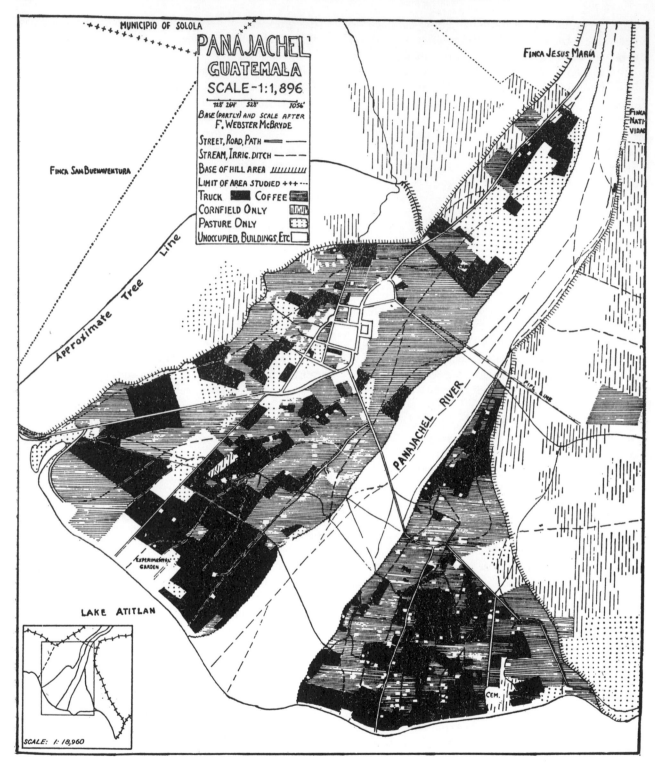

MAP 4.—Land use.

map 4, and comprises by my calculation, [22] 1,530 acres of land surface, divided as follows:

	Acres
Delta	580
West hill	420
East hill	530

[22] Based on laborious calculations on the map itself, with corrections for slopes, checked by information on areas of all of the individual pieces of land. McBryde's maps (see McBryde, 1947) and personal advice were helpful. Figures on hill lands are subject to much greater error than those on delta lands, both because the survey problem is much greater and because the importance of the delta lands is reflected in correspondingly more information.

The use of this land, as estimated for 1936,[23] is summarized in chart 2. The west hill rises more precipitously than the east, is more rocky and barren, and is unwatered. In places near its summit it is lightly forested, a source of firewood. Corn grows only in a few small fields near the base of the hill north of town, and a large one

[23] The figures and description, unless otherwise noted, are all for the base year 1936. The present tense is frequently used with reference to that year.

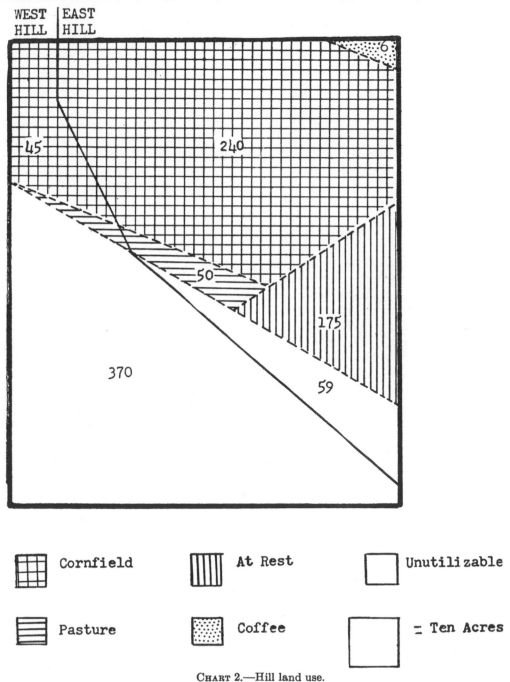

CHART 2.—Hill land use.

high above the delta. A piece of land is used for pasture. Otherwise the west hill is sterile. The measure of its unproductivity is the fact that in 1936 only about 50 acres, 45 cornfield and 5 pasture, produced more than firewood and perhaps a few wild plants. Very few more than these 50 acres, certainly less than 12 percent of the whole, is utilizable agriculturally.

A much greater proportion of the east hill, more irregular in its rise, can be put to agricultural and pastoral uses. The entire slope is not part of the territory of Panajachel, or included in this study; perhaps the upper third is land of the neighboring *municipio* of San Andrés. The 530 acres of Panajachel land, including territory from the base of the hill to the San Andrés line and from the boundary with Santa Catarina to the plantation "Natividad," are not all shown on map 4, but their limits may be seen in the insert map.

The figures in chart 2 are accurate to within a few percentile points except for the uncertain line between the land "at rest" and unutilizable, which is little better than a guess. The cornfield land classified as "resting" had been used before 1936, as evidenced by the land itself and specific information from many informants, and some of it has been planted since 1936, while other cornfields have since lain fallow. The unused land, like that which is never utilizable agriculturally, is meanwhile a source of firewood and useful plants.

This east hill is watered by three streams and a spring that is tapped for the town's water supply. In 1937 a small fraction of an acre of land watered by the largest of the streams, in a relatively level pocket half way up the hill, was utilized for vegetable growing in the dry season. By 1941 this vegetable area had grown to several acres. By 1941 also, the hillside acreage devoted to coffee had grown to 50 or 60 acres, at the expense of cornfields.

If fallow land, including pasture, is called agricultural, it may be said that all potentially agricultural land was so utilized in 1936. No case appeared in which apparently suitable land was said to be left indefinitely untilled for any reason. This is not to say that all land was used optimally. Evidence to the contrary is the fact that after 1936 some was cultivated more intensively by replacing corn with coffee and vegetables. Nor do I have a way of knowing if some of the land that was resting should not really have been planted, or that some

that was planted should not have been resting. But it seems clear that by and large all suitable hill lands are, over the course of years, put to agricultural uses.

DELTA LAND

It is with somewhat more confidence that I turn to data on the delta portion of Panajachel. First, because the area is much more easily delimited (as shown on map 4) as being confined by the two hills, the lake, and the boundries of the fincas to the north. Second, because the land, being level, is relatively easily paced off; the topography presents few problems, even to one not expert in such matters. Third, because once the area is mapped to scale, the accuracy of the dimensions of plots of land, as furnished by informants, can be checked by measurements on the map itself.[24]

The area of the delta comprises about 581 acres, divided as follows:

	Acres
West of river bed	319
River bed	130
East of river bed	132

The river bed is an expanse of stones, sand, and gravel; although in places small foliage has taken root, the whole of it may be considered sterile waste. A few garden beds made during the dry season on reclaimed patches at the east edge of the river bed occupy less than a fifth of an acre. A generation before, according to all reports, the river bed was only a half or a third of its 1936 width; and it has continued to widen by erosion of the fertile banks. At the time of study, stone walls near the right bank helped to protect it (the other was without any protection at all); since then, a flood serious enough to be reported in the United States has doubtless made this statement obsolete.

Aside from the river bed, almost all delta land is utilizable agriculturally. During one rainy season an avalanche of rock and water from the

[24] The delta was originally mapped, with the help of natives and of a simple compass, in April of 1936. Data on land use, and ownership, as well as houses and other features, were plotted. When this map, reduced and printed, was shown to Dr. F. W. McBryde, 4 years later, and compared with a sketch of the same area that he had made in September 1936, it was apparent that revisions would be necessary. Therefore in 1940–41 the map was revised in the field; McBryde himself came to Panajachel in the course of his work and together we checked a number of points. Later, using McBryde's revised map (see McBryde, 1947, map 23) as a base, I went over every part of the delta and made further small corrections. Map 4 is thus the result of collaboration between McBryde and me; but final responsibility for errors is mine.

east hill rendered a strip of land useless. Some of it had been reclaimed by 1936; some 3 acres remained untilled and presumably untillable. In two places on the west side of the delta, irrigation ditches had cut small ravines and rendered fractions of an acre unsuitable for farming. In addition, land within a few feet of the lake edge cannot be cultivated because of the sweep of the waves. Otherwise all of the land is utilizable for agriculture. However, as seen in the following estimate, 48 acres are diverted from agricultural purposes for buildings, roads, irrigation ditches, etc., not counting the narrowest footpaths and irrigation ditches or the little land occupied by fences and land boundaries, which are themselves frequently paths and ditches.

Acreage not utilizable agriculturally:

Buildings, cemetery, houses and patios, etc.	31
Streets, roads, larger paths	13
Main irrigation ditches	4
Unsuited to agriculture: river bed	130
Otherwise unsuited to agriculture	7
Total	185
Potentially agricultural-pastoral	396
Total acreage of delta	581

Of the 396 acres remaining for agricultural uses, only about 10 were not so used in 1936. In other words, almost 97 percent of potentially agricultural land, almost seven-eighths of nonsterile land, and about two-thirds of *all* delta land, including the river bed, were used agriculturally or pastorally. As will be seen below, not all this is so used during every month of each year, but if the information compiled is correct, all of it was used during at least part of 1936, and the general picture had not changed by 1941. Actually, somewhat more than the mentioned seven-eighths of the nonsterile land is regularly in production, for in the patios and gardens of the houses are always to be found fruit trees and flowers, and even vegetables, with commercial value; and lining the roadsides are numerous fruit trees.

The proportion of land in cultivation is greater on the east side of the river than on the west by about 4 percentage points, owing chiefly to the fact that the Ladinos, whose houses and patios occupy much more space per family, live almost exclusively on the west side. The large white spaces west of the river shown on map 4 are the houses, stores, and hotels owned by Ladinos (and one Ladino-owned piece of land used in 1936 as a public playing field and since brought under cultivation). It is a main thesis of this section that land use cannot be discussed without reference to the class of owner, for the questions resolve themselves into discussion not so much of "What kinds of land are used for what purposes?" but of "To what uses do different kinds of people put their land?" Suffice it to say here that the geographical differences are less important than the "racial," and that specifically the Indians cultivate a much greater proportion of the land at their disposal than do the Ladinos.

The following summary, dealing only with land put to agricultural-pastoral uses, classifies it somewhat arbitrarily:

	Acres	Percent
Truck	142	37
Coffee	193	50
Cornfields only	14	4
Pasture only	38	10
Total	387	101

The classification "coffee" is clear, for occupation by coffee bushes is visible and year-round. The term "truck," on the other hand, requires explanation. On the irrigated land of the delta a wide variety of vegetables is grown, with growing seasons of 2, 3, 4, 6, or 11 months. In a large number of cases this land, devoted to onions, garlic, beans, etc. in the dry season, is planted with corn during the rainy months. In some cases this program is carried out year after year. In any case, I have called such land "truck" even though I would prefer that the word not include corn. Some land, however, is never cultivated except during the rainy season, and then is planted only with corn. This land, usually of different quality from truck land, I have classified separately as "cornfield only." The land called "pasture only" is land that was not cultivated in 1936 but on which animals regularly grazed. Animals also grazed along the edges of the river bed and the lake shore, on a few parcels of the truck lands for several months during the year, and in the dry months also on land devoted to corn in season. This land of course is not classified as "pasture only."

A thesis will be developed that in general Panajachel lands are utilized as intensively as possible, especially those owned by Indians. Explanation of the 38 acres of land used only for grazing is therefore required. It is not far to seek. About 4 acres are unsuitable for agriculture, or marginal: 2 acres near the lake shore are marshy, another acre was affected by the wash of a few years before, and two other small pieces are stony. One of the latter might be tilled, but the owner happens to have sufficient better land for his needs. The remaining thirty-four-odd acres of pasture that could have been tilled in 1936 belong almost entirely to Ladinos who own a few cattle, who thus need the pasture, and who are wealthy enough to be able to divert part of their land to this use. One large piece was in family litigation in 1936 and could not therefore be rented to Indians for vegetable growing as it has been since. Disregarding such an exceptional circumstance, it appears to be true that only when a man owns considerable land, and happens to need pasture, will he sacrifice some of it to the purpose. That Indians are rarely in such a position explains why only five Indians had pasture land in 1936. Two of them owned the stony marginal plots alluded to above. The third, a land-rich Indian, had a small piece on which to keep his mule. The fourth, a dairying Indian with sufficient land, had a small pasture for his cattle. I do not have data on the fifth case, involving less than one-fifth acre. The exceptional cases help make it clear that the Indians tend to use all their land as intensively as possible. Statements by Indians suggest that such use is explicitly valued.

The smallness of the percentage (3.6) of delta land confined to the cultivation of corn also confirms the tendency, especially among Indians, to more intensive cultivation. Most "cornfield only" lands are at the foot of the hillsides, chiefly the west hill north of town (map 4). This land is often irregular, stony, and not irrigable and thus not suited to vegetables. The plot at the base of the east hill was rendered unsuitable for gardening by the wash a few years before. The two pieces of land in the delta interior happen also to be too irregular and stony for the easy cultivation of vegetables. Some of the "cornfield only" land, however, appears to be suitable at least for coffee, and by my argument should not be left for corn. The largest single piece (7½ acres) is owned by a relatively poor Ladino family, and I do not know why they do nothing more profitable with it. Another piece is owned by a Ladino who actually has coffee planted in all but this corner of a large

parcel of land. The remaining hill-base cornfields are owned by three Indian families, and two Indian families share with a Ladino the two parcels in the center of the delta. The five Indian families are all well above the average in the amount of land they own and control and so can, perhaps, afford to make less intensive use of these marginal lots. Perhaps the ultimate explanation is that sacrifices are frequently made for the sake of corn growing, since corn is of such great importance in the kitchen.

The statement that land is usually devoted exclusively to corn only when it is unsuitable for more intensive use also explains the cornfields in the hills, most of which are good only for rainy-season *milpa*. It is significant that parts of the hills suitable for coffee or vegetables are being more and more converted to such crops. This fact suggests another point about the delta. It seems likely that in years past more land was less intensively used than was the case in 1936 and that the continuing tendency has been to cultivate more and more coffee and vegetables, and to leave less and less land idle or planted only with corn. Informants talk about "new land"; i. e., land with no recent history of vegetable growing; and, as do the other facts available, they indicate that such new land is disappearing. Some of the new land of course is now in coffee, but a good part of what there evidently was, especially on the west side of the delta, is now devoted to truck gardening.

COFFEE OR TRUCK

The reason why lands are alternatively devoted to coffee or to truck demonstrates contrasts between the economies of Indians and Ladinos. Some land may be more suited to coffee than to truck (probably never the reverse); however, the land of the delta is sufficiently homogeneous to make it unlikely that this limiting factor is important. Certainly it is negligible compared to the easily demonstrable fact that the Ladinos tend to grow coffee and the Indians truck. The large blocks of coffee lands shown on map 4 are seen by a comparison with map 6 to be also blocks of land owned by Ladinos; and those where vegetables are grown are predominantly Indian-owned. Chart 3, *a*, a comparison of the two sides of the delta, shows that there is no great difference in the distribution of crops geographically. On the other hand, chart 3, *b*, as clearly shows that coffee is grown very much more on Ladino land than on Indian land. Actually, 78.3 percent of the delta coffee land belongs to Ladinos, while 73 percent of all truck land is Indian-owned. If the land rented by Indians from Ladinos is added, the Indians indeed have 82 percent of all of the truck land. The difference between Indian and Ladino is the overruling factor in the use of land: *wherever* Ladinos own land they tend to grow coffee; *wherever* Indians own land, they tend to grow truck crops. In order to test this rule in detail map 5 compares the relationship in sections of the delta that were divided arbitrarily for another purpose. The figures (table 5) show that there is an exception to the rule; the following analysis both explains the exception and gives additional insight into patterns of land use.

TABLE 5.—*Location of Indian and Ladino coffee and truck lands*

| Section | Acres owned | | | |
| | Ladino | | Indian | |
	Coffee	Truck	Coffee	Truck
W1	46.56	6.04	2.29	6.19
W2	18.45	6.18	3.12	9.94
W3	19.90	4.75	.58	10.76
W4	22.33	5.53	6.17	5.95
W5	3.03	6.28	4.75	32.45
E1	11.88		3.51	7.40
E2	7.67	1.83	5.63	9.33
E3	4.95	1.07	6.00	8.48
E4	2.95	2.11	8.88	11.76
E5	13.34	.24	1.06	2.26
Unknown				.36

(1) The Ladinos consistently own much more coffee than truck land. The notable exception is in section W5 where almost all the coffee-truck land, including that of Ladinos, is in truck. The land involved here is dominated (and was in the past even more dominated) by nonresident Indians from San Jorge la Laguna. Both in San Jorge and Panajachel they grow vegetables and no coffee. All of their land is in truck, and this may influence the local Indian and Ladino W5 landowners in that direction. However, another factor is the relative "age" of various sections. Truck gardening is the traditional Panajachel occupation, coffee having come in relatively recently. The east delta without any doubt was always heavily populated and intensively cultivated, while the west delta was more thinly popu-

lated and less intensively cultivated. Indians recall when on the west delta there were large forests of cane so thick that animals and even people became lost in them. One of the reasons why Indians took to replacing truck with coffee is that the land was no longer producing truck crops abundantly. This must have been especially true in the east delta, a fact that is part of the explanation of why the Indians have a larger percentage of their land in coffee in the east delta than in the west. Conversely, the Indians talk about the land of section W5 as "new land," and one concludes that it is devoted almost exclusively to vegetables partly because of the Jorgeño tradition, and partly because it has been producing truck products most profitably.

(2) There is a tendency for the Ladinos to have a greater proportion of their land in coffee where they own a greater percentage of the land; but the proportion of their land in coffee is greater east of the river than west (table 6).[25]

TABLE 6.—*Location of Ladino coffee land*

Section	Percentage of land owned by Ladinos	Percentage of Ladino-owned land in coffee	Section	Percentage of land owned by Ladinos	Percentage of Ladino-owned land in coffee
W1	86.1	88.5	E5	80.3	98.2
W3	72.7	80.8	E1	52.1	100.0
W4	69.6	80.2	E2	38.9	80.7
W2	65.3	74.9	E3	29.3	82.5
W5	20.0	32.5	E4	19.7	58.3

(3) There is some tendency toward a constant relation between the proportions of land devoted to coffee and truck by Indians and by Ladinos. Thus in five sections (W1, W2, W5, E1, E5) the proportion of Indian coffee to coffee-plus-truck is about a third the proportion of Ladino coffee to coffee-plus-truck. In two sections (E2, E3) it is about a half, and in two others (W4, E4) higher. Only one section (W3), exceptional in most respects, is unique—the proportion being about one-sixteenth. If it is assumed that the proportion of one-third is "normal," it is seen that sections E2, E3, W4, and E4 have (by alternative interpretations) either an abnormally large percentage of Indian coffee to truck, or of Ladino truck to coffee. In terms of the first statement,

[25] The fact that the sections east of the river do not run in as smooth order in this respect as those west is doubtless partly due to the smaller universes involved. Thus, for example, the Ladino land of section E1 is all owned by three families who happen to be coffee producers and who have virtually no truck land anywhere.

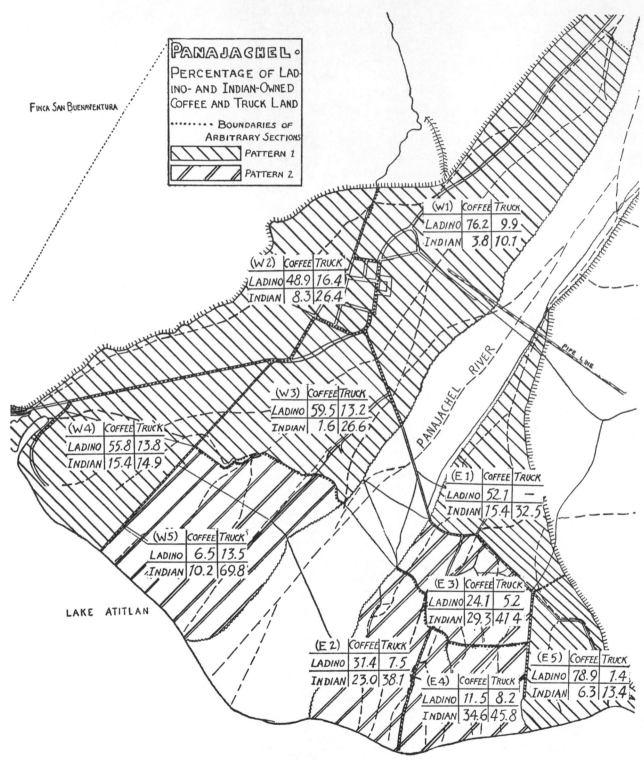

MAP 5.—Coffee and truck lands.

the pertinent facts in explanation are (*a*) that in these sections there are more Indian houses than in any others, and (*b*) the Indians favor coffee around the house site because children and animals damage gardens close by.   In terms of the second statement, the explanation might be that truck, the crop of the group dominant in the ownership of E2, E3, and E4, influences the crop of other owners in the same direction (as in the case, above, of section W5).   This explanation could

not cover W4, however, where Ladinos own almost 70 percent of the land.   Nor would such a rule be applicable in the contrary direction, since it is not true that the largest proportions of Indian coffee are in sections most dominated by Ladinos.

(4) Two dominant patterns may be identified. In one, comprising sections W1, W2, W3, W4, E1, and E5, the Ladinos own the great bulk of the land and have it largely in coffee, while the Indian land, smaller in extent, is largely in truck. Section

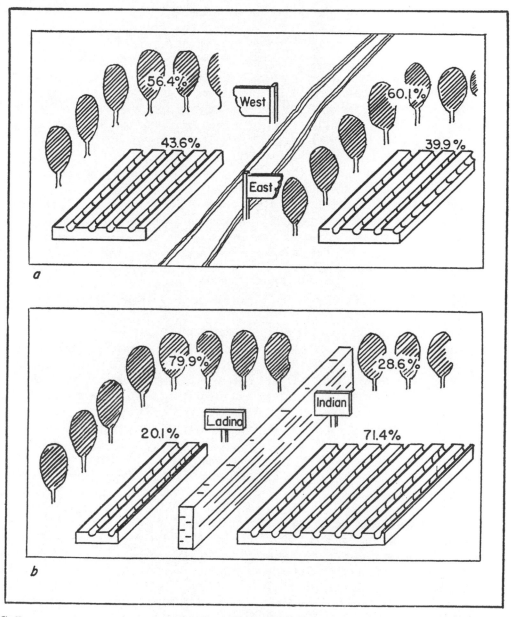

CHART 3.—Coffee vs. truck acreage.   *a*, East side and West, crop distribution much alike; *b*, Ladinos grow coffee, Indians grow truck.

E1 is atypical only in that the land is almost equally divided between the "races." E1 and E5 are unusual in that the Ladinos have extraordinarily large proportions of their land in coffee: the statistics are upset by the fact that in each section there happens to be a coffee plantation accounting for a large part of Ladino-owned land. Section W4 is atypical in that the Indians, instead of having a large percentage of their land in truck, actually have a little more in coffee than they have in truck. Most of the disproportion is accounted for by one large-land-holding Indian family that came to Panajachel from Sololá two generations ago and has planted coffee on most of its land. In the area of the delta comprising sections W3, W4, and W5 the soil tends to be sandy rather than black. The Indians say that until recently they thought it was not very suitable for vegetables. They were proved very wrong, but the fact remains that vegetables were not grown much in the area. Sections W3 and W4 are particularly stony, since the river once flowed through them, and probably little cultivated until coffee (easier to plant under the circumstances than truck) was introduced. It is likely that the family of Sololá Indians (whose coffee groves are indeed very old) planted most of the land in coffee because at the time any other course seemed impracticable. In any case it will be seen that there are good reasons for a large landowner to plant a large proportion in coffee.

In the second pattern, comprising sections W5, E2, E3, and E4, the Indians own the great bulk of the land and have it largely in truck, while the Ladino land, smaller in extent, is largely in coffee. Section W5, atypical in that the Ladinos reverse their usual condition of having more coffee than truck (although they still have three times as much of their land in coffee as the Indians do) has been discussed above.

TRUCK LANDS

The specific uses to which truck lands are put are exceedingly complex, differing with the class of owner, the season, and to some extent the kind of land. Most of the data obtained concern lands used by resident Indians whose use patterns are also described below in connection with agricultural practices. In anticipation some general points are pertinent.

A given piece of truck land is utilized in one of three ways:

(1) Corn may be grown during the rainy season, in which case the soil is prepared much as in the hills. The milpa occupies the land for about 7 months. Sometimes while the corn is drying the cucumberlike melon locally called *pepino* is planted between the corn plants. The land is not otherwise utilizable during those 7 months.

(2) *Pepinos*, usually planted in small individual hills, occupy the land for from 9 to 11 months; with the exception noted above, it cannot be otherwise used during that time.

(3) Most frequently the land is made into the rectangular garden beds, called *tablones*, in which are grown onions, garlic, sweet cassava, sweet-potatoes, and various other vegetables including cabbage, carrots, radishes, etc. These crops have different growing seasons, and some—notably the tubers—are grown simultaneously with others. Thus there results great complexity. But where and when there are *tablón* crops, neither corn nor *pepinos* are grown.

Between crops, some land is usually idle. How much land is idle in a particular case depends upon the crops customarily planted by the owner. There are several very common patterns in this respect, which may be listed as follows:

(1) A season of corn followed by a crop of garlic, and repeated. This sequence crowds the land, for since garlic grows for at least from 5 to 6 months, and corn for at least from 6 to 7, obviously the planting of one must coincide with the harvesting of the other. The land is never idle. This sequence is not considered favorable for the garlic, so frequently corn succeeds garlic, but another crop succeeds the corn.

(2) A season of corn followed by a crop of beans, and repeated. This is a popular sequence, especially with the rich (notably Ladinos). It usually allows 2 months' rest for the land each year, and no doubt is preservative of the richness of the soil; it is not an economically intensive use of the land.

(3) A season of corn followed by one or two crops of onions and other vegetables, and repeated. Depending upon the amount of onions grown, there may be 2 or 3 months of rest, or none.

(4) The whole year devoted to onions and other vegetables. Onion nursery grows for 2 months, the transplanted onions for another 3, and the

tablones allowed to go to seed for another 5 or 6. Since it is a rare individual who can regulate his time and land perfectly, part of such land is usually idle for a month or two once or twice a year. In most cases very little is planted during the rainy season, so frequently there are 4 or 5 idle months during that time.

(5) A crop of garlic followed by a crop or two of onions and other vegetables. As in the case above, there is apt to be considerable idleness of the land during the rainy season.

(6) A crop of *pepinos*, occupying most of the year, followed by one of the various yearly patterns mentioned above. Most frequently, perhaps, *pepinos* are alternated with one of the combinations including corn, and in such cases the *pepinos* may be planted while the corn is still in the field. Pepinos are rarely grown in consecutive years on the same land.

A particular landowner may follow several of these patterns on different plots of his land. For example, it is frequent among Indians for a man to use two pieces of land in manner No. 6, but to alternate them so that in any one year he has both *pepinos* and the other crops growing.

Notwithstanding such complexity, it is possible with some confidence to calculate how the truck land is used in any one year, for particular families and "race" groups usually follow consistent and commonly known patterns. Table 7, which brings together the myriad items of land-use data, calculated for every plot of land, reports the acreage devoted to each of the important truck crops during the year.

The situation whereby so great a proportion of idle land is to be found during the rainy season when *tablón* crops are relatively few could be avoided if all the land were planted with corn during the rainy season. Actually, the Ladinos do plant corn on virtually all their *tablón* land, and their idle land is found rather in the dry season; this results in less intensive cultivation of the most valuable money crop of the dry season, onions. Most Indians cannot afford this. Garlic and corn might seem the optimum combination from this point of view. But garlic supposedly cannot be grown year after year in the same land; it is also said that garlic land should be prepared months in advance to allow the turned-under grass to rot, so that a repeated sequence of garlic and corn is uncommon. Of course continual use of land is not the only measure of intensity of use; as will be seen later, when compared with corn or any other crop, the labor and the gross income involved in vegetable growing is out of all proportion to the acreage involved.

Table 8 compares the percentage of acreage devoted to various crops throughout the year (the arithmetic mean of the monthly figures) on Ladino lands, resident Indian lands, and those of outside Indians virtually all of whom live in San Jorge. The comparison is instructive: unlike the resident Indians who strike a balance, the Jorgeños devote almost 57-percent of their land to onions (and grow neither corn nor garlic) and the Ladinos the same proportion to corn (and grow no *pepinos*). In the case of the San Jorge residents, the explanation evidently is that they have acquired these lands *for* onion growing; on the one hand they doubtless have cornfield lands back home that occupy their rainy season time and give them the grain they need, and on the other, onions rather than garlic are a traditional crop in San Jorge. The case of Ladinos, who grow so much corn on truck

TABLE 7.—*Panajachel truck acreage*

| Crop growing | Number of acres on 1st of month | | | | | | | | | | | | Total | Total ÷12 |
	January	February	March	April	May	June	July	August	September	October	November	December		
Corn	2.8				29.7	53.0	53.0	51.5	48.7	48.7	45.3	25.2	357.9	29.8
Corn with *pepinos*								1.4	4.3	4.3	4.3		14.3	1.2
Pepinos	16.6	16.6	16.6	12.7	6.3		3.8	8.6	12.4	12.4	12.4	16.6	135.0	11.2
Onion seedlings	5.5	3.4	1.3	1.2	1.2	.6	.9	1.4	1.9	4.6	5.4	5.4	32.8	2.7
Onions	57.8	58.2	51.7	47.5	37.6	31.3	29.3	27.6	27.1	31.4	49.7	54.9	504.1	42.0
Onions for seed	7.5	7.5	5.9	4.5	2.9		1.1	1.1	7.5	7.5	7.5	7.5	60.5	5.0
Garlic	22.8	22.8	22.8	21.7	14.6					.4	10.7	19.8	135.6	11.3
Vine beans	4.5	8.0	10.4	10.4	8.0	.7						.7	42.7	3.6
Ground beans	1.4	8.8	19.0	19.0	8.1	.7							57.0	4.8
Cabbage	.6	.6	.8	.8	.7	.3	.1				.1	.5	4.5	.4
Carrots	.3	.3	.5	.5	.3	.1	.1					.1	2.2	.2
Other vegetables	.3	.3	.5	.5	.3	.1	.1	.1				.1	2.2	.2
Idle	16.4	10.0	7.0	17.7	26.8	49.7	48.1	44.9	34.6	27.2	1.1	5.7	289.2	24.1
Total	136.5	136.5	136.5	136.5	136.5	136.5	136.5	136.5	136.5	136.5	136.5	136.5	1,638	136.5

lands, is particularly illustrative of the difference in economies of the local Indians and Ladinos. Corn is the important breadstuff to both, and it is advantageous to grow at least enough for household needs. But only the rich are able to do so. Few Indians, but most Ladinos, are independent enough of the need to earn a livelihood through money crops to be able to grow corn instead. (The same may be said of beans, another food staple, which are grown disproportionately by Ladinos.) A complementary reason for the difference is that Ladinos depend upon Indians for agricultural labor, hence prefer crops that depend less on intensive labor. Another case is the noted Ladino preference for coffee as opposed to truck.

TABLE 8.—*Truck-land use of Ladinos and resident and nonresident Indians*

Crop	Percentage of year-acres of delta truck land			
	All	Resident Indians[1]	Absentee Indians	Ladino[2]
Corn	21.8 ⎫ 22.7	17.8 ⎫ 19.1	---	56.5
Corn with *pepinos*	.9 ⎭ 9.2	1.3 ⎭ 10.0	---	---
Pepinos	8.3	8.7	14.8	---
Onion nursery	5.0	5.0	9.0	.8
Onions	27.8	30.9	38.3	6.9
Onions for seed	3.6	2.9	9.4	.8
Garlic	8.3	9.9	---	11.5
Vine beans	2.6	2.0	3.5	3.8
Ground beans	3.5	3.7	---	6.1
Vegetables	.6	.8	---	---
Idle	17.6	16.6	25.0	13.5
Total	100.0	99.6	100.0	99.9

[1] Including that rented from Ladinos.
[2] Excluding that rented to Indians.

The reason why the Jorgeños use their land to only 75 percent of capacity while the Ladinos use theirs to 87 percent of capacity is that, as mentioned above, corn grown in the rainy season, when onions are at low ebb, uses land more continuously. The difference in this case would be more striking except that the Jorgeños grow so many *pepinos*, which themselves occupy the land much of the year. No doubt the Jorgeños gross more from their pattern of truck-land use than do the Ladinos; it will be seen later that the resident Indians have struck a happy medium.

Chart 4 depicts graphically the use of sixty-odd acres of truck land owned or rented by the local Indians for which fairly reliable information was obtained. This is a $^{12}/_{17}$ sample of all resident Indian land and probably gives a good picture of the whole.

Since the Indian pattern is median, the picture

that emerges is not unlike what would appear for all truck land in Panajachel.[26] The chart represents the area of each crop on the first day of each month; but the interpolated impression of the annual cycle of each crop must be fairly realistic.

There are differences in the use to which truck land is put in different parts of town, but as may be inferred from table 8, the class of the owner of the land again is at least as important a differentiating factor as the geography. For example, the Ladinos grow corn, beans, and garlic on their truck land no matter where it is located. Nevertheless, such a fact as that *pepinos* are grown more on the west side than on the east must be explained by common belief that they produce better in the less-exhausted land of the west side. Very much more corn is grown on resident Indian truck lands of the east side than of the west; this in a negative way can also be attributed to this presumed geographic factor. The reason why a greater proportion of resident Indian truck land is in garlic on the east than on the west side may also be a matter of the soil, since much sandy soil—said to be unsuited to garlic—is west of the river. But it is still clear that the most essential determining factor in the use of the land, insofar as it is not uniform, is the custom of the group to which the farmer belongs. For whatever the origin of such custom, and whatever its geographic and economic base, the people of one element of the population tend in general to use their land, no matter where located, in much the same way.

The details of truck-land usage among the Indians for which such details are available are so complex as almost to defy generalization. Variations on the patterns of truck-land usage that have been listed above are many, for within the limits set by the agricultural habits of the community, there is sufficient leeway to permit a large number of crop combinations. The way a particular farmer uses his land depends upon the total available to him, and whether it is owned, on pawn or rented; what he supposes to be the nature of the soil and the requisites of the crops; the immediate past crop history of the land; market prices of various products when plans for the next crop or next year are being made; and so on. In addition, the financial state of the landowner—his consumer needs, his obligations and debts—helps him determine how he should plant his land. Table 9,

[26] Such a chart could be made from the data of table 7.

organizing information for 161 pieces of Indian-planted land, will give an idea of their kinds and relative frequencies.

In the section where the value of the various crops is discussed (pp. 108–116), some light is thrown on the problem of the relative efficiency of some of the uses. But since other factors besides profits during a year must be taken into consideration, that discussion is hardly definitive. The crop combinations favored by individuals appear little related to their total wealth. A thorough comparison of the truck crops planted and of total land wealth, or truck-land wealth (for which data are available) is not made because a quick survey shows that this would probably not be worth the effort. Examination of the crops planted by 25 of the poorest, 10 medium rich, and the 8 wealthiest families shows little difference except that the

rich, having more land, tend to plant one piece more uniformly than the poor and achieve the same variety by planting different pieces with different crops. I looked for the rich to plant more corn in their truck lands on the same principle that Ladinos do, but the difference is not obvious.

AGRICULTURE

THE MILPA

In the milpa, or cornfield, grow maize, beans, and squash or pumpkins. Beans are rarely if ever planted in delta cornfields; but in about two-thirds of the hill cornfields they are planted with every fifth or sixth corn plant.[27] Beans are

---

[27] In some places in Guatemala beans are planted not only together with the corn, so that the vines climb up the cornstalks, but also in rows between the rows of corn.

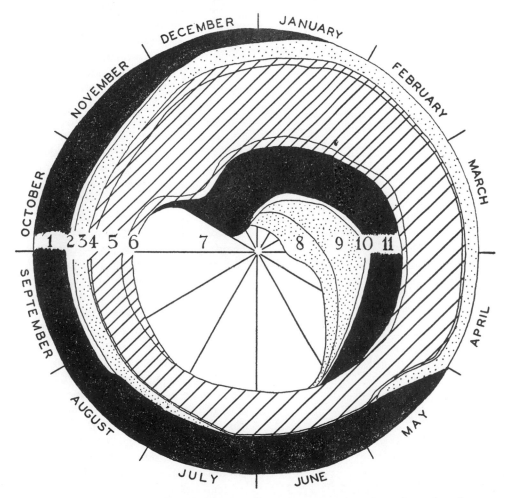

CHART 4.—The use of truck land by resident Indians: 1, Corn; 2, corn-pepino; 3, pepinos; 4, onion nursery; 5, onions; 6, onion seed; 7, idle (resting); 8, vine beans; 9, ground beans; 10, miscellaneous vegetables; 11, garlic.

also widely grown in the delta in the dry season entirely apart from corn, in separate gardens; these beans will be discussed separately. Squash, of the kinds called *ayotes* and *chilacayotes*, are very infrequently grown in the delta cornfields, but almost universally in the hills, planted between the rows of corn at wide intervals, and never except in cornfields.

Corn is grown only in the rainy season [28] on the hillsides, where it is virtually the only crop

[28] Occasionally a rich Indian plants a few stalks of corn in irrigated delta fields during the dry season. The Indians recognize the practice as uneconomical; some insist that for some reason such out-of-season corn does not produce.

TABLE 9.—*Resident Indian truck crop patterns* [1]

Crop(s) normally planted	Number of cases				
	Land planted exclusively with crop(s) listed	Crop(s) listed followed by milpa		Crop(s) listed alternated with *pepinos*	
		On whole piece	Only on part	Alternating halves	Alternating years
Total (161 cases)	91	31	9	12	18
Onions	[a] 33	3		[b] 5	
					2
Part onions, part beans	[c d] 4	2	[a e] 2		
					[f] 2
Part onions, part garlic	3	1	[a] 2		[b] 2
				[g] 2	
					[b d] 2
Onion seed	6				
Part onions, part seed	10				
Part onion seed, part garlic	[h] 16				
Beans	[a i] 5	12		2	1
				[j] 2	
Garlic				[k m] 1	
		5			[n] 3
Part garlic, part idle	2				[k] 2
Part garlic-onion sequence, part beans	[o] 3	4	[o] 2		[b] 2
					[b] 2
Part garlic, part beans		4	[o] 2		
Part beans-idle, part onion seed			1		
Strawberries	1				
Pepinos (rented land changed annually)	[p] 8				

[1] In reading the table, the columns (but not the figures) are "cumulative." For example (last column, ninth row) it is seen that there are 2 cases in which all of the land is planted with onions and garlic, but part of it with milpa in season, every other year; in alternate years *pepinos* are grown instead.
  [a] 1 case, part of land idle.
  [b] 2 cases, less than half *pepinos*.
  [c] 1 case, beans all year; others, beans followed by more onions.
  [d] 1 case, also vegetables.
  [e] 1 case, milpa only every second year.
  [f] 1 case, beans on all the land part of year.
  [g] 1 case, 2 pieces of land changed off.
  [h] 3 cases, garlic land idle after harvest; others, onions fill in the year.
  [i] 1 case, beans all year; in others, the land rented from Ladinos for only the bean season.
  [j] 2 cases, part of land idle.
  [k] 1 case, less than half *pepinos*.
  [m] Land idle after garlic harvest.
  [n] In 1 case there is an onions-milpa sequence and in another case a beans-milpa sequence replacing the garlic-milpa sequence every third year; in these cases *pepinos* are grown only every third year.
  [o] 1 case, only 1 of the 3 crops (beans, garlic, or onions) grown in a year, and each one every third year. 3
  [p] 1 case, *pepinos* grown consecutive years, producing no crop the third year.

that is planted, and also in the delta where for the growing season it is permitted to displace other truck crops. The growing season is about 8 months, from May through December, including the 6 months of the rainy season and the first 2 months or so of the dry season, during which the ears ripen.

The tools used in milpa agriculture are the ax, machete, occasionally the pickax, a wooden harvesting nail, and above all others the hoe. Neither plows nor draught animals are ever used. Trees need rarely be felled in preparation, so axes are much less used than machetes (imported, broad-bladed knives some 18 inches long with 6-inch handles), used to cut small trees, bushes, and brush. The hoe is used not only to turn over and break up the soil, but also to chop away and scrape off undergrowth of all kinds. Typical is the broad-bladed hoe; but for some purposes a hoe with a small blade (once a large one, worn down by use) is employed.

No fertilizer from outside the field is normally added. Exceptionally animals graze on hillside land between crops and while it lies fallow; otherwise fertilizer is never added, although after the harvest the cornstalks and leaves are allowed to rot, or are gathered and burned to enrich the soil. Delta land, used the year-round, is fertilized, but not especially for milpa; it is planted with one crop or another year after year without becoming exhausted. Hillside land presumably does become exhausted; it is then allowed to lie fallow for a number of years, during which wild vegetation grows, to be cut and burned when use of the land is resumed. Such land is called "new land"; it may remain fallow so long that many forget that it was ever cultivated. I cannot say for how long land may be uninterruptedly planted with milpa and still produce a crop. Indians talk about "tired" vs. "fresh" or "new" land, and differences in yields between the two; the criterion for "exhaustion" (i. e., at what point a field would not be considered worth planting again) is not clear. The life of land depends in part on its inclination; the more level the land, the longer it can be used. I have cases of gentler slopes which produced profitable crops after 12, 15, and 25 years of continued planting. This contrasts with a piece on a steep hillside that had been planted for "about 10 years" and given up to rest because exhausted, to remain unplanted for "about 6 years."

On new land in the hills, the trees and brush are cut away with machetes during March and early April, and burned over during the last of April, when it is ready for planting. On land used the year before, the soil is thoroughly hoed and the weeds and old cornstalks piled and burned. Ashes are thought to be good fertilizer. Seed has been kept on the ear from the year before, carefully selected by picking over. Seeds from the same piece of land are usually planted each year, for each altitude and region has its appropriate variety. After the first rains of May, a number of men plant together, each with a small-bladed hoe and a small bag in which the seed is carried. A 6-inch hole is dug with the hoe and five or six seeds are carefully placed in it, after which the hole is covered over with the hoe and the earth patted down. Every fifth or sixth plant, chosen so they will not form rows, is planted also with three or four beans. [29] Squash are planted (between the corn plants) only after the corn is up.

On a slope, planting is begun at the top, and the rows follow the contour lines, apart either a *vara* and a half (4.1 feet) or a *vara* and three-quarters (4.8 feet), apparently depending on the practice of the farmer rather than on the type of soil. The distance between plants in a row is the same as between rows. Some Indians say that on new land, known to be richer, the distances are reduced by a foot, but the few data I have do not seem to bear this out. I have seen corn growing on slopes as steep as about 45°. In irregular fields, odd niches of soil are utilized simply by planting as many stalks as the space permits; no land is ordinarily neglected if it can be planted.

Until the seed sprouts, at least, the fields are carefully guarded against grackles, mice, etc. Scarecrows and traps of various kinds are used; but children are frequently on the field a good part of the time. Seeds which do not sprout are replaced. After the danger of small animals is past, the milpa need be visited only every few days. The field is usually cultivated twice, sometimes three times: when the plants are about a yard high, the field is weeded and the earth hilled around each plant to a height of about a foot; then with the second weed-

ing (when the "points" begin to form on the plants) the mound is built to about a foot and a half; at the same time the leaves of the bottom of the stalks are often cut away. Like the planting, each cultivation is done by a group of men with hoes. When the ears are formed, some are usually picked for eating or sale and the leaves around them cut for use. When the ears are fairly ripe, the tops of the stalks may be cut off for use as fodder. Now in delta fields the stalks are nicked above the middle and the tops bent over so that the ears point downward. The tall corn in the delta is particularly vulnerable to wind; the reason given for "doubling" it, however, is that it protects the ears from the birds and the last rains which otherwise rot the grain. While the grain ripens, the field is especially protected from the larger animals: deadfall traps are used.

In December, the men harvest, again work in groups, each with his shoulder bag, a large mesh bag,[30] and a harvesting nail, a 6- to 8-inch hardwood or bone spike with which he separates the ear from the husk to remove the bare ear. Large ears are taken with the husk. Harvesting begins at the upper edge of a hill so that ears that fall can be retrieved later (the poor later are permitted to glean anything left). The harvesters carry the corn back at noon and at night, emptying the bags in the courtyard of the house where the ears dry for several days before being stacked on the ear in the granary. Practically every part of the corn plant, from the stalks to the silk, has important uses which need not be detailed here. Of course the grain itself is the basic food staple.

CORN YIELDS

The corn yield varies not only from year to year but with differing terrain and soil fertility, hence also on the length of time the land has been in use. Indians ordinarily report their harvest in number of bags whose content varies with their size and, since they are filled with whole ears, with the quantity of grain on an ear of given size. Since the land harvested is also not exactly measured, it is little wonder that official statistics (not themselves too carefully gathered) should

---

[29] There is no fixed plan for the distribution of corn and beans. The planter actually places about 2 pounds of corn and a half pound of beans (for a *cuerda*— 0.178 acre) in his bag and draws out a handful for planting. If there happen to be less than five or more than six kernels of corn, he makes a correction. If there are one, two, or three beans, he plants them—provided that he has not planted beans in the immediate vicinity. What goes into each hole, is therefore, partly a matter of chance.

[30] Made of maguey fiber in towns outside of Panajachel, and bought in the markets. The bags are closed at both ends by means of drawstrings. They differ in size, depending on the number of meshes and the size of each. According to informants, those most commonly used in Panajachel are of meshes 50 by 10 or 50 by 9. Some are 40 by 10 and 36 by 12. One informant uses bags of 56 by 12, but he says these are uncommon.

be unreliable.   Production of corn in the Department of Sololá in 1935–36 was officially estimated at 62,249 hundredweight on 4,694 *manzanas* of cultivated land,[31] or about 13.7 bushels per acre, next year at 136,484 hundredweight on 5,952 *manzanas*,[32] or 23.6 bushels per acre. According to the same source the yield per acre in the Republic as a whole dropped from 17.2 in 1935–36 to a little less than 16 in 1936–37. Even were these estimates reliable, the yield in Panajachel might be quite different from that of the Department of Sololá.

In Panajachel the Indians consider "three bags per *cuerda*" an average yield; they say they may get only half of that or as much as four bags or more. Offhand they say that one bag gives 100 pounds of shelled corn,[33] so that their "three bags per *cuerda*" may be translated 30 bushels per acre. This yield is attributed to hill land, unfertilized except by the yearly wild growth and the cornstalks burned or turned under. Town land is known to produce more because it is level and usually fertilized with rotted leaves of coffee bushes. Indications are that the Indians figure too optimistically. In delta truck lands where the soil is fertilized, the field easily guarded, and the plants can even be watered if necessary, it is true that the yield is high. A reliable informant for 15 consecutive years harvested from a *cuerda* (0.178 acre) of such land as much as 46 bushels per acre, which appears to be about the maximum. Judging from other data, the worst yield from that piece of land is about 20 bushels per acre. My only other information on delta yields comes from an experimental milpa we planted in 1936;[34] the area was small and the year bad; too much reliance must not be placed on the results. The yield for the whole plot was at the rate of 25 bushels per acre, the range between 57 and 4. In the portion planted in the same manner

as the Indians normally do in the delta, the yield was about 30 bushels per acre. However, the experimental plants suffered extraordinary vicissitudes. It seems on the whole probable that the normal yield in the delta is well over 30 bushels per acre, and that it ran to about 35 in 1936.

The yield on the hillsides is certainly less. Three reliable informants furnished the following information on their own harvests over a period of years:

(1) Ten *cuerdas* (1.78 acres), near the foot of the East slope; medium incline; stony soil (considered good); the land had been at rest up to 1934, when the vegetation had been felled and burned and milpa planted. In 1935 the informant sowed this second-year land in the usual manner, half with yellow and half with white corn. The weather during the growing season was favorable. The yield was at the rate of 28 bushels per acre for the yellow corn, 20 bushels per acre for the white; *average yield, 24 bushels per acre.*

(2) Same land as No. 1; planted in 1936 with yellow corn only. The weather conditions were less favorable than in 1935; *average yield, 25 bushels per acre.*

(3) Thirty *cuerdas* (5.34 acres) on the East slope; the soil is black and loose, with few stones; since 1914 it had been used annually for milpa, but the cornstalks were always turned back into the soil, and only occasionally were the leaves removed from the field. The higher part of the field is much more inclined than the lower, which is almost level; a barren rock cliff also shades part of the higher portion. In 1937 the informant planted one-half of the piece, including high and low portions. Cultivation was as usual, except that hard places (in which clumps of grass grew) were hoed up. Fourteen of the fifteen *cuerdas* were sown with yellow corn; the other, at the highest edge of the land, at the foot of the rock cliff, was sown with white corn. The harvest of yellow corn was at the rate of 14.3 bushels, of white corn, 20 bushels; *average yield, 14.7 bushels per acre.*

(4) Same land as No. 3, but the entire piece planted by the informant and his family. Cultivated in the same manner as usual, in 1938 white corn was planted in a strip along the higher edge, occupying 8 of the 30 cords. The rest was planted with a yellow corn that a local Ladino is supposed to have brought from Puerto Barrios (on the Atlantic coast) 2 years before and planted in Panajachel. The land was divided across the contour into four equal strips, each planted by one member of the family. The yellow corn yielded 22.5 bushels per acre, the center strips 24 bushels and the other, 19.6 bushels per acre. The white corn did very poorly, yielding at the rate of 5 bushels per acre; *average yield, 17.8 bushels per acre.*

(5) Same land as No. 4, planted in 1939 entirely with yellow corn. Beans were also planted, but yielded nothing for lack of rain. The weather was very unfavorable. One outside strip yielded 18 bushels per acre, the other, 16.5; one inside strip yielded 16.5 and the other, 11.4 bushels per acre; *average yield, 15.6 bushels per acre.*

(6) Four *cuerdas* of 34 *varas* (0.784 acre) on the hillside,

---

[31] *Memoria*, Dept. Agri., 1937, p. 332 (Guatemala, 1938).

[32] *Memoria*, Dept. Agri., 1938, p. 213 (Guatemala, 1939).

[33] Estimates of casual informants ranged from 60 to 150 pounds for a "large" bag. In good harvests, with more and larger kernels to the ear the net weight of the grain is greater per bagful of harvested ears. Since bags differ in size, it is difficult to be satisfied in the matter. I helped thresh only one bagful of corn, so must depend upon statements of three reliable informants. They seem to agree that in times of good harvest a standard 50 by 10 bag—the numbers refer to the number of meshes—holds enough ears to give 100 pounds of shelled corn. One says that a good harvest gives 115 pounds from a full bag of this size, but that in bad years the yield is only 100 pounds. Another, who uses oversize (50 by 12), bags, gets 120 pounds, but that in the poor year 1939 each bag yielded only 95 pounds.

[34] The experiment and its results are outlined in my microfilmed notes, pp. 149–194.

near the lake shore, of San Buenaventure; stony soil that had been used for seven consecutive years. Informant planted milpa in 1939, burning the old cornstalks and using no other fertilizer; sowed the yellow Puerto Barrios seed referred to in No. 4, at intervals of 1¾ *varas* instead of the more usual 1½. Weather unfavorable; *average yield, 19.5 bushels per acre.*

(7) Three and a half *cuerdas* (0.623 acre) at the foot of the east hill and the lower part almost level; soil clayey; protected on one side by neighboring milpa, and below by truck garden. The land had been continuously cultivated with milpa since 1924 by the informant, who burned the stalks and leaves each year as its only fertilizer. Planting yellow corn in the usual manner, except that he cuts away the first growth before the "first cultivation," and at intervals of 1¾ *varas*, the informant says that good harvests have yielded 287 pounds. This is at the rate of 29 bushels per acre. In 1939, however, when the weather was very unfavorable, the yield was at the rate of only 15 bushels per acre. *Probable average annual yield, some 25 bushels per acre.*

(8) Four and one-half *cuerdas* (0.8 acre) contiguous and similar to No. 7. This land has the same history as No. 7, except that from 1933 to 1937 it was mortgaged to and used by another Indian who, according to the informant, planted the same seeds by the same methods as he does himself. This was planted in 1938 with the same yellow seed; *yield, 23.1 bushels per acre.* In the year 1939, with unfavorable weather, the harvest was like that of No. 7; *yield, 15 bushels per acre.*

These are records of informants. In 1940 I was able to check some of them:

(9) The owner of the land of cases Nos. 7 and 8, who planted the whole 8 *cuerdas* (1.42 acres) in 1940, measured off a *cuerda* in the center of the field and harvested the corn of this section separately. The harvest consisted of three 50 by 10 mesh bags, one containing small husked ears, the second large ears in the husk, and the third some of each. I could not shell the corn (for the owner would have no way of storing the grain), but I weighed the bags on an accurate balance. The first bag weighed just 150 pounds, the second 140, and the third (which was not full) just 75. We carefully calculated that we should reduce the total by 40 pounds for the bags, husks, and cobs. The remainder was 325 pounds of grain, which meant that the measured *cuerda* yielded at the rate of *32.6 bushels per acre.* The measured-off *cuerda* obviously yielded better than the field as a whole, as the center usually does. We calculated, simply by counting the total number of bags husked and of unhusked corn and assuming that they weighed the same as did our samples, that the yield of the whole field, including white maize that did poorly, was at the rate of just *25 bushels per acre.* This is just what we had previously calculated from his information alone.

The informant said that the yield in 1940, that we had just measured, was about the same as that of 1938, and much better than that of 1939. A glance at the figures of cases Nos. 7 and 8,

independently collected in 1939, will show how nearly correct his judgment was. There seems little question that the yields mentioned in these last three cases are very nearly correct. It is especially significant, therefore, to note again that this land began to produce corn in 1924 and without the addition of any outside fertilizer in 1940 it still yielded 25 bushels per acre.

(10) An informant who had not previously supplied me with information allowed me to weigh the harvest of corn yielded by what he said were 3 *cuerdas* (0.54 acres) of steep Santa Catarina hillside which he had rented. I did not see or measure the land, but I saw the five small bags of corn that it produced and noting that they were equal, we shelled but one of the five and weighed the grain. The grain weighed 65 pounds, so that it may be calculated that the total yield was 325 pounds, or at the rate (if the land area was correctly calculated) of *11 bushels per acre.* Unfortunately, I neglected to ask the informant how much corn he had eaten before the harvest; since he is poor, it may be that such a factor was important in the case.

A casual informant said that his 1940 yield from 4 *cuerdas* was four large bags, each containing 150 pounds, or at the rate of 20 bushels per acre. A very reliable Indian told me that a certain 30 *cuerdas* (5.4 acres) planted for the second year, yielded 48 large bags; if the bags averaged (as in case 9) 130 pounds of shelled corn, the yield per acre on this large piece was 21 bushels per acre.

If such records are typical, the yield of hillside corn rarely if ever reaches 30 bushels per acre. The range in cases reported is from 29 down to 11 bushels per acre (leaving out the disastrous white corn of case No. 4), the average of good and bad years about 20 bushels per acre. In the long run "bad" years may be less frequent and the long-time average yield closer to 30 than to 20 bushels, as the Indians believe. Nevertheless, for 1936 I have set it at 20 bushels. It should be emphasized that Panajachel hill land is not exhausted as quickly as reputed here and elsewhere using the same system of agriculture. (McBryde, 1947, pp. 17–18). The land of cases 3, 4, and 5, in use continuously since 1914, yielded 22.5 bushels per acre of yellow corn in 1940, compared with the yields of 28 and 25 bushels per acre for second and third year land (cases 1 and 2). Cases 7, 8, and 9, in continuous use since 1924, show a yield of 25 bushels per acre in 1940. The evidence is not conclusive; soil analyses were not made; it is also conceivable that the Indians who say that animals were never grazed on the land err in their historical accounts.

The normal return in corn appears to be close to two-hundred-fold in the hills and four-hundred-fold in the delta. The Indians' report that they sow about a pound of seed to the *cuerda*, or 5.6 pounds to the acre, appears reasonable. Kernels of corn suitable for sowing run 100 to 120 to the ounce; if planted 5 kernels to the stalk at intervals of 1.5 *varas* (4.1 English feet), some 7 pounds would be used to the acre. The difference between this figure and 5.6 pounds may result because usually not every foot of the acre is utilizable. Even on the basis of 6 pounds of seed to the acre, a conservative normal hill yield of 20 bushels gives a return one-hundred-and-eighty-seven-fold, and a minimum normal delta yield of 30 bushels, a return two-hundred-and-eighty-fold. No account is here taken of seeds used in replanting, which would lower the relative return.

In all the cases cited, five grains of seed per plant were used. In cases Nos. 1 through 5, the distance between the plants was 4.1 feet, in the remainder 4.8 feet. Assuming that in each case the seed was planted throughout at even intervals, that 7 pounds of seed were used per acre in the first cases and 5 pounds in the others, the returns were:

No. 1:
    Yellow_____ Two-hundred-and-twenty-four-fold.
    White_____ One-hundred-and-sixty-fold.
No. 2_____ Two-hundred-fold.
No. 3:
    Yellow_____ One-hundred-and-fourteen-fold.
    White_____ One-hundred-and-sixty-fold.
No. 4:
    Yellow_____ One-hundred-and-eighty-fold.
    White_____ Forty-fold.
No. 5_____ One-hundred-and-twenty-five-fold.
No. 6_____ Two-hundred-and-eighteen-fold.
No. 7:
    Average_____ Two-hundred-and-eighty-fold.
    1939_____ One-hundred-and-sixty-eight-fold.
No. 8:
    1938_____ Two-hundred-and-fifty-eight-fold.
    1939_____ One-hundred-and-sixty-eight-fold.
No. 9:
    Whole area_____ Two-hundred-and-eighty-fold.
    Measured por- Three-hundred-and-sixty-five-fold.
      tion.

In the one case of the delta land mentioned above, the yield was four-hundred-and-sixty-fold. The return in those portions of the experimental milpa planted more or less after the Indian fashion was two-hundred-and-twenty-eight-fold. Probably the normal delta yield is well above three-hundred-fold.

BEAN-SQUASH YIELDS

Information on milpa beans is scant. In one case, the farmer harvested 1 pound per plant (112 pounds per acre) of black, white, and red beans, all of which yielded equally. Another said that his yield of black beans on new land in 1935 came to 88 pounds per acre, and that an additional (unknown) amount had been stolen. In 1936 the same land yielded at the rate of 53 pounds. Another Indian reported having planted 84 bean plants per acre, 50 of black, and 17 each of white and red, from which he harvested (he said) 28 pounds of black beans, and an unreported quantity of the others. Another said that from 10 *cuerdas* (1.78 acres) he harvested 25 pounds of beans. In case No. 5 (above) the beans yielded nothing at all because of "lack of rain." On the basis of such data it is difficult to form a judgment as to average or normal yield. As calculated from official figures, the yield in the whole Department was 663 pounds in 1935–36 [35] and 933 pounds per acre in 1936–37.[36] But these reports must include ground beans as well as milpa beans. I estimate that the harvest of beans planted with corn in Panajachel hill milpas in 1936 averaged 75 pounds to the acre.[37]

Data on the yields of squash are also inadequate. In the seven cases recorded—none from trained informants—the number of plants ranged from 17 to 33 per acre, and the yield between 3 and 5 *chilacayotes* and between 5 and 10 *ayotes* per plant. From this information I estimate an average yield of 50 *chilacayotes* and 100 *ayotes* per acre.

TRUCK FARMING

The chief crops in irrigated fields in the delta (besides corn) are onions and garlic, beans, and such vegetables as cabbages, carrots, turnips, radishes, etc., sweet cassava and sweetpotatoes, and *pepinos*. Garlic and *pepinos* have fixed planting and harvesting times; the others may be found at any time at any stage of development. Beans may be grown at any time, but in practice are generally planted in delta milpas between

[35] *Memoria*, Dept. Agr., 1937, p. 332.
[36] *Memoria*, Dept. Agr., 1938, p. 214.
[37] There is also the question of the effect of milpa beans on the corn yield. On that point there is no information from the Indians; but from the inconclusive results of the experimental cornfield it appears that beans do adversely affect the corn yield. In every case where beans were planted, the corn yield was smaller (and in all but one case much smaller) than in corresponding plants without beans.

milpa seasons to fill in the remaining 4 months. The tools employed in truck farming are the pickax, the hoe, a pointed wooden stick, and a tin basin or a gourd for watering. In general the techniques employed are those of a home gardener; a great deal of meticulous hand labor is involved.

All except a few plants, especially *pepinos* and tomatoes, are grown in rectangular garden beds called *tablones*. These beds, neatly and sharply raised above clean straight troughs that separate them, are characteristic of the irrigated lands of the town. Singly or in patches of a dozen or two they are to be found in all parts, surrounded by coffee and fruit trees. The amount of land available sometimes limits the length (ideally 32 *varas* or about 88 feet), but rarely changes the width from its apparent optimum of three *varas* (about 8 feet). If a bed is wider than this, it is difficult to reach the center from the gutters; if narrower, too much space is wasted by the gutters. The standard is a bed 3 by 32 *varas*, with eight beds to a *cuerda*. Most of the working time of the Indians, at almost any time of the year, is spent in making the beds or planting, transplanting, watering, weeding, or harvesting the vegetables.

In the dry season, the land is first thoroughly flooded; the softened soil is then dug up with a pickax and the raised rectangles are formed by moving earth from gutters to beds. Even a bed that is remade from an old one is carefully dug up to a depth of 2 feet and the soil turned. Every twig and stone is removed, but leaves and rubbish are left for fertilizer. The edges are carefully tamped down, work that requires the greatest skill. After a few days the bed is watered and then smoothed: every lump must be broken and the bed made perfectly level lest water collect in depressions.

ONIONS

If seed is to be planted, the bed must be especially carefully smoothed and even small pebbles removed. A pound of onion seed is sprinkled evenly over the surface, the planter moving along the trough, then covered with an inch of damp black soil containing rotted coffee leaves, and the whole carefully covered with broad leaves to keep off the sun. Every 3 days the leaves are lifted and the bed is watered. Watering is always done by standing in the flooded trough and with a tin basin or a gourd sprinkling from above. When

the plants come up, in about 9 days, the leaves are removed; then the plants are watered daily with a fine spray until 2 inches high, after which they are watered only once in several days, or when the plants seem to need it. In 2 months the seedlings are ready for transplanting. Beds for transplanting have been readied, and now with the aid of a pointed stick the plants are uprooted and placed in a basket. Half of the head and a quarter of the green is cut off, and dried leaves are removed. The seedlings produced in one *tablón* are sufficient to plant eight *tablones* of onions.

Transplanting is usually women's work. Each seedling is, with the aid of a stick, inserted in the earth with the thumb. The onions are evenly spaced 4 inches apart, unless large onions are desired, when 5 inches are left between. Onions (or other vegetables) are also usually planted along the oblique edges of the bed. Some people, when they transplant, sow seed of other herbs on the bed at the same time, and the best of these are left to grow with the onions. As the onions grow, they are regularly watered and weeded. When they begin to flower, the tips of the greens are cut off. Before harvesting, the ground is softened with water. After pulling up the onions, the hairy root and any wilted leaves are cut off (and often left on the bed for fertilizer), the onions are graded by size and tied into bunches of 10 for market.

Some beds of onions are allowed to go to seed, almost always in October so that the seed may mature during the dry months. They are fenced off and carefully watched, and the soil is fertilized with the droppings of barnyard fowl. At the time that seed replaces flowers, the field is flooded for an hour or more. Seed is produced from mature onions in about 5 months, thus from seed in 10 or 11. When ripe, half the stalk is cut off, and a number of stalks are tied together and hung heads down in the kitchen to dry. When dry, the seeds are removed from the stalks and painstakingly husked with the fingers, the chaff picked out by hand. Seed is sold as well as used. A *tablón* of seed is enough to grow about an acre of onions.

Yields.—The yield of a standard *tablón* of onions varies considerably according to the soil, the care, the weather—hence the season—and the health of the plants. Onions may be graded as "large," "medium," and "small" and a *tablón* normally yields onions of different sizes. Actual counts in a number of *tablones* show that there are about 5,000 to a standard all-onion *tablón*. The proportion of onions of different sizes was carefully worked out with a reliable farmer and checked against other data. The yields per onion bed (1/45 acre) result as follows:

Good harvest	3,333 large onions.
	1,667 medium onions.
Fair harvest	2,500 large onions.
	1,667 medium onions.
	833 small onions.
Poor harvest	1,667 medium onions.
	3,333 small onions.

Since there is no reason to believe that 1936 was an abnormal year, I am supposing that yields on Indian onion lands approximated these figures. We also calculated that about

10 percent of all *tablones* yield nothing.
20 percent of all *tablones* yield poor harvests.
30 percent of all *tablones* yield medium harvests, and
40 percent of all *tablones* yield good harvests.

Using these figures, which I believe are as good as could be had except with enormous effort not worth the possible difference, it may be concluded that an average acre of onions (containing 45 *tablones*) yields:

Large onions	93, 750
Medium onions	67, 500
Small onions	41, 250
Total	202, 500

GARLIC

Garlic, the second most important truck crop, is grown (in this region) almost exclusively at Panajachel. It takes about 6 months from the beginning of November to April for garlic to grow. Since garlic is supposed to thrive better in land that has been at rest, a greater proportion of *tablones* than in the case of onions are probably made in new land. Garlic also requires considerably longer use of the land, for not only is the growing season longer, but the land is usually prepared several months in advance to allow the weeds and other vegetation to rot thoroughly.

Since garlic is planted not with seed but with sections of the bulb, neither nurseries nor seed beds are involved. The growing of garlic thus corresponds to the growing of onions from onion seedlings. After the beds have been prepared, the sections of garlic are inserted at 4-inch intervals with the fingers, and left uncovered. If the soil has been properly prepared, only one weeding is required; otherwise two. Watering is done as for onions, except that after the plants reach the surface they are not watered for 3 weeks; after that, every 3 or 4 days. Preparing the harvest for market is a long task, often saved for evenings and rainy days, when the greens are carefully braided into bunches for market.[38]

BEANS

Beans are the third important *tablón* crop of Panajachel. Both vine (pole) and shrub beans are grown. Most often planted in January and February where a corn crop is harvested, beans not picked green for market mature in 3 or 4 months. The garden beds are prepared as for onions or garlic, and three or four beans are planted at intervals of about 9 inches. Since they grow for the most part in the dry months, watering must be frequent and regular; they are weeded once. Shrub beans require considerably less labor than vine beans, both because the growing season is shorter and because poles have to be gathered and set for the vines to climb.

OTHER VEGETABLES

Other vegetables of relatively minor importance that are grown in Panajachel are huskcherries, cabbages, radishes, peas, lettuce, carrots, beets, turnips, kohlrabi, *metabel* (a beetlike plant), and swiss chard. Occasionally part or even a whole *tablón* is occupied with one of these crops. More often they are grown along the edges of beds of onions, garlic, or beans, or (for their nurseries) interspersed among these other plants, thus grown incidentally and involving no easily separable expenditure of effort. Huskcherries actually grow like weeds and are allowed to mature during the rainy season in the garlic beds. The other vegetables are planted from seed imported from the United States. Cabbages and beets are planted in nursery beds and transplanted like onions. Cabbages are planted either 18 inches apart in a bed, or at 54-inch intervals along the edge of a bed of another crop. A cabbage bed is weeded twice, beets only once; swiss chard and *metabel* are also transplanted, but I have no details on their culture. Radishes, carrots, and turnips are planted in nurseries, weeded once, and thinned only as they are harvested.[39]

[38] For yields, see p. 112.
[39] For estimates of yields of these vegetables, see infra, p. 114.

TUBERS

Sweet cassava and sweetpotatoes are grown along the oblique edges of the garden beds (as are several varieties of peppers) about a dozen of the first and 140 plants of the second in each of most onion *tablones* in town. They are planted from shoots, sweetpotatoes some 9 inches apart (usually in December for August harvesting) and sweet cassava about 6 feet apart. Since cassava grows for as long as 2 years, it is planted at any time; the other crops of the field are harvested and the *tablones* remade while it grows.

PEPINOS

Pepinos, with onions, garlic, and beans, are the fourth major truck crop, and a Panajachel specialty. They are rarely grown in *tablones*, almost always in individual hills in an open field. They require, like garlic, relatively fresh land, so are not usually planted in remade *tablones*. They grow from July to June; the crop occupies the soil for a year, therefore, or sometimes even more, since on new land the soil is first prepared in May. After the soil has been turned with a pickax and pulverized, and stones and weeds removed, circles 2 to 3 feet in diameter are marked off about 2 yards apart and shoots of *pepino* bushes inserted in the center of each. At this point a special soup made of the hoofs of cattle is put on each plant. The field is usually fenced. When the rains stop, the plants must be frequently watered because *pepinos* are usually grown in sandy soil. Watering is done by flooding the field between the plants, the hills of which are carefully ridged and reridged to keep the bushes growing inward and to keep the water from running off. A monthly weeding adds to the labor required. Plants bear fruit different in both size and number, both varying with the quality of the yield. Results of calculations made with one thorough informant checked so well with other data that I had that I am basing my estimate of yields on the conclusions we reached:

Pepino yield:

Best ------------------------------	52,552 large.
	56,594 medium.
	60,637 small.
Average ---------------------------	33,249 large.
	30,318 medium.
	35,270 small.
Worst -----------------------------	13,946 large.
	4,042 medium.
	9,903 small.

The best harvests come on rented land, for renters look for "new" land. On land that has not been planted with *pepinos* for 2 years, the harvest is average. If land is planted in consecutive years, the harvest will "surely" be poor the second year. (People who do this "know no better.") If *pepinos* are planted too late, I was told, a sickness attacks them and the yield is very poor. These rules hold for any year, it was said.

The list of garden plants cultivated is by no means exhausted; there are a number of herbs such as coriander, rue, mint, and *cintula*, a few additional vegetables such as peas, tomatoes, and cucumbers, and some miscellaneous plants such as strawberries. But those of any considerable economic importance have been discussed, and for the rest the data available are too scant for inclusion even if discussion should be warranted.

COFFEE

Coffee grown by Indians is found exclusively in the delta, virtually all of it on land that might otherwise be used for truck. The techniques used are similar to those of local Ladinos, which probably do not differ much from those practiced by small producers elsewhere in Guatemala. Groves are begun with saplings that are either found in the fields where they have sprouted and grown wild, or have been planted in nurseries. Even when nursery-grown, however, they most frequently are planted not from seed but from wild seedlings transplanted to nursery when 2 or 3 inches high. The nurseries are simply garden beds less carefully made than for vegetables. The seeds or seedlings are planted from 4 to 7 inches apart usually at the beginning of the rainy season. One weeding is usually required. During the ensuing dry season the bed is watered twice weekly. At the beginning of the following rainy season, the saplings, now a foot or two high and with four or five branches, are ready for transplanting. The bed is flooded for an hour or two, the young bushes carefully pulled out, and the roots wrapped in banana "bark" (layers of the trunk) and bound with fibers of the same. The bushes are frequently sold to Ladinos.

Meanwhile, in the field destined to receive the coffee, holes about 2 feet square and deep are dug at intervals of from 5 to 7 feet. The bushes are unwrapped, carefully set into the holes, and the earth stamped down around them. Other trees, including banana and other fruit trees, but especially silk-oak, are planted from 10 to 15 feet apart, in holes that are a little larger than those for coffee. Silk-oak seedlings are sometimes planted in nurseries, but most trees are simply transplanted from their wild state. Bananas, of course, are easily planted from shoots.

When the coffee bushes are still young, corn is frequently grown on the same land. Occasionally, vegetables are. But after the second year the amount of shade makes this impracticable. Some people occasionally water the young bushes. In the third year there are some berries, and the annual work of caring for the grove and harvesting the berries has begun. Twice yearly, once in the rainy season and once just before the harvest, the grove is weeded and cleaned; the underbrush is removed from between the rows so that berries fallen during the harvest are more easily retrieved. Men, women, and children alike do the harvesting, which begins in November and continues through January. No special tools are used, except a hooked pole to pull down pliable branches and a ladder used by children. The berries are picked one-by-one, carefully, or (when the worker is paid by the quantity harvested) carelessly by running the hand down the branch. They are collected in baskets or bags. The same grove must be picked over several times as the berries ripen.

To remove the beans from the pulp, women use the grinding stone; but many families own hand pulping machines and others rent them by the day. The beans are then placed in earthenware pots buried in the ground. The next day water is added. On the third day the beans are placed in baskets, washed, and then sunned on mats for about 3 days. Then they are ready to be sold. Alternatively, they may be shelled of their outer parchment on the grinding stone or in a mortar hollowed out of a tree stump, after which they may be sold at a higher price or else consumed.

The yield varies from field to field (depending partly on the age of the bushes and the care they receive) and from year to year—usually alternating between heavier and lighter yields. A good informant said that in the third year after transplanting, a *cuerda* produces 20 pounds, the next year 50, the fifth year 75, the sixth, 100, the seventh, 125, and the eighth, 150 pounds. Then for 2 or 3 years the yield drops to 125 pounds and after that to 100 pounds (562 pounds per acre)

for as many as 30 years (with good care). His own yield, in the past few years, ran from 75 to 150 pounds per *cuerda* (422 to 843 pounds per acre); but his grove is old. Another owner of an old grove harvested but 87 pounds per *cuerda* in 1936. Two other informants said their groves produce from 200 to 250 pounds per *cuerda* (1,125 to 1,406 pounds per acre); another, that when the harvest is good, he gets 125 pounds per *cuerda* (703 per acre), and otherwise a little under 100 pounds (562 per acre). Official statistics show that in 1935–36 the yield in the whole Republic was at the rate of 456 pounds per acre and in the Department of Sololá, 409,[40] and in the next year 455 and 443 pounds per acre respectively.[41] It is hardly conceivable that the Panajachel yield should be two or three times the general yield; yet it must be above average. Most probably the Panajachel yield in 1936 ran to some 100 pounds per *cuerda* or 562 per acre.

FRUIT

Very few fruit trees are actually planted by the Indians; most of them grow wild. Sometimes the seeds of papayas, peaches, oranges, *limas*, limes, and Spanish plums are planted in onion nurseries and the seedlings later transplanted. Occasionally a seedling of a cross-sapodilla is found and brought to the house to be planted in the yard. Bananas and occasionally other fruit trees are planted in the coffee groves. But mostly fruit just grows. Likewise, the trees receive almost no attention. Some people occasionally weed and fertilize the ground around young trees, which three or four times during the dry season are also watered by the women or children of the house. It is the custom to smear honey, vinegar, or lard on appropriate trees during Holy Week. That is the main care they receive.

Harvesting of the fruit takes most of what effort is needed. The most common method is to twist off the stem of a fruit such as an orange with a long notched pole. Or the tree may be shaken so that the fruit drops. Or one may climb the tree and pick the fruit by hand and deposit it in a bag. The time involved depends upon the kind of tree and the extent to which it is laden. For example, it takes about an hour to gather 100 oranges, but if the tree is heavily laden, 300 may be gathered

40 *Memoria*, Dept. Agri., 1936, p. 330 (Guatemala, 1937).
41 *Memoria*, Dept. Agri., 1937, p. 211 (Guatemala, 1938).

in the same time. Spanish plums, growing much more thickly, are gathered by the thousand rather than by the hundred.

VEGETABLE-PEAR

The vegetable-pear vine is quite another matter. Planted from seeds or shoots in only a few minutes, the young plant is frequently fenced in and usually a trellis is built for it to climb and small pots are suspended to encourage the growth of large fruit. After the first harvest, in October or November, the vine is pruned. Then it must be watered occasionally until, in March or April, there is another harvest. After 2 years, fruit is usually no longer produced until the root, which has grown large, is harvested. Then for 2 or 3 years fruit grows again. Roots can be cut twice before the vine dies. Each year, therefore, there are two harvests of fruit, and every 2 years one of roots.

Agriculture is what Panajacheleños think of when they think of the land. For the most part, when they think of agriculture they think of business. In The Business of Agriculture (pp. 108–132) there is extended discussion of costs and returns in this main Panajachel business.

LAND OWNERSHIP AND PRACTICES

COMMON LANDS

Four kinds of land are in some sense publicly owned:

(1) The law of Guatemala [41a] claims for the Government 200 meters of the shore of such navigable inland waters as Lake Atitlán, so that legally the State could dispossess the private owners of land along the lake shore. But the traditional owners, at least through the time of this study, were permitted to retain and use this land and to buy and sell it at will. I have heard, but not verified, that foreigners (but never Indians or local Ladinos) who have bought such land on which to build homes have had to make financial arrangements with the central Government on what appears to be a rental or lease basis. Local people have titles to their lake-shore land and appear to

suffer no interference, although one lake-shore landowner was denied exclusive wharfing privileges and during the period of study the Government set aside a piece of shore land as a public bathing beach. Neither of these events deprived Indians of land, although a road-building program in 1941 did.[42] In the following discussion, I shall treat lake-shore land as privately owned, as, practically, it is.

(2) Streets, roads, main paths, and main irrigation ditches are publicly owned. So also are the church and cemetery (which are not church property), the plaza, and the edifice housing the town hall, post office, etc.

(3) The sterile river bed may be considered public. Anybody may collect firewood or stones from it, and when stones are collected commercially for building purposes, permission must be had from the town authorities. Since in the past generation the river has continually eroded its banks there are legal titles to land that "the river has taken away." But the owners appear to consider such land as irrevocably useless and do not raise the question of its ownership. Nobody seems to know if reclaimed lands would be returned to the original owners. Since none has been reclaimed,[43] all the river bed is best treated as publicly owned.

(4) There is one piece of truly communal land on the west hillside. Generations ago all hillside land, at least, was probably communally owned and parceled out to different families who obtained permission to plant their cornfields on it, as in other towns. If this is true, communal tract on the west hill is doubtless the last remnant of such land in Panajachel, not allotted because it is not utilizable agriculturally. Whatever the history, this piece of land is universally recognized as communal property.

This tract of land is divided into two parts, however. A strip at the foot of the hill is usually thought of as privately owned, and only the upper part is legally, practically, and indisputably communal. The private owners of land at the base of the hill claim as their own from 300 to 600 feet of adjoining slope, but the town officials have established the rights of the municipality over it

---

[41a] *Decreto* No. 483, 1894, Article 16, which provides that 200 meters from the shores of navigable lakes are reserved to the public domain. The local impression is that the figure is 100 meters; perhaps the law has been changed, but I find no subsequent laws relevant to the point in *Leyes Vigentes*, Guatemala, 1927.

[42] The right to take land for roads was recognized in the then Guatemalan Constitution (Article 28); although compensation is mentioned as mandatory, for some reason none was given in this case.

[43] Except a miniscule portion on the very edge of the river bed which has been reclaimed for truck.

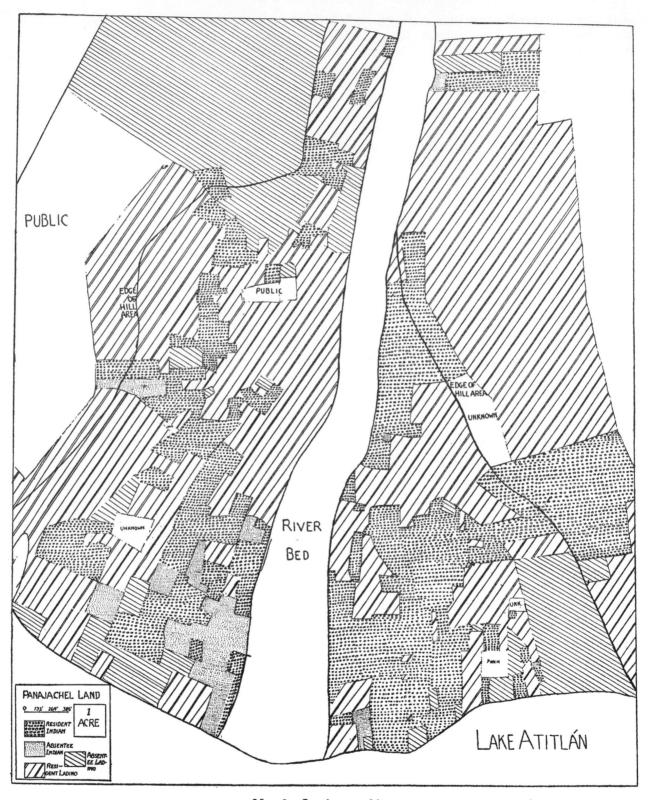

MAP 6.—Land ownership.

and in the only case where such disputed land is utilized agriculturally, the "owner" is required to ask permission of the authorities to plant his cornfield. In one case a claimant actually included about 300 feet of the rocky hill base in the deed of land that he sold, but since the land is worthless, the minor dispute that arose was, and appears to remain, purely academic. Nevertheless, most people seem to think that this disputed strip has individual owners, and for practical purposes it has. On map 6, and in most of the following discussion, this land is therefore treated as if it were privately owned.

Chart 5 separates private from public land, as classified above. About 23 percent of the land is publically owned, or 19 percent not counting that which is privately claimed and used. Almost

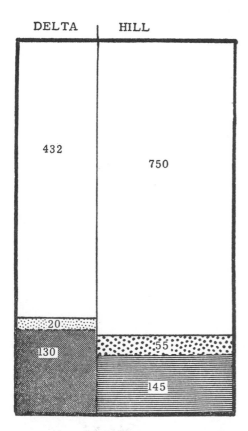

DELTA   HILL

432

750

20

130

55

145

Privately Owned

Privately Claimed

Communal Land

Roads, Buildings, Etc.

River Bed   = 20 Acres

CHART 5.—Land ownership.

26 percent of delta land has no private owners; 21 percent of hill land is communally owned or claimed, but the undisputed (and agriculturally useless) part constitutes but 15 percent of all hill lands. Of the public lands of the delta, 87 percent consists of the sterile river bed. Of the remainder, most (65 percent) is taken up by streets and roads and the smaller portions by irrigation ditches (20 percent) and public buildings, the plaza, and the cemetery (15 percent).

PRIVATELY OWNED LAND

Chart 6 shows graphically how the privately owned and claimed land of the area studied was distributed in 1936 [44] among Ladino and Indian landowners, both resident in Panajachel and absentee. It shows clearly that the Ladinos own the lion's share—so much so that even the absentee Ladino landowners own a third more than all the Indians combined. This is a fact of importance, for the Indians of Panajachel depend upon the land almost exclusively for their living, and they constitute more than two-thirds of the resident population. Nor is this the whole picture of the disparity, for the Ladinos to an extent not at all approached by the Indians own land outside the area studied. At least eight resident Ladino families have large landholdings not included in this study; indeed, the acreage of lands outside owned by local Ladinos is far greater than the entire area of Panajachel studied. (Probably all the absentee Ladino owners own more land in other places.) On the other hand, the resident Indians own relatively few acres of land outside of Panajachel. (Again absentee Indian landowners no doubt have larger holdings elsewhere.) In the area studied, however, the disparities are not as great as the gross figures would indicate,

[44] Unlike crop distributions, which can be observed, ownership information must come from informants. On the original work map, made in 1936 with a scale of 40 inches to a mile, land boundaries were plotted as exactly as possible, with the help of several native informants. In 1940 independent information on the size of Indian lots was obtained from informants and compared with corresponding data taken from map measurements. At the same time, the base map was corrected to conform to Dr. McBryde's findings, and the land boundaries—now corrected in some instances to conform to informants' statements—plotted again on the new base. The map was then rechecked on the ground, and with Ladino estimates of the size of Ladino plots. Most inconsistencies were ironed out so that, finally, the sum of the extensions of the lots of a given small area as given by informants, about equaled the extension of that area as measured on the map. This was considered a final check on the accuracy of the individual land boundaries as plotted on the map. The sizes of resident Indian holdings are probably more accurate than those of the other classes, however, for only for resident Indians was the information of informants obtained entirely independently of the original and corrected maps.

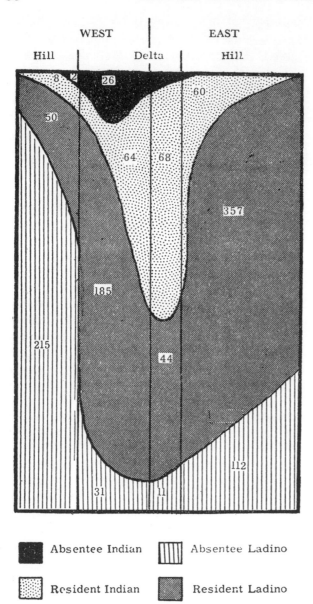

WEST   EAST

Hill   Delta   Hill

8   2   26   60

50

64   68

357

185

215

44

112

31   11

◼ Absentee Indian   ▦ Absentee Ladino

▨ Resident Indian   ▨ Resident Ladino

CHART 6.—Distribution of privately owned land.

Absentee Ladino holdings are not nearly as valuable as the gross acreage figures would indicate. Not only are they primarily (89 percent) on the hillsides as opposed to the delta but three-fifths of the total (actually one large piece) is located on the nearly sterile west hill. In the delta as well, the absentee Ladinos make less productive use of their land, agriculturally, than do the resident Ladinos, or, for that matter, than any other class (chart 7). Almost one-fourth of their land (as compared with 12 percent of that of resident Ladinos) is idle or occupied by buildings, including the chapel quarters of the American missionaries and the houses and gardens of outsiders who maintain vacation homes here. On the other hand, absentee Ladinos devote a larger proportion of their tilled land to truck and coffee than do the resident Ladinos, chiefly because they own considerable lake-shore land especially suited to truck farming, including a large experimental farm and orchard owned by a foreigner.

With their high proportion of coffee to truck crops, with their truck land rented to Indians, and the remainder disproportionately planted to corn, it has been shown that Ladinos cultivate their land less intensively than do the Indians, probably because (1) they have more land to cultivate; (2) they have other sources of income, hence less need to make the most out of their soil; and (3) since they require more hired labor than do the Indians, they find intensive cultivation both more difficult and less profitable than do the Indians.

Land owned by Indians, as compared with that of Ladinos, exists in very small parcels. Hill lots are much larger than delta lots, but in hill and delta alike Ladino parcels are fewer and larger than Indian [45] (chart 8). Likewise delta lots of the west side are consistently larger than those of the east. This is so despite the fact that 111 of 157 Ladino delta lots (71 percent) and 192 of 325 Indian (59 percent) are on the west side. Nevertheless, one reason is that the east side is where most resident Indians live and own land, and it has long been cut and recut by inheritance. The Ladino land of the east delta is in relatively

for Indians own a greater share of the more valuable delta lands. They own only 18.7 percent of all land, but 37.2 percent of delta land. For resident Indians the figures are 16.2 and 30.5 percent. The Ladino advantage is far greater in the least valuable lands than in the most valuable, and the rule continues to hold as one analyzes the delta lands alone: the Ladinos have progressively larger proportions of coffee, milpa, and pasture land, and a smaller proportion of the intensively cultivated high-income-producing truck lands.

[45] Fifteen of the total of five hundred and seventeen lots extend from the delta onto the hill and for purposes of this chart are called two, one a delta lot and the other a hill lot. The case of an absentee Ladino hill lot of 215 acres hides the fact that most parcels of land owned by resident Ladinos are larger than those of the absentee owners. The number of Ladino hill lots (21) is too small for statistical treatment. The fact remains despite some exceptions, however, that Ladino lots are much larger than Indian lots and that hill lots are very much larger than delta lots.

small parcels because much of it was acquired by the foreclosure and purchase of Indian plots. It will be recalled, also, that the land of the east delta has been in intensive use for a longer time, and was thus valuable at a time when (like the hill lands today) much land of the west side was not producing or was less intensively cultivated.[46]

It is seen in chart 9 that the average of 47 resident Ladinos who own Panajachel land owns

8½ times as much land as the average of the 127 resident Indian landowners, but the disparity is only 5 to 1 if the question concerns owners of delta land alone (45 Ladinos, 127 Indians). When only resident owners of coffee and truck lands (34 Ladinos, 126 Indians) are considered the disparity is again slightly larger not because Ladinos own a larger proportion of such land, but because they are few in number. In general the disparity in average landholdings of absentee owners (for all land, 30 Ladinos and 32 Indians; delta land, 25 and 32; and coffee-truck land, 12 and 32) follows

---

[46] As late as 1894 (Maudslay, 1899, photograph) the river passed through what is now the west side of the delta. The land of the west side is still stony; no doubt much of it has only recently come into production.

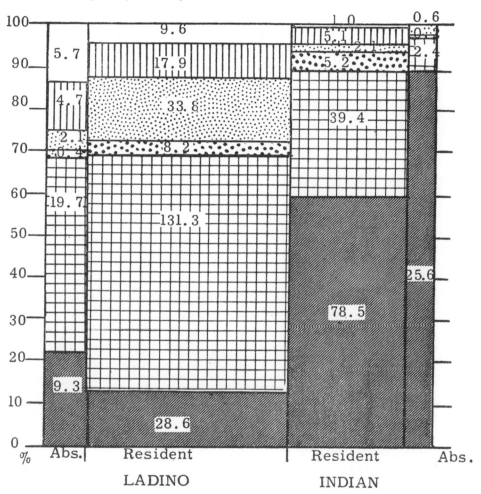

CHART 7.—Delta land use.

the same pattern, but residents who own land in Panajachel own more each than absentee landlords. Neither among Indians nor Ladinos is the land equally distributed. In each class a few families tend to own a large proportion of the land, but this is more true for Indians than for Ladinos. Chart 10 and table 10 summarize the distribution of land owned by resident Ladinos and Indians. (There is no point, of course, in discussing distribution of Panajachel lands among the absentee owners). It should be noted again that the data on Indian lands are more reliable than those on Ladinos. These were independently and completely checked with informants, while the sizes of Ladino parcels, determined originally by mapping to scale and measuring, were only partially verified in other ways. It will be noted that within each class the disparities are less in the case of delta lands than of all lands or of coffee-truck lands.

LADINO OWNERS

Thirty absentee Ladinos own 40 parcels of land in the area studied: one of them four pieces, two others three apiece, and three others two

apiece; the remaining 24 own one lot each. The average acreage per owner is 12.3 acres, the distribution as follows:

1 owns 215 acres, all hill land.
1 owns 80 acres, all hill land.
1 owns 22 acres, 12 of which are hill land; 10, delta.
1 owns 10 acres, all hill land.
1 owns 8 acres, all delta land.
1 owns 5 acres, 3 of which are hill land; 2, delta.
1 owns 5 acres, all hill land.
1 owns 2 acres, all hill land.
5 own from 1 to 5 acres, all delta land.
17 own less than 1 acre, all delta land.

TABLE 10.—*Comparison of land distributions*

| 20ths of population (families) | Percentage of Panajachel land owned | | | | | |
| | All land | | Delta land | | Truck-coffee land | |
	Ladino	Indian	Ladino	Indian	Ladino	Indian
1	52.3	30.6	32.8	21.5	38.0	21.1
2	16.2	19.7	20.0	13.8	19.5	13.3
3	10.5	11.3	13.8	10.4	13.0	11.0
4	7.0	7.5	9.5	9.5	10.6	9.7
5	4.3	5.9	8.0	8.1	8.0	8.4
6	3.2	5.1	5.4	6.6	3.8	6.8
7	2.7	4.0	3.4	5.7	2.7	5.7
8	1.4	3.4	2.6	5.0	1.7	5.1
9	1.0	2.9	1.6	4.2	1.4	4.2
10	.6	2.4	1.3	3.7	.8	3.8
11	.5	2.2	1.2	3.1	.2	3.0
12	.4	1.7	.5	2.3	0	2.2
13	.15	1.2	.3	1.9	0	1.8
14	.1	.9	.2	1.5	0	1.4
15	.08	.6	.15	1.1	0	1.0
16	.05	.5	0	.9	0	.8
17	0	.15	0	.3	0	.15
18–20	--------	--------	--------	--------	--------	--------
Total	100.48	100.05	100.75	99.6	99.7	99.45

Twenty-five persons thus own the 42-odd acres of absentee Ladino land in the delta, an average of 1.7 acres for each. The largest delta holdings are of 10 and 8 acres; six are from 1 to 5 acres each; and of the 17 who own less than an acre apiece, 4 have only house sites 0.05 to 0.13 acre each.

Eleven of the absentee Ladino owners live in Guatemala City, nine in Sololá, three in the Pacific lowlands, two in San Andrés, and one each in Quezaltenango, S. José Chacayá, Agua Escondida, and the United States. The last is the North American missionary group operating in Panajachel, where it owns two pieces of land. In its role as a resort Panajachel draws landowners from as far away as Guatemala City, and in recent years even from the United States. The number of such owners has increased from 1936, for which year the figures were prepared, to 1941 (when the study ended), and probably since. Because of its interest to tourists, as the most accessible spot on the lake, Ladinos of nearby towns are also invest-

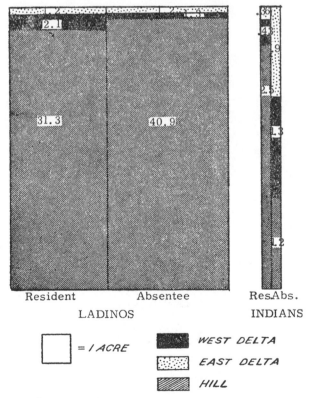

2.1

31.3   40.9

Resident   Absentee   Res.Abs.
    LADINOS   INDIANS

☐ = 1 ACRE   ▓ WEST DELTA
               ▒ EAST DELTA
               ▨ HILL

CHART 8.—Average acreage of individual lots.

ing in Panajachel land. But many of the Ladino owners from such neighboring communities as Sololá and San Andrés have long owned Panajachel land, especially hill land, for reasons other than the resort potentialities of the place.

A not-too-careful census counted 62 Ladino families in 1936, besides officials, teachers, missionaries, and others not permanently resident. Of these 62 families, 15 owned no Panajachel land at all, while 2 families owned 22 (and 9 families, 48) of a total of 140 lots. Including the landless families, the average of 13.6 acres per landowner

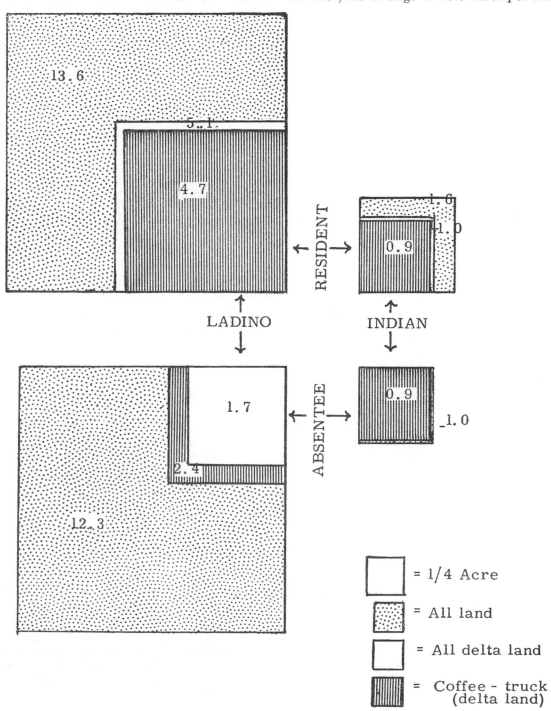

CHART 9.—Average acreage per land-owning family.

is reduced to 10.3 per family. But among the landowners themselves, one family alone owns 230 acres, or 36 percent of all Ladino-owned land. Eight families own 75 percent of the land, while 21 own more than 95 percent of all Ladino holdings in Panajachel. These figures include the less productive hill land as well as delta land; but, although the order of individual owners changes

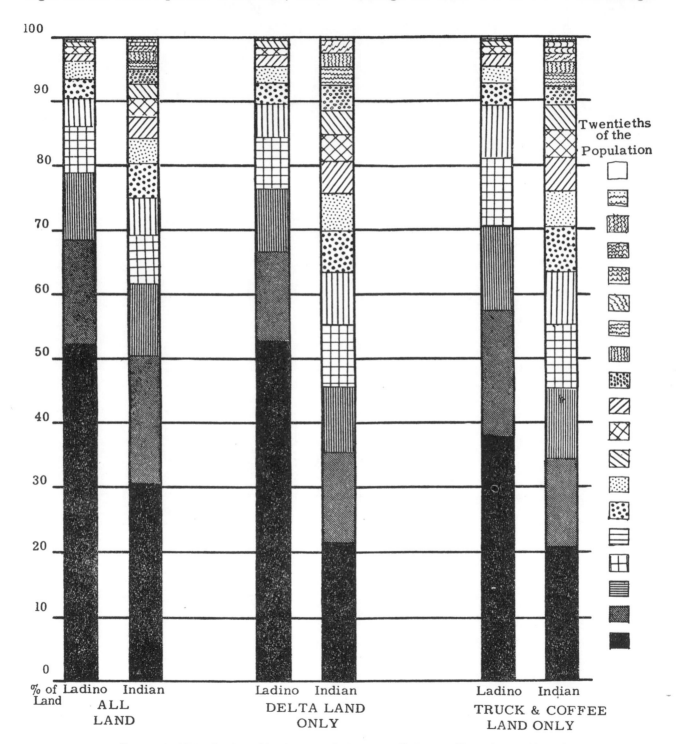

CHART 10.—Distribution of land among Ladinos and Indians. (Data from table 10.)

when delta lands alone are counted, the general picture remains pretty much the same, as seen in chart 10 and the following summary:

    6 families own more than 51 percent.
    12 families own almost 75 percent.
    19 families own almost 90 percent.
    25 families own more than 95 percent.
    34 families own 99 percent, leaving
    11 families owning together only 1 percent of the land, and 17 families landless.

Put another way, less than 10 percent of the Ladinos of Panajachel own more than 50 percent of Ladino-owned delta land, while on the other end of the scale almost half of them own together but a hundredth of the total. Even less evenly distributed are the very valuable coffee and truck lands of the delta, of which

    5 families own almost 51 percent.
    11 families own more than 76 percent.
    17 families own about 91 percent.
    21 families own about 95 percent, and
    30 families own 99 percent, leaving
    4 families owning together 1 percent, and
    28 families without any.

Since the Ladinos are usually only partly dependent upon agriculture for their living, this distribution is only a partial index of the distribution of wealth among them. Moreover, land owned by Ladinos outside of Panajachel are not included. Since the large landowners of Panajachel tend also to have other sources of income, and to own land outside of Panajachel, inclusion of additional data would probably show even greater difference in the wealth of the rich and the poor.

INDIAN OWNERS

It has already been pointed out (charts 6 and 7) that Indians own only 18.7 percent of all Panajachel land, but twice the proportion in the delta (37.2 percent), and that the proportion of Indian land in intensive cultivation is relatively great. What land they do not own probably passed from Indian into Ladino hands in the past two or three generations. This seems likely both because there were virtually no Ladinos in Panajachel before about 1850, and because they would have had little incentive to exploit such land as is found in Panajachel until coffee became a commercial crop. Probably as much as half of what Ladinos own came to them in the two decades preceding this study, which was the period of increasingly

profitable coffee culture, as well as of the arrival of city families who found on the shore of the lake sites for hotels and chalets. Indeed, a good part of their land was lost by the Indians during the depression years of the thirties when they defaulted on debts or were forced by some necessity to sell. The general rule is that transfer of land from Indian to Ladino is a one-way process: Ladinos obtain Indian land, but the reverse is rarely true.[47] However, at the time of study the peak of such transfers may have passed, for there was growing resistance to sell land to outsiders, and when an Indian needed money he seemed to go first to other Indians.

It should not be supposed that with so much land alienated, the Indians have been reduced largely to working for Ladinos. Among compensating factors are (1) that the Indians are able to rent a large proportion of Ladino land; (2) the diminution of Indian holdings was accompanied by a decrease of Indian population (from 2,092 in 1893 to 1,145 in 1921[48]) as many no doubt migrated to plantations;[49] and (3) increasingly greater exploitation of and larger returns from the sale of their fruits and vegetables to the growing Ladino population.

Nor does the transfer of lands to Ladinos necessarily mean that there are more landless Indians now than formerly, since before the land was so monopolized by Ladinos, a few rich Indians may have owned as much.

Absentee owners own 13.8 percent of Indian land, and 18 percent of Indian delta land. Their proportion in intensive cultivation is higher than that of the resident Indians (their proportion in truck a third greater—see chart 7) and they have a particular preference for onions and *pepinos*.

All but four of the absentee Indian owners live in neighboring San Jorge, the hamlet of the *muni-*

[47] A few cases of sales of land by Ladinos to Indians were noted. Both groups seem to follow the custom of offering land first to a previous owner, or one who owns adjoining land. Thus I have a note (November 1939) concerning an Indian who supposes that the Ladino owner of land formerly his did not offer it to him before others because he was presumed too poor to be able to buy it back. I had assumed this custom to be Indian until an Indian recalled that one of the ways the first Ladinos enlarged their holdings in Panajachel was by suggesting to their Indian neighbors that—to be good neighbors—they should offer land to them first.

[48] 4th Census, Part I, Guatemala, 1924, p. 186. From 1921 to 1940, the number of Indians increased again to 1,524 (5th Census, 1942, p. 222).

[49] In some cases they probably left when for some reason they lost their lands and in others they doubtless went to plantations for other reasons and then more readily sold their Panajachel lands. In 1936–37 several Indian families freed from plantation obligations by new laws returned to Panajachel; but having no land, and no way of making a living, they soon left again.

cipio of Sololá that is half way up the road to the city of Sololá. Although Jorgeños and Sololatecos have almost identical language and costume, and presumably culture, San Jorge has been recognized as a separate community since the earliest recorded times.[50] Panajacheleños say that a Jorgeño obtained Panajachel land about a century ago; his name is known, and so are some of his descendants. He is said to have owned most of the lower west delta when it was almost uncultivated pasture land with large patches of cane. He planted vegetables on some of the land and sold or rented other parts to his compatriots for the same purpose. His descendants, some of whom live now in Panajachel and are counted as resident Indians, still own some of the land.

Besides the Jorgeños, three Sololatecos and an Indian living in the hills above San Andrés own Panajachel land. The number of Jorgeño land-owners depends on the exact ownership of two of the pieces of land said by local people to be owned by "about three" and "about eight" Jorgeño families, respectively. If the "about" is dropped, there are 28 Jorgeño owners, thus 32 absentee Indians who own a little over 31 acres of Pana-jachel land, almost 29 in the delta. The average of something under an acre compares with 12.3 acres for absentee Ladinos. In the delta the average holding of 0.9 acre compares with 1.7 acres for absentee Ladinos, 4.7 acres for resident Ladinos, and 0.9 acre for resident Indians. The average coffee-truck acreage is however relatively high (chart 9). The land of the absentee Indians in 1936 was the most intensively used in Panajachel, in most striking contrast to that of absentee Ladinos. It may be said that outside Ladinos own land in Panajachel while outside Indians have farms in Panajachel.

RESIDENT INDIANS

It is with the land of the resident Indian community that this study is chiefly concerned. Data on resident Indian land ownership as well as population are both more complete and more accurate than on that of other classes.

[50] Diego de Ocaña wrote, in 1662, that the town called "San George" had been located at the lake shore until, 20 years before, it had been destroyed by a river and had been rebuilt half way up the slope (Vásquez, 1937, vol. 1, p. 191).

[51] In table 4 the number is shown as 157, but that includes the dual households of two polygynous men; for purposes of land distribution, each of the dual households is better treated as one.

In 1936 the 155 Indian households in Pana-jachel[51] owned slightly less than 200 acres of Panajachel land and about 24 acres outside the area studied. Only 127 of the 155 families owned land, however, so that the average of 1.5 acres per household is increased to almost 1.8 acres per landowning household, as compared with 10.3 and 13.6 acres, respectively, for resident Ladinos.

Almost two-thirds of the landowning families own at least two parcels. Indeed, almost two-fifths of them own at least three. At the other end, 10 percent own from 5 to 15 pieces each. The parcels in the delta are usually very small— 90 percent of them under an acre (table 11)—but by purchase or inheritance the family typically accumulates several of them.

Of the resident Indian lands, 6 households own almost 25 percent (chart 10 and table 10); 15 almost 50 percent; 38 about 75 percent; and 105 more than 95 percent. As with the Ladinos, 10 percent of the households own half the land, while at the other extreme more than a third of the people own less than 1 percent. Delta lands exclusively are less unequally distributed:

26 families own about 50 percent,
54 families own about 76 percent,
82 families own about 90 percent,
100 families own more than 95 percent, and
116 families about 99 percent, leaving
11 families with 1 percent and
28 landless.

TABLE 11.—*Size of Indian delta lots*

Size of lot (acres)	Number	Percent
Under 0.5:		
Under 0.1	24	7.9
0.1–0.2	87	28.7
0.2–0.3	39	12.9
0.3–0.4	59	19.5
0.4–0.5	5	1.6
Total	214	70.6
0.5–1.0	59	19.5
1.0–1.5	24	7.9
1.5–2.0	4	1.3
2.0–2.5		
2.5–3.0	2	.7
Total	303	100.0

Or, to put it another way, a wealthy 17 percent of the families own half the land while a poor quarter of the people together own a hundredth. The distribution of coffee-truck lands is similar to that of all delta land.

This inequality is less if one omits from the reckoning immigrant families who have come to Panajachel as laborers or artisans. Of the 20 such families, only 2 own land in Panajachel, and only one-fifth acre between them. It is also useful to leave out of account two Jorgeño families resident in Panajachel; they own land and are farmers as are the Panajacheleños, but they enter into local life hardly more than do their relatives who live in San Jorge. The remaining "Panajacheleños" (as opposed to "foreigners") number 132 families.[52]

_____
[52] Including two dual (polygynous) households here counted as one apiece.

They own about 222 acres, 129 of which are in the delta; the average per household is 1.7 acres for all land, and just under 1 acre for delta land.

Of the 132 Panajacheleño households, all but 9 own land. Of these 9, 2 are not really landless; their inheritance had simply not been turned over to them in 1936, although they worked the land. There were, then, 7 families of the 132 with no land resources. The distribution of the land of

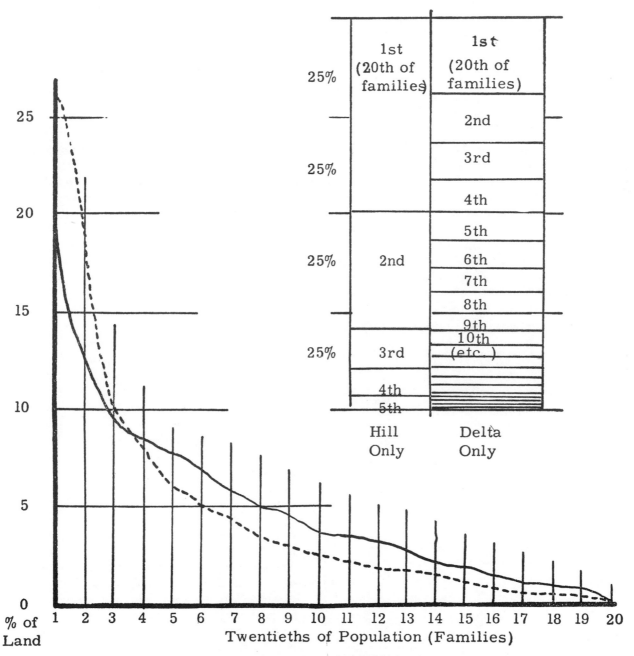

CHART 11.—Distribution of Panajacheleño land.

the Panajacheleños giving equal shares to house-holds sharing land (chart 11) may be summarized as follows:

Of all land:

    6 families own 25 percent,
    16 families own 50 percent,
    39 families own 75 percent,
    68 families own 90 percent,
    85 families own 95 percent, and
    109 families own 99 percent, leaving
    7 families landless.

Of delta land alone:

    9 families own 25 percent,
    26 families own 50 percent,
    53 families own 75 percent,
    80 families own 90 percent,
    94 families own 95 percent,
    116 families own 99 percent, leaving
    9 families with 1 percent and
    7 families landless.

In other words, an eighth of the families own half the land, while at the other end a sixth of them share a hundredth of it. But the distribution of valuable delta land is much more equitable: 27 percent of the families own half of it while at the other extreme only a ninth of the households are left with the last hundredth. The difference results because only a fourth of the families own all Panajacheleño hill land, including that in other communities.

Table 12 shows the distribution of Panajacheleño land wealth with areas of different types

TABLE 12.—*Distribution of all Panajacheleño land, areas reduced to value*

20ths of population	Percentage of land owned		Percentage of land controlled	
	By house-holds	By per-sons [1]	By house-holds	By per-sons [1]
1st	18.5	17.1	21.5	19.6
2d	12.2	12.3	12.4	12.2
3d	10.1	9.9	10.5	10.1
4th	8.9	9.0	8.8	9.6
5th	7.8	7.7	7.2	7.0
6th	6.6	6.5	6.1	6.4
7th	5.5	5.9	5.4	5.4
8th	5.0	5.0	4.8	4.9
9th	4.6	4.7	4.5	4.4
10th	3.7	4.0	3.6	3.8
11th	3.4	3.6	3.1	3.4
12th	3.1	3.3	2.6	2.9
13th	2.7	2.8	2.3	2.4
14th	2.2	2.3	2.0	2.1
15th	1.9	1.9	1.7	1.7
16th	1.4	1.3	1.3	1.4
17th	1.0	1.1	1.0	1.2
18th	.92	.86	.83	.86
19th	.46	.64	.39	.55
20th	----------	.12	----------	.12
Total	99.98	100.02	100.02	100.03

[1] Calculated not on the basis of individual ownership or control, within the household, but simply by dividing the land owned or controlled by the household by the number of persons in the household, excluding servants.

of land reduced to dollar value (below, pp. 82–84), the families reduced to the number of individuals, and with pawned land (below, pp. 80–81) counted as the property of the pawnee rather than of the nominal owner. This gives a more realistic picture of the distribution of land wealth which, in Panajachel, is the basis of virtually all wealth.

With delta land worth so much more than hill land, the distribution by dollar value is not unlike the distribution of delta acreage. A comparison of the four distributions shown in table 12, however, demonstrates two further points of some interest: (1) The land controlled by the various families is more unevenly distributed than the land actually owned. This might mean that in the process of pawning lands, the rich are becoming richer and the poor poorer. However, as will be seen, there is no such general rule; one wealthy family has obtained control of so much land as to skew the distribution. (2) The distribution of land owned or controlled is more even when the individual is taken as a unit than when the household is. This is because, in general, the most land-poor families tend to be small while the richest households are large. This fact, of some importance in discussion of wealth mobility, will be referred to again.

TENURE AND TRANSFER

If more of the hill land was communally owned in past generations, the system of allotment was probably similar to that in San Pedro across the lake, where there is much more (Rosales, 1949). Individuals who prove need receive the use of land from the town authorities in exchange for a small quantity of the harvest per unit of land (the same rental, actually, that is paid to private landowners). The authorities use the proceeds to pay secular and ceremonial expenses. In Panajachel there exists no problem of use of the piece of hill land still commonly held, because it is useless. For practical purposes all of the land of Panajachel is privately owned, and wholly alienable, and landowners are free to do whatever they wish with their holdings. Public opinion to some extent limits the individual's freedom to dispose of his land: it is better to sell to an Indian than to a Ladino, if possible, and it is better to sell to one who owns adjoining land than to anybody else, especially if he is a former owner. More important as a limitation is the high value placed on ownership of land: to buy it increases and to sell it decreases not only wealth but prestige. Finally, the individual's freedom is restricted by his family: if a man's children object strongly enough, he may desist from selling his land, especially since public opinion supports their argument that he is wrong to fritter away their inheritance. With these qualifications, ownership is unrestricted: land can be bought and sold, rented or mortaged, or given for security for a loan.

There are apparently two kinds of legal title to lands, and two kinds of corresponding transfer of title. Deeds prepared by lawyers may be registered in and transferred through a Government land office in Sololá, in which case taxes are paid on the land. Or titles may be privately drawn up and transfers privately arranged, in which case an amateur lawyer draws up the papers of transfer on stamped paper, they are signed by the principals and witnessed and kept in the possession of the purchaser. Such unofficial transfers are apparently legal but not considered very safe and watertight. The proportion of Panajachel lands the ownership of which is registered in the land office in Sololá is probably small. The three cases in which I was a principal to a land transaction were all cases of unregistered documents. (I do know what happens if an owner of lake-shore land attempts to transfer title in Sololá, since legally the land there is of the public domain.)

Land can be, and is, owned by individuals regardless of sex; thus part of the land of a family may be owned by the husband and part by the wife, each of whom has separately inherited it or acquired it in some other manner. Men in general own more land than women, both because they are often willed more and because the husband rather than the wife takes title to land bought by the family. Young sons and daughters may under certain circumstances own land, but if they are living under the power of their parents or stepparents the latter actually use the land for them until they become independent and come into their inheritance. In a similar manner, the husband as agriculturalist generally controls the use of the land of his wife. Neither husband nor wife is sole master of the home or the family purse, and neither is likely to buy or sell land without the other's permission. Certainly neither can sell

what belongs to the other. In one case a prospective buyer erred seriously when he approached a man about land which his wife owned; whatever the real reason may have been, the wife subsequently refused to sell at any price even though her husband seemed to favor doing so. After that he refused even to talk about the land except in his wife's presence. In another case an Indian obtained his wife's permission to sell a piece of her inheritance to a Ladino; the sale was consummated, but the wife's mother then objected so strongly to her duaghter that she induced her husband to return the money.

In general, Indians appear to be loathe to sell their land, and sell only when they deem it absolutely necessary. One class of exceptional cases has come about in recent years with the willingness of outsiders to pay high prices for lake-shore land. Indians have in such cases sold land, but have bought other land to replace it. There are also cases in which people have sold land to pay for prolonged drinking, and even (after coming into a substantial legacy) to live an easy life. Such selling of land is not only unusual but frowned upon in the community. It is generally felt that parents should keep their land for their children. In one case where a land-rich Indian sold all of his land, I heard nothing but censure for him who had had so much and who left nothing to his children. I have several notes on similar cases: I shall cite three that seem especially significant.

(1) An informant described how a man who had been left considerable money and land by his father quickly spent the money and then eventually pawned or sold almost all the land. He added, "Now he is not even able to work well; his physical weakness is undoubtedly an infirmity sent him by his father because he has lost all the land."

(2) I tried to buy a piece of land from an Indian friend. "What would I have to leave my children?" he asked, and added, "You can dig and dig in your land, and the land is still there. Put in fertilizer and the land grows. But money . . .?" Several months later he was still reiterating this position; he told me that others also wanted to buy the land, but that he would not sell. He said that he was considering trading it, however, for a larger piece in a less favorably situated place.

(3) An American in Guatemala City who was trying to buy a certain small piece of land from a local Indian asked me to intervene. The land was

the wife's inheritance. For a time I thought she was holding out for more money, but when she refused to sell even for 10 times what the land was worth by local standards, I became convinced of the sincerity of her insistence that she wanted it for her son.

It is true that there are special objections to selling to Ladinos and to foreigners, but in too many cases they proved too weak to interfere with negotiations to suppose that they were the major consideration in the last two cited. In 1941 an Indian proved anxious to sell me a piece at a very moderate price; mistakenly thinking that I had bought it, an Indian who lived on adjoining land complained at its having been sold to a foreigner. But the fact remains that had I wished, I could have made the purchase (nor was the seller a friend of mine: I did not know him before negotiations began). In the case of a family that did sell to foreigners, some Indians blamed them for the opening of several new roads which took away the land of others; but nobody seemed to take the matter to heart. I tried in vain to get a serious condemnation of sales to outsiders from the richest landowner in town (who himself had never sold land) or from almost any body else. What feeling there is is both mild and sporadic. The facts are that for generations land has been sold to Ladinos and to foreigners, that Indians if they must sell prefer to sell to other Indians, but that they almost surely put money (in this matter) above sentiment.

Until recently when lake-shore land began to bring high prices from foreigners, so that some sold it to better themselves by buying larger areas of agricultural land elsewhere, it could be said that Indians do not sell land for business reasons but only because they need or want the money for consumptive purposes. Cases that I have, as well as statements of informants, all indicate that sickness, death, and the assumption of municipal or religious office are by far the most important events leading to loss of land. Even if land is not immediately sold in such circumstances, debts eventually lead to its sale, or to its loss by being pawned and never redeemed. Protracted drinking, which also often leads to debt, is itself frequently begun at funerals and during the performance of duties connected with civil and religious offices. There are cases in which land is sold in order to liquidate debts, and these may

in a sense be called sales for business purposes. In one case cited below, one of two pieces of land was sold to enable the owner to redeem the other. In another, an Indian was anxious to sell a heavily mortgaged piece of land, having no hope of redeeming it, to enable him to pay other pressing debts. But I have never heard of land's being sold to furnish capital, probably because land itself is the only really profitable investment available to a Panajacheleño.

The last land to be lost, if all is lost, is almost always the house site. If it is pawned, the family continues to use the house—the creditor using only the land; but if it is sold, the family can remain only by the kindness of the new owner. There were only five cases in 1936 (besides that of a man who kept a second wife and family in a "borrowed house") in which families who owned land did not live on their own property. In none of these cases was the house site sold or otherwise given up before other land, and the evidence is clear that such would be an extraordinary practice. On the contrary, landless Panajacheleños buy land first from a desire for a home site. This means, of course, that while land is the source of wealth and economic security, it also makes possible an owned home site, desire for which may be as important as desire for wealth. In other words, Indians do not live on borrowed land in order to make the most, agriculturally, of their own land.

While it is true that the sale of Indian land to Ladinos and outsiders is in general a one-way process, our notes record six cases of the reverse, four of them in very recent years. It is, obviously, a matter of relative wealth: Ladinos usually are not forced to sell land, and when they do sell, it is apt to be in quantities that Indians cannot afford to buy, and often for prices higher than they will pay. Of the six cases, four concerned wealthy Indians, and the other two poorer Indians who bought very small lots from relatively poor Ladinos. Most of the land that Indians buy is purchased from other Indians. The number of such transactions, probably four or five a year, is difficult to estimate from my incomplete notes, partly because in all-Indian transactions the line between pawned lands and purchased lands is very hazy. Discussion of pawning is anticipated in the following cases inserted to show the confusion that often surrounds land transactions among the Indians.

(1) Norberto and Petrona Salanic were brother and sister, the latter widowed and with one son, Leandro Rosales. Petrona and her son had no land, and lived in various borrowed houses. Norberto, sorry for them, gave his sister 2 *cuerdas* (0.4 acre) of coffee land on which to build a house; this was half of a certain piece of land he owned. The whole piece had been pawned to a Ladino for $50, so Norberto could not give his sister immediate legal title. Instead, he took her to the town hall, and there, before witnesses, turned over the land. Shortly afterward, in 1936, Petrona died. Her son Leandro inherited the land, which had never come into Petrona's possession. In order to pay for his mother's funeral, Leandro pawned the land for $20 to Agustín Yaxón, the informant. No document was turned over, but there was a witness. Norberto paid to the Ladina $33 to apply on his debt of $50; he expected to pay the remaining $17 that year, and thus redeem the land and turn the half of it over to his nephew, Leandro.

In September 1937 Norberto himself died, leaving as sole heiress to his property a daughter, grown but unmarried. She recognized that half of the land had been given to her aunt, Petrona, and now belonged to her cousin, Leandro, who had meanwhile gone to the lowlands to look for work. However, she did not have money with which to bury her father, and she now made an agreement with Ventura Lopez (her father's father's brother's son): she would give him her half of the land mentioned and he would pay the funeral expenses and also repay the $17 still due the Ladina. Ventura accepted, and after the funeral tried to sell the land. He asked $50 for the 2 *cuerdas*, and nobody would buy it. Then he went to Sololá, where lived the Ladina to whom the land was pawned, and offered to sell it to her. The woman had not previously heard of Norberto's death. Now she arranged to repay Lopez the funeral expenses and to keep possession of the land herself. A few days later she came to Panajachel and in the presence of Norberto's surviving relatives took possession of the entire 4 *cuerdas* of land (to which she had the document), refusing to recognize Norberto's gift to his sister, hence Leandro's rights to half the land.

Now Yaxón, worried about the $20 he had given to Leandro, received a letter from the latter, who had heard of what had happened, asking if it were true, and if he should come to Panajachel to try to reclaim his land. This letter was answered to the effect that Leandro should come, and 2 weeks later he did come and was unsuccessful in his suit in the local courthouse. He then went to Sololá to complain of the lack of justice, but nothing ever came of the matter. Meanwhile, Yaxón forgot about the land itself and simply obtained recognition by Leandro of his $20 debt to him.

It would be difficult to conclude from this account whether any land sales were involved, and yet there were several land transfers—all but one in the end illegalized.

(2) Quirino and Vicenta Quiché are two of several grown and married children of Santiago Quiché, a rich Indian.

Quirino is married to one Elena Rosales (Juan Rosales' father's sister). On November 12, 1936, he explained to Rosales difficulties he was having with his father, Santiago. Elena's mother long ago ceded to her a *cuerda* (0.2 acre) of truck land with the proviso that she should not take full possession until after her (the mother's) death. Before she died, however, the mother pawned this piece of land to Santiago Quiché for $3.33. When she died, Santiago let Quirino use the land "because it really belonged to his wife (Elena) anyway." Some years later, Quirino and Elena pawned the land to Vicenta, Quirino's sister, for another $1.67. When Santiago heard of this, he told Quirino that since he and Elena now considered the land theirs to pawn, they should repay him the money he had given Elena's mother with the land as security. Quirino had no money, however, and suggested that his father pay Vicenta what she had given him (Quirino) and take full possession of the land himself. To avoid difficulties, Santiago did so.

Years later, Santiago divided his lands among his children, stipulating that this particular piece should go to Vicenta. Now Quirino reported that he had $5 in his possession and wished to redeem the land. He said that he had offered the money to his father but that they had quarreled when his father refused it, saying that the land now had a new owner, Vicenta, with whom he should deal, while he himself insisted that since the money had been borrowed from Santiago, it should be returned to him. He added that no written documents were involved in the transactions, nor witnesses, and that he was considering going to the courthouse in the matter.

On January 7, 1937, Santiago Quiché told Rosales his side of this story. He said that 18 years before, Elena's mother had sold him the *cuerda* of land for $3.33, the deal made without documents and only before witnesses. Now in his old age he had divided his lands, and had given this piece to his daughter, Vicenta. But now Elena, the daughter of the woman who had sold him the land, had come to claim it, offering him $3.33 and saying that the land had not been sold, only pawned. "The worst thing is that she who is quarreling with me is my daughter-in-law." Santiago went on to say that he could not give her the land, for he has other heirs to consider; besides, he continued, both Quirino and Elena had sold lands inherited from their parents, because they do not work. He added that if Elena went to court, he would not only prove his case but would shame her by recounting all that she and her husband had done to their parents.

Elena won her case (having obtained the original documents) and on July 20 Vicenta Quiché reported to Juan how badly she had been wronged by her. She said Elena had taken away the land, her inheritance, because of personal animosity. She added that her hope now came from the fact that another brother (Rafael) had promised to give her a *cuerda* of coffee that was part of his inheritance; and the purpose of her visit was to ask Rosales to draw up a document for this so she would have no further trouble.

There are probably few pieces of land without some confusion in their histories, for most are the objects of transfers of one kind or other—frequently without written evidence—and disagreements as to the nature of the transfers are easy and common.

INHERITANCE

The rules of inheritance are simple, but too flexible to be easily stated. Land is usually the most important property inherited. As a general rule it is divided equally among all the children, male and female. But the parent may divide his land while still living (the division to take effect either before or after his death) in which case the division may be unequal and a child may even be disinherited. Since such divisions are rarely made with full legal procedure, a disinherited son cognizant of his legal rights may still get a share after his father's death. However, every child should get some of the land of his parents; usually only one who has left town permanently, or has fought seriously with the parents, is deprived of his share. The shares should be about equal, but sons are often favored over daughters, and it is sometimes thought proper that the eldest son get more than the others, especially if family responsibilities come to him. It is a rule, frequently broken, that the eldest son inherits the house and house site of his father, even though the division in terms of value is even. The whole matter is complicated by the frequent division of lands before the death of the parents, and the separation from the family of one or more sons who are then given all or part of their inheritance while their parents still live. Thus, the eldest son frequently builds his house elsewhere; then when the parents die, a younger son inherits the parents' house; thus if the parents live long and several sons are set up independently, there may even be a complete reversal of the rule so that in practice the youngest one inherits the homestead.

What actually happens to land in the course of two or three generations can be shown by a few case histories.[53]

THE INHERITANCE OF HOUSEHOLD NO. 49

Juan Yach had three children growing to maturity: son Santos, daughter Tomasa, and youngest son Nicolas (chart 12). Santos and Tomasa received their inheritance when they married, and when they died (before their father) the land went to their children. Nicolas still lived and worked with his father when the latter died, at which time the land remaining came to Nicholas without question. It consisted of two pieces: the inherited house site of a little less than a half acre, on which Nicolas continued to live; and a quarter-acre piece on the river's edge which Nicolas had helped his father buy in his later years.

[53] Summarized from fuller accounts in my microfilmed notes, especially pp. 109-131.

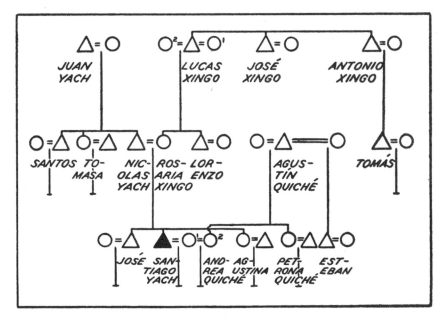

CHART 12.—Genealogical reference to the inheritance of household No. 49.

Nicolas married Rosaria Xingo, the daughter of Lucas Xingo who owned considerable land, long distinct from the holdings of his brothers, not divided between his two children. Nicolas and Rosaria had been long married, and had a family when Lucas (who had drinking debts) sold to Nicolas a piece of land (1½ acres, mostly hill) at the foot of the east hill for 40 silver pesos, a bargain "because he did not wish to leave his daughter without any remembrance of him (i. e., inheritance)." Lucas' brothers competed to buy the land; Lucas refused them because "they were already rich." Nicolas, though poor, obtained the money and gave it to his father-in-law in the presence of the brothers and thus avoided later quarrels. Nicolas was grateful to his father-in-law for selling him land cheaply which might have come to him later by inheritance, and when he died, Nicolas showed this gratitude by furnishing the coffin. Cousin Tomás later inherited a piece adjoining the land that Lucas had sold to Nicolas. Tomás pawned this land for 300 pesos (paper) (now $5). The boundary between Nicolas' and Tomás' land was not well marked. A boundary dispute arose between Nicolas and the pawnee of Tomás' land. Then "since they were relatives," Tomás permitted Nicolas to redeem the land for him and take deed to it.

Nicolas thus in his lifetime acquired four pieces of land: the two parcels of hill land, now considered one, had come in some measure through his wife, another was his inherited paternal house site, and the last had been purchased by his father with his help. When José, the eldest, married, he and his wife stayed with Nicolas for the few years until he died. His widow married again, and their daughter did not live to maturity. José had not owned land; there was no problem of inheritance. Nicolas died suddenly in the midst of negotiations for his second son's marriage to Petrona Quiché, and Rosaria survived him by only a few months. Santiago, his wife, and his young sister Agustina were thus left with undivided house and lands. Petrona died in a few years; a young son did not long survive her. Petrona's father had not divided his land, which went on the death of Petrona and her son to Petrona's only sibling, a boy. Santiago gained no land by this marriage.

While Petrona still lived, Augustina married (against Santiago's wish) a drinker who soon sold all of his own land; the couple lived with Santiago and Petrona without working until made to move. After Petrona died Agustina brought action in court for a division of the inheritance. Santiago claims that Agustina virtually bribed the Ladino judge; whatever the reason, the settlement forced on Santiago was nearly an equal division. Agustina obtained half of the house site (but not the part where the house stood) and the whole of the quarter-acre piece near the river; Santiago kept the 1¾-acre piece at the foot of the hill, including a quarter-acre of delta land.[54] Agustina immediately sold or pawned to an Indian for 600 pesos the river land (since eroded completely away), and her half of the house site land for 350 pesos. She and her husband then left, and (with their only child) died.

Not until years after his second marriage did Santiago discover that his wife, Andrea Quiché, owned land. Andrea had a brother Esteban and a sister, Petrona. Their father had divided all his land among the children on condition that they treated him well for the rest of his life. Petrona later quarreled with her father, and he sold her portion and left her nothing. Andrea's share consisted of a piece of coffee land and a piece of truck land, each about 0.18 acre. When he was ill before he died, the father pawned the coffee land for 600 pesos ($10) and Santiago had supposed that it had been sold. The truck land had been used for years by Esteban, who claimed the right to use it because—he said—he had lent his father 200 pesos. After a quarrel with Esteban, Andrea told Santiago about both pieces of land; they then sold the coffee land for 1,000 pesos, repaid the debt on it, paid Esteban the 200 pesos he claimed, and took possession of the piece of truck land.

Santiago and Andrea thus own three pieces of land: the house site inherited by Santiago, which is half of the "original" house site left by his father; the land at the base of the hill which his father was able to buy because of its connection with his mother's inheritance; and the piece remaining of Andrea's inheritance. They were never able to buy land. On the contrary, in 1936 Andrea's land, a coffee-planted piece of the house site, and half of the hill land were all pawned, and another piece of the house site had just been redeemed.

THE INHERITANCE OF HOUSEHOLD NO. 58

Manuel Cululén (chart 13) was widowed and then died himself while son Santiago and a female ward (parentage unknown) were still children. The orphans took residence with Miguel Quiché (their mother's brother) who also had children of his own. Manuel had about two-thirds of an acre of truck land (including his house site) on the west side of the delta. Miguel took the furnishings and utensils from the abandoned house, a bull that Manuel had left, and the use of the land, as if they were his own. However, nobody questioned that the land belonged to Santiago and (presumably in smaller share) his foster sister. When the girl matured, she married and lived on the coast and both she and her husband eventually died without ever claiming any of the land left by Manuel.

Santiago stayed with his uncle until the latter died, then remained with his cousins until they quarreled, when he went into the service of the local priest under whose influence he learned Ladino ways, continued to work the land left him by his father, and saved some money. He eventually left the priest, married Francisca Matzar, and built a site of his father's. For some

reason they later left this house and after living for awhile with Francisca's parents on the east side of the river, built another on a quarter-acre (also on the east side) which Santiago bought. He sold the land that his father had left him, partly because of the difficulty of working it during the rainy season, and with the money bought from Lorenzo Matzar (who later became his wife's step-father) another third-acre a little above his house site. There was money left for the burial of his four eldest children who died within a relatively short period. (All together five of his six children died without reaching maturity.) Later Santiago was able to buy another fifth-acre near his house site.

Although Francisca's parents owned seven or eight acres of land, besides two steers, Francisca inherited nothing. Apparently her father did not divide the land before he died. When Francisca (the youngest of three) married, her brother Jorge and sister Micaela remained at home, both of them married. When the parents died they began to sell land "in order to eat well and to drink." Francisca at first demanded her share; but Santiago told her that he would provide more land if they needed it, and her sister and brother would suffer later for the wrongs done her. He did however remove from pasture and sell one of the two steers to pay for a mass for her deceased parents.

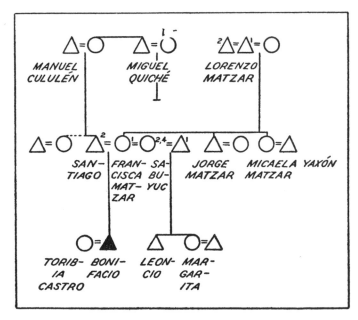

CHART 13.—Genealogical reference to the inheritance of household No. 58.

Eventually both Jorge and his family and Micaela with hers went to the coast, where both Jorge and Micaela died before Santiago did.

Francisca died, leaving Santiago with the one surviving child Bonifacio (the informant) still a young boy. Santiago married a woman named Sabuyuc who had a son, Leoncio, who came with her, and a married daughter, Margarita. She owned some land, part of which she had already given to Margarita. After a short while they separated, but when Santiago's third wife died, she returned with Leoncio who, like Bonifacio, was now a young man. When she in turn died, Leoncio continued to live with Santiago and Bonifacio. Leoncio's mother left a small piece of land which Santiago pawned for 60 pesos to pay for her funeral. Meanwhile, Margarita had pawned to Santiago two-thirds of an acre of hill milpa land for 30 pesos.

Now Bonifacio married Toribia Castro and moved to her house, leaving Santiago and Leoncio alone in bachelor housekeeping, buying their food ready-made, and working Santiago's land. Until he died, five years later, Santiago refused to give Bonifacio any land. Bonifacio therefore helped work his father-in-law's land and also worked for others.

Santiago left three pieces of land, all bought during his lifetime, totaling four-fifths of an acre; but two of the pieces were now pawned for 240 pesos ($6) to pay for his burial. He also left control of the piece of land pawned by Margarita Sabayuc for 30 pesos (50 cents). Santiago had left no indications as to the disposal of his land. His only living child was Bonifacio; but his stepson Leoncio had been living and working with him.

Leoncio came to live with Bonifacio; they agreed to work the land together and pay off the debts, whereupon Leoncio would receive the land left by his mother and also one of the three pieces left by Santiago, the other two to remain with Bonifacio. However, the two men quarreled, and after 8 months Leoncio went to live with Margarita, whereupon Bonifacio worked alone, redeemed the two pieces of pawned land, and kept all three pieces of land that his father had left; while Leoncio alone redeemed his mother's land and gained possession of it. Since Leoncio went to live with his sister, Bonifacio returned to her the land she had pawned to his

father. After some time living with his wife's parents, Bonifacio built a house on land destined to be Toribia's inheritance, near the river's edge. Eventually the river washed this land away, and he built a house where his father's had fallen into ruin. Thus, he now lives where he was born.

Bonifacio thus inherited the three pieces of land that his father had owned, and his right to them has not been questioned. His wife, Toribia, brought him no land that still exists. Her parents had owned considerable land, but almost all of it had been washed away by the river, and only a small piece remained to her widowed mother at the time this study was made. Since she had six living brothers and sisters, including a brother living with the mother, Bonifacio thought it most unlikely that she would ever inherit anything. (As it turned out, Toribia died before her mother; and when their grandmother died, Bonifacio's children inherited nothing.)

Bonifacio has five sons living. Only one is married, and now has two children. He has not sold any of his inheritance. He added to it in 1937 when he bought about five and a half acres of cornfield hill land. Before making this purchase, Bonifacio thought of dividing his land as follows (assuming that all of his sons continued to live and work with him and to respect him): the one-third acre farthest from the house to the two eldest sons equally; the nearer one-sixth acre to the third son; and the one-fourth acre house site to the two youngest equally, with the houses themselves going to the youngest.

THE INHERITANCE OF HOUSEHOLD NO. 55

Manuel Rosales was born in San Cristóbal Totonicapán. As a young merchant in the 1830's or 1840's, he came frequently to Panajachel to buy produce to sell in markets in the west. In Panajachel, he stayed with one Francisco Quiché, and eventually with the help of this family he bought a piece of Panajachel land, married Antonia Quiché, the daughter (chart 14), and settled down. He built a large adobe and tile-roof house and prospered and continued to buy land. The five children (José Gil, Antonio, Bernadino, Tomasa, and Coronada) remained in the house working for and supported by their parents. When Manuel became old and infirm, he willed that upon his death his property remain for his wife to divide when and how she would decide.

Soon after Manuel died, son Bernadino, who was married, asked for land on which to live independently, and was given a half acre on the original home site (from which the parents had since moved). Bernadino was dissatisfied, and bad blood arose between him and the rest of the family. Therefore before she died the mother legally divided the land in 1888–89. She gave most of the property to the four children who remained with her because "Bernadino had received his inheritance previously; because he had, without consulting her, sold a mare worth 10 silver pesos; because, unsatisfied with his share he had in a state of intoxication come to fight with her and had struck her; and because he had, after she had already taken to her bed, fired a shot at his blind uncle, Ventura Alinán—and only luckily had not killed him." She directed that her son José Gil should keep daughter Tomasa's share for her until she should marry and should always manage daughter Coronada's share because she was blind. She also left a mule and 5 pesos to her brother's daughter, Francisca Alinán, in gratitude for having served as a grinder in the house "in spite of her being a mute," and 12 sheep and 5 pesos each to two adopted orphans—Andrés Can and María Saquil—whom her husband had "bought for three silver pesos" and were living with the family. She also directed these orphans to leave the house at her death so that they would not be mistreated by their foster siblings.

The will named and identified each of 10 pieces of land totaling about 131 acres.[55] Tomasa received three delta lots: one of 0.6 acre (part of her Antonia's own inheritance) valued at 6 silver *reales* (¾ peso); one of 1.4 acres that Manuel Rosales had bought for 10 silver *reales* (1¼ pesos); and one of 1.1 acres that Manuel had bought for 1 silver peso. She also received 50 sheep and images of Santo Domingo, San Pablo, and Santa Eulalia.

Blind Coronada was left one piece of delta land of 2.2 acres (part of Antonia's inheritance) valued

---

[55] There were also at least 124 sheep, 6 debtor laborers, 5 images of saints' a credit of 100 pesos (paper) owned by a Ladino on 8.9 acres of delta land he had bought for 200 pesos. Half this money was to be used for Antonio's funeral.

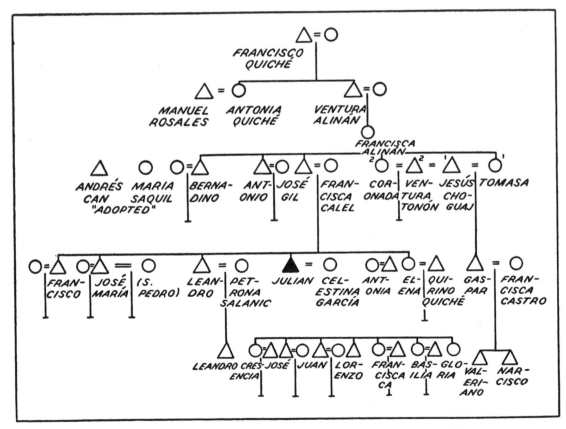

CHART 14.—Genealogical reference to the inheritance of household No. 55.

at 2 silver pesos; 50 pesos (paper for clothing); 50 sheep; images of San Francisco, a Christ, and the Holy Ghost; and 6 debtor peons, 3 each of San Andrés (owing a total of 9¾ pesos) and Santa Catarina (14½ pesos) who, if they returned to work, were to serve Coronada.

José Gil (the eldest) was left more than the others "because since the death of her husband, he had taken care of his mother's and his sisters' expenses." Three pieces of land came to him: a 41.7 acre piece of the delta (now virtually all part of the river bed) that had been bought by Manuel and Antonio and was worth 75 silver pesos; a piece of equal size in the municipio of San Andrés, worth 100 silver pesos; and a 27.8-acre piece on the east hill, bordering lands of Santa Catarina and coming down to the lake, worth 50 silver pesos.[56] He also received images of San Antonio and San Sebastian, and 50 sheep.

Antonio was left one piece of land, of 8.9 acres. Bernadino was left two pieces of land. One, the remainder of the parcel already received, now totaled 2.8 acres. The other, also in the delta, was the same size.

Shortly after Antonia died, Tomasa married Jesús Choguaj and took possession of her land. José Gil bought her sheep for three reales each, and, since the couple had no place to keep them, he also kept Tomasa's three images. Soon after son Gaspar was born to the couple, Jesús died. A few years later Tomasa married Ventura Tonón, at which time Gaspar went to live at the house of a local Ladino, where he learned to read and write and eventually married an Indian servant of the house, Francisca Castro, by whom he had two sons, Valeriano and Narciso Castro, who now live and work in Guatemala City.

Meanwhile, because of sickness, Tomasa gradually sold to José Gil all three pieces of land, after which she and Ventura remained on one of them by arrangement with her brother. When Tomasa died, Ventura became a laborer in José Gil's house. The blind Coronada was still living with her brother, and when he discovered that she was with child by Ventura, he gave them Coronada's inheritance and they lived together openly. Coronada's one child died at the age of 8, when she began to sell her sheep to José, followed (when her husband died) by the land.

So, finally, José Gil came into possession of all but three pieces of his parents' lands, all five of their images, and all of their sheep. Meanwhile, he had himself bought a large amount of land. His wife brought him no land, for she was of a poor family, her mother having been a servant in the Rosales home. But by the time he died in 1906, he was (on local standards) fabulously wealthy, owning some 700 acres of land, as well as numerous domestic animals and a hoard of silver money, and having many laborers in debt to him. His lands, as nearly as they can be reconstructed with data available, consisted of at least the following:

1. Chimucún, 41.7 delta acres worth 75 pesos [57] (inheritance).
2. Chilocón, 41.7 hill acres worth 100 pesos (inheritance).
3. Tzansiguanay, 27.8 hill acres worth 50 pesos (inheritance).
4. Chisoloyá, 0.6 delta acres worth ¾ peso (bought from sister).
5. Chuarramos, 1.4 delta acres worth 1¼ pesos (bought from sister).
6. Panaj, 1.1 delta acres worth 1 peso (bought from sister).
7. Chimatzar, 2.2 delta acres worth 2 pesos (bought from sister).
8. Chitonon, 2.5 acres for 7 pesos (purchased).
9. Chisanto, 4.4 delta acres for 16 pesos (purchased).
10. Chuichimila, 0.7 delta acre for 4 pesos (purchased).
11. Chialinán, 1.2 delta acres for 50 pesos (purchased).
12. Chigertrudis, 1.1 delta acres for 200 pesos (purchased).
13. Pachichiyut, 53.4 hill acres for 150 pesos (purchased).
14. Tzampetey, 400 acres near San Lucas (purchased).
15. Tzantzajcap, 100 acres near San Lucas (purchased).

No Indian in Panajachel today owns nearly that amount of land. Nor, in fact, does any Ladino own as much Panajachel land as did José Gil Rosales. If the present study had been made 40 years earlier the figures on the distribution of lands would have been quite different, largely because of the extraordinary extent of the lands of José Gil Rosales, many of which have now passed into Ladino hands.

José is recalled as a miser who spent little on himself and his family. He died there clutching

---

[56] Contradictory information says it was only 3.6 acres in size and worth but 6 pesos.

[57] Values and purchase prices are given in silver pesos, not the paper money of lower value that came into use later. The valuations put on the inherited land are seen to be much lower than purchase prices of other land. A partial explanation is the time factor: the valuations put on inherited land came down from previous generations when prices may have been much lower, while purchases occurred when Ladinos were already in Panajachel (some of the land was bought from Ladinos) and land had increased in value. José Gil Rosales was the first coffee planter in Panajachel, and the coming of coffee may also have sent land prices up.

the key to a chest in which he had two or three thousand silver pesos. He had not divided any of his land or chattels. He left no will except directions that he be buried in Sololá rather than in the local cemetery which was always in some danger of being washed out.

Besides his widow, José was survived by four sons and two daughters. The sons, in order, were José María, Julián, Leandro, and Juan Francisco; the daughters were María and Elena. The first three sons were married. All were living at home except Julián, who married against his parents' wishes and quarreled with them when he asked for a share of the land. The widow, Francisca Calel, thus found herself the head of a considerable establishment with much money which (according to the disaffected son, Julián) they were not averse to using. Several years of neglect of the properties, and fiestas shared by many Ladino friends, and the 30-odd laborers attached to the household, end with the money gone and the family selling mules and small parcels of land.

Son Julián then stopped the sale of property and invoked the laws of inheritance by which the widow received half and each child one-sixth of the other half. In general the widow and daughters were given lands closest to town, the sons the lands farthest away. In general also the larger pieces were split several ways among the heirs while the smaller ones remained intact. Tools and utensils were divided between men and women according to their use.

The widow survived José Gil 22 years, and died in 1928. She continued to sell her property, part to others and part to son Julián (the only child to increase rather than lose his heritage), and died owning no land at all. José María, the eldest son, kept two families—one with a San Pedro woman. He gradually sold all his land, and in 1932 he died in poverty, leaving four daughters. Four of five children by his first wife, meanwhile, lived on plantations on the coast and the fifth, a woman, married in Panajachel; none inherited land.

Leandro did not long survive his father. What remained of his property went to his wife, Petrona Salanic, and young children, who continued to live with Francisca and to sell land. Petrona married again. Eventually she and her son Leandro lost the rest of their land, and when widowed again Petrona became one of the poorest women in town. Young Leandro went to work on the coast.

The two daughters, Elena and Antonia, married and eventually lost their inheritance. Antonia died early, childless. Elena married Quirino Quiché and they still live with their surviving children. Quirino as well as Elena inherited land, most of which they sold. Now they own but one small piece of land (No. 10 above) inherited by Elena.

The youngest son, Juan Francisco, was a child when his father died and remained with his mother even for a time after he married. When she died, he sold what remained of his land and became a day laborer for his brother Julián. At the time of this study he was landless and homeless and "not quite right," working for José Rosales, Julián's son.

Julián was independent of his parents when his father died. He soon had much of his inherited land under cultivation and began to augment it and to buy livestock, including cattle. His success aggravated the strain of relations between him and his mother and sisters who (he claims) employed black magic to destroy him. Eventually the rest of the family became sufficiently reconciled to sell land to him rather than to outsiders so that he recovered a large part of his father's estate. By 1928, at the apex of his fortunes, Julián was probably as rich as his father had been, possessing less land, but more of it in cultivation, and having more domestic animals.

He owned at least 60 acres of delta land, including the parcels above numbered 1, 8, 9, 11, and 12, (the first was flooded by the river in about 1924 and rendered nearly useless) and seven or eight hundred acres of hill land including the lots numbered 13, 14, and 15. He grew large quantities of corn, beans, anise, chile, coffee, and vegetables. Some 20 laborers were in his debt, each as much as 8,000 pesos (paper, now worth $133.33). He had 5 riding horses, 2 or 3 pack mules, 20 head of cattle, 5 milk cows, 6 sheep, and a canoe. The profits from his operations he put back into the land, for domestic expenses were paid by his wife from the sale of fruit, of the eggs of her 60 chickens, and of the ducks and rabbits and of the 10 pigs she fattened.

Celestina García, Julián's third wife, was the mother of all seven of his surviving children, three sons (José, Lorenzo, Juan) and four daughters (Cresencia, Francisca, Basilia, Gloria) who could have looked forward to a rich inheritance. But of a sudden Julián's fortunes turned and in 8 years he lost literally all that had taken generations to accumulate. In 1926 he sold Tzampetey (No. 14) and invested in cattle. The enterprise failed in some way. In 1928 his wife sickened, and he spent a lot of money in a vain attempt to cure her, even taking her to the hospital in distant Quezaltenango. On her death he began to drink. He opened a tavern and lost interest in his farming. He let his laborers go. He entertained his Ladino friends, took up with a woman, became estranged from his sons, and began to run up debts. One piece of land after another was pawned to Ladinos and eventually lost. In 1936 son Juan bought the last piece (the house site) to keep it in the family; there Julián lived in 1936, sobered but not embittered, earning his living as an entrepreneur on a small scale. He died in 1942, leaving nothing to his children. José (an industrious worker) bought land after his marriage, with the aid of his wife's inheritance. Juan (who had gone to school in the city as a child) is not a member of the local community, though he owns the home site. Lorenzo is a professional soldier in the Capital. Cresencia is married to a Ladino and lives on the coast; Basilia was married to a local Indian, but she died recently. Antonia is married to a local Indian and they have become medium-rich. Gloria, the youngest, is a servant in a Ladino household.

SUMMARY

In spite of the free market in land there is clearly a family feeling about it. If it must be pawned or sold, it is desirable that it go to a close relative—especially one who would fall heir to the land if it were not alienated. One should not leave his children landless, but conscience in the matter appears to be salved if the heirs are permitted to buy the land. This is a method by which aged parents obtain support from their children when they are no longer able to work. The parent demands money from a son or daughter due to get the land with the threat to sell it if the money is not paid. A bargain price frequently indicates that the transaction is not purely a commercial one. In one case when an old widow demanded support from a son, arguing that he was using her land, and the son pointed out that he had bought the land, she retorted that she had sold it to him very cheaply. This practice does not so much indicate unwillingness to support the aged (probably no Panajachel Indian would let his parents starve) as a desire on the part of parents to justify demands less on the ground of filial duty than of moral or legal, even commercial obligation. In the same way the heir who has supported his parents and paid for their burial has greater claim to their land than his brothers and sisters. Likewise, the son who stays at home and helps his father work the land and hence buy more land is entitled to a greater part of the inheritance than one who works for himself. This is one reason why daughters, who more frequently than not marry away, get less of the family land than their brothers. But all of the children, including the daughter or son who has lived independently, are considered entitled to some of their parents' land.

The following generalization of rules of inheritance is all that the data permit.[58] All personal property is inherited. Except for the clothing in which the body is dressed, nothing is destroyed at death. All privately owned land is wholly alienable, but it is thought good to keep it for one's children if possible. The children are all entitled to a share, but sons—because they generally remain with the parents to work the land—to larger shares than daughters. The eldest son ideally becomes the head of the household when the parents die, and usually gets a larger share. The portions of young siblings, and especially of girls until their marriage, are given to the eldest son to hold in trust for them. He frequently takes advantage of them, but in any event he is not expected to turn over to them the profits of the land—only their shares of the original land itself—on the theory that he is supporting them meanwhile. Sons and less frequently daughters are sometimes given all or part of their inheritance some time after marrying. The practice is not by any means always accompanied by quarreling. Thereafter they may also buy land from their parents (as well as from others). A surviving widow usually keeps control of all

---

[58] To learn more about the rules of inheritance one could obtain the history of the ownership of each piece of Panajachel land for several generations back. Or, short of that difficult task, one could with data at hand relate the distribution of lands owned by the Indians to their genealogies. The result of such a formidable task would be subject to much error, since it cannot be assumed that two brothers owning adjoining lots in a district where other members of their family also own land have both inherited rather than bought the land.

not hitherto-divided land, but the death of the father tends to hasten the further division. A dependent son who dies without heirs generally has no real property to leave. If he has, it presumably (I have no cases) goes back into the family pool. If he dies with heirs, and before he has received his inheritance, his share belongs to his children; but if they are young, and years pass before the division is made, they are likely to get less than a fair share.

The laws of the country are infrequently applied.

LAND AS COLLATERAL

I know of three ways by which money is borrowed with land as collateral. (1) The title is deposited as informal security; (2) the land is mortgaged; and (3) most commonly the land is given in pawn to the creditor.

In the first case, an Indian borrows money, usually at interest, and leaves with his creditor the deed to a piece of land without making any agreement concerning the land. The document is left as an evidence of good faith; for without it the land cannot be sold or pawned. Thus in a number of cases where Indians came to borrow money they brought titles to land to leave with me. A case outside personal experience demonstrates that no question of forfeit of the land is involved. An Indian borrowed $5 from a Ladina, at 5 percent per month payable monthly,[59] and left with her the deed to a piece of land. For 5 years interest was paid pretty regularly, and receipts given. Then the Indian took sick and stopped paying interest. Two years later, his creditor (the son of the Ladina, who had died in the interim) took the matter to the local courthouse where, after the Indian showed he had paid more in interest than the amount of the original debt, the remainder of interest was canceled and he was given 3 months to pay the $5. He paid, and received the deed to his land. In the litigation the Indian had assured the Ladino that he would pay because he wanted his document returned. No question was raised of forfeiture, and during the years that the debt ran, the Indian continued in possession of the land.

Mortgaging of land, with a stipulation that the land may be forfeited, is not common and perhaps never occurs among Indians. However, I have

record of three cases in which Indians mortgaged land to Ladinos. The Indians continued to use the land, simply paying interest on the money borrowed. In all three cases, the Indians finally lost by foreclosure; in one, the Indian lost his home.

LAND PAWNING

By far the most common way of borrowing large sums of money is by giving to the creditor the use of the land for the loan period or until the money is repaid. I know of no case in which the land was forfeited by any legal process when the term of the loan expired, although Ladinos are reputed to foreclose in such circumstances. (However, there are cases in which the land has been pawned again by the person who has it on pawn.) What happens instead is that after a long time even the owner or his heirs forget that it only has been pawned and not sold, and the community thinks of the land as having changed hands. In such cases, with deeds not registered, the land has in fact changed hands.

The custom of pawning land was probably the only way Indians borrowed on land in generations past when written documents were not common. It is convenient. There is no problem of collection of either interest or principal. The creditor simply takes possession of the land until the money is repaid. The fruit of the soil is so profitable a return that the investor does not care if the money is never repaid. Indeed, with land virtually the only profitable investment in Panajachel, and control of land the way to wealth, people with money are anxious to lend it on these terms. The wealthiest Indian of Panajachel obtained his start this way. The converse is that Indians pawn land only when they think they must, knowing that loss of their land curtails earning power and makes redemption of the land difficult. They are therefore motivated to borrow less rather than more money on a piece of land, to redeem it more easily. Borrowed money is usually spent for food, medicines, and liquor, at times of sickness, death, or the assumption of office, when cash is needed at a time the earning power is reduced. With the abolition of debt peonage in 1936, advance payment for labor became illegal. This left borrowing as the only way to get money for emergencies, and the easiest way to borrow is to pawn land. Possibly the pawning of land has therefore increased

---

[59] Such a rate is now illegal, though in informal contracts interest is often higher than the legal maximum.

in recent years. From 1935 to 1938 the average number of pawnings of Indian lands was about eight per year and the number of redemptions about four. In 1936 the number of contracts generally known to be in force was 38, the oldest of them dating from about 1930. Thus more than 11 per cent[60] of the 330 Indian-owned lots were wholly or partly in pawn in 1936. Of the 38, 27 were pawned to other resident Indians, 5 to Indians of other towns, 5 to resident Ladinos, and 1 to the author. Lands pawned totaled about 20.6 acres (table 13) including more truck land than coffee. Indians own twice as much truck as coffee land, but pawn almost 2½ times as much, for two reasons: (1) The lender prefers truck land, which brings him more income than coffee land and his bargaining power is greater than that of the borrower with a sudden need; (2) many Indians sell their coffee crops to Ladinos long before the harvest as a way to get money without borrowing; nobody is likely to take on pawn land which will yield nothing for over a year.

TABLE 13.—*Pawned land*

Pawned to—	Acres of land pawned, 1936			
	Total	Delta coffee	Delta truck	Hill milpa
Resident Indian	16.7	2.7	7.2	6.8
Absentee Indian	2.9	.4	.9	1.6
Resident Ladino	1.0	.5	.5	
Total	20.6	3.6	8.6	8.4

In all cases that Indians pawn land to Ladinos (I have none of the reverse) a term of years is written into the contract. Among Indians alone the duration of the contract often is "until the money is repaid." Of 24 cases on which there is information to the point, only 13 include a time limit. Of these, five are for 4 years, four for 4 years, two for 3, and one each for 1 and for 7 years. Informants have said that the larger the amount, the longer the time; and that when the pawner is very poor, no time limit is set; but the cases do not clearly support them. It should be repeated that since Indians do not foreclose, time limits have little significance.

The pawning of land is not a sign of poverty, only that there are no liquid assets in time of emergency. But Indians who have pawned their land are often in process of losing it, and are

meanwhile losing an important source of income. They are becoming poorer. Facts about land pawning are therefore significant in discussion of wealth mobility in Land and Wealth (pp. 192–193).

LAND RENTING

Of the several ways in which Indians obtain use of houses or land belonging to others, renting is the most obvious. Renting of houses, however, is not common. There were in 1936, 33 families occupying houses that did not belong to them, and of these only 6 paid rent, 5 of them immigrant artisans who rented houses in town, following (as they did in other respects) Ladino custom, and the sixth an immigrant woman who worked as a day servant in Ladino homes and rented a house for herself and her family. The rental was probably no more than a dollar a month in any case.[61] Nine of the remaining 27 who paid no rent lived in houses furnished by their employers, the remainder in "borrowed" houses, 4 of them rather permanently, and 9 occasionally changing their residences. In addition 5 landowning families lived not on their own land but in their own houses built on borrowed land. The remaining 122 families lived on land that they owned.

Agricultural land is much more frequently rented. In 1936 only 5 families used land furnished rent-free by their employers. On the other hand, 50 families (including 4 landless families and 3 who owned land but did not live on it) regularly rented land. In 1936, the Indian community rented from outsiders about 17.5 acres of hill milpa to add to their own 94 acres, and about 12 acres of delta truck land to add to their 78.5. Coffee is never rented, since the annual crop is almost pure profit.

Most commonly there is an annual cash rental on a specified piece of land, giving sole rights to it. Such agreements are generally verbal. Frequently the rental is paid not in advance, but throughout the year or when the harvest is in. In at least one 1937 case the rental fee was worked off. Hill land, used only in the rainy season, is valuable in the off-season only for pasture; since both the owner and the renter welcome the fertilizing effects of such use, it is an academic question whether the

[60] In terms of value, about 8 percent.

[61] In 1940 we rented a good little house from an Indian for $1 a month, and certainly overpaid. We also rented a Ladino's house for $5 (in 1937); Indian friends thought that we were paying $2, which they considered outrageously high.

rental period is a year or only a season. In the case of truck land, on the other hand, the time is important. While most frequently the land is rented for a whole year, there are cases of rentals for but 3 or 4 months—the growing season for onions. One rich Indian habitually rents out land only for the bean-growing season (4 months) in exchange for one cornfield stint of labor for each *cuerda* rented. Between bean seasons, he plants corn on the land. Coffee land is never rented because, of course, the annual crop is almost pure profit.

Very often a renter keeps the same land year after year. This is convenient for both parties; certainly the renter planting onions finds it inconvenient to break into the annual cycle at any point. On the other hand, *pepino* growers usually rent a different piece of land each year in the conviction that "new" land gives a better crop. The most common practice among Indian renters is to seek to rent appropriate land for a particular purpose. The fact that each tends to rotate crops after a favorite pattern is a motive to keep one piece of land for several years.

The right to harvest a crop still growing when the rental period is over, appears to be recognized by the Indians. In 1936 an Indian pawned a piece of truck land to a Ladino who then rented it on an annual basis to another Indian. In 1941 the land was redeemed and the Indian owner took possession. The renter had harvested a crop of beans, but still had sweet cassava growing on the edges of the *tablones*. He worried over what might become of it, but the owner recognized his right to the plants; he planted corn and no technical problem was presented.

In 1936 there were 72 pieces of land rented by the Indians. Of these, 43 involved cash rental. Seven cases required the payment to the landowner of half the crop. All these involved delta land, but in one the land was used only for corn. The other 22 cases required payment in labor— the planting of coffee or shade trees, or a certain number of stints in the cornfield or the coffee grove. In general it may be said that the renter comes out most favorably by paying cash, and least favorably by sharing his harvest. Payment with labor is cheaper than cash when the owner rents cheaply to assure himself labor when he needs it. Table 14 summarizes the cost of the rental in the various arrangements recorded.

Neither the very rich (who have more of their own than they can manage) nor the very poor (who have neither the money to rent land nor the time to work it) rent much land. Land renting as it relates to wealth is discussed in the section on Land and Wealth (pp. 192–193).

LAND VALUES

How much Panajachel land is worth depends first of all on its kind and location. Hill land useful only for cornfield is worth less than hill land that is relatively level, or has a water supply, and can be used for coffee or truck. Delta land is worth more than hill land, but delta land good only for cornfield is worth much less than delta land suitable for vegetable growing. Land on which coffee is standing is worth more than any other kind. In recent years, land along the lake shore has become especially valuable. Land in the center of town, where the Ladinos have their stores and houses, is more valuable than other land except that on the lake shore. Furthermore, there is one scale of prices (however vague) for sales of land to Ladinos and foreigners, especially by Ladinos, and quite a different scale governing sales within the Indian community. Finally, the price of land perhaps more than anything else is influenced by particular circumstances surrounding each sale. Thus, an Indian in sudden need who can obtain money only by selling a piece of land is not likely to get as much as another who is approached to sell a piece that he would just as soon keep.

Although I shall evaluate lands by standards of

TABLE 14.—*Rental costs in 1936*

Number of cases	Total acres	Kind of land	Rental arrangements	Calculated cost per acre
14	10.7	Hill milpa	25 cents per *cuerda*	$1.41
9	5.9	----do	1 milpa stint per *cuerda*	.93
2	2.7	----do	1½ stints per *cuerda*	1.40
1	.2	Delta milpa	Half the crop	[1] 3.06 [2] 12.25
6	1.5	Delta beans (4 months)	1 milpa stint per *cuerda*	[3] .93 [4] 2.79
14	2.8	Delta truck	$6 per *cuerda*	33.75
9	3.9	----do	$5 per *cuerda*	28.12
3	3.2	----do	$4 per *cuerda*	22.50
2	.4	Delta *pepinos*	Half the crop	[1] 46.11 [2] 169.80
4	1.2	Delta truck	----do	[1] 108.06 [2] 119.50
4	3.2	Hill milpa	Dig holes to plant coffee	4.69

[1] Value of labor and seed invested in the half paid as rent.
[2] Value of the crop of the half paid as rent.
[3] Per acre-crop, or for 4 months' use.
[4] Per acre-year.

what Indians pay for them, it is interesting to note first the differential for outsiders. Hill land, as we shall see, is normally worth from $2.50 to $8.50 an acre. In 1940 a Ladino owner offered to a foreigner a large piece of such land (extending to the lake) for a sum that figured to $33.33 an acre; there were indications that he would come down as low as $17.05. Another Ladino offered a large piece of hill land (parts of which were planted in coffee and vegetables) at the rate of $126.84 an acre. When the prospective buyer, a North American, refused, the owner half regretted not having come down in price; but the lowest price he would have considered came to $84.56 an acre, and he was sure that the land for its coffee yield would eventually be worth more than that to him.

Delta truck land is usually sold for from $50 to $150 an acre. When favorably situated it was sold to foreigners for much more in 1940. One well-situated piece of land of 1.4 acres sold at the rate of either $813.75 or $1,968.75, depending upon which of two countrymen who were involved in the deal I chose to believe. Another North American paid a Ladino at the rate of $525.58 an acre for a piece of lake-shore land. He refused to pay a broker $562.50 an acre for an adjoining piece, and finally offered the Indian owner at the rate of $1,135 an acre and was unable to buy it. Another Ladino was asking a sum that worked out to $562.50 an acre for a very small piece of land overlooking the lake. Perhaps the clearest example of what is happening to land values near the lake is this: In 1935 a Ladino offered me a hillock (8 acres) on the lake shore between Santa Catarina and San Antonio for $90. Eventually a German in Panajachel bought it for $80. In 1940 he told me that he had turned down a North American's offer for $500 for a small piece of this land, and that he valued the whole at $5,000.

Obviously, Indians cannot begin to buy land at such prices; and they buy, even from Ladinos (but not lake-shore land) for much less. The following evaluations of land according to the Indian standard are based on both statements of informants and a number of cases.

HILL LAND

Only ordinary hill land, useful for growing milpa in season, is owned by Indians. Informants usually set its value as between about $5.50 and $9.50 an acre. I have records of three sales, two of them of Santa Catarina land to Panajachel Indians, well below the lowest figure ($3.94 and $4.30), but none above the highest figure. (For a time the Santa Catarina Indians were in great need, and sold cheaply.) I have two well-authenticated cases of purchases of Santa Catarina land at $9.35 an acre, and one at $8.50. I was offered by a Ladino a piece of Panajachel hill land at $8.50; a Panajachel Indian wanted me to help him buy it at that price. In another case I assisted an Indian in the purchase, from another Indian, of 5.4 acres of Panajachel hill land at $9.35. It seems reasonable to set the usual value of hill land, in Panajachel or Santa Catarina, at about $8 an acre.

There are also records of the pawning of six pieces of hill land. Two parcels of Santa Catarina land were pawned to Panajachel Indians for $5.13 and $5.76 an acre, respectively. Three pieces of Panajachel land were pawned—Indian to Indian—for $4.16, $5.15, and $5.62 an acre, respectively. A fourth and similar piece was pawned at $1.87 an acre. Of course, minimum pawning-prices are of no significance in this discussion; but since people would not usually lend more on a piece of land than it is worth, it is obvious that hill lands are considered worth at least $5.62 an acre. Pawning values thus check fairly well with sale values.

It has been noted that hill milpa land rents, for cash, at $1.41 an acre. Using the figure $8 as the value of such land, the relation of annual rental to the value of land is 1 to 5.7.

DELTA TRUCK LAND

Irrigated land in the delta not planted with coffee is valued by informants (in 10 cases) from $56 (2 cases) to $235 (1 case). The value in 5 cases was given as $187.50, in another as $140.63, and in the last as $78.12. One Indian, who has been buying land from others, and from Ladinos, told me he usually expects to pay at the rate of $140. One may discount the statement of an Indian that long ago he had bought a *cuerda* for $5 ($28 an acre); more probably he obtained the land on pawn. The lowest price otherwise noted figures to $62.50 an acre; this land was bought from a Ladino many years ago. Another piece was said to have been bought at the rate of $93.75 an acre. The other prices, including those in all recent transactions, range between $112.50 and $187.50. Perhaps overinfluenced by the roundness of the figure, I have set the value of truck land at the average of these extremes, or $150 an acre.

Records of money lent with pawned land as security indicate that this is at least not too low. I have 25 cases of the pawning of truck land. The amounts were at the rate of:

	Per acre		Per acre
2 cases	$22. 50	1 case	$62. 55
4 cases	28. 12	1 case	67. 42
3 cases	37. 50	1 case	79. 68
1 case	43. 00	1 case	93. 63
7 cases	56. 25	4 cases	112. 50

The cash rental price of truck land has been noted as between $22.50 and $33.75, with the norm near the higher figure. If we consider the usual rental price as $30, it is seen that—using the valuation of $150 an acre—the proportion of annual rental to land value is 1 to 5, not far from that of hill land.

I have only one case by which to judge the value of delta land that is useful only for milpa. In that case, the figure given comes to $28 an acre. Comparing this with the value of hill milpa land, it seems about right. The yield on such land is considerably higher than on the less level hill land, it lasts much longer (if not indefinitely) without fertilizer, and, being closer, such land requires less work time than do hill lands. If this delta land is thought of as potential coffee land, it should probably be valued even higher.

COFFEE LAND

Land on which coffee is already growing should be worth more than truck land, depending on the condition of the coffee. One informant set the value of coffee land as double that of vegetable land, but he also set the value of vegetable land unusually low. Other informants estimated coffee land to be worth from $85 to $187.50 an acre. I have but two cases of sales of coffee land, one at $215 and the other at $225 an acre. In both cases sales were to non-Indians, and it would probably

be safer to set the value of delta coffee land at about $175 an acre.

Recorded are only 10 cases of money lent on pawned coffee land. In one case the sum was $28.12, in three cases $37.50, in two cases $56.25, and in one case each, $75, $84.37, $93.75, and $112.36. The amounts tend to run, therefore, about the same as for truck lands. (From one point of view they should run higher, since the money lender without much labor is able to harvest about $34 worth of coffee each year he has the land; but for the same reason the pawner ought not to ask for more, so that he can redeem the land quickly.)

Since the land on which Indian houses are built is unproductive, it has no value comparable to that of coffee and truck lands. But since before it became a house site, and after it ceases to be one (if it does) it was or will be good truck land, it may be given the same value—$150 an acre, not including the improvements.

The total value of lands recorded as belonging to resident Indians in 1936 may therefore be summarized as follows:

Hill lands (at $8 per acre):	
In Panajachel, 68 acres	$544. 00
Elsewhere, 26 acres	208. 00
Delta lands:	
Coffee (at $175 per acre), 39.38 acres	6, 891. 50
Truck (at $150 per acre), 78.52 acres	11, 778. 00
House lots (at $150 per acre), 5.08 acres	762. 00
Other (at $28 per acre), 8.35 acres	233. 80
Total	20, 417. 30

Of these totals, 0.45 acre of coffee land, 1.8 acres truck land, and 1.6 acres hill land—with a total value of $361.55—were pawned to Ladinos or others outside the local Indian community. The value of the land owned and controlled by the resident Indians in 1936 was, therefore, $20,045.75. In addition, they had on pawn at least $86.18 worth of hill land and about $150 worth of truck land in Santa Catarina. They therefore controlled land with a total value of about $20,282. This figure takes no account of lands borrowed or rented from Ladinos or others.

LABOR

THE USE OF TIME

Besides the land, nature gives to the Indians of Panajachel, as it does to others, 24 hours a day for 365 days a year. How are they used? To answer the question would require a complete description of the round of life of the society. In a book on the economy alone it may better be asked how time is used in relation to production. In doing so it may appear that a position is taken that the more time spent adding to wealth, the more "efficient" is the use of time. This is nonsense (since presumably in most contexts wealth has ends other than itself) as is the position apparently taken in the section on land (pp. 34–47) that land ought to be in production, the more intensively the better. I do not mean to take either. In the case of the land, the site where the house stands is not wasted, nor only a necessity; nor are the yard and its flowers luxuries. In the case of time, likewise, the hours spent sleeping and eating are not wasted, or merely necessary; nor is the time spent in church or in a drinking bout a luxury stolen from work. Nevertheless, with this understood, it is still useful to consider how efficiently from the point of view of production the community of Panajacheleños utilizes both its main resources—land and labor.

Table 15 classifies the way the entire community spent the year 1936. Whether the percentage for economic or strictly productive activities is high or low compared with other people, or the differences in this respect between men, women, and children one cannot say without comparative data. My suspicion is that Panajacheleños work more than is typical either of primitive tribesmen or of urbanites. Where they fall within the range of peasant and rural peoples—in comparison with Chinese or Roumanian villagers, or Bantu or Iowa farmers (or for that matter the Indians of neighboring Sololá) remains a question. Panajachel is probably more hard-working than its neighbors who depend chiefly on the growing of corn, in which work is seasonal. How it compares with neighboring communities which have industrial specialties I do not know. In comparison with North American farmers, it seems probable that the difference is that here the farmers work longer (and much harder) during some seasons

than in Panajachel, but that in general more time is taken with recreation, visiting, school, and study. The Panajacheleños "waste" time by bits, American farmers in large doses. But such a comparison is better made by those with closer acquaintance with American farm communities. I have no data enabling me to handle quantitatively the question of intensity of work; however, the Indians of this study would surely be described as slow, easy-going workers whose pace is not comparable to that of industrious northern workers.

A description of how Panajacheleños use their economically devoted time is the main subject of this section. Full documentation of the time *not* devoted to economic activity would require description of the social, political, and religious practices and institutions of the society. What is given here is less than a brief summary.

The total amount of time available to the Panajachel Indians in 1936 was simply the population multiplied by the number of hours in the year. In working over the data, however, it was found expedient to subdivide the population by sex and age, and to reduce the hours to units of 9-hour "days." The 9-hour day was standardized because the usual work day in Panajachel is 9 hours. The data (e. g., table 15) are reported in these units. Insofar as in this description the quantities are reduced to proportions the unit is immaterial.

Little more than a third of the total time is potentially usable for productive purposes because, first, none of that of infants can be included and, second, everybody must eat and sleep. Although such information may seem to presuppose considerable private knowledge I am confident that little error is involved in the estimate of eating-sleeping time. Adults and children alike normally retire at about the same time, from 8 to 9 in the evening, and rise at from 5 to 6 in the morning. Doubtless everybody sleeps a little less in the season of short nights, which happens to fall in the dry months when there is also more agricultural work and more vending in the markets; but the average throughout the year is almost surely close to 9 hours. The three meals a day take something less than 3 hours, but additional time is usually taken, especially after the evening meal, with rest.

TABLE 15.—*The use of time*

Activity	Number of 9-hour days in year					Percentage of community time				
	Total	Men over 15	Women over 15	Children 4 to 15	Infants under 4	Total	Men over 15	Women over 15	Children 4 to 15	Infants under 4
Economic activities (chart 16)	240, 921	101, 615	99, 706	39, 600	___	31.7	13.4	13.1	5.2	___
Community service (table 16)	8, 334	8, 033	289	12	___	1.1	1.1	___	___	___
Personal and social activities (table 18)	25, 433	5, 567	11, 913	7, 953	___	3.3	0.7	1.6	1.0	___
Eating-sleeping, etc. (13 hours daily)	457, 920	[1] 133, 153	[2] 143, 597	77, 714	[3] 103, 456	60.2	17.5	18.9	10.2	13.6
Not accounted	28, 521	361	9, 967	18, 193	___	3.7	___	1.3	2.4	___
Total [4]	761, 129	248, 729	265, 472	143, 472	103, 456	100.0	32.7	34.9	18.8	13.6

[1] 253 men, since the 2 in military service are not counted. From the total 9-hour days, are subtracted 200 for less time spent eating-sleeping on market trips, 100 for the ceremonial time of officials that cuts into their sleeping, and 300 for less sleeping time at wakes, fiestas, etc.
[2] From the total are subtracted 50 9-hour days for less sleeping time by the wives of officials and their helpers for ceremonial cooking, etc., and 150 for less sleeping time at wakes, fiestas, during sickness, etc.
[3] All infant time is included here.
[4] Number of persons (table 3)×366 days×24/9 hours.

Sleeping, eating, and resting incidental to meals and in the evening take, on the average, about 13 hours a day.[62]

"Community service" (table 16) accounts for all time devoted to obligations to church and state, including military service, sporadic assistance on public works (60 percent of the total, and five-sixths of what is done locally), and service in the formal political-religious organization (table 17). The distinction between religious and civil functions is not clear-cut. The civil duties are police and administrative, centered about the town hall; the religious duties are performed in connection with the local church and the cult of the Saints. Individuals in their lifetimes "ascend the ladder" of a single hierarchy of offices, with more menial functions at the bottom and more honorific ones at the top, usually alternating between the religious and the civil offices. Beyond the lowest office, marriage is required, and wives occupy the positions in some sense jointly with their husbands. The men are principals in all ritual, the women in a few ceremonies; but the women prepare ceremonial food and drink. Every normal person is part of the system; a man of the household serves for a year after which no service is required for 2 or 3, when again the man (or another in the household, depending on who is ripe for service in relation to the particular needs at the time), enters another year of service further up the ladder. The offices are unpaid; on the contrary

[62] Even a small error here, multiplied by all the people and every day of the year, is the most likely single source of error in the number of days left unaccounted for in the whole community. Such an error would effect only the proportions of time spent eating, sleeping, and resting relative to that not accounted for. If the block of time devoted to eating, sleeping, etc., and that which is unaccounted for, are left out of consideration, only 12.3 percent of the remainder is "noneconomic" (chart 15), and community obligations account for three-fourths of this time.

they require expenditure of both time and money. The system thus distributes economically costly obligations through the community; each year different individuals become devoted to public service.

TABLE 16.—*Community service*

Kind	Number of 9-hour days in year			
	Total	Men	Women	Children
Road work for central Government [1]	960	960	___	___
Military Service (2 men full time)	1, 952	[2] 1, 952	___	___
Training of military reservists	90	90	___	___
Public works assistance by private individuals [3]	200	200	___	___
Public officials' chiefly civil duties (table 17)	4, 081	4, 081	___	___
Public officials' chiefly religious duties (table 17)	1, 051	750	289	12
Total	8, 334	8, 033	289	12

[1] Assuming that half of the men—not counting exempt office holders—worked in 1936.
[2] *All* of the time of the 2 men, including that spent eating, sleeping, etc., is here included, since they are outside the community.
[3] Repairing irrigation ditches, controlling the river, installing decorations, etc.

TABLE 17.—*Time of officials*

Officials	Number of 9-hour days per year					
	Total	Men			Women	Children
		Total	Chiefly civil	Chiefly religious	Chiefly religious	Chiefly religious
24 *Alguaciles*	2, 787	2, 787	2, 787	___	___	___
4 *Mayores*	481	472	460	12	9	___
2 *Auxiliares*	238	236	230	6	2	___
4 *Regidores*	435	426	404	22	9	___
2 *Sacristans*	239	237	___	237	2	___
2 *Fiscales*	35	33	___	33	2	___
4 *Cofrades*	118	67	___	67	51	___
9 *Mayordomos*	225	125	___	125	100	___
Voluntary helpers	120	20	___	20	100	___
30 *Principales*	220	220	200	20	___	___
4 Rocket burners	24	22	___	22	2	___
30 Dancers	160	160	___	160	___	___
12 Crucifiers	20	20	___	20	___	___
12 "Apostles"	30	6	___	6	12	12
Total	5, 132	4, 831	4, 081	750	289	12

The class of activities labeled "Personal and Social" (table 18) attempts to catch all other non-productive activities. Although each figure is the result of close calculation on the basis both of case materials and general impressions, some are subject to greater error than others.[63] The first item assumes that a woman spends about 2 hours a week on personal hygiene, a man but an hour, because women wash and dress their hair frequently, and bathe more often in the sweat bath—a time-consuming operation. In the matter of sickness, I was reduced to pretty rough calculations, assuming that on the average everybody is sick at home or in bed 2 days a year; that nursing (chiefly by women) takes an average of 3 hours a day from other activities; and that in each of the 200 cases that a shaman is called, a day's time is lost to call for and accompany him.

That in each of the 74 cases of births the woman loses an average of 10 days' time is probably a sound statement, for the lying-in period is recognized and I have a number of cases in my notes. That in each case a father—to call the midwife, assist her, and register the birth, etc.—loses 2 days, is not nearly as certain. In the matter of baptism, it is assumed on the basis of a few cases that the parents each lose a day and the sponsor a half day. In the estimated five cases of marriage, consequently five "askings" and courtships, it is calculated that both sets of parents, and the principals, each lose 24 hours, and that six other men and women each lose 6 hours.

The time that funerals cost is based on knowledge of customary differences when adults, children, and infants die. It is supposed that the people of the family (on the average a man, woman, and two children) each lose 3 days at the death of an adult, 2 at that of a child, and 1 at the death of an infant; and that (on the average) five other men and five other women lose 2, 1, and a half day, respectively, in such cases.

Only general observation and more scattered cases are the basis of the other figures; yet it seems to me wholly unlikely that the totals of table 18 are off more than about 20 percent.

Chart 15 omits sleeping–eating time, and that

[63] And sometimes greater error than would have been the case had I known I was going to use the data in this manner. For example, I did not get official data on attendance in school which would have been available, and which might have been more accurate than my extrapolations.

TABLE 18.—*Personal and social activities*

Activity	Number of 9-hour days in year			
	Total	Men	Women	Children
Bathing, hair washing, hygiene, etc.	4,917	1,405	3,022	490
Sickness: patients' and nursing time	2,361	818	1,184	359
Childbirth: family's time	1,052	148	904	
Baptisms: parents' and sponsors' time	154	77	77	
Care of infants: feeding, etc.	4,287		4,287	
School attendance	6,000			6,000
Courtship and marriage	100	50	50	
Funerals	832	369	369	94
Noncommercial fiesta-celebration and Sunday and holiday rest by private persons	3,385	1,400	1,250	735
Informal visiting, gossiping, drinking on no special occasion	670	250	270	150
Formal visits, gift bearing not included elsewhere	225	100	100	25
Fighting, quarreling; time in court and jail and worrying	200	100	100	
Business errands	200	150	50	
Rainy days when no work in house; caught on road, etc.	1,050	700	250	100
Total	25,433	5,567	11,913	7,953

unaccounted for, to show that 87.7 percent of all the time available to the community is devoted in one manner or other to getting a living. Description of how this time is used necessarily involves differences associated with sex and age because (for example) the 87.7 percent in chart 15 hides a difference between men (88.2 percent), women (81.8 percent), and children (60.2 percent) which becomes more and more significant as the categories are broken down. Thus, for instance, men devote 80 percent of their usable time to gainful employment and commercial production, but women only 28.6 percent and children a trifle less. The women meanwhile spend their time on cooking, laundering, and the making of clothing.

Chart 16 therefore, confined to the distribution of time devoted to economic activities, distinguishes the use of time by sex and age.

Agriculture (the techniques of which are discussed on pages 47 to 57 and the business aspects on pages 108 to 132) is obviously the only real source of livelihood; especially since three-fourths of the labor done for Ladinos is agricultural labor and most of the marketing involves marketing of home-grown agricultural produce. Table 19 shows how the time was divided between different crops and animals grown by Indians. In contrast a miniscule 500 days, including 15 of women and 155 of children, is spent on hunting, fishing, and the like.

Women spend 51 percent of their time in household tasks, and an additional 5.5 percent in weaving, sewing, and repairing clothing; house

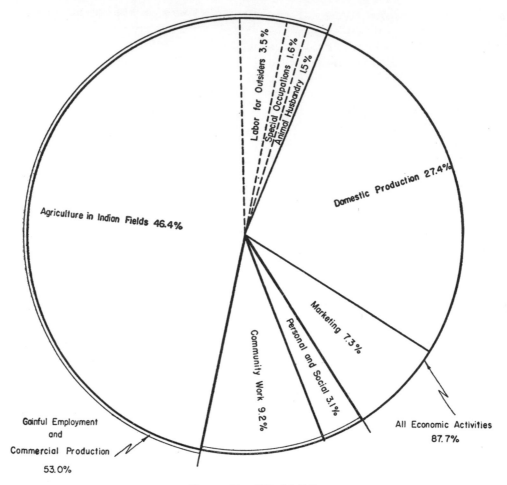

Labor for Outsiders 3.5 %
Special Occupations 1.6 %
Animal Husbandry 1.5 %
Domestic Production 27.4%
Agriculture in Indian Fields 46.4%
Community Work 9.2%
Personal and Social 3.1%
Marketing 7.3%
All Economic Activities 87.7%
Gainful Employment and Commercial Production 53.0%

CHART 15.—"Usable" time.

building and maintenance, and cutting and bringing firewood, are equivalents for men, but not of course in importance. Although payment of rent is not required, men generally work for money and use the money—rather than their time—to supply household needs.

Buying and selling is a major enterprise of both sexes, for men second only to agriculture and for women on a par with the making of cloth and garments. Indeed, in the context of the culture, marketing is even more significant than the proportion of time devoted to it, for selling the produce (rather than harvesting it) is the real culmination of the cycle of agriculture, just as buying, where the prerogative of choice is most clearly enjoyed, is the beginning of social living.

Practices in the hiring of labor, and the role of specialists in the society, follow a description of the more general division of labor.

TABLE 19.—*Time devoted to agriculture and domestic animals by sex and age*

Kind of work	Total man-days	Men	Women	Children under 14
Agriculture:				
Milpa	6,055	5,755	100	200
Onions from seed	83,195	55,195	20,000	8,000
Onion seed from seed	6,437	5,337	800	300
Garlic	10,576	5,776	3,300	1,500
Beans	4,113	3,263	650	200
Vegetables	1,720	1,160	460	100
Pepinos	6,198	4,198	1,600	400
Coffee	2,144	1,714	280	150
Fruit	416	316	50	50
Total	[1] 120,854	82,714	27,240	10,900
Domestic animals:				
Fowl	352		282	70
Pigs	167		137	30
Goats and sheep	173	73		100
Cattle	2,513	1,313		1,200
Horses-mules	550	400		150
Total	3,755	1,786	419	1,550
Grand total	124,609	84,500	27,659	12,450

[1] From table 39; the totals are larger in chart 16, which adds 2,000 woman-days and 5,000 child-days (to take account of the extra time put in by women and children to accomplish their "man-days") and subtracts the labor done by outsiders (450 from men's, 160 women's, and 90 children's).

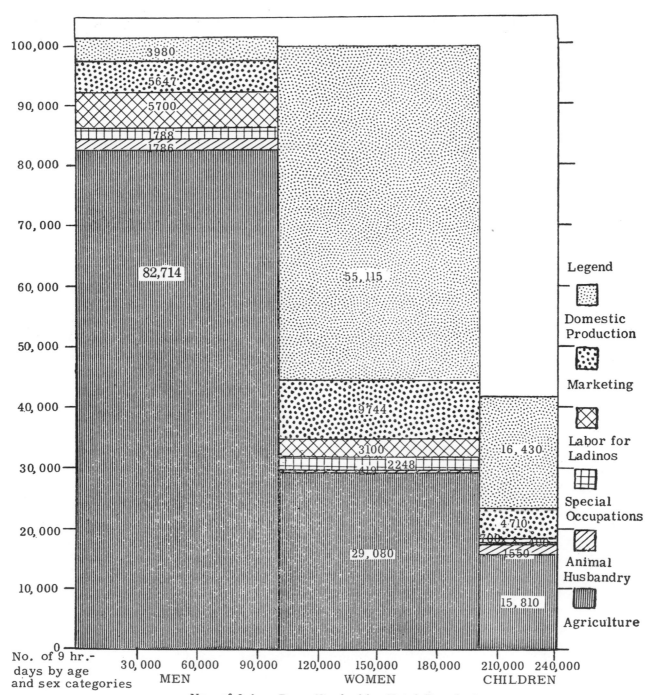

CHART 16.—Time spent on economic activities

DIVISION OF LABOR

Chart 17 summarizes the sex division of labor in Indian Panajachel.

	Men	Women

Milpa growing	Preparing soil
	Planting
	Cultivating
	    Harvesting
	      Storing
	      Graining	

Truck gardening	Making beds
	    Planting
	      Transplanting
	  Watering
	      Weeding
	  Harvesting
	  Preparing crop	

Coffee growing	Transplanting Cleaning grove Harvesting Preparing beans	
Fruit	Harvesting	

Animal husbandry	Pasturing
	    Feeding
	    Killing	

Firewood	Felling trees
	  Cutting branches
	     Gathering	

Housing	Building Repairing Furnishings	
Clothing	Sewing	Weaving Laundering
Housekeeping	Fire making Sweeping	Cooking Grinding Dish washing
Marketing	Distant markets Nearby markets	Local market
Load carrying	Large, heavy Small, light	Infants

CHART 17.—Sex division of labor in ordinary work.

While only women are expected to work in the kitchen, it is not true in Panajachel that only men are supposed to work in the fields. Indeed, the only broad generalization that can be made about the sex division of labor is that men do not normally cook, carry water, spin, weave, or wash dishes and clothing; while only men do certain agricultural tasks considered too difficult for women—preparing the soil for corn, making garden beds, planting coffee bushes; and only men (using the tumpline) carry heavy loads.

The ax and the hoe, and to a lesser degree the machete, are the men's tools. Men cut down trees and turn over the earth. Women, in agriculture, use their hands or sticks and the watering basins. The work that can be done without heavy tools is done by either men or women. But it is the heaviness of the work rather than the tool that sets the pattern. Women do not lift great weights, or swing axes, picks, or hoes. They do not climb trees, or roofs.

Men travel greater distances than women. A man may carry his load 50 miles to market; a woman rarely more than 5. Women work the fields in the delta, men in the hills. But this is because most of the agricultural work in the hills is heavy work connected with the milpa rather than because of their distance. The milpa, perhaps because most of the work involved is heavy, is the most typically men's job. But there may be an element of tradition here too, as well as of distance.

Domestic tasks—cooking and washing and the making of clothing—are almost exclusively women's work. It is typical for the man to be off in the fields or on a business trip and the woman to care for the home. But women no less typically engage in agricultural work and in taking their wares for sale in the market. In a broad sense, the women do all the kinds of work that men do, and in addition care for the house and prepare the food. They are breadwinners as well as breadmakers.

The degree to which these statements are true, to which the division of labor along sex lines is fixed and unalterable, will be discussed (following the order of chart 17) after considerations of age differences.

AGE DIFFERENCES

A child of 2 or 3 is carried on the back of mother or sibling, except in the house, and there is little sign of sex distinctions. By the age of 4 or 5, he is carried only on long trips. By this time costume distinctions have set in: a boy dresses much like his father, a girl like her mother. Whatever the sex, however, he stays in and near the house, helping the women folk with minor errands. "Bring me a piece of firewood" the mother is apt to say to the boy or to the girl. Now also the child of either sex begins to carry and watch his younger sibling. At 6 or 7, the child frequently accompanies his parents to their delta fields, and although he plays more than he works, he is asked to help in little ways. "Let the water flow in the ditch," the parent might say to a child playing in the water, and the youngster will direct the water into the proper channel with his hands. There is still little sex distinction; either girl or boy accompanies either parent to the field. A child of 8 or 9 (assuming he is not in school) still works both around the house and in the fields, caring for younger siblings, sweeping and doing other chores in the house, and helping in the fields. But now the sex distinction is more important. A boy will have a small hoe, and when in the fields will help his father make garden beds, while a girl will have a small water jar and will be sent for water for the kitchen. The boy is now home much less frequently than the girl; more and more he accompanies his father to his work. The girl may still go with her father, or her mother, to the fields. But she is much more closely attached to her mother and hence to the kitchen. By now she is frequently setting up toy looms with coarse fibers.

At the age of from 10 to 12 the sex division of labor is virtually complete. Now a boy will not stay home to help in the kitchen. He goes as a helper with his father to the fields; if he goes with his mother, he goes as a coworker. He does the kinds of work his father does, even if on a smaller scale. He uses the tumpline to carry small loads nearby, but when he accompanies his parents to a market outside he is more apt to carry the lunch in his bag. A girl of 10 or 12, on the other hand, no longer goes with her father to the fields; at home and in the fields she is under her mother's direction. She now helps very considerably in the house. She may make the fire and is expected to be able to make coffee; of course she carries water. She also can weave small things of limited usefulness because the work is defective. She alone, and not her brother of like age, cares for the younger children and sweeps out the house.

At 14 or 15 the young man is more a man than a boy. He enters his first municipal office and tends to do a man's work. He now smokes and begins to drink. He carries medium loads with his tumpline and goes to nearby towns. He frequently accompanies his father or an older brother to more distant markets. He does all kinds of heavy agricultural work. The girl of similar age has not quite to the same degree reached woman's estate. She now grinds, and can prepare the meal of the family if it is small; but her tortillas are far from perfect. If she has been taught to weave, she makes only small things, neither very speedily nor very well. But of course she now dedicates her time more and more to such tasks, while her mother is freer to work longer in the fields and to sell more frequently in the market. If the girl goes to market, as she does, it is usually in the charge of an older woman, if not her mother, who helps her.

At the age of 18 a youth is a man or a woman, and may be expected to do all of the work of his sex. The young man may go alone to the most distant markets, he will work for others by the day at a man's wage, and will carry full loads. The young woman can do every kind of housework well, and can do the women's work of the fields for the family or for hire. If she does not go freely to market to sell, it is only because young women should be protected from escapades. She is ready for marriage.

There is normally no age limit for work. Except that sickness tends to take a greater and greater toll of one's time with advancing age, the old work side by side with the young, earning a living by the same means. In practice, it is rarely true that an old man works as much as a young man. If he is not enfeebled by sickness, the custom of prolonged drinking acquired during his public career takes his time and saps his strength, or he has acquired sons enough to make his own hands less necessary, or has become wealthy enough to hire hands so that he himself undertakes more the direction of work than the work itself.[64] By the time a man is old—say 60—he has usually completed all of his civil and religious obligations which were in the past a very significant expense, and now he requires less and is hence richer. By this time, too, he frequently is little interested in accumulating more land, and is apt to live off his capital. Hard and steady work is therefore frequently not necessary.

The same may be said, in general, for women. Since women outlive men, there are more old women than there are old men. They continue to the end of their days to do the work of women, but

---

[64] A rich old Indian (now deceased) who was at least 75 at the time, said in casual conversation, "I personally no longer do any work because my arms cannot stand it, but my son Rafael is the one who does everything necessary, or I send *mozos* and only direct them. But I still sometimes take up my ax or my hoe to do a simple task because I am ashamed to be always sitting in my house watching my (third) wife work in the fields. Sometimes I tell her to get herself *mozos* to clear the onion patches and other fields, but she answers me that she too is ashamed not to do anything because my children (her step-children) and neighbors might think that she wanted me only for the advantages. And so it is that we are both ashamed to do nothing. Look now, for example, she has gone to the Sololá market to sell and to buy the necessary things, and I remain to watch the house; but I always go out to my fields."

again they work less long and less hard. An old woman no longer has children to care for. Her eyes are frequently too bad to permit much weaving. There is no large family to cook for. Like men, old women tend to be ill more frequently and for longer periods, and they, too, sometimes lose time in prolonged drinking, to which their public life has habituated them.

SEX DIFFERENCES

Most of the ordinary work of the community is done, therefore, by men and women between the ages of about 18 and, say, 50. Older, the quantity of work diminishes, the kinds and the sex distinction remain the same; younger, the kinds of work also change and the distinctions between the sexes diminish and (with young children) disappear. Since agricultural work of both women and children tends to be "light," children's work resembles rather women's work than men's. Thus women rather than men transplant onions; but one may as well read it, "women and children" even though more especially girls than boys. Men do less on light tasks than women because more of their time is turned to heavy tasks that they alone can do; thus the practice of youngsters, who are necessarily cut out of the heavy work, is like that of women.

THE MILPA

I have never heard of a woman's helping to fell trees, clear and burn brush, hoe the soil, or anything else to prepare the cornfield; nor have I ever heard of a woman planting or cultivating. Women only harvest, frequently going alone to cut leaves or a few green ears, especially if the field is in the delta, when a woman even goes alone to harvest a few ripe ears. Most frequently, however, men take the lead in harvesting and women accompany them, if at all, only to assist, partly because large loads must be brought home, mainly because of a feeling that milpa is men's work. To harvest a large field laborers are hired to join what members of the family are available, perhaps including women;[65] but women are never hired, as men are, to help.

Stacking corn in the granary is done by all the family under the leadership of the man of the house. Removing the grain from the cob is primarily women's work. When (infrequently in Panajachel) corn in quantity is grained by beating a bagful of ears with sticks, men do most of the work. Generally each day's grain is taken off with the fingers before use, hence is a kitchen task of women. Nevertheless men often do this chore in idle moments around the house, and men rather than the women grain seed corn before planting.

Beans are removed from the pod (usually by beating) by both men and women.

TRUCK GARDENING

Only men make garden beds, or *pepino* hills. Boys but not girls or women help the men; it may be said that this is work of males, as grinding is of females. The only other gardening tasks exclusive to men are planting onion seed (which evidently requires expertness which no women have developed), and planting *pepinos*, which involves carting fertilizer and making holes. Otherwise work in the truck gardens is done by both sexes, one or the other predominating in each process.[66] Probably women plant more garlic, transplant more onions, and possibly plant more beans than do men. They certainly do more weeding as men do more watering. Men harvest more onions, garlic, and beans (which require some strength for the pulling), but women probably cut more *pepinos*. These differences are not matters of custom but of circumstance. Thus, men usually harvest the quantities of *pepinos* or green beans they take to the wholesale market and women cut those they will sell locally. But husband and wife (and others) are apt to go together both to the harvest and to the market. Onions, garlic, and vegetables are prepared for market by the whole family, with little distinction of sex. Women doubtless wash vegetables more, since in general each vendor prepares his own load for market but women help their husbands wash the larger quantities. Women go to market more frequently than men, but carry considerably less.

---

[65] In one case the wife and 10-year-old daughter arrived at the distant cornfield at 10 a. m. with lunch and remained the rest of the day to pick beans and gather together the ears of corn. In another case a wife and daughter did some harvesting, in a nearby field, alone, and later accompanied the man of the house to do more.

[66] A man and wife are often found together, perhaps transplanting onions in the same garden bed. Women are frequently seen working with babies on their backs. When these cry, they are given the breast. Where there are other children, an older sibling may relieve the mother of her burden while she works, but of course the infant must remain close by to be fed. A wealthy woman may hire a nursemaid to keep the baby in the shade nearby.

COFFEE

Division of labor in the coffee nurseries follows the usual garden pattern. Only men transplant coffee bushes from the nursery bed, work which involves digging holes; pulling, binding, and setting both coffee and shade trees. Again, only men clean the grove. Both sexes harvest coffee, and women as well as men are hired for the purpose. In Indian groves women probably harvest more than men, for small groves are often picked over by the women and children of the house. Men exclusively use the depulping machine, women the grinding stone. Men do more than women washing and sunning the beans, especially if the quantity is large; on the other hand when the parchment is removed from the beans before use or sale, it is done on the grinding stone, by women,[67] and roasting and grinding coffee is women's work, done in small quantities for daily use in connection with other kitchen work.

FRUIT

Planting vegetable pears and harvesting their root are peculiarly men's tasks, involving some ritual. Otherwise the work of the "orchard" is little differentiated by sex. Fruit harvesting that requires climbing is done by men, but most fruit is collected by other methods, and by both sexes. Quantity is a factor: a man (perhaps helped by his wife) is apt to strip a whole tree of its fruit, but a woman usually brings down the fruit that she plans to take to market. In this work children are of special assistance.

ANIMAL HUSBANDRY

The few horses, cattle, sheep in town are cared for by men and boys who lead them to pasture, move them occasionally, and lead them back in the evening. Women may feed such animals at the house, but their care is the responsibility of men. Pigs and fowl, on the other hand, are the province of the women (and children) of the house. Though men may and do handle them, women generally do all the chores connected with them. "Chicken raising is the woman's work; the man has nothing to do with it," is the usual view. Pigs are killed by professional butchers, but the housewife usually kills a chicken for the table. Turkeys are killed only for fiestas, when usually

men have charge of their ceremonial slaughter together with that of roosters. Men also clean and dismember the fowl used ceremonially, women those for the house.

FIREWOOD

Firewood in quantity is prepared by men and boys. Women never cut down trees, though they frequently chop branches into kindling. Women and children perhaps more than men, collect faggots in the river bed and in the fields. The distinction is between "making" and "collecting" firewood.

HOUSING

Building of all kinds is in the province of the men, assisted by boys. Women do not help. Materials which are not purchased are obtained generally in the hills, systematically by the men. Setting up the house is heavy work, but women do not participate even in building small structures like chicken coops, or thatching low roofs; probably they lack the techniques. Nor do they mix mud for mass-adobe walls, which is neither heavy nor skilled labor.

CLOTHING

The little cotton spinning still done in Panajachel is strictly women's work. Men rather than women twist maguey fibers for special uses, and when maguey textiles were made, the men did it as they still do in other towns. Women, never men, do weaving. Exceptions are two men who have learned a non-Indian belt-weaving technique.[68] A few men (no women) have also learned to make fish nets. But textiles for common use and by the usual processes are strictly in the female sphere.

Men usually tailor their own cloaks from woolen cloth that they buy, though women sometimes do this for their husbands. They also repair their own clothes, especially if they are unmarried. It is no shame for a man to use a needle. Yet women do virtually all sewing done in Panajachel: they fashion the textiles that they weave (for themselves, the menfolk, and the children) and some-

---

[67] A 12-year-old boy was once observed helping his mother at this, but he was not grinding.

[68] Once a boy of about 10 learned to weave cotton belts when his father was in prison in Sololá and he took food to him and stayed all day; he watched the prisoners making belts and went home and began making them for sale to Ladinos. Since then he has earned a few dollars a year; he also has learned to make nets.

times tailor shirts of bought material, they also sew .their own skirts (of bought material), the largest operation. They also do most of the mending.

Women do virtually all the laundry, and have regular wash days. Men are ashamed to be seen washing clothes (especially young men who have no female relatives they can ask), but they do it.

HOUSEKEEPING

On the road men do all work necessary to sustain life—building fires, making coffee, cooking meat and soup, washing dishes, etc. But at home such tasks are done by the women. Cases of temporarily womanless households in which men have done their own grinding and even tortilla making are not only aberrant but provoke mirth. Women usually rise first and build the fire; a man at home might do this if his wife were ill, but rarely otherwise. Grinding and cooking are (with weaving) the most definitely women's tasks. Such others as curing utensils, preparing leaves for tamales, washing dishes, etc., are included. Men do virtually nothing in the kitchen.

Except that a *cofradía* house is swept by the men officials, all interiors (including Saint's houses) are cleaned by women and children. But men and boys—not women—normally sweep the patio.

Marketing is the subject of special discussion in the following sections. Briefly: Panajachel men do not patronize the local market; both women and men buy and sell in nearby markets; and usually only men go to distant markets.

LOAD CARRYING

Men and boys never carry loads on the head, as women and girls carry produce (in baskets) or water (in earthenware vessels). Men and boys rarely carry any other way than with the tumpline.[69] Locally, women sometimes carry as much as 100 pounds—with the help of two others, to get the basket onto the head; the usual maximum is 50 or 75 pounds, and women carry as much as 50 pounds uphill to Sololá or San Andrés (5 miles). The normal load of a man is roughly double that of a woman.

Women (never men) carry babies on their backs in a cloth slung over a shoulder. Men do not

ordinarily carry babies, but if a child tires on the road, and the wife is carrying an infant, her husband may place the child on his load.

Only men (but not very many), and sometimes boys, paddle canoes. I have heard of a woman's helping only in one extraordinary case. Women simply do not "know how." Once when an Indian brought home his corn harvest by canoe, accompanied by another man and by his mother and sister, the north wind blew them off course. "The women wanted to help, but of course they didn't know how," the man told me later.

SUMMARY

Table 20 reduces the total time distribution to hours in the day, showing how the "average" man, woman, and child spend an "average" of those which include every day of the year: week days, Sundays and holidays; sunny days and rainy days. It is seen that on the average a man spends 8½ hours working in the fields. With less work on Sundays and during festivals, and in periods of sickness and of rain, this means that most days of the year the average man works well over 9 hours a day in Indian or Ladino fields; and with artisans, officials, and the aged in the fields much less, it is apparent that for this average to maintain, most men actually work in the fields close to 10 hours on a normal weekday.

Women, on the other hand, average 5 hours in the kitchen and in clothing manufacture and care and 2¾ hours in the fields. These averages are less meaningful than corresponding statements for men because relatively few women spend whole days in the fields while relatively more devote themselves more exclusively to domestic tasks. As might be expected, children of both

[69] There is a Totonicapeña married into the local community. Following the custom of her community, she sometimes carries with a tumpline. The local Indians were heard to remark about this. The Indian women of Patanatic (also originally Totonicapeñas) frequently bring firewood to town on their backs.

TABLE 20.—*Average day of average Indian*

Activity	Hours and minutes		
	Man	Woman	Child
	Hr. Min.	Hr. Min.	Hr. Min.
Hunting, fishing, etc.	---- 02		---- 02
Agriculture in Indian fields	8 03	2 38	2 39
Animal husbandry	---- 10	---- 02	---- 16
Special occupations	---- 10	---- 12	---- 04
Agricultural labor for outsiders	---- 26	---- 14	---- 05
Domestic and other labor for outsiders	---- 07	---- 03	---- 02
Domestic production	---- 23	4 59	2 43
Marketing	---- 33	---- 53	---- 47
Community work	---- 35	---- 02	
Personal and social	---- 32	1 05	1 20
Eating, sleeping, etc.	12 56	12 59	13 00
Not accounted for	---- 03	---- 54	3 02
Total	24 00	24 00	24 00

sexes divide their time about evenly between kitchen and field. The average work time of children as they grow to adulthood undoubtedly approaches that of men and of women, respectively, for the average here given includes the young children who do much less work.

If my information is nearly correct, the average time devoted by men, women, and children to military training, all religious activity, fiesta celebration and Sunday and holiday rest, and the carrying on of social relations is relatively so little that even adding in the time not accounted for—which includes the idleness of young children and the aged—it amounts to but 45 minutes a day. To add to their working time substantially, therefore, the community would need to cut the 13 hours used in sleeping, eating, and resting with meals; while on the other hand, to add greatly to their leisure time for education, recreation, or greater participation in national, social, or political life, the time devoted to making a living—if levels were to remain the same—would have to be decreased by (1) improving agricultural techniques, (2) relieving women of kitchen burdens through technological improvements, and/or (3) improving facilities for buying and selling (which might, however, reduce the recreation afforded by the market with relatively little gain in time).

SPECIAL OCCUPATIONS

Simple societies are usually characterized by economic homogeneity. Each family earns its living much like every other. In that respect Panajachel is simple; so of course is a community of workers in a factory, and for the same reason. Panajachel is a unit in a system where regional differentiation and local homogeneity are correspondingly significant. By and large, every Indian family in Panajachel earns its living in about the same way: by agriculture. This is especially true when one leaves out of account "foreign" Indians who tend to have special occupations, as will be seen below. In 1936 only four of the 157 households—including Panajacheleño and foreign—did not derive their chief income from the soil; all four were households of emigrants. As far as could be determined, only 50 other individuals engaged in any pursuit at all besides farming, farm laboring, the care of domestic animals, and the sale of agricultural produce. And most of these special occupations were of

little economic importance. Thus only 3 percent of total time spent on productive tasks in 1936 was so occupied. The relative importance of each of the occupations is shown in tables 21 and 22. Table 23 shows what occupations are practiced by the 54 persons (in 50 households) with specialties. The combinations of special occupations are frequently but not always consistent. Thus, while two men are both shamans and bloodletters, another is a bloodletter, an animal caponizer and a masseur, a third is a mason and a carpenter, and a woman is a midwife and childcurer, there are also such combinations as (a)

TABLE 21.—*Time devoted to trades, professions, and special occupations*

Occupation	Number of 9-hour days in year			
	Total	Men	Women	Children
Mason-carpenter [1]	760	760		
Adobe maker	25	25		
Barber	5	5		
Butcher	320	250	70	
Baker	7	7		
Netter	5	5		
Canoe business	75	75		
Weavers [2]	1,800		1,500	300
Restaurateurs	500		400	100
Messenger-carrier	300	300		
Marimba player	80	80		
Flageolet-drummer	150	150		
Shaman [3]	118	118		
Midwife	275		275	
Curer	7	4	3	
Caponizer	9	9		
Total	4,436	1,788	2,248	400

[1] Masons: 2 full time, each 250 days; 2 part time, each 40 days. Carpenter: 120 days. Mason-carpenter, 60 days.
[2] Including only the specialized weaving of *huipil* figures.
[3] Calculated on the basis of performance of 234 rituals, of which 00 were away from Panajachel. Time lost by drunkenness begun in performance of duty is not counted.

TABLE 22.—*Income from trades, professions, and special occupations*

Occupations	Total	Within community	Outside community
Mason-carpenter [1]	$420.00	$30.00	$390.00
Adobe maker	6.25	3.00	3.25
Barber	5.00	2.00	3.00
Butcher	305.00	150.00	155.00
Baker	7.00	5.00	2.00
Netter	2.00	.50	1.50
Canoe business	25.00	12.50	12.50
Weaver [2]	200.00	200.00	
Restaurateur	50.00		50.00
Messenger-carrier	40.00		40.00
Marimba player	30.00		30.00
Flageolet-drummer	30.00	15.60	14.40
Shaman [3]	210.00	156.60	53.40
Midwife [3]	135.00	114.00	21.00
Curer	7.50	7.50	
Caponizer	4.00	3.00	1.00
Total	1,476.75	699.70	777.05

[1] Masons: 2 full time each $150; 2 part time each $20. Carpenter: $50. Mason-carpenter, $30.
[2] Including only the specialized weaving of *huipil* figures; the figure of earnings includes gifts.
[3] Assuming that the ceremonial food is worth $1.

adobe making and barbering, (*b*) fish-net making, baking, running a canoe business, and playing the marimba, and (*c*) decorative weaving and curing children's ailments.

TABLE 23.—*Persons with special occupations*

Occupation	Number of practitioners			
	Total	Full time	Part time	
			No other specialty	Combining specialties [1]
Artisans:				
Masons	4½ (5)	[2] 2	[2] 2	½
Carpenters	1½ (2)	—	[2] 1	½
Adobe makers	½ (1)	—	—	½
Butchers, beef	2 (2)	[2] 1	1	—
Butchers, pork	3 (3)	—	2+[2] 1	—
Bakers	¼ (1)	—	—	¼
Barbers	½ (1)	—	—	½
Netters	¼ (1)	—	—	¼
Weavers	6 (8)	—	4♀	½+½+½+½♀
Business:				
Canoe renting	1¼ (2)	—	1	¼
Restaurateurs	3 (3)	[2] 1♀	2♀	—
Messenger-freight	1 (1)	—	1	—
Musicians:				
Marimba	3¼ (4)	—	3	¼
Drum	1 (1)	—	1	—
Flageolet or "caña"	2 (2)	—	2	—
Practitioners:				
Shamans	9 (11)	—	7	½+½+½+½
Midwives	1½ (3)	—	—	½+½+½♀
Curers	4½ (6)	—	3♀	½+½+½♀
Bloodletters	5⅓ (8)	—	3	½+½+½+½+⅓
Masseurs	⅓ (1)	—	—	⅓
Bone setters	1 (1)	—	1	—
Caponizers	1⅓ (2)	—	1	⅓
Total	53	4	36	13

[1] In each fraction, the numerator indicates the number of persons practicing the occupation, and the denominator the total number of special occupations he practices. The total of the column is the arithmetic sum of the fractions.
[2] Indian native of some other town.
♀ Female; all not marked are males (except in "total" column where sex is not indicated).

It will be noted that merchants are not included in this list. It will also be seen that some of the practitioners (notably curers) are not professionals in the sense that they are paid; they are included for completeness and because they are sometimes given gifts for their favors.

ARTISANS AND MISCELLANEOUS BUSINESS

The two full-time masons, Totonicapeños who moved to Panajachel evidently for the purpose, work almost exclusively on Ladino and municipal jobs, either by the day or more usually on contract. Neither has any other local source of income and both work steadily, earning about 50 cents a day. On contract they must take into account idleness because of weather or shortage of materials or help.

The carpenter without other specialty in 1936, a Pedrano who also rented land for cultivation, was too poor a craftsman to earn (chiefly from Ladinos) the 75 cents a day that a good carpenter-cabinetmaker does. The local Indian who is a part-time mason-carpenter devotes most of his time to his land.

Since most Indians make their own adobes, the part-time adobe maker works almost exclusively for Ladinos. Like masons and carpenters, adobe makers hire laborers out of a contract price, generally $1.50 per hundred adobes. When large constructions are undertaken the Ladino contractors usually import adobe makers. The adobe maker learned the barbering trade while in military service; tourists in later years kept him very busy and prosperous, but in 1936 his customers were few. Indians come to his house on appointment for a 5-cent haircut; for whatever he can get he goes to the homes of rich foreigners.

Only one Indian beef butcher (from Atitlán) followed the trade in 1936. The following year a second Atiteco opened shop. However, a local Indian owns to the trade. Before the depression of the thirties cut down extravagances, he was called to butcher steers for private and *cofradía* Indian fiestas. The one Indian butcher competed in 1936 with a local Ladino as well as with butchers in Sololá; he usually killed but one animal a week, which he traveled to the coast to buy, which he slaughtered and butchered with the aid of a part-time (paid) assistant and of which, with the help of his wife, he processed and sold the meat, tallow, and hides. After 1936 the shop prospered, and the butcher took larger quarters and hired a full-time assistant.

Of the three part-time pork butchers in the community in 1936, only one—an Indian from Mixco—practiced his trade. The other two, both local Indians (one a large landowner), knew how to butcher, but in 1936 killed no pigs. The Mixqueño only occasionally bought pigs for slaughter, and processed them and sold the meat, lard, and cracklings.

The baker learned his trade from a Ladino, but he bakes only for Easter week when there are special demands for bread. Then he is at his oven day and night, making "bread" (we would call it coffee cake) of materials (including firewood) furnished by the customers. The same man learned to make fish nets from a local Ladino. He probably makes a net every 2 years or so, chiefly for his own use, of cotton thread and lead-weights which he buys. (In 1937 he was a sacristan in the church and worked much more at it.) The same man is one of two Indians who own canoes, which they use for themselves for carrying passengers and for rent. The two canoe owners are brothers-in-law and were close friends and rivals in 1936 (but only rivals in later years) and competed with only one Ladino in this business. The first owned a $20 canoe in 1935; the next year the other bought a larger one for the same amount; not to be outdone, the first in 1937 sold land to buy a new and larger one for $35, and in 1941 was thinking of buying an outboard motor for it. Canoes are not great money makers (passage across the lake costs from 6 to 10 cents, and a canoe can be rented for 20 cents or 25 cents a day); both men depend largely on their lands for a living and happen to be well-to-do.

Many women know how to weave, but only six know all the processes, and these are called upon by others at least to weave the figured design into their blouses. Six others take in ordinary weaving.

One woman, from Nahualá, has a permanent restaurant in the market place; most of her clients are passing merchants. In addition, two Panajacheleñas regularly bring coffee, tortillas, etc., to the markets, each a few hours of most days. Other women only occasionally bring cooked food to market.

The one "messenger" is a very poor Indian who lost an arm several years before the time of this study, and took to carrying freight and messages between Panajachel and Sololá almost every day, chiefly for the Ladinos. He was our closest neighbor for two seasons, and we came to know him well, but could never learn accurate details of his earnings from this business because we were customers. The family has a little additional income from the labor of the wife and daughter, and the man sometimes profits by transactions in fruit.

The only local marimba (of the gourd type) was bought communally by four young men a year or two before the period of study. In 1937 one dropped out and the group was reorganized. It plays locally and in 1936 had at least one outside engagement, playing in the *cofradías* and at taverns during fiestas. Besides cash fees musicians receive liquor; they sometimes work by the hour (at 50 cents for the company), sometimes are paid by the customers in the tavern for each piece played, and

sometimes they contract to play (say for a day and a night) in a *cofradía* for a fixed sum, with or without food.

One Indian who plays the flageolet is not included in this study; he is a Panajacheleño without living relatives who is a hotel servant, owns no land or house and is not part of Indian society. Of the three listed, one plays the drum, one the *caña* (a simple reed instrument), and the third both the *caña* and the flageolet. They play only for religious fiestas and are paid cash fees (usually 20 cents apiece for a dawn to dark day) with food and liquor.

PRACTITIONERS

The business affairs of shamans remain pretty much a mystery. We came to know two quite well, but both are very unreliable informants, especially on this topic. One is agreeable but evasive, the other even more agreeable and very talkative but a great braggart. Some shamanistic activities are illegal; hence there is some evasion. I could not determine how many cases they have or how much they earn from each. The work of shamans is of course irregular, and part of their compensation is in food. At least one of them has a large practice outside the local community (while the local Indians frequently call shamans from other towns) so it is difficult to get much information by indirect methods.

Although in some other towns there are shamans who probably devote all their time to their profession, in Panajachel all are primarily agriculturists. Some, however, have more clients than others. The 11 shamans fall into four groups according to the reputation (and hence amount of practice they have). The two top shamans probably did something like a ritual a week each (this does not mean they had new cases each week) and they are the only ones who were frequently called out of town. The next three probably had practices half as extensive; the following four performed rites but once a month; and the last two were just beginning in 1936 and probably had no more than two occasions for practice all year. What the shaman does takes him 3 or 4 hours (almost always at night), or 7 or 8 for out-of-town cases (I have never heard of a local shaman going beyond the lake and neighboring towns). Additional time is lost by drunkenness begun at work, at least by some shamans sometimes.

Judging from the few cases of which I have record, the usual fee is about 50 cents for a visit or ritual, plus food that is worth about 40 cents. Liquor worth 60 cents is consumed during the ritual. Calculations on this basis of an average per man-day of 80 cents is high by local standards, but considering the nature of the work not incredibly so.[70]

In addition to the three Indian midwives practicing in Panajachel in 1936, there was a Ladina midwife who infrequently served Indians (who prefer Indian midwives). The Indian women treated Ladinas as well as Indians. Some Ladinas are delivered by the Sololá physician. Of the 103 births recorded for the whole *municipio*, these 3 Indian midwives probably attended 80 births— 70 Indian and 10 Ladino. One probably attended some 40, the second, who had passed her prime, 30, and the third (who attended births chiefly among her relatives and neighbors) only 10. How many cases of abortions and other ailments they served I cannot guess.

The time that a midwife spends at the delivery is, of course, variable. Sometimes she is not called until the birth is imminent, but more frequently there is at least one consultation during pregnancy and often four or five. After the birth, she comes daily for 4 or 5 days, then two or three times more, until the 10-day lying-in period ends. Including time for the trip, and for gossip, the midwife takes about 2 hours for each ordinary call. The average at the time of birth is probably about 6 hours.[71] Fees are fairly uniform. A midwife is paid either entirely in cash, with a smaller sum plus food; but the value of the food roughly makes up the difference. In the case of Indian patients who follow old customs there is an added gift of food (and liquor) prepared for a fiesta 20 days after the birth. The usual fee is 50 pesos (83 cents) if the child is a

boy, and 40 pesos (66 cents) if a girl;[72] in case of a stillbirth the fee is halved. A Ladino is usually charged a dollar because no ceremonial food is involved. My estimate is that the total received from each case varies between 41 cents (a stillbirth) and $1.83 (for a male Indian birth) which would make their rate of pay 50 cents a day, high for a woman but not as high as that of a shaman.

There are various *curanderos*, Indian and Ladino, in Panajachel. Four old women (one also a midwife) know how to cure the evil-eye in children; one of them is also expert in curing worms and a certain kind of indigestion; a fifth woman cures sore eyes. One man at the time of this study was becoming known as a bone setter and healer of bruises. More important were bloodletters; of these there were eight (all men), four of whom were also shamans and another also a masseur and caponizer. This was the only masseur in town, and his specialty was to rub down persons in the sweat bath to cure them of certain ailments. There were also at least eight Ladino women engaged by Indians to cure certain ailments. None of these curers charges a fee. The patient or his relative "asks a favor." After the cure, however, the family sends to the curer— Indian or Ladino—a gift of food. My notes do not tell me how many such gifts are received by the Indian practitioners, but I hardly doubt that enough Indian families have a case or two of sickness each year for which a curer is called to make an average of two or three per curer reasonable.

The two caponizers in town, one of whom has no other specialty, presumably geld most of the pigs bought for fattening, and an occasional bull as well. Hence they probably worked on forty-odd animals. The usual fee is 10 cents, to which is added refreshment, usually alcoholic.

AGRICULTURAL LABOR

Hands are indeed hired for such tasks as house building and load carrying, especially by Ladinos; there are also Indians who are domestic servants and (women) who hire themselves out as corn grinders to Indians as well as Ladinos. Common labor is also expended as a public service for repairing roads and irrigation ditches, and the

---

[70] In San Pedro across the lake Rosales reports that the payment for a rite in town, which takes a maximum of 3 hours including travel to the place of the rite, is 25 cents plus food worth from 40 to 50 cents. That works out to about the same rate of pay calculated for Panajachel and is some check.

It should be noted that in some cases in Panajachel when the patient was a close friend or relative, the rate was reduced—in one recorded case from 50 cents to 25 cents—or no charge was made at all, in which case the patient simply sent a gift of food in the single such incident recorded. In one case a shaman from Santa Catarina was paid 25 cents. An informant reported that "some shamans charge $1.50 or even $3 and do not even give medicines" but it is not clear if this fee covers one visit or ritual or the entire cure.

[71] I have records of only 17 cases (5 women) of the period of labor, ranging from an hour to 29 hours, with the gross average 10.5 hours; but of course the midwife is frequently not called until the last few hours of labor.

[72] Some Indians report other prices, but most of such cases reported occurred years ago. One Indian thus reported a fee of 12 pesos (18 cents) long ago, and fees of 20 pesos (33 cents) and 40 pesos (67 cents) more recently. In 1941 another informant said the usual fee was $1 for a boy, 83 cents for a girl.

lower public officials perform such tasks as sweeping, carrying loads, and the like as part of their unpaid duties. But as might be expected in an agricultural community where there is great disparity in the distribution of land, by far the most significant use of hired labor is in the fields.

The system of agriculture requires a great deal of hand labor, some more and some less skilled, in differing amount for different crops. Thus milpa-growing requires from 36 to 57 man-days of relatively unskilled labor per crop-acre; coffee growing a little over 50 man-days of much less skilled labor; and truck farming from 197 man-days (shrub beans) to 1,878 man-days (the onion cycle) of relatively highly skilled labor. Actually, since in the case of most truck crops the growing season is only 3 or 4 months, so that there may be three crops a year, the labor required in truck farming is usually not less than about 600 man-days per year-acre, and in most cases much more. If an acre of land should be devoted to onion nursery exclusively for a year, over 7,000 man-days of labor would be devoted to it! This certainly is only a hypothetical situation, but it is evident that a farmer rich in delta land requires much more labor then he and his family alone can supply.

Both Ladinos and Indians in Panajachel hire labor, and in both cases the source of this labor is both the local Indian (and in rare cases Ladino) community and neighboring communities of Indians. We shall be interested here only in (1) resident Indians who hire out to either Ladinos or other Indians, and (2) persons, Indian or Ladino, from whatever community, who are hired by resident Indians.

Since by definition "resident Indians" do not include whatever Panajacheleños may be living and working on plantations, there are few who can be said to be full-time laborers. Since, also, Indians living and working in the local hotels—who are in virtually all cases Indians from other towns—have not been included in this study, there are few who will be counted as domestic servants. Actually, in 1936, Indians of 17 of the 157 households of the Indian community fell into the classification of full-time laborers and domestics (table 24). All these households were landless.[73]

[73] They account for all but nine of the landless Indian households. Of the remaining nine (eight foreign and one Panajacheleño) five were families of full-time artisans, and one of a carpenter who also rented land. On the residual three, including the Panajacheleño family, information is lacking.

There are, of course, a great many more families members of which work part time for other Indians and for Ladinos. Indeed, it is probable (see pp. 195-199) that all Indian families except those of the upper quarter in land wealth sometimes have members working on the land of others. At the same time almost all families of the land-richest half of the Indian population hire hands, regularly or occasionally. The result is that there are a number of families whose members are both employers and employees; these families tend to be in the second-richest quarter.

TABLE 24.—*Full-time laborers*

Type	Number of households		
	Total	Foreign	Panaja-cheleño
Lived in house of Ladino employer; man worked for him as permanent employee	9	[1] 7	2
Lived in rented or borrowed house; man sought work where he could	6	3	3
Lived in rented house; no man; woman a domestic in a Ladino household	1	1	....
Lived in borrowed house; no man; woman worked as domestic where she could	1	....	1
Total	17	11	6

[1] In 1 case the man was also a drummer, part time; in another, the woman of the household kept a full-time restaurant.

There is a considerable supply of labor from neighboring Indian communities, some of it skilled for work in truck farming, the total probably well over a hundred from Concepción, Santa Catarina, San Jorge, Sololá, Tecpán, and other places. Some of these are regular workers attached to local Indian or Ladino employers; of such the best estimate is that 60 [74] are employed by Indians, many more by Ladinos. Others are transients, chiefly from Santa Catarina, who seek work (and advances on their wages) almost house to house, although of course they know who is likely to hire them at a particular season, such as for the coffee harvest. All of the outsiders together put in a total of some 730 days of work in Indian fields (500 days in coffee groves, chiefly harvesting, 185 in milpas, and 45 in truck gardens),[75] no large portion of the total required.

[74] Based on a 1941 estimate that 20 Catarinecos and 10 or 12 Concepcioneros regularly came for the coffee harvest; 15 and 8 to 10, respectively, in Indians' cornfields; and 4 or 5 Catarinecos in truck gardens; and on an incomplete tabulation of cases, by households, showing that some 35 Concepcioneros, 15 Catarinecos, 6 Jorgeños, 4 Sololatecos, and 2 Tepanecos were known to work for different Indians.

[75] Calculated with an informant, carefully considering for which of the various processes of work in all of the local crops the outsiders are hired, and the total required in Indian lands (table 39).

Conversely, the local Indians hire themselves to employers outside their own community (i. e., Ladinos) for a great deal more time. Besides the 17 landless families, who worked about 4,350 days for Ladinos,[76] other Indians of families without much land worked occasionally in the fields of outsiders, to bring the total to about 7,500 days (table 25) chiefly in truck gardens where the local Indians have over most others the advantage of skill. (The truck-gardening Jorgeños generally hire other Jorgeños to help them.)

Rosales writes (and the Indians frequently say) that "the local Indians do not like to work as laborers for Ladinos, and few of them do. They work in the fields for Ladinos only in 'deals' involving work-for-rent. The poor Indians prefer to look for work among richer Indians. Other Indians speak ill of those who have Ladino patrons." This is a meaningful statement of the Indian attitude, but the statement of fact is exaggerated. In 1937 three of the four families with whom we had closest contact worked more or less regularly for Ladinos. All three are very poor, and probably not exceptional among people of their economic level who work, in general, for anybody who asks them, Ladino or Indian. Another poor Indian who in 1941 supplied infor-

mation on the work he had done during the previous year (which I never got straight!) worked as much for Ladinos as for other Indians. Nevertheless, the Ladinos do tend to hire Indians from other towns, especially in milpas and coffee groves, partly because of a shortage of local labor which comes because Indians *do* prefer to work for other Indians.

LABOR PRACTICES AND WAGES

Wage-work hours are normally from 7 to 12 a. m. and from 1 to 5 p. m., a 9-hour day which was the legal day during the period of study.[77] The Indians usually take their lunch to the fields or have it sent by a child of the house. When working for an Indian employer the laborers are generally given food in his house, if close to the fields, or else brought to or cooked in the field itself. A laborer attached to a Ladino patron sometimes complains that he is worked more than 9 hours (in one case from 5 a. m. to 7 p. m., an Indian said after he had changed employers).

When working in their own fields, hours are more irregular. Sometimes the Indians water their gardens by moonlight. They frequently rise at dawn to do some of their own work before breakfast and before beginning work for an employer. They rise very early to begin a journey to a market, and frequently work late the night before to prepare their loads. On the other hand, when working for themselves they not infrequently idle part of the day. But on the average, they probably work the same 9 hours a day that is customary when working for others.

The work week is 6 days. Laborers are rarely hired for Sunday work. In 1936 we needed labor for the experimental milpa that we were planting, and tried to hire men for Sunday; we found men who were willing to come on Monday, but none accepted for Sunday; as reasons they gave that (1) they needed rest and (2) it is a sin to work on Sunday: "those who do so are very niggardly and miserly and do not want to set aside even 1 day for their God." Actually, Indians do a lot of work for themselves, if not for others, on Sunday. It is the day generally devoted to the cutting of firewood for the family, and gardens that need

TABLE 25.—*Local Indian labor in Ladino fields*

Work	Approximate number of 9-hour days			
	Total	Men	Women	Children
In milpas	1,500	1,500		
In truck gardens	4,000	2,500	1,500	
In coffee groves	2,000	500	1,000	500
Total	[1] 7,500	4,500	2,500	500

[1] Since the Ladinos almost never work their own fields, the chief problem involved in this calculation is how much they actually depend upon Indian laborers from outside towns, and how much the local Indians do. On their 151 acres of hill milpa, 156 acres of coffee, and 26 acres of truck (on which last they grew 14.6 acres of corn, 2 of onions, 0.2 of onion seed, 3 of garlic, 1 of vine beans, and 1.6 of shrub beans), the number of man-days required, according to calculations based on Indian agriculture, were:

Hill milpa	7,555
Delta milpa	526
Truck	4,041
Coffee	8,689
Total	20,811

Since without much doubt Ladinos are justified in their frequent plaint that Indians work more slowly and poorly for Ladinos, the total was probably nearer to 25,000 man-days. Using that figure, and a breakdown by crops, and knowing that a minimum of some 4,350 man-days were done by resident Indians, it is not too difficult to calculate, with some degree of security, how many more than that minimum must have been done by local Indians.

[76] Based on a family-by-family analysis, using as a basis that "full time" means 300 days a year. The figure includes work in the fields, not in domestic tasks, difficult as the distinction sometimes is with a full-time employee who runs errands and all kinds of work. It includes the work of one woman, but not of an Indian "overseer" on Ladino land, since the actual labor was done by others.

[77] It is sometimes said that working hours are from sunrise to sunset with a rest period of one-half or three-quarter hour at lunch time. During short winter days this may be close to the 7-to-5 schedule generally followed. The lunch period may be shorter than 1 hour, however, depending upon where and how it is taken.

watering on Sunday are watered without any hesitation. Furthermore, Sunday is the big market day in town, and people often rise early to harvest and prepare fruit and green vegetables, for market. The Indian who gave me an account of his time indicated clearly that he spent most of his early Sunday mornings cutting firewood and that he frequently watered his gardens Sunday morning or afternoon. Another Indian, from whom I took household accounts, stated flatly that every Sunday morning is devoted to bringing firewood from the hills. And of course we had occasion to see that many Indians were watering their gardens on Sundays. There is a distinction between "hard" and "easy" work in the matter that may be interpreted as a difference between "work" and "chores." Getting firewood, watering gardens, preparing produce for the market are "chores" and may be done on Sunday or on holidays.

But even heavy work is occasionally done on Sundays and holidays. A poor neighbor made garden beds one Sunday morning; I asked him if that were not sinful and he explained that he had worked for only a short time in the morning and that it was a necessity with him. "Where there's no work to do," he said, "one should rest on Sunday because it is a day of rest." Yet later I noticed that the sons of the richest family in town spent the whole day making gardens; I chided them but obtained no response. The next day I asked an Indian friend about this, and he was not only not surprised but said, "yes, that is their day; during the week they have to work for their father."

Some seem to think that it is worse to work in the afternoon of a Sunday or holiday than in the morning; but others have the opposite view. Holidays especially sacred on which work is forbidden are Epiphany (January 6), Esquipulas (January 15), Thursday, Friday, and Saturday of Holy Week, Ascension Thursday, Corpus Cristi, and the day of the local patron, San Francisco (October 4). One Indian said it is very dangerous to work on Esquipulas (and indeed a boy who cut firewood on that day in 1941 injured his leg with the ax) but said it is all right in the afternoon. Although we witnessed Indians watering their gardens during the mornings of both Holy Thursday and Good Friday, I doubt if any of them would do other work those days. We were told on Epiphany that it is a holiday on which no hard work is permissible; but we saw people watering gardens, and one Indian weeding, and a Ladino had hired laborers to cut coffee. An Indian friend who was that day harvesting coffee for pay said, "Oh, we are only cutting coffee; that isn't hard work."

During the period of study, the basic rate of payment for an adult man in agricultural or any common labor was 10 pesos, the equivalent of 16⅔ cents. Payment for the 6-day week thus came to an even dollar; for one day, 16½ cents; for 2 days, 33 cents, and so on. Ladinos paid these rates without question, and Indians accepted them.[78] Normally an Indian would not work for less.[79] But some employers, to avoid labor shortages, paid more. Laborers were paid 20 cents a day on a bridge being built in 1940; two contractors building houses at the same time also paid 20 cents. When corn was high in 1937 Rosales wrote that laborers were talking about asking wages in proportion to the cost of corn (30 cents a day), but there is no indication that they obtained any such sum.

The corresponding wage for a woman hired in the fields was 8 or 10 cents; I have cases of both, but cannot explain the difference. A boy of 10 or 12 could usually be hired for 5 cents, and one of 14 or 15 for 10 cents.[80] Very frequently, however, Indians (and rarely Ladinos) hire labor for a smaller cash wage and include the day's food— three meals—as part of the payment. A man then earns from 10 to 13 cents in cash, a woman 4 or 5 cents, and a young boy 2 or 3 cents. In two cases Indians who paid 16⅔ without food told me they paid 10 cents with food. With one of them I calculated together the value of the food, and it came to just 7 cents (1 pound of corn, at 1½ cents, a half pound of meat, worth 3 cents, a half cent each of coffee and *panela*). When only lunch is served the laborer, the cash wage is of course higher. Since the Indians know the value of food,

---

[78] These rates prevailed in the Panajachel region. In Chichicastenango the day labor rate in 1935 was 8 pesos (or 13 cents) and in 1940 it had dropped to as low as 10 cents. In 1936 a plantation on the coast was offering 16 cents a day plus a ration of corn and beans, and it furnished grinders to men without wives to cook for them.

[79] It will be noted below that one Indian frequently worked in 1940–41 for 15 cents a day for Ladinos. He needed the work, and he was usually indebted to his employers.

[80] The little information on wages paid to women hired as full-time servants shows that food is the most important element, the cash wage ranging from $1 to $3 a month. One Indian girl when she quit work in a Ladino home complained that the food was poor and she was paid nothing at all.

the wage usually is little different whether it is paid all in money or part in food. However, some employers are known to feed their workers well and so either pay less in cash or have a better labor supply. Thus the biggest Indian employer pays only 8 cents a day and food, but he feeds the men well "because" (according to a man who frequently works for him) "he wants them to have strength for the hard work."

Although the local Indians are frequently paid with food, which appears to be a method preferred by the laborers, Indians from other towns are often refused work except for cash. Rosales writes (September 7, 1937) that "People have been coming from other towns like Santa Lucia Utatlán for a long time looking for work here. They want work with meals because food is what they are after. People here do not like to give it." Twice he writes that Sololatecos came looking for work, payment to be made partly in food, but it was refused because Sololatecos are notoriously big eaters. (Rosales adds that he has observed the same.) Probably no more than 300 of the 730 man-days of outsiders are paid with food.

Workers at the corn harvest usually earn more than usual in food. A fiesta spirit prevails, and not only is the work lightened with gaiety (an employer laughingly described the day's harvest so: "We had a good time working all day, shouting back and forth; one laborer stumbled and somersaulted twice down the hill with a bag of corn on his back!"), but the food is better than usual. Meat is frequently included, as well as beans, bread, and coffee. Or some employers (including the richest Indian and one other that I know of) serve ordinary food; but after the harvest serve *atole*, or send it to the homes of the harvesters. Even when laborers are paid entirely in cash, they are served *atole* of the new-harvested corn at noon. During one coffee harvest a neighbor family who had been working in the fields of the richest Indian brought home quantities of food and explained that this employer does not require that they eat it there.

The following is a description, by one of his laborers, of this richest Indian's treatment of his employees. This employer is not only wealthy, but the first man of the community politically; he tends to be an old-fashioned Indian, wearing the most conservative clothing and insisting that his sons do, too.

Miguel advances money to those he knows comply and they work it off when he needs help. When they do not comply, he just never gives them money again when they need it. (So I never let him down.) He warns the *mozos* when he advances the money that they must not disappoint him when he needs them. He alternates his *mozos*, calling some one week and others the next, giving them time to get their own work done. He calls them only when he has much work: otherwise only he and his sons do the work.

He gives plenty of food for lunch so that the *mozos* have strength to work and says it is so they will have strength to work. He tells them to eat slowly and enjoy their food.

He doesn't let them work fast because then it would be done poorly. His motto is: Do little and do it well. When they are picking coffee, he keeps telling the men to do it well and slowly and without breaking the branches. If one does break a branch, Miguel reprimands him a little and in a moment is again pleasant. Often he tells them funny things, so they are always happy working. He himself and his sons work along with the *mozos*—and he jokes and tells them old things that he knows.

His sons don't talk when he speaks, but laugh at his jokes; and when they talk he listens and laughs; when they finish he can start again. Sometimes the *mozos* talk too.

Miguel has the old way of talking—saying opposites; if a field is good, he says it is no good and he will lose money, etc.; if an animal is rapidly growing and fattening, he says it is not growing and he will lose the money invested in it. So also he tells the *mozos* that their work is very bad and he will never give them more money; so he talks to me, but always gives me more money. But if a *mozo* doesn't understand he becomes confused and doesn't come back. On the other hand when the work is bad, he compliments the *mozo* and tells him he will never lose him; but when the man asks for money Miguel says he has none.

The question of wages is complicated by the fact that piece-work arrangements are frequently made. Except for work in the milpa and occasionally the making of *tablones* Indians pay exclusively by the day; but Ladinos often make other arrangements with Indian laborers. The unit of work, called the *tarea*, differs with different jobs. A *tarea* of firewood is a pile 2 *varas* high and 2 *varas* wide (the pieces of firewood are from a half *vara* to a *vara* in length—but this is immaterial because the labor is the same); a *tarea* of stones is a cone with its base 2 *varas* in diameter and its height the same. In the milpa—and in general with the hoe and pickax—the *tarea* is a *cuerda*, 32 *varas* square. The making of a *tablón* 32×3 *varas* is a *tarea*. In coffee picking, a *tarea* is 105 pounds of berries, and there are baskets holding that much and also half that much, so that the baskets themselves are units. In the corn harvest 3 bagfuls picked and carried home is the *tarea*.

Units for miscellaneous work are agreed upon by employer and employee. For example, a price is arranged for the felling and cutting of a certain tree; in one case in my notes an arrangement was made to haul 100 stones by canoe for 30 cents.

The *tarea* is the amount of work that a man is expected to do in a day (except in such work as gathering stones and cutting firewood where a number of *tareas* make a day's work); and when a man is hired by the day he is expected to do that amount just as, when he is hired by the *tarea*, he expects to do his *tarea* in a day. Actually, however, a worker by the day—unless supervised—does not always do his *tarea*—and that, doubtless, is why Ladinos more frequently pay by the piece. Rosales notes that an Indian hired by the day made 10 trips with firewood in each of 2 days; on the third day he was paid 1 cent a trip and by 4 p. m. had already made 15. Another time he hired Indians for the corn harvest; they did only two bags apiece the first day; the next morning he accompanied them and the four harvesters filled and transported six bags; then in the afternoon, unsupervised, they managed only four. Again he notes that he hired an Indian to fell a tree and cut it up; the pay was for the whole job, so the man started at 5 a. m. by the light of the moon and by 8 a. m. had felled and stripped the tree. An Indian who hauled stones at first worked by the day (20 cents) and then by the *tarea*, by which arrangement he earned 30 cents a day.

Ladinos almost always pay for coffee picking by the *tarea*, paying 10 cents for a full basket. One Indian woman complained that she had to fill a 5-cent basket very full; she said she was also paid 8 cents for a coffee sack full. The Indians sometimes bring the whole family, the women and children stripping the lower branches, the men the higher ones. The children, helping to fill the baskets, hence earn money without any special wage agreement.

There is one other complexity in the wage system: laborers frequently work for less than normal wages because either they accept favors of an employer (such as living on his land) and are under obligations and lose part of their bargaining power, or they receive money in advance for future work. In time of need the Indian asks for, and receives, some money; no interest is involved, but it is understood that he will work off the debt when the other needs him. That time

comes, and the employer asks him to work. The Indian, conscious of the favor done him, is not apt to be very demanding. Nevertheless, of course, he does not work for less than the lower figure in the pay range. The employer is usually interested more in getting labor when he needs it than in saving a few pennies in wages.

Almost all labor is done on some kind of cash basis. There are three kinds of communal labor which are unpaid. First, there is the time of the political and religious officials during their periodic years of service. The only officials whose duties entail occasional manual labor, such as sweeping and running errands, are the *alguaciles*, who are young unmarried men. Two shifts of them work alternate fortnights; while on duty they can earn money occasionally, for private persons may ask to have them run errands for pay. Second, there are cooperative enterprises such as the annual cleaning of the irrigation ditches; each Indian family concerned is expected to furnish a man, and the Ladinos are supposed to hire men for the purpose. Occasionally there are special tasks that fall into this category; the river on a rampage may require sudden action, and the people are called to help; or people may be asked to contribute labor as well as money to repair the church. The religious officials also customarily ask Indians to carry the *santos* in procession, and when the wives of the officials prepare food for a fiesta they ask other women to help. In the last instance helpers are given food in return for their services.

The third kind of communal labor is road work. In accordance with Federal law, every man between the ages 18 and 60 is required to work on the highway 1 week (6 days) every 6 months without pay. If he wishes, however, he may pay $1 instead of working a week. Since the rate of $1 for 6 days happens to coincide, in Panajachel, with the usual labor rate, the working class of Indians usually work and those who do not customarily work for others usually pay instead.

Within a family (the group with a common kitchen, that is) work is communally done. The land is worked in common and one member of the family does not pay another to work, say, on a piece he happens to be especially interested in. But such a communal attitude stops with the simple family, the economic household. When a father and son, or siblings, live separately, they may work together, but the one whose land is being worked will invariably (according to all informants, observations, and cases) pay the other at prevailing cash rates. The impoverished son of a wealthy man, for example, frequently works as a farm hand for his father as if they were not related. Another example is that of a woman who came to plant onions for her brother at 10 cents a day. However, I do not know if relations—other things being equal—work for each other more or less than do nonrelatives.

Only one case of work exchange not on a cash basis came to my attention. A young Indian told me that he sometimes works for either of two friends of his, and instead of being paid for his day they work for him the following day. He told me he had never heard of other people doing this in Panajachel although he volunteered that in neighboring Santa Catarina "everybody does it both in the milpa and in house building." It may be added that this informant (the poor young man of the next paragraphs) also works for cash for the same friends with whom he exchanges labor.

The following account of work sequences of the above Indian is illustrative of the variety of work arrangements and wage differences in Panajachel. Felipe in April 1940, had 7 tablones (4 with pole beans and 3 with pepinos but later planted in corn) of his own; in addition his young sister had a miniature tablón which she planted and cared for. He rented from Ladino M. G. at 50 cents each 8 tablones (2 with pole beans, 4 with garlic, 2 with onions; when these crops were harvested the rental term was over), working off the $4 rental by cleaning 24 cuerdas of coffee land at 10 pesos each (240 pesos equal $4). He rented from Ladino A. R. for $3, 4 tablones, with pepinos; when they were harvested he did not re-rent the land. He rented 3 cuerdas (0.54 acre) of hill corn from Ladino J. F. A. for which he had to grow an equal amount for the owner. Finally, he had on pawn another 0.54 acre of hill corn in Santa Catarina.

Until March 15, 1940, he was an alguacil in the town hall. During his alternate fortnights on duty he averaged about 10 cents a week carrying messages, and could work in his fields about 3 hours each morning. In his fortnights off duty he worked for Ladinos M. G. and J. F. A. at 15 cents a day; but he could not work the first Monday of his free fortnight. Therefore, from the first of the year to March 15 he worked only about 22 days for pay.

From March 16 through 19 he was in jail, together with his fellow ex-alguaciles, because a pickax that had been in their charge was missing. On the 20th (Wednesday of Holy Week) all he did was make a load of firewood, and the rest of the week—holiday, of course—he did only a little work in his own fields.

Then for 2 weeks (12 days) he worked on the bridge-construction job at 20 cents a day. This brought him to April 6. He quit that job to work in his own fields for 2 weeks, and they refused to hire him again at the bridge. For the next 2 weeks—until May 4—he therefore worked for J. F. A. at 15 cents a day, 6 days a week. During the whole of the following week he prepared and planted his milpa.

Then he began to work again for J. F. A., cultivating his milpa. He did 6 tareas of this, at 15 cents each; but partly because of bad weather and partly because he also did some of his own work, the job actually took 12 days, until May 25. During the next 2 weeks he cultivated his own cornfield and made tablones. But on Tuesday of the first week he went to Sololá to sell, and on Friday of the second week to San Lucas.

Then, on June 10 he began to work off a $1 debt owed to Indian L. S. He worked 20 days (to and including July 2) for 8 cents a day, plus food. Thus he earned $1.60, but he bought from his employer one-half pound of onion seed for $1.50, so when he stopped working he still owed 90 cents. Until Wednesday, July 17, he did his own work. That day, then, he went to sell his produce in Tecpán, and returned on Friday. Each of the following 2 weeks he followed the same program, doing his own work but spending from Wednesday to Friday on selling trips to Tecpán. He was back early on Fridays, but too tired to work.

On August 5 he began 2 weeks (12 days) of work for Indian E. S. at 8 cents a day, plus food. For the next 3 weeks he worked for Indian J. J.; paid 12 cents (without food) to make each tablón; it took him 18 days to make 20 of them. On the Monday following (September 9) he began 2 weeks of work for Ladino M. G. to pay for the rented land. Because of bad weather, in 9 days he did only 6 tareas of coffee-grove cleaning, at 16 cents a tarea. But when it rained he braided his garlic, and he did other chores at various times. The next week he spent his required second week working on the highway, then had 2 days in his own fields (planting vegetables) before the titular fiesta began on October 2. All he did then until Monday, the 7th, was water his gardens, cut firewood, and so on. That day he went with Indian L. S. to spend 2 weeks (but they returned week ends) in Cerro de Oro, across the lake, to cultivate 2.67 acres of corn that L. S. had there. It was a 12-day job because the land is very stony. He was given 8 cents a day, plus food; but because of his debt, he received in cash only 6 cents a day. Then for 3 days he worked in his own milpa and in the following 6 workdays he made 7 *tablones* for Ladino M. G. (at the rate of 12 cents a *tablón*) in part payment of the rented *tablones*. [81]

Then, All Saints' Day holiday intervening, he celebrated on October 31 and November 1 and wound up in jail on November 2. Released on the 4th, he weeded his own vegetables on what remained of November 4, and on the 5th and 6th. The rest of that week he helped thatch Ladino J. F. A.'s house, and earned 15 cents cash each of 3 days. On the 11th, 12th, and 13th he earned 70 cents carting stones in a canoe. The next day he worked in the garden of his Indian friend L. S., and 2 days later the favor was returned; in the intervening day he did his own work. Meanwhile he began to pick coffee for Ladino J. F. A. and in 2 weeks picked 30 5-cent baskets. During these same weeks, however, he earned $1.16 making *tablones* for an Indian (J. J.) who discounted 70 cents still owed him.

Not until November 30 did he get back to his own work, and even then he worked with me in the morning; but not until December 3 did he finish picking J. F. A.'s coffee. Most of the next 3 weeks he spent making his own *tablones*, etc., and harvesting his milpa (on December 16–17 with the help of three laborers). The last 12 work-days of the year he spent making *tablones* for Indian V. L. who paid him 6 cents a day plus food.

Most of the first 3 weeks of 1941 he spent picking coffee for Ladino M. G. who paid him either 13 cents or 15 cents per hundredweight—I never did get this straight. In each week there was a 1-day holiday (January 1, 6, and 15) but he worked

right through, except that on the 6th he stopped early. He collected 1,200 pounds of coffee in this period, and received all but 50 cents, which was applied on a dollar debt, in cash.

The week of the 20th he devoted to his own fields, harvesting corn the first days and planting onions the last. Then during the last week of January and the first two of February he worked around the house of Ladino M. G. cutting trees for house posts, making and combing *tablones* and planting nursery, cutting firewood, carrying stones and adobes, fencing, helping to make a duck pond, etc. On the days he worked he earned 15 cents a day, but of the *tablones* he made, three were for himself and another three for his employer in lieu of rent. In between times he also did some work of his own, spending 3 or 4 days making a hard *tablón*. He also took a day off cutting firewood for Ladino J. F. A.

Then he obtained steady work on the construction of a large house, and he continued to work there at 20 cents a day to the time I took this information, on April 8th.

During these weeks, when I spoke with the informant almost every evening, I could obtain a good idea of how much of his own work he could do early mornings and late afternoons. Sunday mornings he had to report for military training, but before that he almost always "made" a load of firewood. Twice he watered his gardens instead, and once he prepared firewood in the morning and watered in the afternoon. Usually, however, he did not work Sunday afternoons. During each week he watered his gardens once or twice before going to work and sometimes in the midweek he prepared firewood in the afternoon.

FREEDOM OF LABOR

Chester Lloyd Jones concludes a discussion of the labor history of Guatemala, in which he shows that from early Colonial days there was virtual labor slavery in one form or other, with the statement that the more the system changes, the more it is the same thing (Jones, 1940, p. 164). He describes how the abolition of the *mandamientos* was followed by a system of debt peonage, which kept the highland Indians still bound to lowland plantations, and argues that the 1935 substitution of antivagrancy legislation for debt peonage had the same effect.

---

[81] Up to this point I had to depend upon the memory of the informant and there were many mix-ups; doubtless there are inaccuracies enough in the account I present, but they give an idea of how this man's time is spent. After this point I was in contact with him, and my own diary checks his statements. I took his statement independently, and I found that he tends to have a poor memory for sequences; but I was able to straighten out most matters.

For the whole of Guatemala, I am not prepared to say more than that Jones was probably unduly pessimistic; but from the point of view of the Indians of Panajachel alone, it is evident that he was mistaken and that (1) the *mandamientos* worked far more hardship than did the subsequent system of debt peonage, and (2) labor became in effect quite free in Panajachel after the abolition of debt peonage.

The following is a brief description of the system of *mandamientos* from the Panajachel point of view.

The system existed during the administration of President Manuel Estrada Cabrera, and with greater force a few years before World War I and the earthquakes of 1918. After these events, the *mandamientos* gradually disappeared and, with the fall of Cabrera, ended. Under the *mandamientos*, the plantation owners of the coast, especially those who were beginning or extending operations, hired Ladino or foreign contractors to find for them laborers in their own or other towns. The contractor was paid a specified sum for each laborer he was able to line up. The contractors then asked the President of the Republic for an order to obtain laborers from one or more Indian villages. This order was given the Jefe Político of the Department, and then passed on to the *alcaldes* of the towns involved. The contractor then obtained a large sum of money from his employer, and this money was left at the local *juzgado* for advance payment, at a very low rate, to the Indians, who would then be forced at a later date to work 20 or 30 days on the plantation. The local authorities then assigned the Indians to the task.

The Indians had to comply whether they had work or not; if they objected, they were bound and taken under guard to the plantation. Sometimes a man would not yet have returned from one *mandamiento*, and at home there would already be an order for him to go back to a plantation. Upon his homecoming, he would then have to leave the following day while his family suffered along on the reduced wage he was earning. It was even worse when the man had a civil or religious office and still had to comply with his obligations. The laborers who came to the plantations on *mandamientos* were given the worst jobs, and that is one reason why some Indians decided to sell their lands in Panajachel and go to the plantations with their families to live as *colonos*.

In the autobiography of a middle-aged Indian (taken in 1941) there is a description of how the system worked out in his family.

When I was about 4 years old, my father was sent to the coast on a *mandamiento*. I remember that the *alcalde* left money on the ground in the patio and told him he had to do it. My parents were very angry. . . . The next day my father went to San Andrés to bring corn for the journey, and the following day mother began to make *totoposte*, I recall how she ground the corn while father went to make a load of firewood. The making of the *totoposte* took 3 or 4 days. . . . In about 10 days, the *alcalde* returned to tell father that in a few days he would start with the others. Then father went to buy corn to make . . . tortillas and large tamales for the road. And early one morning he went to Tzanjuyú (where he met the others) to take the launch for Atitlán to begin his journey. Mother cried, because the money that had been left was not enough for all the corn and things—and where would the money come from for the expenses at home? She also worried that father might get sick on the coast. . .

I do not remember how long father was gone that time (but a good worker usually could return in about 3 weeks). I do recall that he returned rather soon, and was very happy that he had come so quickly. . . . Mother had ready some cash from the sale of father's crops that she had harvested, and she sent (my brother) José to buy him a drink. The next day father picked up his work where he had left off. Of course he had brought no money, having simply worked off that which had been advanced.

Every few weeks he would have to go. I remember that at first he was sent, and paid, for 15 or 20 *tareas* at a time; but during the time I was in school, they began to demand 30 or 35 *tareas*. Then father took José with him; but José was too small to help much, and they were often gone a month or so at a time. Then nobody was left at home to help mother, and little work was done. Mother watered the gardens herself, and weeded and transplanted when necessary: sometimes I did a little before school in the morning, or stayed out of school for a day. . . . Then when father returned he worked hard to prepare many *tablones* so that if he should be called away soon again, there would be something for mother to plant.

This went on for the rest of father's life. Toward the end, after José died, I used to go with father; and then when he died, I had to go, alone. . . .

When the *mandamientos* ended, the authorities could no longer force an Indian to go to work outside, unless he owed a debt. The abuses of the ensuing system of debt peonage are very well known.

Many Indians were virtually bound to plantations by a system of advance payments on contracts to work that were practically impossible ever to liquidate. The plantation-owners paid to so-called *habilitadores* commissions for supplying Indian labor from the highlands. These men, usually Ladinos or foreigners, advanced money to Indians on condition that they work off the debt on their employers' plantations. Many Indians came to live permanently on the plantations, and others worked off their debts seasonally. Each laborer had a little book in which the employer helped him to keep accounts. The Indians, almost always illiterate, were generally suspicious that they were being cheated, but there was little they could do.

The following account of how the system worked from the peon's point of view, appears in Rosales' diary just after the system was abolished. Six strangers, who turned out to be Antoñeros, slept in the Rosales portico the night of May 18, 1936. One of them asked Rosales to read him the balance of debt in his little book. When told it was 1,633 pesos ($27.22), he said that his employer was a thief, and recounted his story:

His father, dead 15 years (on the plantation) had once been well-off in his village, but he gave up his properties to support his family while he went to do *mandamientos*; he finally took permanent employment on a plantation which was then better than living in his village. His family, together with others from San Andrés, Panajachel, Sololá, and Chichicastenango thus took root in the plantation. When he died, the contracted debt was on the shoulders of his sons, and the one who was telling the story thought *his* sons too would have to carry the debt when he died. But "how happy we were when we learned," he continued, "that the President actually had ordered our freedom, and that we would no longer have to pay off these old, old debts!" He went on to say that for every 10 pesos received every month or so, 30 or more were entered in the account book, and they had to work even on Sundays, the debt never decreasing, only rising more and more. When the peons realized this injustice, they resolved not to take any more money. Afterward they learned that the manager received money for them biweekly from the owner, which he had pocketed and (as Rosales could see) not credited to the laborers. Now when the peons heard of the new law, they met with the owner; he told them that henceforth they owed nothing, and should continue to work. A committee of 10 of the laborers instead went to the Jefe Politico to verify the law and to see if the patron could not be made to conceal rather than burn the books, for none of them wanted to stay on the finca; they wished either to find new employers or to go home.[82]

On May 7, 1934, the system of debt peonage was abolished by National legislation.[83] Effec-

tive in 2 years, all such debts still outstanding were to be canceled and it would henceforth be illegal to advance a laborer more money than sufficient for his journey to the plantation. Since such a law might by itself be expected to make difficult a regular labor supply, it was immediately supplemented with the "Law of Vagrancy,"[84] which obliged any person not having a trade or profession or not possessing a certain amount of cultivated land to seek employment for 100 or 150 days of the year, depending upon the amount of land owned. This law was also to take effect in 2 years. As interpreted by the Secretary of Agriculture in June of 1937[85] (a year after the law of vagrancy went into effect), the land requirements were set up as follows:

No laborer shall be considered a vagrant, nor be obliged to seek employment with another if he personally cultivates at least three *manzanas* of coffee, sugar cane or tobacco, or three *manzanas* of maize in the warm country or four in the cold country, or four *manzanas* of wheat, potatoes, garden-stuffs, or any other crop in whatever zone.

The laborers who cultivate less than this, but not less than ten *cuerdas* of twenty *brazadas*, are obliged to do 100 man-days of work on outside plantations.

And the laborers that have no crops of their own must, in order not to be considered vagrants, do 150 man-days of labor annually in outside plantations.

Three *manzanas* are equal to about 5.67 acres, and four *manzanas* to about 7.56 acres. Ten *cuerdas* of 20 *brazadas* (40 *varas*) are equal to about 2.78 acres. Since the Indians of Panajachel rarely possess such extensions of cultivable land, under the law virtually all of them are obliged to work for outsiders at least 100 days of the year. But since an acre of Panajachel delta land, especially if in truck, requires all of the time at a man's disposal and also earns him a tidy living on local standards, a man who owns even 1 acre can hardly be considered a vagrant.

To facilitate enforcement, the Vagrancy Law was implemented by a law[86] requiring every laborer to purchase (for 2 cents) a *libreto* (little book) in which his employer could note the number of days of labor done. The local authorities were to enforce the law through the evidence of the little books. The law took effect in May of 1936, and the books were available during the next months. When the Indians worked for Ladinos the employers entered their days; when

---

[82] A few days before, Rosales had heard two Indians discussing the freeing of the laborers on the plantations. One said that the unfortunate owners of the *fincas* are losing their money; the other replied, "No; it is right that a poor workman should be freed after working 20 years only so that his employers might sit smoking and eating well at the expense of the sweat of their workmen."

[83] *Decreto Legislativo* No. 1995. I am unable to reconcile this fact with the following note, dated October 7, 1936, in Rosales' diary: "A representative of the plantation told me that he is looking for a certain Indian here to go to the plantation to work in accordance with an agreement made in the town hall before the fiesta (of October 4) when he advanced money on 30 *tareas* that the Indian promised to work off. The man said he is authorized to sign up Indians of Panajachel, San Antonio, San Jorge, San Andrés, Concepción, and Sololá (not Santa Catarina "because Catarinecos are poor workers and are dishonest.") He will stay in the Highlands two months to recruit labor . . . . He says he gets a small salary plus a few cents per man that he hires."

[84] *Decreto Legislativo* No. 1996, May 8, 1934.

[85] *El Imparcial*, Guatemala, June 16, 1937, p. 1.

[86] *Acuerdo* of September 24, 1935.

they worked for each other, the Intendente did so. In May of 1937 the Intendente examined the books. There were immediate difficulties: some of the Indians had no books at all; those who had begun to use them in June or July learned that they should have begun on May 15; and in general many of the Indians had not worked for others the required number of days.

The Indians sought to settle matters first with the local Intendente who however wished (as they understood him) to enforce the law literally, even suggesting that only work for Ladinos could be counted. Threatened with jail, the Indians then organized a committee to call upon the Jefe Politico in Sololá. Although this official promised them satisfaction, the Indians were left without a decision. Since they were subject to arrest for not having a properly certified booklet in their possession, they were impatient and resolved to call upon the President Ubico. After a series of meetings of the *Principales* called by the Indian officials a commission was appointed and

it did see the President. For this visit, the Indians spent a day together preparing a document designed to show how on their small parcels of land local Indians were both kept busy and made their living. This document (to prepare which Rosales acted as secretary) is translated as Appendix 1; it serves both as a basis for and a summary of discussion of how the Indians use their time. The President gave to his callers from Panajachel an order to the local officials, who eventually agreed to accept a slightly smaller land-unit and to admit to their booklets labor of Indians done for one another.

By 1941 it had worked out that the Indians who had enough land to keep themselves busy were not required to work for others; and those who lacked sufficient land (and in any case would have to seek work) could work for Ladinos or other Indians as they wished and when they pleased. Except for the bookkeeping—since most of the Indians were required by law to have certified the labor they did for others—labor was now essentially free.

THE BUSINESS OF AGRICULTURE

AGRICULTURE

As will be seen, the Indians do not quite measure every economic activity by its money value. But they come close. On this measure, the value of land and of effort devoted to agriculture are clearly demonstrable. Domestic animals, it will be seen, are unimportant in Panajachel because they are uneconomical. The same may be said of some crops. In this discussion it is taken for granted that since the community is near a subsistence level, activities which take more time are preferred to those which take less time and bring correspondingly less return; and that time not otherwise usable is economically spent even when the return is small.

THE MILPA

Table 26 summarizes the money returned by an acre of cornfield crops in 1936. The labor required varies not only between hill and delta, but (in hill fields) between new land and land previously planted; in small degree with the distance from the farmer's home, the type of soil, the weather, and the protection afforded from marauding birds and animals; and (slightly) with different practices of individual farmers and the quality of the work they demand. Yet it is relatively uniform and knowledge of it is shared very generally in the community. The labor is reckoned in terms of *tareas*, each the unit of work that an able-bodied worker is expected to do in 1 work day,

TABLE 26.—*Cost and gross and net return per acre of milpa, 1936*

Item	Per acre	
	Hill land	Delta land
Cost of crop:		
Labor [1]	[2] $8.33	$6.00
Seed	.18	.10
Ceremonial	.08	.02
Total	8.59	6.12
Value of harvest:		
Corn	14.00	24.50
Beans	1.20	
Chilacayotes	1.50	
Ayotes	1.50	
Total	18.20	24.50
Net return	9.61	18.38

[1] In this and subsequent tables, the cost of labor is calculated at 16⅔ cents per man-day.
[2] Assuming that 90 percent grew on old land in 1936.

and close enough to enable us to translate it as 1 man-day.

Table 27 sums up the number of man-days of work that are required, on the average, for three types of fields.[87] Estimating that 9 out of 10 acres of hill land planted are old land—data directly bearing on the question were not obtained—it may be concluded that the average number of man-days required for an acre of hill milpa is about 50, as compared with the 36 required to grow an acre in the delta. The cost of this labor may be definitely fixed at 16⅔ cents a man-day, whether the farmer does his own work or whether he hires hands. Since in Panajachel a man can virtually always obtain work himself at the same rate of pay at which he hires labor, a farmer's time has a definite cash value. The cost given in table 26 glosses over a few irregularities: for example, the rich Indian who, in exchange for 1 man-day of labor, allows his regular helpers to plant a crop of beans on a *cuerda* (0.178 acre) of his delta land;[88] or the few Indians and Ladinos

TABLE 27.—*Labor required to grow 10 cuerdas of milpa*

Work process	Number of man-days		
	New land	Old land	Delta land
Cutting trees, etc. (*rosar*)	20		
Making fire lanes	2		
Burning fallen trees, etc	2		
Stubbling (*rastrojear*)		10	
Cleaning (*chaporrar*)	10	10	10
Planting	5	5	5
Replanting where needed	1	1	1
First cleaning (and hilling)	20	20	20
Second cleaning (and hilling)	20	20	20
Harvesting	5	5	5
Carrying home (if far)	10	10	1
Stacking corn in granary	3	3	3
Threshing beans	3	3	
Total per 10 *cuerdas*	101	87	65
(Total per acre)	(57)	(49)	(36)

who allow their regular laborers the use of land, rent-free, as a matter of good will and to assure a regular labor supply. To such the cost of labor is certainly a little higher than the stipulated day wage.

Compared with the cost of labor, other agricultural production costs are minor and on the whole unimportant. Most of the cost of seed, fertilizer leaves, poles, etc., really represent labor costs, and from the point of view of the community as a whole should be treated only as labor. However, for a comparison of the costs of various crops it is necessary in some cases to add certain items to the cost of the labor. In this case, to the cost of labor must be added the value of the seed used and also certain ceremonial expenses in connection with the harvest. The latter consist of candles and incense, frequently burned in the field during or after the harvest, and food, given or sent to the laborers who help to harvest. Since the amount of such gifts varies greatly, and since families doing their own work are free of the expense, the amounts mentioned are necessarily rough approximations. The average expense for these items is smaller in delta cornfields because, since they are small, it is rarely incurred.

Depending upon the distance between plants, hence partly on the quality and type of the soil, and upon weather conditions which largely determine how much replanting must be done, the amount of seed sown in the cornfield probably ranges between 5 and 10 pounds per acre. The average cost of the corn seed therefore is about 10 cents an acre.[89] Where beans are also grown, the cost (of 3 pounds per acre) comes to some 5 cents. The value of squash seed, for from 10 to 25 plants per acre, must average about 3 cents an acre. In the estimate of the value of the produce in table 26, some items of value are not taken into consideration. The green leaves removed from the plant, the cornstalks, the dried corn plant, and the cornhusks all have important uses, and are occasionally sold. I do not know how much income they produced in 1936.

Since costs remain virtually stationary from year to year, it is apparent that the yield and the price determine the profit or loss.[90] In 1936, with

---

[87] This and similar tables (following) are based on information of at least three careful informants and on the Report prepared for the President (Appendix 1). Since the Indians were interested in showing how much work is required, one might expect that they overestimated. Such is not the case, however, for on checking the figures with others I obtained from several Indians where the purpose was to figure out the profits from agriculture, I find that there is general agreement, and only a few cases in which the "official" figures are higher than those I obtained. The figures of the tables represent what a "good worker" does, and what a paid laborer is expected to do. There are, of course, variations in practice due both to efficiency and to differential soils, etc.; but they do not appear to be great. The totals do not include time spent in guarding the milpa (usually done by children), in making traps, etc., and in visiting the fields to see that all goes well.

A man-day in these tables is defined as the work done by a full-grown man in 1 working day of about 9 hours; 10 man-days of labor may be the labor of 1 man for 10 days or of 10 men for 1 day.

[88] Nobody rents bean land for cash, so that it is difficult to calculate the value of this "favor" to the workers. Since beans are not profitably grown on irrigated land, and they also probably return something to the soil, the owner's labor costs may not actually rise by this arrangement.

[89] Commodity prices are discussed below, and summarized in Appendix 2.

[90] In a wide economic sphere, of course, yield and price tend to be inversely proportional; but in a community like Panajachel the relationship is not as close, and it is possible (although not usual) for a poor local yield to coincide with a low price in the country as a whole, hence in Panajachel.

corn at 70 cents a bushel in Panajachel, any hill cornfield that yielded as little as 12 bushels of corn, and a few beans and squash, paid its cost. In the delta, only 9 bushels per acre were needed. Data on yields make it clear that from the point of view of the individual farmer, and of the community as a whole, milpa was in 1936—and is in general—a paying matter. This does not take into account the value of the land, however. If hill land is rented at the usual rate of $1.41 the total cost comes to just $10, and a yield of 14 bushels of corn is needed to break even. This is a safe chance. If the contract calls for payment of half the crop (of which there were no cases in 1936) the share cropper should still do a little better than break even. If it requires the digging of holes for the planting of coffee, the farmer must harvest some 18 bushels of corn to break even; and this becomes doubtful. In 1937 some Indians contracted (and others refused) to plant coffee in the cornfield in exchange for the use of the field for milpa for the 2 or 3 years while the bushes were small. The value of the labor paid for rent under such an arrangement comes to about $9.37. If the farmer can plant corn for but 2 years, he again needs to harvest about 18 bushels a year, but if he can plant for 3 years, he need harvest but 16 or 17 bushels to break even. Such deals are not very promising. In the case of rental of delta cornfield for half the crop, the cost of labor rises to $9.18. This is not serious, for the share cropper still breaks even if he harvests 13 bushels—virtually a certainty in the delta. Thus, even when rent must be paid, it usually pays to grow corn in Panajachel.

While there is no doubt that it pays to grow corn in the delta, it will be seen below that other crops pay even better, both from the point of view of furnishing the owner with more employment and from the point of view of net profit. It will become apparent that if all delta truck lands were occupied with corn from May to December, the Indian community as a whole would be forced into idleness and its income would be tremendously reduced. The total amount of land available is too small to permit the use as cornfield of a large proportion of delta land.

TABLÓN CROPS

It is necessarily difficult to calculate the profits from the complicated combinations of truck crops.

ONIONS

Onions are both the most complicated and the most important. Table 28 summarizes the costs involved, separately for seedlings, mature onions, and onion seed, all of which have their prices. The matter is complicated further because of differing practices. It is seen that the producer does best if he produces his own seed for planting, and next best if he at least grows his own seedlings for transplanting. This is because there is some net profit at each stage.

There is probably considerably more variation in time required in truck farming than in the milpa; yet even here the work is pretty well standardized. The figures given in the tables on truck farming, based largely on the report to the President (Appendix 1), with corrections, represent the normal time required with the error in no case more than 10 percent. In some cases, however, they do not give a good picture of the kind of labor involved. For example, the great labor required to transplant onions is very often done by women who can do the work as well as men but whose time is usually considered only half as valuable. Women also do considerable watering; and boys and girls help. The labor required for onions, which accounts for the bulk of the cost, is summarized in table 29. The total includes the entire process of growing a *cuerda* (or acre) of onions, from seed to seed, including making the

TABLE 28.—*Cost of growing onion products (per acre)*

Method	Item	Seedlings	Onions	Seeds
Grown from home-grown seed.	Labor	[1]$237.71	[2]$114.90	[3]$304.27
	Fertilizer and leaves	35.93	4.49	4.49
	Total	273.64	119.39	308.76
Grown from bought seed (but onions and seed from home-grown seedlings).	Labor	[4]158.03	[5]108.69	[6]298.06
	Seed	112.50	14.06	14.06
	Fertilizer and leaves	35.20	4.40	4.40
	Total	305.73	127.15	316.52
Grown from bought seedlings.	Labor	--------	[7]90.93	[8]293.25
	Seedlings	--------	45.00	45.00
	Total	--------	135.93	338.25

[1] Item 1, plus 8 times item 2 of table 29, plus 1/6 of total of table 30, times 16⅔ cents.
[2] Total of table 29, leaving out item 4, plus 1/48 of total of table 30, times 16⅔ cents.
[3] Total of table 30, plus 1/48 of that total, times 16⅔ cents.
[4] Item 1 plus 8 times item 2 (except last part) of table 29, times 16⅔ cents.
[5] Total of table 29 leaving out item 4, times 16⅔ cents.
[6] Total of table 30 times 16⅔ cents.
[7] Total of items 1, 3, and the last part of item 2 of table 29, times 16⅔ cents.
[8] Total of items 1, 3, and the last part of item 2 of table 29, plus total of table 30 minus first item times 16⅔ cents.

TABLE 29.—*Labor required to grow onions from seed*

Item	Process	Man-days Per cuerda	Per acre
1	Making beds. (On land in use, 16 per *cuerda*: on new land, 3 days additional for scraping and soaking. Assuming throughout that ⅓ of all garden beds are made on new land)____	17	96
2	Nursery for ⅛ of area (enough for item 3):		
	Fertilizing____	2	
	Sowing and covering seed____	2	
	First weeding (cleaning)____	4	
	Second weeding (cleaning)____	4	
	Watering: daily for 45 days, every 3 days for 15 days. 50 times at ⅛ day each. (Assuming ⅔ grows in dry months)____	7	
	Harvesting and preparing seedlings____	¹ 4	
	Total____	23	129
3	Growing onions from seedlings:		
	Smoothing soil and transplanting____	16	
	First weeding (cleaning)____	16	
	Second weeding (cleaning)____	16	
	Watering: Twice weekly for 4 months; 34 times at ½ day each. (Assuming ⅔ grows in dry months)____	12	
	Harvesting and bunching onions____	16	
	Total____	76	427
4	Growing from onions enough seed for item 2 (¼₈ of total of table 30 omitting first item)___	5	28
	Total____	121	680

¹ 22.5 per acre.

garden beds, the necessary nursery bed, and the preparation of sufficient seed for the nursery needed for the final crop of onions. This does not mean that any Indian tries to come out even with his seeds, seedlings, and onions. Since onions are bought and sold at all stages, it makes no difference.

Besides the labor (and tool depreciation) the only costs entering into the onion-growing complex are for fertilizer and for leaves, frequently purchased from Ladinos. About 1,200 pounds of coffee-leaf fertilizer are normally used in a *cuerda*, or 6,740 pounds per acre, worth $3.40. The six loads of large leaves used to cover the planted seed in a nursery bed cost at the rate of

TABLE 30.—*Labor required in growing onion seed*

Work process	Man-days Per tablón	Per cuerda	Per acre
Work that has gone into growing the mature onions____	12.7	102	574
Weeding, fertilizing the bed to go to seed____	2.0	16	90
Fencing (including gathering materials)_	1.5	12	67
Flooding when seed comes____	.5	4	22
Periodic weeding and watering (¼ day twice a week, 5 months)____	11.0	88	495
Cutting and hanging for drying____	2.0	16	90
Cleaning, weighing, packaging seed____	10.0	80	450
Total____	39.7	318	1,788

about $1 an acre. Cornstalks used for fencing are gathered, not purchased; the value of the time involved is too small to count.

The cash value of onions in Panajachel varies according to whether they are sold by the *tablón*, the buyer harvesting and preparing, or by the thousand or hundred, the producer preparing them for market. About 10 percent of the onions produced by resident Indians (chiefly Jorgeños) are regularly sold by the *tablón*. Since the difference in price reflects the cost of labor in harvesting and is thus a difference in cost-of-production, it may for the time being be disregarded. Concern about the proportion of onions produced in different seasons, when the prices are different, likewise does not seem necessary; for since the season of plentitude is the season of low prices, and vice versa, the average is naturally weighted. Using as a basis the 1936 "normal" prices in Panajachel (see Appendix 2), the cash value in Panajachel or Sololá of the yield of an average acre of onions may be simply calculated:

Large onions____	$103.12
Medium onions____	33.75
Small onions____	7.43
Total____	144.30

A comparison of these figures with those of table 28 shows the following net profits:

Onions grown from home-grown seed____	$24.91
Onions grown from bought seed, but home-grown seedlings____	17.15
Onions grown from bought seedlings____	8.37

Thus normally it pays fairly well to grow onions. If a particular field suffers extraordinary vicissitudes, obviously the farmer might lose rather than profit. On the other hand a farmer's profits may occasionally soar, if his yield is good when prices are high. Such circumstances must be rare; for if in one field in a terrain as small and homogeneous as the Panajachel delta yields very well or especially poorly, the others are apt to do the same, and market prices will be affected. (But the market price depends on yields in other areas as well.) It is obvious, however, that the care given the onion fields is of great importance; for that must definitely be reflected in the yield of a particular plot.

It is also apparent that it pays to rent land for

the growing of onions. The lowest cash-rental price is $22.50 an acre (table 14) on which the farmer gets three crops grown from home-grown seed, or four crops from bought seedlings. Even with higher rental prices, it usually pays better than appears at first sight, for it is the best land that is usually rented. On the other hand, it definitely does not pay to rent land for onions in exchange for half the crop. Assuming that onions exclusively are grown, from bought seed to the finished product, the renter would lose (in the value of his labor) about $55 every time he grew a crop! Yet there are well-authenticated cases of such agreements.

A standard *tablón* of onion nursery should yield from a pound of seed, about 48,000 seedlings for transplanting, enough for eight *tablones* of onions. The seedlings themselves are frequently sold, when the buyer gathers them for transplanting in his own fields. The virtually universal price is 25 cents a *vara* the width of the *tablón*. Since there are 32 *varas* to a *tablón*, the yield in money is $8 per *tablón*, or $360 per acre. Since (table 28) the cost of growing the seedlings is either $305.73 or $273.64 per acre, the apparent net profit is $54.27 or $86.36. (But nobody grows more than a small fraction of an acre.) An individual farmer may realize profits at this rate if the nursery produces as it should. However, the nurseries are said frequently to fail wholly and in part, and the farmer may lose instead of gain. Many Indians prefer to buy their seedlings rather than to grow them because of the risk involved. It is impossible to get reliable information on the point, but I judge that in the community as a whole something like 10 percent of expectable onion nursery production fails to materialize. Where bought seed is planted, a 10 percent loss is enough to wipe out the profit.

A standard *tablón* of onions allowed to go to seed yields as much as 10 pounds of onion seed. On the other hand sometimes the harvest is entirely lost. The average yield in seed, all things considered, seems to be about 6 pounds, or at the rate of 270 pounds per acre. The 1936 value of this yield, per acre, may be set at $675. A comparison of this figure with the costs shown in table 28 shows a net profit per acre of $366.24, $358.48, or $336.75, depending on from what the onions for the seed are grown. (But again, onion seed is produced in quantities much smaller than acres.)

An individual farmer who grows seedlings, onions, and onion seed exclusively for a year profits as follows from an acre of land, assuming that he grows the same proportions of each that are shown on chart 4:

Seedlings, 0.071 acre at $86.36 _____ $6. 13
Onions, 0.512 acre at $25.91 _____ 13. 27
Seed, 0.017 acre at $366.24 _____ 6. 23
                                                    _____
    Total, 1 acre _____ 25. 63

He can do better than this if he manages his agriculture so that less land is idle between crops, while awaiting seedlings to transplant, etc. But it is unlikely that anybody is so efficient that his profits rise to beyond about $40. Looking at it in this way, obviously a rental of from $22.50 to $33.75 for the acre (table 14) leaves a slim margin of net profit.

GARLIC

Garlic costs (table 31) are all charged to labor, since the seed is almost invariably home-grown. In a standard *tablón* are planted 2,400 sections of garlic taken from the best heads of the previous harvest, which average 10 sections each (the yield, in most general terms, being thus 10 for 1). A few of the best heads have only large sections, all suitable for planting; the next best, from which most seed comes, have five or six large sections (for planting) and four or five small ones (consumed or sold). So, roughly 10 percent must be added to the labor cost to supply the seed.

The work of braiding is usually done by the family during time that would otherwise not be economically used: evenings and during rainy spells, etc. Not counting the time needed for braiding, the cost comes to about $85.32 an acre.

All garlic that is planted normally produces. A good harvest, usually on "new" land rented from Ladinos, produces uniformly large heads; a medium harvest produces medium-sized heads; and a poor harvest yields very small heads. The large and medium sizes are bunched for sale, 60 heads to a bunch; and an acre yields 1,800 bunches. A poor harvest of small heads (sold by the measure sufficiently uniformly so that they may be treated as if they were sold by the pound) produces about 2,250 pounds per acre. Calculated from the normal 1936 prices (Appendix 2), the cash value of the yield in 1936 was, per acre:

Good harvest _____ $144.00
Medium harvest _____ 72.00
Poor harvest _____ 52.50

TABLE 31.—*Cost of growing garlic*

Work process	Man-days per *cuerda*	Cost	
		Per *cuerda*	Per acre
Valuable-time labor:			
Making beds (assuming that ¾ of garlic is planted on "new land"), average	18		
Preparing the seed	2		
Planting	8		
Weeding (cleaning)—(only once)	16		
Watering (twice a week, after first 3 weeks, for 6 months, ½ day each time)	23		
Harvesting and carrying	8		
Cleaning and arranging garlic for storage	8		
Additional for seed (10 percent of above)	8		
Subtotal	91	$15.17	$85.32
Braiding for market: 15 bunches per day (assuming yield is 320 bunches per cuerda)	21	3.50	19.68
Total	112	18.67	105.00

An individual would thus lose $32.82 per acre (not counting braiding time) if the harvest on his land is all poor. An acre is much more than any Indian plants, but the loss would still be considerable for a *cuerda*. If the harvest is all good, on the other hand, the profit would be tidy, even counting the time for braiding. From calculations made with two informants, I judge that in the community as a whole about 40 percent of the garlic beds deliver good harvests, 40 percent medium, and 20 percent, poor. Using these figures, the average net loss, counting the cost of braiding, is $8.10 per acre, or the average net profit, leaving out the cost of braiding, is $11.58. It must be concluded that Panajachel farmers can hardly expect to break even on garlic. This does not even count the value of the land. Paradoxically, however, it probably pays to rent land for garlic, because in general the Indians rent for the purpose only "new" land which yields large heads of garlic. Thus even if $33.75 is paid as rent for an acre (table 14) there will be a net profit for the garlic crop of $5.25 even counting the braiding cost; and of course the renter in addition has the use of the land for the months between garlic crops.

BEANS

Beans grown in irrigated fields (table 32) also have all costs charged to labor, the seed coming from the previous harvest. With 67½ pounds sowed to the acre, and the yield 800 pounds of shrub beans or 1,400 pounds of pole beans [91] the ratio is $\frac{1}{12}$ or $\frac{1}{21}$, respectively. This assumes of course that none of the beans are picked green. The value of the harvest, meanwhile, $12.80 and $22.40, respectively, leaves a net loss of $22.80 for shrub beans and $27.26 for pole.

Any way one does the bookkeeping the result is the same, and there can be no doubt that growing beans in the delta is a losing business. The reason it must be is that the price of beans is set on the basis of the rainy-season product grown with the milpa. The labor of making *tablones* and watering increases the cost tremendously without any corresponding increase in yield.

These figures and this discussion concern the growing of mature beans. However, an estimated 30 percent of Panajachel farmers sell part of their yield of shrub beans while still green, and virtually every one sells most of his vine-bean crop in that stage. No labor is saved by cutting the beans green since none would be required for the maturing beans; on the other hand the cost of cutting green beans is more than the cost of harvesting and threshing dry beans. If *all* delta beans should be harvested green, the total labor per *cuerda* would rise from 38 and 53 man-days to 40 and 56, worth $37.49 and $52.49 per acre, re-

TABLE 32.—*Man-days required and cost of growing beans in garden beds*

Work process	Man-day per *cuerda*	
	Shrub	Pole
Making beds (assuming that ⅓ of beans are planted in "new land")	17	17
Planting	2	2
Weeding (cleaning)—once	3	3
Watering (except first 3 weeks; then twice weekly for 3 and 4 months respectively, ½ day each)	10	14
Gathering poles (16 days every third year)		5
Setting up poles		8
Harvesting and carrying dry beans	1	1
Sunning and threshing dry beans	2	1
Labor that has gone into seed	3	2
Total	38	53

	Cost	
	Per *cuerda*	Per acre
Shrub beans	$6.33	$35.60
Pole	8.83	49.66

[91] A good informant helped me calculate for shrub beans a range of 675 to 900 pounds; in an independent case recorded the rate was 844 pounds. The range for pole beans was calculated at 1,125 to 1,665 pounds.

spectively. The green beans harvested would be worth an average of $33.75 for shrub beans and about $45 for vine beans, for some loss. This hypothetical case (no Panajachel farmer harvests all of his beans green) indicates that it does not pay to grow beans no matter how they are harvested.

VEGETABLES GROWN FROM IMPORTED SEED

Vegetables grown from imported seed (4 cents a package) are planted in such small quantities (on pieces of garden beds or at the edges) that calculations are best made per package of seed (table 33), which occupies some 3 square *varas* (1/32 of a *tablón* or 1/1500 of an acre). A package of beet seed yields 200 beets, transplanted to about 1/750 of an acre; cabbage seed, a hundred heads transplanted to 1/45 of an acre. The total costs come to about $93.60 per acre of cabbage; $135, beets; $165, carrots, radishes, and turnips.

The cabbage yield per package ranges from 100 large and 50 small heads to only 50 small heads; the normal yield is said to be about 50 large and 50 small heads. Beets are said always to yield well "because they are fertilized"—100 large and 100 small beets. The best carrot yield per package is said to be 100 large and 200 small, the usual 80 large and 200 small, and the worst 60 large and 200 small. Radishes are said to yield 100 per package. When good, they are all large, when poor all small. Turnips yield 200 per package—all large when the harvest is good and small when it is poor. It is apparent from table 33 that only cabbage gives promise of much profit—and correspondingly it is risky.

ROOT CROPS AND PEPPERS

The profits from truck farming in general are greater than indicated because sweet cassava, sweetpotatoes, and peppers are grown along the edges of the garden beds and although they take virtually no extra time to produce, they yield good income. In an acre grow about 540 cassava plants, 90 percent of which produce after 2 years. Each plant yields 2 to 3 pounds, so that the annual product is about 600 pounds per acre, worth $9. Simultaneously some 6,300 sweetpotato plants can grow on the acre. But since most farmers grow these only on two edges of each *tablón* (onions or garlic on the others), the average number per acre is probably only 4,500, 80 percent of which live to

TABLE 33.—*Returns from vegetable growing*

Item	Man-days of labor required			Cost (per package of seed)			Return (per package of seed)		
	Per *cuerda*	Per acre	Per package of seed	Labor	Seed and fertilizer	Total	Poor	Normal	Good
Cabbage	91	522	2.9	$0.48	$0.04	$0.52	$0.17	$0.92	$1.67
Beets	115	647	.85	.14	.05	.19		.18	
Carrots, radishes, and turnips	109	614	.43	.07	.04	.11	.09	.11	.12

yield from 1 to 2 pounds per year, for a total of 6,400 pounds, worth $64. The several varieties of peppers planted like sweet cassava are not a common crop. Perhaps the added income from peppers raises the total income from *tablón*-edge produce to $80 per acre per year. Probably a fourth of all Indian *tablón* acreage has these crops and yields this extra income. However, they take the place of about 1,500 onion plants, where they grow, and thus reduce the onion yield by 30 percent. It may be estimated that 20 percent less onions are grown in the community than the onion acreage would indicate.

PEPINOS

Pepinos are evidently a very profitable crop when grown on "new" land, for if the costs (table 34) are compared with the estimated yield (see p. 55), it will be seen that an acre at its best produced a net of $237.38. An average harvest, at 1936 prices, grossed $206.70 for a net of $114.48. The poorest yield, grossed $69.76, for a loss of $22.46. Evidently it paid well to rent good land.

COFFEE

To the cost of labor in growing coffee (table 35) might be added that of the fertilizer used when the coffee is transplanted from nursery to grove. Amortized over 30 years, it cannot add more than a few cents. If the owner has no husking machine, the rental (for husking a yield of 562 pounds) comes to 57 cents, the total cost thus rising to $9.86. Against this cost was an income of $33.72, for a net of $23.86 per acre.[92] To this should be added about $1.40, the value of the berry pulp, used as fertilizer. In fact, however, the poorer Indians profited less than this, for they sold their coffee as futures for $3 and $4 a hundred pounds.

[92] Calculated on the basis of yields discussed above (p. 56) and the $6-a-hundred price that Panajachel coffee brought in Panajachel in 1936.

The average obtained by Panajachel Indians was probably about $4.50. Even at the lowest figure,

TABLE 34.—*Cost of growing pepinos*

Items of cost	Man-days per *cuerda*	Cost per acre
Fertilizer		$0.55
Labor:		
Scraping the land	1	
Digging and making hills	4	
Making the holes for planting	2	
Carrying and placing fertilizer	2	
Planting	1	
Watering (twice weekly during 6 dry months, 1 day each time)	52	
Weeding (once monthly, ten times, 2 days each time)	20	
Cutting posts for fence	1	
Planting posts of fence	1	
Gathering vines for the fence	1	
Cutting and carrying cornstalks for fence	5	
Making the fence	3	
Harvesting (little by little), estimate	2	
Cutting shoots for planting	1	
Total	96	[1] 91.67
Fertilizer and labor		92.22

[1] Rarely the farmer buys (instead of using his own) branches of *pepino* bushes to plant. The additional cost (at 10 cents per *cuerda*) would be 56 cents for the acre.

TABLE 35.—*Cost of an acre of coffee*

Items of cost	Man-days per *cuerda*	Cost per acre
1. Cost of planting coffee:		
a. Nursery (1 *tablón*): [1]		
Making the garden bed	0.2	
Fertilizing and planting	.1	
Weeding	.1	
Watering (semiweekly in 6 dry months, 1 hour each time)	.5	
Flooding, harvesting, binding seedlings for removal	2.5	
b. Planting bushes: [2]		
Digging holes for coffee, 2,000 at 25 per day	4.0	
Digging holes for shade trees, 500 at 25 per day	1.0	
Carrying coffee and shade seedlings (assuming 1 kilometer distance)	2.5	
Planting coffee and shade trees	2.5	
Total	13.4	
Total man-days×5.6 acres×$0.16⅔ per hour÷30 years [3] amortization		$0.42
2. Annual cost in mature grove: [4]		
First cleaning	1	
Second cleaning	1	
Gathering berries	3	
Husking and separating berries	2	
Washing beans	1	
Drying beans	1	
Cleaning beans	.5	
Total	9.5	
Total×5.6 acres×$0.16⅔ per hour		8.87
Total		9.29

[1] Except for the last item, this labor is not included in the report to the President (Appendix 1). The information was supplemented by a reliable informant in 1941.
[2] Information chiefly from Appendix 1, which is inaccurate in saying that shade trees require the same labor as the coffee, for only a fourth as many shade as coffee trees are planted.
[3] This figure was given by Ladinos, and it checks fairly well with the little reliable case material available. Most Indian coffee has not been growing for that long. One Indian, 46 years old, recalls that coffee now producing for him was planted when he was a child, which indicates that the 30-year figure is a minimum. This informant said that 40 years is the maximum.
[4] From Appendix 1, and probably almost perfectly accurate, since work in coffee groves is standardized much like that in cornfields. However, it may be noted that the time consumed varies with the method of payment of hired labor (it is less if piecework is paid).

however, the net came to about $7 an acre. Against this must be accounted the investment and the value the land might have for other purposes.

FRUIT

Table 36 is based on a hasty count, with a reliable informant, of fruit trees owned by each family in 1941. A census of a sample of a few households indicated that the count consistently tended to understate the number. Visible trees had been noted, but an almost equal number were apparently hidden. Table 36 therefore includes a correction, but the calculations may err as much as 25 percent. It is assumed that the fruit situation did not materially change from 1936 to 1941.

Fruit yields are very variable, depending on the kind, size, and quality of the tree; the estimates here given are based on calculations made with one good informant, checked against other information more casually obtained. The prices are from Appendix 2. Ranges in yields of most fruits are not great; for example, mangos yield from 800 to 1,000, cross-sapodillas from 300 to 400, white sapodillas from 600 to 700 (half of which rot on the tree), *limas* from 100 to 150, limes from 500 to 600, etc. The greatest variation is in papayas, peaches, oranges, and sour oranges, the yield vary-

TABLE 36.—*Time consumed in and income from fruit growing, 1936*

Fruit	Number of trees	Costs			Gross income		Net income
		Hours per year (each tree)	Total man-days per year [1]	Labor costs	Yield per tree [2]	Total	
Vegetable pear	200	3	67	$11.17	[3] 125	$104.00	$92.83
Orange	310	2	69	11.50	300	232.50	221.00
Sour orange	150	1	17	2.83	150	21.00	18.17
Lima	210	1	23	3.83	125	52.50	48.67
Lime	85	2	19	3.17	550	46.75	43.58
Avocado	150	3	50	8.33	400	199.50	191.17
Cross-sapodilla	100	3	33	5.50	350	117.00	111.50
White sapodilla	40	1	4	.67	325	26.00	25.33
Spanish plum:							
Petapa	100	3	33	5.50	2,500	125.00	119.50
Chicha	60	3	20	3.33	2,500	60.00	56.67
Corona	25	2.5	7	1.17	2,000	33.25	32.08
Mico	10	2	2	.33	1,500	3.00	2.67
Tamalito	45	3	15	2.50	3,500	31.50	29.00
Panchoy	10	2	2	.33	2,000	10.00	9.67
Papaya	40	1	4	.67	22	8.80	8.13
Peach	70	1	8	1.33	75	6.30	4.97
Mango	60	3	20	3.33	900	108.00	104.67
Banana	1,000		20	3.33	5	40.00	36.67
Sugarcane	25	1	3	.50	[4] 40	7.50	7.00
Total	2,690		416	69.32		1,232.00	1,163.28

[1] Calculated on the basis of a 9-hour working day.
[2] Calculated on the basis of prices in Appendix 2.
[3] 125 fruits, 7 roots.
[4] 40 sections.

ing 100 percent. In the case of some varieties of Spanish plums, the number of fruit is greater than shown, the remainder eaten by the birds.

Since so little cost is involved, the profit from fruit is considerable. The Panajachel Indians devote their energies to agriculture, but a good part of their living comes from the sale of fruit which comes near to being a free resource.

SUMMARY: COSTS AND PROFITS

The total cost of the harvests produced by resident Indians, on land exploited for themselves, came to a little more than $24,000 (table 37). About 95 percent of this amount represents the cost of labor which was almost entirely of the Indian community itself. Only the small remainder was spent in cash outside the community— for labor, tools, a little fertilizer and a few seeds, a few dollars worth of candles and incense, and rent paid to outsiders.

The total value of the produce harvested by the Indians on the same land was over $26,000 (table 38). From the apparent net profit of $2,146.90 must be subtracted $380, the value of produce given as rental; about $320 for market taxes, bus fares, etc.; and about $900 for the value of the time devoted to selling the produce. Actually, of course, all this sum need not be subtracted from the profit, for the value of the produce was figured on the basis of Panajachel prices, and the merchandise sold outside presumably brought enough more to make up the value of the time

TABLE 38.—*Value of agricultural products*

Product	Total value	Consumed in community [1]	Sold to outsiders
Corn	$2,051.00	$2,051.00	
Beans	[2] 360.70	360.70	
Squash	135.00	80.30	54.70
Onions	[3] 12,929.28	113.63	12,815.65
Onion seed	2,430.00	1,574.72	855.28
Garlic	1,626.72	36.80	1,589.92
Vegetables [4]	276.60	181.41	95.19
Root crops and peppers	1,800.00	161.31	1,638.69
Pepinos	2,377.05	13.54	2,363.51
Coffee	1,052.00	418.32	633.68
Fruit	1,239.60	417.42	822.18
Total	26,277.95	5,409.15	20,868.80

[1] Cf. table 67. Except in items where there is special reason for not doing so, for convenience it is falsely assumed that the local product is consumed first, then additional supplies bought from outside. This is not true in all cases. For example, Panajachel producers sell most of their green-bean crop and in other seasons buy green beans; and throughout the year also buy dry beans. Thus the space for beans "sold to outsiders" should not be blank, while in table 67, the items under beans and green beans "produced in community" should be correspondingly less. But since the result is the same in the final bookkeeping, I am doing it this way.

[2] This figure assumes that 85 percent of shrub beans and 50 percent of vine beans are permitted to ripen.

[3] Assuming that the total onion acreage is reduced by 20 percent for the growing of root crops and peppers.

[4] Assuming that 0.4 acre of beets were grown and that miscellaneous vegetables besides beets produced 10 cents worth of vegetables per package of seed planted.

expended. On the basis of the figures presented here the net profit from agriculture was evidently something like $1,500. That is to say that if the Indians owned no agricultural land and worked exclusively for outsiders (and could always obtain work at the prevailing rates) they would be about $1,500 poorer—or its equivalent in goods purchased—than they actually are at the end of each year. Their agriculture not only gives them steady work, but a little extra as profit.

Roughly 80 percent of the $26,000 crop is sold for cash outside the community, and only the small remainder is consumed. Almost $13,000 in cash is realized from the sale of onions alone and amply explains why the people of Panajachel consider onions the basis of their economy.

SUMMARY: TIME CONSUMPTION

The total number of man-days devoted to agricultural production on resident Indian lands, owned and controlled, and rented, came to some 120,854 man-days in 1936 (table 39), including work done by the men, women, and children of the community as well as that done by hired laborers—virtually all Indian—living outside the community. It assumes that all work is done by adult men. The times given are calculated on the basis of what an industrious man can do in a day. Since women and youths of both sexes do a good part of the agricultural work, it is neces-

TABLE 37.—*Total cost of agricultural products*

Product	Value of labor	Seed, fertilizer, leaves, etc.	Cash rent outside	Annual tool cost	Outside labor	Total
Hill milpa	$781.67	$25.41	$25			
Delta corn	195.00	3.90				
Onion nursery	3,480.05	560.51				
Onions	[1] 12,430.71	502.88				
Onion seed	1,095.59	16.16				
Garlic	1,638.00	163.80	360	$216.77	$121.67	
Shrub beans	416.94	34.75				
Pole beans	224.73	10.10				
Vegetables [2]	258.38	100.87				
Pepinos	1,054.17	6.32				
Coffee	340.00					
Fruit	67.67					
Total	21,982.91	[3] 1,424.70	385	216.77	121.67	$24,131.05

[1] It is assumed, as in table 38, that the onion acreage is reduced 20 percent by the growing of tubers and peppers in onion beds. The labor is reduced by only 5 percent, however (and that reduction has here been made) because only the transplanting and preparing-for-market items are affected.

[2] Assuming that 0.4 acre of beets were grown in 1936.

[3] Of this total, about $200 is for fertilizer and broad covering leaves, $100 for packaged seed, and $10 for candles, incense, and food consumed in connection with harvests of corn. The total of $310 is spent outside the community. The remainder, $1,104.70 is really chargeable to local labor, $400 for fertilizer and leaves locally produced, and the remainder for fencing materials and especially home-grown seeds.

sary to distinguish agricultural work done by the two sexes and by people of various ages, for the value of a woman's or a child's time is less than that of a man. If it could be assumed that a woman or child, as compared with a man, accomplished work in proportion to their wages, the distinction from the point of view of costs would not be important. But this is not always true. A boy cannot work as fast as a man in the making of a *tablón* or in the various processes of the milpa; but a boy can probably replace a man in other cases. For example, three men usually make a *tablón* together; the most skilled, certainly a grown man, guides the others, but if a boy of 12 takes the role of one of the others, the work is probably not slowed appreciably. Likewise, a woman can probably transplant as fast and as well as a man, or do the weeding of an onion bed with equal efficiency, or braid garlic as fast. Yet, their time is considered worth less than that of a man, and their wage is smaller. These distinctions have been made in table 19, from which it may be concluded that adult males did a total of about 83,000 man-days and women and children about 38,000; men thus did some 70 percent of the work in the fields. Since women and children work more slowly (in some employment) than do men, the 38,000 "man-days" probably took them 45,000-odd full days of work, and the total time spent by Indians in their fields was actually 128,000 work days. From this total,

TABLE 39.—*Time devoted to agriculture*

Crop	Acre-crops [1]	Man-days per acre-crop [2]	Total man-days in 1936
Hill milpa	[3] 97.7	[4] 50	4,885
Delta corn	[5] 32.5	36	1,170
Onions from seed	127.6	652	83,195
Onion seed from seed	3.6	1,788	6,437
Garlic	16.8	629	10,576
Shrub beans	12.7	214	2,717
Vine beans	4.7	297	1,396
Cabbage	1.5	522	783
Beets, etc	.5	647	323
Carrots, etc	1.0	614	614
Pepinos	11.5	539	6,198
Coffee	[6] 38.5	55.7	2,144
Fruit (table 36)	---------	---------	416
Total	---------	---------	120,854

[1] These figures were derived by estimating the number of acres of the crop growing on the first of each month of the year (cf. chart 4) and, totaling these acres for the year, dividing by the number of months in the growing season. In cases where there is one crop in the year, the highest monthly figure was taken.
[2] From tables 27, 29-36.
[3] Includes hill milpa lands owner-controlled, and rented (hence used) in 1936, within and outside the area of study, by resident Indians.
[4] Assuming that 9/10 of the cornfields were planted on old land.
[5] 28 of truckland milpa plus 4.5 of cornfield in nonirrigated delta land.
[6] The total Indian coffee acreage (39.4) less than pawned to outsiders (see p. 81).

however, must be subtracted 730 days that Indians from outside the community are calculated to have worked on resident Indian lands.

ANIMAL HUSBANDRY

In comparison with agriculture, animal husbandry is extremely unimportant in Panajachel. As will be shown, it is also uneconomical. Although one or a few families once counted more sheep and mules in its possession, pastured on land outside of Panajachel, the numbers were never large. A count (table 40) in 1940 shows that the order of numbers is such that no family depends for its living on the raising of animals. Actually (table 41) 38 families kept no animals whatsoever; another 36 had only dogs or cats; and of the remaining 81, 4 had only nonproductive horses or mules (in addition to dogs). In general, the wealthier the family (table 80) the more domestic animals it keeps. "Foreign" Indians, for the most part artisan town-dwellers, kept almost no animals but horses, dogs, and cats. Of Panajacheleños, 24 families without any animals fell into the groups owning least land. Half of the households had chickens or other fowl, a little over a fifth, pigs. In both cases the land-rich tended to have more than the land-poor. Cattle, horses, goats, mules, and sheep were owned by relatively few people, and in the higher wealth brackets; none of the poorest quarter had such animals. Three-fourths of Panajacheleño families kept dogs or cats, or both; and again the number owned varied with the amount of land.

FOWL

Almost any Indian will say that "Every housewife has her chickens." Therefore, it is significant that in fact 95 out of the 155 households do *not* keep them and only 24 have flocks of 15 or more birds, one of them the maximum of 44.

Chickens, kept in small coops fitted with poles for roosting, often run loose during the day, except when everybody of the house is busy in the gardens, or away at market. They are fed corn at least once a day and frequently twice. Laying hens require special care, and there is considerable technology (as well as magical practice) involved in the keeping of chickens. Ducks, and one kind of pigeon, are also bred; a second pigeon is caught wild or more frequently bought caged and its wings clipped when it is accustomed to the house so that it can be given the freedom of the yard. These wild pigeons are occasionally allowed to multiply in the house. Probably the women and children who care for the fowl a few minutes at a time dribble away only about an hour a week in their care.

TABLE 40.—*Value of domestic animals owned*

Kind	Number	Average value (each)	Total value
Chickens, young	365	$0.10	$36.50
Hens and roosters	445	.20	89.00
Ducks	14	[1] 1.75	5.25
Pigeons	22	[1] 1.50	5.50
Pigs	40	2.50	100.00
Goats	14	1.50	21.00
Sheep	13	1.12	14.60
Bulls or steers	8	7.50	60.00
Cows	8	13.50	108.00
Calves	8	4.00	32.00
Rabbits	6	[1] .20	.60
Guinea pigs	10	[1] .10	.50
Colmena bees	14	[2] 1.00	14.00
Coxpin bees	4	[2] .10	.40
Horses and mules	20	12.50	250.00
Dogs	198	.30	59.40
Cats	61	.10	6.10
Total			802.85

[1] Per pair.
[2] Per hive.

Because they are important in belief and custom and a "good" housewife is expected to keep them, it is noteworthy that turkeys are absent and chickens sparse, and that this fact coincides with the fact that it does not pay to raise chickens in Panajachel. One careful informant estimated that his flock of 2 roosters and 17 hens ate 480 pounds of corn in 1936, worth $6; during the year he lost 4 chicks, worth 40 cents. Thus, not counting the value of the time expended in caring for the fowls, building the coop, etc., the cost was $6.40. At the same time the value of the flock increased (by natural growth) by $1.60—counting the four chicks that died—and produced 360 eggs worth $4.50, for a total of $6.10 and a net loss of 30 cents. Data from several other informants make it clear that at best one breaks even on the raising of chickens. Thus a household owning 5 roosters, 16 hens, and 18 chicks casually reported that the flock consumed 2 pounds of corn daily ($9 worth a year) and increased in value by $3.40 in the year while some 400 to 500 eggs (worth $5 to $6.25) were produced; another with 6 hens reported that each laid 18 eggs monthly for 6 months for a total of 648 during a year (worth $8.10) and that the flock ate 2 pounds of corn daily ($9.12 a year).

The Indians appear to know that it does not pay to raise chickens, and that perhaps explains why so many do not. Certainly they do not raise turkeys for that reason, for they frequently say that a turkey eats as much as a pig while at the same time the fowls are delicate and often sicken and die. But, aside from the feeling that a household is not complete without chickens, there is a recognized reason why it is desirable to raise them. During the rainy season when money is scarce and corn must be purchased, the sale of chickens is a source of emergency income. On August 15, 1936, Rosales noted in his diary that many women were selling chickens in order to buy corn and sugar because money was scarce; "The onions are all gone and only garlic is left, and its price is low." An Indian reported before All Souls' Day that he took chickens to Sololá to sell in order to buy things for the fiesta. We frequently noticed that when the need for money arose, a single hen or rooster was offered for sale.

TABLE 41.—*Combinations of domestic animals* [1]

Animals	Total	Number of households owning each combination
Dogs	106	__ 33 11 7 6 __ 4 3 __ 2 2 2 2 2 2 2 2 __ ... 1 1 1 1 1 1 1 1 1 1 1 1 1 1 1 __ 1 1 1 1 1 1
Cats	33	__ __ __ 7 __ __ 4 3 __ __ __ 2 2 2 2 1 ... 1 __ 1 1 1 1 1 __ 1 1 1 __ 1 1 1
Chickens	60	__ __ 11 7 6 6 __ 3 __ __ 2 2 2 2 __ 1 ... 1 1 1 1 1 1 1 __ 1 1 1 1 1 1 1
Ducks	3	__ 2 __ 1 __ 1 __ __ __ __ __ __ 1 1
Pigeons	5	__ __ __ 2 __ 1 __ __ __ __ 1 1 1 __ 1 1
Pigs	29	__ 6 __ 4 3 __ 2 __ 1 __ 1 1 1 1 __ 1 1 __ 1 1 1
Goats	4	__ 1 __ 1 __ 1 __ 1 __ 1 1
Sheep	6	__ 2 __ 1 __ 1 __ 1 __ 1 1 __ 1
Bulls—steers	7	__ 1 __ 1 __ 1 1 __ 1 __ 1 1
Cows	6	__ 2 2 __ 1 1 __ 1 1
Horses	19	__ 2 __ 2 __ 2 2 __ 2 __ 1 __ 1 __ 1 __ 1 1 1 __ 1 1
Colmena bees	4	__ 1 __ 1 __ 1 __ 1
Coxpin bees	3	__ 1 __ 1 __ 1 1
Rabbits	2	__ 1 __ 1
Guinea pigs	1	__ 1
Total	155	38 33 11 7 6 6 4 3 2 2 2 2 2 2 2 2 1 1 1 1 1 1 1 1 1 1 1 1 1 1 1 1 1 1 1 1 1 1 1 1 1 1 1 1 1 1 1

[1] To read this table, begin with the numbers in the "Total" row and follow them up. Thus, 38 households have no animals (for all the other spaces are blank), 33 households have only dogs, 11 have only dogs and chickens, etc. The column headed "Total" shows how many households have each species of animal.

When it was pointed out to Indians that it did not pay them to raise fowl, their most frequent reply was that it is good to have chickens for sale when money is needed.

HOGS

Hogs, not bred in Panajachel, are bought when young and fattened for sale. Of the 29 families that were fattening hogs in 1936, 11 had 2 head each, and none had more than 2. An 8-month-old pig bought at about a dollar,[93] is sold after 7 or 8 months for from 3 to 6 dollars, and a young one bought to replace it. Pigs are rarely allowed loose, since the houses are surrounded by gardens; their diet is therefore chiefly kitchen waste and corn. An hour a week by the wife and children probably takes care of them. Hogs are certainly very poor business. Some of the Indians who realize this give it as the reason why they do not raise them. Others, although they know hogs are not profitable, may not realize how much they actually lose, and raise them as a means of investing money when corn is more plentiful, for liquidation when money is scarce. A wealthy Indian with two pigs estimated that they consumed 1,400 pounds of corn (worth $17.50) and 10 pounds of salt (worth 15 cents) in the fattening process. In addition, he spent a dollar to make a pen and 26 cents to castrate and keep the young boars in good health. He did not figure the additional cost of rope, which came to about 24 cents, or the value of the time involved. Including the original cost of the pigs (but not time spent), he had invested $20.15 by the time they were fattened, and the pigs were worth but half of that. This man, who grew his own corn, perhaps did not calculate his losses; certainly the factor of saving money does not enter in his case, for he is wealthy and usually has cash on hand. Juan Rosales recalls that in his wealthy father's house when he was young they once took to raising pigs; when they had 2 or 3, the amount of corn consumed by the pigs was not noticed particularly; but when the number soared to about a dozen, they saw that the corn supply was rapidly dwindling and then did some calculating and thereafter never raised pigs! There are other similar cases in my notes; certainly many Indians know that a pig's consumption of 3 or 4 pounds of corn daily for 8 months makes hog raising unprofitable. A young Indian of a poor household learned his lesson in 1941. About November 1, 1940, he told me proudly that he had a pig fattening. It cost him $1 and in from 4 to 6 months would be worth $4. He thought it was a good practice: "It is no good if people eat all of their corn every day; give some to the pig, and it grows and you get money out of it. You don't notice the daily expense in corn, and later when you need it, you will get a large sum of money." He said that the pig ate 3 pounds of corn daily. When we calculated the cost (as he himself had not done) he was surprised. In 6 months the pig would consume $6.50 worth of corn! But he still thought it was a good way to save money. On January 11 he complained that (although 3 weeks before, he had turned down an offer of $2.50 for his pig, now quite fat) he was offered only $1.50. On February 5 he told me that the pig weighed 150 or 175 pounds and he was getting no offers for it, the butchers apparently all going to Atitlán to buy hogs. On March 23 he finally sold the animal to a local butcher for $3; he said he was tired of feeding it corn while waiting for a better price. A week later the butcher killed the pig and found it diseased and the young man had to return $1.50 of the purchase price. He swore that he would never buy a pig again.

GOATS AND SHEEP

Goats are bought when young for about a dollar and sold for twice that when grown. Sheep similarly are worth 75 cents when young, $1.50 when grown. Like pigs, they are simply fattened, although in times past they were sometimes bred. The goats are not milked, but the sheep are occasionally shorn and the wool sold or used in the house in pillows. Since goats and sheep are pastured in the river bed, along the roadsides, and in the hills, virtually their only expense is the value of the time taken incidental to other tasks, no more than, say, 3 hours a week. Occasionally a sheep is fed corn-dough water that is left in the kitchen, but that has no money value. On the whole, there is probably little gain or loss in fattening goats and sheep.

CATTLE

At least four of the six families owning cows (one of them owning three) also owned a calf of

---

[93] They are usually bought in Sololá, but they are sometimes bought more cheaply elsewhere. In 1940 I was told they sold for 40 cents at the annual fair in Chichicastenango, and at least one Panajacheleño went there to buy a pig.

each cow. Cows are kept for milk, sold chiefly to Ladinos, and are also bred—for which purpose all but one dairy must rent a bull, usually from a Ladino. Bulls or steers are bought as yearlings to fatten for sale; they are frequently gelded (by a professional). A calf, bought for 5 dollars, doubles in value in about 2 years when it is ready for sale. A female calf costs about $7, and a milk cow is worth about $20. A calf new-born is valued at about $3, and of course increases in value.

Cattle are pastured during the day and brought in at night incidental to other work by men, boys, or old men. As one informant put it, such animals "are good for a rich old man like Nicolas Chivalan who cannot work hard and who directs his *mozos* and cares for his animals and little else." Cows, however, receive special care, especially when they calve. The steer-fattening families spend some 20 hours a week each on their cattle; the cow-owning households, about 35.

For a few months in the dry season the cattle owner, if he owns no pasture land, frequently rents some from Ladinos, at 50 cents a month. This seems inordinately expensive considering the rental cost of land for planting corn and taking into account that pasture land is enriched by use. In the rainy season there is sufficient free foliage along the lake shore, in the river bed, and along the roadsides.

Only the value of the manure produced makes it possible for the business of fattening steers to pay. In 2 years a steer consumes 50 cents worth of salt, 30 cents worth of rope, and 3 or 4 dollars may be paid for pasture privileges. With these expenses, the value increases only $5; and meanwhile 200 man-days of time (with a normal value of $33) may easily be consumed. Although much of the time has less cash value, it hardly seems worth while to raise cattle. The explanation is that most cattle owners own milpa or pasture land and thus not only pay no rent and enrich their own soil, but collect and sell (or use) the manure of the stable or yard. Cows are probably better business. They are fed the water of corn dough, which amounts to kitchen waste.[94] Milk (sold for 5 or 10 cents a liter) and calves should make worth while the added time consumed in caring for the cows and their offspring. Recent sanitary

regulations, however, have put something of a crimp in the business.[95]

Rabbits (kept for pleasure as well as food) and guinea pigs (also eaten) are to unimportant for extended discussion; they are cared for by the children, and eat kitchen waste.

BEES

Coxpin bees (or wasps) are one of several varieties of wild bee found nearby, and the only one now brought to the house in its hollow log. The hive is valued at 10 cents probably because it produces wax of that value in a year. The children sometimes eat the sour honey, but it has no commercial value. The only honey-producing bees now kept are the colmena bees of European origin, hives of which are bought at about $1 each. The only expense connected with their care is the planting of flowers in the yard (which many have anyway). But the disadvantage of keeping bees is that they may leave the hive and house. They produce about a dollar's worth of honey and 30 cents' worth of wax a year.

HORSES AND MULES

The beasts of burden (there are no oxen) are referred to simply as "beasts," but mules are preferred for burdens, and they usually cost more. The beasts are used for riding and for carrying loads. Of the 19 households owning them 3 are foreign Indians who use the animals for riding; 5 others are wealthy families the head of which in each case has a saddle horse. The remaining 11 households have pack animals and use them in trade with distant markets. In these cases the merchant is able to take a larger quantity to market, and the animals may be said to have commercial value. Most Indians doubt that pack animals repay their keep. Since fodder is not plentiful in Panajachel, and the animals are fed considerable amounts of corn, they are probably right; but if the manure is taken into consideration (as it does not appear to be) horses and mules may possibly be profitable investments.

These animals are never bred in town; they are bought and sold fully grown, for a variable price

---

[94] No family keeping cows also keeps pigs, which are also fed this water.

[95] The most important Indian dairyman, who had three cows in 1940, told me in 1941 that he had five cows but no calves, hence no milk, but that even if his cows produced milk he would be unable to sell it without a license, unobtainable unless he built a two-room stable with a cement floor.

running to about $10 for a horse and $15 for a mule. Their care is in the hands of the men and boys who average some 5 hours weekly to feed and occasionally wash them and cure their ailments.

DOGS AND CATS

Dogs and cats are primarily companion animals and have little commercial value. The former help guard the house and cornfield, and the latter kill rats and mice. But their utility is limited, and the damage they do may well balance their usefulness. These animals may be considered luxuries, and are found more commonly among the rich than the poor. The maximum number of dogs in any household in 1940 was 4 (5 cases); 16 families had 3 each, 45 had 2, and 40 had but 1 each. Most of the 49 families which had none were on the lower wealth levels. Six of the 33 cat-owning families had 3 apiece, 16 had 2 each, and 11 but 1 apiece. All but 2 households with cats also kept dogs.

Cats and dogs, sometimes purchased when young, are most frequently raised in the home; the young are often sold, for about 10 cents. A grown dog (though less frequently the object of transactions) is usually valued at about 50 cents. Kittens or cats, not usually found in the market place, are exchanged for chicks or other small things. One Indian valued his cat at 15 cents, another at 20 cents; they were probably high.

Dogs and cats require little care; but they need food beyond kitchen waste and that for which they forage. One wealthy Indian with three dogs and three cats estimated that the former consume a pound of corn and the latter a quarter of a pound daily. If that estimate is near correct, a dog costs $1.50 a year in corn alone and a cat a quarter of that. A female dog makes up part of that cost with the value of its litter, and some people keep a bitch precisely for that purpose, selling the litter in the markets when they go with other produce. But on the whole it cannot be said that dogs are kept for commercial purposes or that they pay for themselves.

SUMMARY: COSTS AND PROFITS

Table 42, which summarizes the costs and returns of animal husbandry, shows that, in comparison with agriculture, the raising of domestic animals is of no importance in Panajachel—economically, at least. The cost of raising animals

is not even 6 percent of the cost of raising crops; the income from animal husbandry is less than 5 percent of that from agricultural produce.

TABLE 42.—*Estimated costs of and returns from domestic animals, 1940*

Kind	Expenses [1]			Income [2]		
	Total	Feed and salt, etc.	Care and cure (value of time)	Total	Growth and increase (net)	Milk, eggs, or rent
Fowl	$178.88	$150	$28.88	$142.50	$30	$112.50
Pigs	363.83	350	13.83	160.00	160	--------
Goats and sheep	18.67	1	17.67	27.00	25	2.00
Cattle	320.50	25	295.50	885.00	85	[3] 800.00
Bees				1.00	--------	1.00
Horses and mules	194.16	[4] 120	74.16	20.00	--------	20.00
Dogs and cats	270.00	270	--------	25.00	25	--------
Total	1,346.04	916	430.04	1,260.50	325	935.50

[1] Pastures not considered; the manure left is considered to balance it; nor are pen- or coop-building costs included.
[2] Manure not taken into consideration.
[3] This figure is based on a guess that the cows average 3 or 4 liters daily.
[4] Based on personal experience in 1937.

DISPOSAL OF PRODUCE

Artisans and professionals sell their products or services in their homes or shops to those who come to buy. Laborers are either sought out by employers, or shop themselves for employment, or enter into relatively permanent arrangements with *patrones*. The discussion to follow is virtually confined to the sale of the agricultural produce which forms the basis of the local economy.

The corn grown by the Indians of Panajachel is practically never sold. Only a few families grow enough corn for their own household uses, and probably nobody harvests a surplus of any size. Possibly some Indians, in need of money for emergencies, sell their corn after the harvest and subsequently buy piecemeal what they need themselves; but no such case came to light. True, Indians occasionally lend corn to friends and neighbors when money is scarce or there is none in the market; but they expect to be repaid in corn rather than money. The problem in Panajachel is not to find a market for the sale of corn but to find the means to buy it. The same can be said, with less assurance, of the other milpa products; for beans and squash are rarely if ever sold. Green beans are an important item of market produce, especially those grown in irrigated land, but mature beans, even those grown in garden beds, are almost never sold. There is a woman who raises a special variety of squash in her gardens (exceptional because squash are rarely grown outside the milpa) to sell. Processed corn and bean foods such as tamales and *atol* are sold by local women. But by and large, the products that are associated with the milpa, with the exception of green beans separately grown, are not for sale by the Panajachel Indians who produce them.

Coffee, to the direct contrary, is almost all sold. Some of the growers of coffee even sell their entire crops and buy what they need during the year. One reason for this is that Panajachel coffee, which is high grade, brings a better price than that which can be bought in the market. Another is that very many poor families sell their coffee "on the bush" long before the harvest. Indian growers do not market their coffee. Instead, Ladinos come to their houses to buy it to send to the capital for export. Some of the wealthier Indians hold out for better prices, but never attempt to market it themselves. The middlemen often profit from these transactions with little risk, since before they buy they know the price to be had in Guatemala City.

It is to the disposal of their vegetables and fruit that the Indians devote their commercial attention. The sale of this produce is effected in several ways:

(1) A large part of the vegetable crop, and to a lesser extent the fruit, is sold to merchants of other towns who make a practice of coming to the homes of the local Indians to bargain for onions, garlic, *pepinos*, etc. The most important business of this kind is in connection with onions (something like half of which may be sold in this way), bought usually by Sololateco merchants who take them to Guatemala City to sell. When onions are in particular demand in the capital, Sololatecos (less frequently Atitecos or others) are seen knocking at doors looking for onions, or harvesting and preparing them, or fixing their cargoes. They often buy them by the unharvested *tablón*, or they pick up smaller quantities from several growers. Onion seed (Panajachel seed is supposed to be especially good) is also bought by outsiders (most frequently from Mixco) who come to shop for it. Nursery seedlings are also occasionally bought for transplanting by Sololatecos, Atitecos, Tepanecos and perhaps others. Although cases of Atitecos' buying cabbages are recalled, other vegetables are less frequently bought in this manner. Very frequently and in great quantities during the very

short season, *pepinos* are purchased by merchants from other towns, especially Sololá, who take them to Guatemala City. Fruit is frequently sold in this manner also. During the Spanish-plum season Catarinecos, especially, buy the unharvested fruit of whole trees, which they then take home to ripen and eventually to sell in other towns. They also buy ripe and harvested fruit. Cases have been noted of Chichicastenango Indians buying plums and oranges, of Luqueños buying green avocados to take to Guatemala City, of Andresanos buying *limas* and oranges at the time of the corn harvest, to give to their harvesters, of Antoñeros buying *limas*, of Jorgeños buying stems of green bananas to ripen and sell in the Sololá market, and so on.

(2) A relatively unimportant means of disposing of the local produce is by house-to-house sales to Ladino families and to hotels, and to traveling merchants passing through, either on the road or at the piers where they embark and disembark. Only women engage in such selling, and they usually offer small quantities of a variety of fruits and vegetables, or eggs and fowl.[96] A few women (none native Panajacheleñas) also sell beef and pork products,[97] and one local Totonicapeña began in 1937 to make a rice-and-milk drink to sell chiefly at the Ladino houses. Most women sell the produce from home, but in some cases they may buy them from others for resale at a profit. One may guess that a fourth of the households are more or less regularly represented by women and girls who sell at the houses, on the roads, and at the piers several days of each week. Since they sell the family produce, their "profits" are not separable from the earnings of agriculture.

(3) The chief means of disposing of produce is in the market place. Every landed family sells at least part of its produce in formal markets. Local Indians sell their own produce or that of other families, which they buy in private to take to market. Exceptionally, they bring produce pur-

---

[96] Local Indian women never sell fowl in the local market; in one case noted a women sold a hen in the Sololá market. Fowl are evidently sold only when the woman is in need of cash, for she prefers the less public method of going to a customer's house.

[97] Especially pork products. Most pigs being butchered by Ladinos, the business is largely in their hands. Beef products are usually sold in connection with the butcher shops, but one Ladino butcher hired a local Totonicapeña to sell beef-belly at the houses. Rosales one day (October 27, 1936), spoke to her when he had bought some and found that she received a cent for each 5 pounds sold. She carried 30 or 40 pounds in a basket on her head, her child meanwhile being carried in the usual fashion on her back. She said she sold on credit, too.

chased in other towns. The markets that are frequented regularly (table 43), are those of Panajachel itself; of Sololá, an hour by foot to the north; of San Andrés, an equal distance to the east; of San Lucas, across the lake; of Tecpán and of Patzún, a day's walk to the east; of Patulul and Chicacao, on the "coast" to the south; of Quezaltenango far to the west; and of Guatemala City. Occasionally, for annual fiesta markets, local Indians visit other towns such as Chichicastenango, San Pedro, Atitlán, and so on; but relatively few go and not at all regularly. On the other hand, although few are real merchants who regularly buy in 1 town to sell in others, only 13 (all landless) of the 155 households never regularly sell anything. They frequent markets for buying purposes, of course, but take nothing to sell. Three of them are "foreign" Indians (2 Totonicapán, 1 San Pedro) with special trades; the others are for the most part families whose adults work as laborers and domestics for other families, Ladino or Indian. In some cases the women could, were they ambitious as some others, buy produce to sell, but they do not.

TABLE 43.—*Number of households habitually represented by vendors in various markets*

Markets	Number of households
Households having no regular vendors	13
Households represented by vendors in:	
Panajachel market only	32
Panajachel and Sololá markets	69
Panajachel and San Andrés markets	6
Panajachel and Tecpán markets	4
Panajachel and San Lucas markets	1
Panajachel and Guatemala City markets	4
Panajachel, Sololá, and San Andrés markets	3
Panajachel, Sololá, and Tecpán markets	2
Panajachel, Sololá, and San Lucas markets	3
Panajachel, Tecpán, and Patzún markets	3
Panajachel, San Lucas, and Guatemala City markets	2
Panajachel, Sololá, Tecpán, and San Lucas markets	1
Panajachel, Sololá, Tecpán, and Patzún markets	1
Panajachel, Sololá, San Andrés, and Tecpán markets	1
Panajachel, Sololá, Tecpán, and Guatemala City markets	3
Panajachel, San Lucas, Chicacao, and Patulul	1
Panajachel, Tecpán, and Guatemala City	1
Panajachel, Chicacao, Patulul, and Guatemala City	1
Panajachel, San Lucas, and Patzún markets	1
Panajachel, Sololá, San Andrés, Tecpán, and Patzún	1
Panajachel, Sololá, San Andrés, Tecpán, Patzún, Quezaltenango	1
Panajachel, San Andrés, Tecpán, Chicacao, Patulul, Quezaltenango	1
Total	142
Total number of households	155

THE LOCAL MARKET

The 142 households that dispose of their produce in markets are all represented by sellers more or less regularly vending in the local market. Except for three recent cases of men selling in the market (including a young boy, but all equally criticized) these families are represented in the market only by their womenfolk. Table 44 and the derived summary of table 45 (the results of a spot check at stated times over a period of weeks) give a precise picture of when local women tend to sell in the local market and what, during one season at least, they bring.[98] Most women come to market at least several times during the week, for an hour or two, morning or afternoon, some of them regularly on certain days at the same time, others only occasionally. Sunday is "market day" when as many as a hundred local women come, usually only for the morning but often for the whole day, going home at noon for a quick lunch.[99] Sunday is also the day when the women do much of their purchasing for the week from the merchants of other towns who come. The next best selling days are Tuesdays, Thursdays, and Fridays, when (en route to or from the Tuesday and Friday market days in Sololá) merchants stop and buy local produce. The number of women coming to sell on these days rises from a dozen to as many as 30. Besides those who sell fruit and vegetables, there are two Panajacheleñas vendors of coffee and prepared foods; this business is not prominent because a resident Nahualeña keeps a restaurant in a corner of the market place, and a woman originally of Concepción regularly sells food at the entrance of town and often in the market place.

[98] Sunday forenoons are not included; count of the large Sunday market was made but once; the results (table 50) are discussed in section on Consumer Goods (pp. 133–154) because the Sunday market is important for shoppers. Ladina women not included in the table; "Foreign" Indian women resident in Panajachel are included, except for the Nahualeña restaurateur and the proprietor of the butcher shop.

[99] One wealthy woman regularly makes two trips to the Sunday market with large baskets of fruits and vegetables. She is notoriously a shrewd woman and is said always to sell out at good prices. One Sunday (December 6, 1936), Rosales noted that she brought large baskets of tomatoes, sweet cassava, sweetpotatoes, beans, cabbages, onions, oranges, *limas*, peaches, etc. It happened that no Atitecos came with fruit from the coast, and this woman had a field day: the Ladinas surrounded her and bought her out at good prices (peaches, for example, at three for a cent). She hired other women to go to her house for more fruit to sell.

TABLE 44.—*Produce brought to the Panajachel market by local Indian women (1937)*

Distribution of produce by indicated number of vendors at time and date shown

Produce	10 a. m., 4/1–7						11 a. m., 4/24–30						Noon, 4/17–23						1 p. m., 4/3–9						3 p. m., 3/27–4/2						4 p. m., 3/13–19						5 p. m., 3/20–26						6 p. m., 3/27–4/2					
	F	S¹	M	T	W	T	F	S¹	M	T	W	T	F	S¹	M	T	W	T	F	S¹	M	T	W	T	F	S¹	M	T	W	T	F	S¹	M	T	W	T	F	S¹	M	T	W	T	F	S¹	M	T	W	T
(number of vendors)	0	5	5	9	7	9	1	1	4	9	12	12	4	4	6	11	9	13	6	5	6	8	3	0	24	6	9	12	10	4	32	6	8	17	6	20	25	1	6	16	14	20	29	5	4	7	5	8
Onions																																																
Garlic																																																
Green beans																																																
Carrots																																																
Radishes																																																
Cabbage																																																
Lettuce																																																
Green peppers																																																
Tomatoes																																																
Huskcherries																																																
Herbs																																																
Sweetpotatoes																																																
Corn																																																
Beans																																																
Vegetable pears																																																
Oranges																																																
Limas																																																
Limes																																																
Avocados																																																
Bananas																																																
Pepinos																																																
Cross-sapodillas																																																
White sapodillas																																																
Coyóles																																																
Cayús																																																
Coffee beans																																																
Panela																																																
Eggs																																																
Pork																																																
Blood sausage																																																
Lard cracklings																																																
Cooked squash																																																
Cooked sweet cassava																																																
Tortillas																																																
Tamales																																																
Tamales-with-pork																																																
Coffee beverage																																																
Pitchwood																																																

¹ Saturday.

TABLE 45.—*Summary of Panajachel vendors in weekday market (1937)*

Time of day	Date	Number of women vendors counted						
		Total	Monday	Tuesday	Wednesday	Thursday	Friday	Saturday
10 a. m.	4/1-7	35	5	9	7	9	0	5
11 a. m.	4/24-30	38	4	9	12	12	1	0
12 m.	4/17-23	47	6	11	9	13	4	4
1 p. m.	4/3-9	28	6	8	3	0	6	5
3 p. m.	3/27-4/2	65	9	12	10	4	24	6
4 p. m.	3/13-19	89	8	17	6	20	32	6
5 p. m.	3/20-26	82	6	16	14	20	25	1
6 p. m.	3/27-4/2	59	4	7	5	8	30	5
Total		443	48	89	66	86	122	32

While their husbands or brothers are off to distant markets, or doing the heavy garden work, good wives (or sisters or daughters) bring to market the produce of the fields—onions, garlic, oranges, *limas*, and avocados, and so on, and thus do their bit selling where they can. Needless to say, selling in the market has its social and pleasurable aspects. Wives of rich men rather than of the poor are those who come to sell in the market during the week—partly because they are not needed in the fields, partly because they do not take longer trips to other markets. Although men do not sell or even frequent the local market place, they often bring to the doorway the merchandise to be sold by their wives and daughters. The number of women who come to the market varies not only with the day of the week, and also with the season, but also with the time of year with respect to the religious calendar. During a fiesta in Sololá, for example, with its accompanying large market, few women frequent the local market place; they have gone to Sololá, and so have most potential buyers. On October 4, the local titular fiesta, they bring to market prepared food and refreshment rather than ordinary produce. The only time of the year when there is no market at all is during the last of Holy Week, especially Holy Thursday and Good Friday.

OUTSIDE MARKETS

Needless to say, most of the produce of Panajachel eventually reaches markets in other towns. Much sold at retail in the local market is bought by merchants who resell it elsewhere, and all that outsiders buy in wholesale quantities from individual producers is exported. However, most Panajachel Indians themselves market their produce in other towns, close and far. There is no shame attached to selling by either sex in other towns. Some travel to several markets at regular intervals, and devote a large proportion of their time to such merchandising. Others, for the most part those with larger landholdings, sell at wholesale to outsiders who come to Panajachel (or to other Panajacheleños to take abroad) or in smaller quantities in nearby markets.

Of the 155 Indian households, 110 regularly sell local produce in markets of other towns. It must be emphasized that table 43 lists only *regular* visits (weekly, biweekly, or monthly) recognized by the community in general. Other markets are *occasionally* visited,[100] and many more households are *occasionally* represented in the towns listed.[101] Not only do certain households habitually go to certain markets, but particular members of the households are generally known to go (table 46). Thus, the Sololá market is a family market, the household frequently going *en masse* on Fridays. Thus, also, the only markets that women generally attend at all are those of Sololá and San Andrés. The more distant markets are frequented by individual men, a man and his son, or two or three brothers of the household. But also, while certain members of the family patronize one series of markets, others as regularly attend others. Thus, while the husband may sell in Tecpán or on the coast, his wife may go to San Andrés. It is because of this duplication that the 110 households that sell in outside markets are actually represented by 149 vending groups.

Most produce taken out of town is grown by the vendor (table 46) but the proportion is much less than in the case of the local market, for many people make businesses of buying produce from others here (in rare cases from other towns) to sell in distant markets. In general it may be said that the rich sell only their own goods, and the poor, not having much of their own, have to buy at least some of what they sell. So also merchandise that is bought tends to go to the more distant

---

[100] Especially during their annual fiestas, when even the smallest of towns attract merchants. Thus, for example, the village of San Jorgé has no regular market, but on January 24 many vendors go there. In 1937, when that day fell on Sunday, the Panajachel market was very small because so many of the usual vendors had gone to San Jorgé instead.

[101] Also generally on fiesta occasions. Thus, on the days of their Saints, such towns as Patzún are patronized by many more Panajacheleños than are indicated in table 49. During Holy Week the whole marketing program is altered, for different towns traditionally celebrate days of that week and of Lent by extraordinarily huge markets which attract special numbers of merchants. In 1937, for example, there was a great market in Tecpán, on March 22, and one in Sololá next day. Chichicastenango regularly has a very large market on Palm Sunday.

TABLE 46.—*Constitution and source of produce of vending groups in outside markets*

Vendors and source of produce	Number of vending groups								
	Total	Sololá	San Andrés	San Lucas	Patulul-Chicacao	Tecpán	Patzún	Guatemala City	Quezaltenango
Vendors:									
Man alone	42	2	----	5	2	18	6	8	1
Woman alone	6	2	4	----	----	----	----	1	----
Brothers	5	----	----	3	----	1	----	1	----
Man and children	8	3	----	----	1	1	1	1	1
Woman and children	1	1	----	----	----	----	----	----	----
Man and wife	5	2	2	----	----	----	----	1	----
Whole family	82	75	7	----	----	----	----	----	----
Total	149	85	13	8	3	20	7	11	2
Source of produce:									
Own produce	93	68	5	5	----	9	1	5	----
Part own, part bought	24	12	4	1	1	4	1	----	1
Bought produce	32	5	4	2	2	7	5	6	1

markets, because men who make long trips tend to be poor or at least poor in land. Wealthy families do not sell in distant places both because they have much to do at home and because they do not need to travel for a living.[102]

The common means of getting to market is walking, men carrying their loads on their backs, women in baskets on their heads. When man and wife (or the whole family) go, the husband carries the larger part of the load, and sells the more important things, although where a woman is known to be a better vendor, she is apt to sell the large items instead. They also take turns selling to allow each some time for buying or loafing. Exceptions to the rule of walking to market are the cases of San Lucas and the coast towns, where canoes and public launches are used to cross the lake, and Guatemala City, to which public truckbusses are patronized by all except one man and his son, who still walk. In the cases of 11 households that own horses or mules, the beast carries the major burden and the merchant walks beside him, carrying an additional small load.

The big day in the Sololá market is Friday; a secondary market day is Tuesday.[103] Most Panajachel Indians leave early in the morning and spend the better part of almost every Friday there. A few go also on Tuesdays. Not all go to sell:

they do much of their buying in Sololá; persons with political business in Sololá usually choose Friday to do it; and many go just for a holiday. Still, it cannot be doubted that more Panajachel produce is sold in Sololá than in any other market. Sololá is an important wholesale center; merchants from various towns buy produce there in quantities, for resale, and Panajachel men habitually bring large quantities of fruit and vegetables to Sololá in addition to that brought by other members of the family. Furthermore, while to more distant markets (such as Guatemala City) some of the Panajacheleños carry produce of other towns, practically everything they sell in Sololá is Panajachel produce, most of it grown by the vendors themselves.

Sololá is not only a "family market" for Panajacheleños but a greater number of families (69) are represented there exclusively than at all other outside markets together. They include all classes of people—rich and poor, Panajacheleños and "foreigners." Sololá in some ways as much as Panajachel is the market center for Panajacheleños.

Although San Andrés is no more difficult of access than Sololá, only 13 Panajachel households send vendors there. Its market days, Sundays and Tuesdays, conflict with those of Panajachel and Sololá. Unlike Sololá, which is a market center, most produce is sold in small quantities for San Andrés consumption. Since only small amounts of onions and garlic can be consumed by those who patronize this market, Panajacheleños take more fruit than vegetables. As at home, the women tend to do the selling. Men often accompany their wives, but rather to buy corn to bring home than to sell produce.

Those who patronize the San Lucas market regularly almost always take the water route.[104] Both canoe-owning Panajacheleños are among the regular San Lucas vendors;[105] the others rent canoes or occasionally go by launch. Perhaps, therefore, a dislike of travel in canoes keeps women from San Lucas. But its market days also coincide with those in Sololá which is preferred for other reasons. It seems also that the

---

[102] With reference to the "good old days" it is often said that the people were rich and "didn't have to make long business trips." It is said that some rich people died without ever having seen even Atitlán across the lake; although there were means of travel, they said that they did not have to know distant towns.

[103] For a good description of the Sololá market, see McBryde, 1933.

[104] The trip by land is not only more arduous, but it takes longer. Nevertheless, when a canoe is not available or when the water is rough, the merchants do occasionally walk. A number of such cases were noted.

[105] A third canoe-owner is a half-Ladino; culturally Ladino, the family does not sell produce in the markets (nor is it included in Indian in this study).

San Lucas market was never patronized by Pana-jacheleños (until recently when the canoes were purchased) except when they passed through on longer trips to the coast. Therefore it is not traditionally a market for other than men. The trip to San Lucas and back is a full day by canoe, from early dawn to afternoon. None of the present-day vendors go on from there to the coast markets, even though two of them are full-fledged middlemen who buy produce both in Panajachel and San Lucas.

The chief "coast" markets patronized by Pana-jacheleños are Patulul and Chicacao, in the plantation country. After crossing the lake in canoes or launches early Saturday, the merchants stop at towns and plantations along the way and sell in the Sunday market of either Patulul or Chicacao. They stop at plantations on Saturday and Sunday evenings when the laborers are at home, and return Monday afternoon to Pana-jachel. On the coast, they travel at night by kerosene lamp, candles, or pitch-wood torches. Panajachel onions, garlic, green beans, cabbages, beets, etc. are in considerable demand, but in recent years much trade of Panajachel merchants has been taken away by the people of Sololá, Concepción, Atitlán, Santa Catarina Palapo, and San Antonio, who either grow vegetables also or make a business of buying them in Sololá and selling them on the coast.

To Tecpán also only men regularly go, leaving at noon or early in the afternoon of Wednesday to arrive in the evening or more usually early Thurs-day morning and have the whole day Thursday (which is the big market day there) in which to sell. Then they often return late Thursday (if they leave Tecpán at noon) or very early Friday morning, reaching home in time to go up to the Sololá market. Many went to Tecpán, especially during Lent to sell vegetables, for Holy Week, before other towns (especially Sololá) began to grow and sell so many of the same vegetables. A great deal of fruit, especially oranges and *limas*, is also taken to Tecpán.

Fewer men (and some of the same ones) go to Patzún than to Tecpán, taking the same produce. Here again competition has reduced the numbers. The big market day at Patzún is on Sunday. Vendors go late on Saturday and return early Monday. Although truck-bus lines pass directly from Panajachel to Patzún, they are not patronized

because (since they do not run on Sundays) the merchants would have to leave Panajachel early Saturday. Furthermore, they often stop in God-ines on the way to sell for awhile, and the trucks do not pass through at the right time. Women do not go to Patzún, partly because they can sell in the local market on Sunday while their husbands are away.

The truck-bus service to Guatemala City takes half a day each way.[106] Before it was available, fully 8 days were often necessary, 6 for travel and 2 for selling. Now the round trip takes no more than 3 days, for the merchant can sell even on the afternoon of the day on which he leaves Panajachel. Yet less people go now than formerly, because with the quick and easy service, people from all over bring onions and vegetables, and prices are sometimes very low. Few Panajacheleños take even *pepinos* to the capital despite the great demand in season and the virtual growing monopoly enjoyed by Panajachel. The reason (or result) is that Indians of other towns make a business of buying them in Panajachel to sell in the city. Although onions, garlic, *pepinos*, and other fruit of less importance are the principal Panajachel products taken to the Capital, one local Indian has worked up a seasonal trade (wholesale) in onion seed. He buys the seed in Panajachel to sell to customers in Guatemala City and Mixco.

In only one case does a man take his wife with him regularly on such long trips. A progressive young Indian takes his wife to Guatemala City (on the bus), probably more because she wants to go than because it is especially good business.

The best market days in both Guatemala City and Quezaltenango are Monday, Thursday, and Saturday. To Quezaltenango the Panajachel vendors go on foot, requiring 4 days for the whole trip. The usual route passes through Nahuala, where vendors often stop on Sunday, on the way up or back, to sell. The principal products taken are onions, green beans, avocados, oranges, jocotes, and *cíntula*. Again, competition by others, chiefly Sololatecos, has reduced the number of Pana-jacheleños on this route.[107]

---

[106] The fare for Indians on the bus was as low as 75 cents one way, with cargo, during the period of study. Later, competition brought it as low as 40 or 50 cents.
[107] Of course both Guatemala City and Quezaltenango have sources of supply other than the region of Panajachel. McBryde, 1947, discusses sources and trade routes at length.

On all long trips, food is taken from home to warm and eat on the way. To keep down expenses, merchants often take food for as long as a week,[108] young men (who prefer to buy along the way or eat in restaurants) less than their elders. Generally even for a day's trip, as to Sololá, at least some food is taken along, perhaps supplemented by purchase. Only on a half-day trip no lunch is taken. Nights on the road are generally spent in the porticos of public buildings in towns on the way, or in private houses where lodging (i. e., a place under a roof to sleep) can be purchased for a penny or a half-cent or a gift of a fruit or the like. Traveling Indians do not usually sleep in the open. To prepare food, they usually build a fire unless they are in a place where they can use someone else's fire.

A particular convenience to merchants is the custom by which they can leave property *recomendado* in the houses and stores of the towns that they visit. This means that a merchant who is unable to sell his goods one day can, without charge, leave it with some acquaintance and return for it the next day or, if nonperishable, the next week. There is generally no charge for such storage. It is also the general custom in the market place to leave purchases *recomendado* with another merchant while shopping for more or doing business in other parts of the market, or town.

Panajacheleños take their produce to be sold, and return either empty-handed or with consumer purchases. They do not buy products to bring back for resale. To this rule there were in 1936 and 1937, a half-dozen exceptions. One man brought fruit from Guatemala City to sell in Panajachel and frequently in other towns; another (with his wife) brought from the capital a variety of merchandise to sell in Panajachel and elsewhere and also fruit from San Lucas to sell elsewhere. A third bought tomatoes in San Lucas to sell in Panajachel and elsewhere and a fourth (with his son) cheese in coast markets for local sale. The fifth was a Panajachel Atiteco whose business I do not know, and the sixth a woman who bought in the Sololá market, for resale in San Andrés, oranges and *limas* originally of Santa Cruz and San Marcos. These were the only people who may be said to be "merchants." Their net earnings, probably nei-

ther far above nor below a hundred dollars a year altogether were additions to the income of the local Indian community.

FARM BUSINESS

The general question of how well the Indians know their business must take into consideration not only land resources and technology, but the use of time in families of differing land resources. It would appear, for example, that the Indians would make fuller use of their land if they grew vegetables where they grow coffee; but the fact is that they would not have time to put all their lands to the intensive cultivation they employ on vegetables. Similarly, while a family with very little land can most profitably put it all in vegetables, one with a great deal of land would find itself limited by the impossibility or inconvenience of hiring the necessary labor. The following paragraphs examine the question crop by crop.

More and better fertilizer and far better—even hybrid—seed would increase the yield of corn. But better fertilizer would mean either more domestic animals for which grazing facilities are inadequate, or chemical fertilizer, produced outside the culture. Likewise, the Indians, like most farmers, are not capable of making radical improvements in the seed. It is invalid to suggest that the scientific knowledge of the civilized world brought to bear on the local milpas would increase the yield of corn. The Indians may well be getting from their soil everything possible with the aids that their culture, or reasonable extensions of it, afford. Certainly their knowledge of the technology involved is very detailed matter-of-fact. For example, an Indian realized fully that the reason he could plant his milpa year after year indefinitely is that it is nearly level.

The kinds of questions that seem to me legitimate are whether they might get larger yields if they planted closer together, or in deeper or shallower holes, or if they did not let the land lie fallow so long, or if they changed the seed every year, or if more beans were planted. Or one might ask if time could not be saved by changes in technique—for example, if the hillocks about the base of the cornstalks are worth the effort. I lack the special knowledge needed to answer such a series of questions. The experiment conducted in 1936 proved little, particularly since it extended over

---

[108] Toasted *tortillas* in the form of *totoposte* will keep many days; ground coffee and a tin pot in which to boil it are part of the merchant's equipment.

only one season.[109] The Indians are not averse to experiment, even in the milpa; they do try fertilizers, exchange seed,[110] and try out seed of other localities; and occasionally vary other factors. It is not unreasonable to suppose that in the course of the many generations they have been growing corn they have found how, within their cultural possibilities, to get the most out of their milpas.

In choice of crop the Indians are usually, but not invariably, economical-minded. It is clear that irrigable delta land is too valuable to be planted with corn; the yield is not sufficiently greater than on the slopes, where vegetables cannot be grown well, to make it pay in comparison with other crops. Yet most Indians grow milpa, during the rainy season, in the delta. One explanation is a desire for corn for home use. Another is that since floods occur in the rainy season, an investment in vegetable gardens is risky. A very few have planted small patches of corn even in the dry season, with irrigation, which certainly is not worth the effort on a dollar and cents basis; indeed Indians say such unseasonal corn does not even grow well. A fair argument may be advanced for growing corn instead of vegetables even when it does not pay; Ladinos and Indians alike use it. Corn, so important in the diet, is not only expensive in the dry season, but sometimes not locally obtainable; therefore it is good to have a supply. The region uses no methods of storing grain except on the ear; it is difficult to buy corn on the ear, for what is brought to market is always shelled; therefore, it is not usually possible to buy a years' supply, and it is worth some sacrifice to grow one's own. The Indians do not grow more corn in the delta despite the shortage of hill milpa land, because they cannot in most cases afford the loss

it entails. They are good enough bookkeepers to make the necessary choice (if the decision is conscious). That they are not perfect bookkeepers will be seen below in the discussion of beans and of pigs.

I suspect that the practice of growing vegetables on hill land (where water is available) will spread and that a fair proportion of the hilly slopes, at least during the rainy season, may get this intensive use. The Indians might in this manner get more out of their land; however, the commonly used coffee-leaves fertilizer is difficult to transport to the hills. It may also be that with intensive cultivation the hill lands would quickly lose their fertility.

The Panajachel Indians believe themselves expert in the garden culture of the delta and find it hard to get good labor from other towns. Among themselves, some are known to be especially skilled at certain jobs. A good deal of pride is involved, and no doubt good workers keep their gardens better appearing than is technically necessary.

The Indians seem to know the virtues of different soils and prefer to plant vegetables in black humus, and *pepinos*, tomatoes, and sweetpotatoes in sandy soils. They also classify the black soil into "hard" and "soft," the first being preferred for garlic and onions, the second for other vegetables and for onion nurseries. I came across no reason to doubt their judgment.

It is apparent that unlike other vegetables, beans cannot be economically grown in irrigated fields because they must meet the price of beans raised with little labor in the rainy-season cornfields. Yet land is consistently uneconomically spent on beans. Possibly all of the Indians are aware of the facts. When I discussed it with them, two friends desisted from planting beans (in 1937), but a third began planting the day after our conversation. It was not pure irrationality. Like corn, beans are an important part of the diet, but the Indians have very few milpa beans. Just at the season when their delta bean harvest comes in, the price of milpa beans is at a peak. When deciding whether to plant beans, the Indians therefore weigh the choice between harvesting plentiful supplies of their own or paying high prices in a short market. An alternative is to buy and store large quantities after the milpa harvest; most Indians do not seem to have enough free money to do so. Wealthy Indians also grow beans,

[109] Although I have notes indicating that this is common practice, a cultural factor may interfere with the free exchange of seed. When Sr. Rosales in 1936 went around trying to buy certain kinds of seed for the experimental milpa, and was almost always turned down, the people saying they had none even when Juan was sure of the contrary. Finally one woman explained why she and the others would not sell. She said that if she sold him seed, his milpa would prosper and hers would not. She was finally persuaded to sell on the condition that the harvest would not be distributed more widely than to himself and to her. (Microfilmed notes, p. 1125.)

[110] As an example of how agricultural emergencies are treated, the following note may be cited. In 1936 the crows had eaten the young plants in the experimental milpa. An old Indian told Rosales that the same had happened to him, that it was not a new occurrence in the history of Panajachel, that the crows did not respect even the large plants, that even scarecrows that he had put up did not help. He said that he had replanted with damp seeds that would germinate quickly. He approved of Juan's other plan to put branches over the seeds to hide them from the crows and he advised also sprinkling the ground.

however; it may be argued that they can afford to take the loss to assure a supply. However, the Indians also argue that beans enrich the soil, so that onions or garlic may be planted immediately with excellent results.

With respect to garden agriculture, at least, the Indians are always willing to try new plants, or different seeds, or new techniques. Among some of them experimenting is a constant procedure. A few examples may be mentioned; in 1936 one Indian reported that he had planted a *cuerda* of each of two different kinds of onion seedlings, and that if one kind did not work out well, he would replace them with the other. A woman planted squash in *tablones* in the fall so they would be ready for market in Lent when the price is very high; other Indians, who had tried to do the same thing with poor results concluded that her success came from the seed she used, and they tried in vain to buy some from her. Indians keep trying to plant onions closer together to get a larger crop; but the onions result too small; nobody has succeeded in bettering the 4-inch distance. I brought a number of seeds from the United States in 1936, and there was a great rush for them among the Indians. Included was broccoli, of which the Indians had never heard. The recipients not only grew it but planted some of their own the next year. An Indian asked me about some kind of fertilizer that had once been brought to town; he said it cost several dollars a bag, but that he wanted to buy some because with only a pinch to each plant, the vegetables grew enormously. Perhaps the best example of pure experimentation is that of the Indian who in 1936 completed an experiment to get better onion seedlings. After planting the seed, instead of covering it with black earth, he brought sand from the river bed and spread it over the watered seeds. The seeds sprouted quickly, grew fast, and the onions were much better than ever before in the same bed. He reported his success to others.

Crops have changed considerably in the memory of people still living. Carrots, beets, turnips, lettuce, and a few others are very recent introductions. A new radish has partly displaced the older variety which is called "native." Cabbage grown from packaged seed is also new; years ago a native cabbage grown from shoots was a very important crop, but consumers preferred the new variety and the other has disappeared. Strawberries were very recent in 1936, and by 1941 the quantity grown by Indians increased so that the price dropped to a third or fourth of what it was. An older variety of sweetpotato is said to have been grown in great quantities in rows; now, less valuable, two new varieties are grown only on the edges of *tablones*. Sweet cassava, now so common in Panajachel, is said to have been brought up from the coast. Chile used to grow much more plentifully than now; it probably went out because of the advantages of the dry red chile sold in the market. Peas were once a most important crop, grown by the *cuerda* in garden beds, or like corn; but they produce better elsewhere and have practically been abandoned. The Indians also say that once anise grew in quantity in Panajachel; but the "spirit" left, and anise now grows in San Antonio. But *pepinos*, which were a San Antonio crop now grow only in Panajachel. I was told the name of the first Panajacheleño to grow *pepinos* by an informant who claimed to have been the second. When the first *pepino* grower reaped a good harvest and got a good price, he asked him for but was refused branches to plant; but when passing through San Antonio later a farmer working in his *pepino* field willingly sold him a carrying frame full of branches. Tomatoes were abundant in Panajachel until Antoñeros began to grow them; they seemed to take away the spirit, so Panajachel tomatoes are poor. Now the Antoñeros are beginning to plant onions, and the Indians are very worried; actually they complain about a sickness attacking onions and garlic.

Discussing such matters at a wake in 1937, one of the Indians remarked the curious fact that although San Antonio lands are near those of Panajachel, and are cultivated in the same way, the onion seed that they produce is no good, while that which is grown by Jorgeños is very good (and better than that of Panajacheleños). When a second opined that perhaps the Jorgeños now have the spirit of the Panajachel onions, or that San Francisco (the patron of Panajachel) likes them better, or Panajacheleños less, as punishment for something, the first suggested that they petition the Minister of Agriculture to stop Antoñeros from raising onion seed so that Panajachel would not lose its only business. A third man argued against this suggestion, saying that the Antoñeros could then do the same and ask that Panajacheleños plant no more *pepinos*; he added his view that business and farming are free, so that what a town plants is not a matter for laws, and that one town has more of a certain crop than others because it produces better there. Some, dissatisfied with this opinion, changed the subject. It may be added as a sequel that since 1939 a local Indian has planted anise successfully; and this crop may eventually pass back from San Antonio to Panajachel. Indian laborers from Santa Caterina, where anise is also grown, showed him how to cultivate the plant.

Coffee is a new crop that has become extremely important. It probably had its greatest boom in the twenties. Coffee requires relatively little labor; but it does not return as much from the soil as do vegetables. The rich therefore find it advantageous to grow coffee in part of their lands, since labor difficulties would arise if they tried to plant all with vegetables, while the poor do better with vegetables which permit them to work more time on their own land and earn more for their time. Most Indians see advantages in diversifying crops; the ideal is some coffee, some vegetables—a little of each kind—some *pepinos*, some milpa, and so on; for then if one thing turns out badly, all will not be lost. This is one reason why, they do not always plant a crop that pays better to the exclusion of less profitable things. The Indians also rotate crops, and let lands rest, knowing they will then produce more.

One point is clear: that while they do not always succeed, the Indians consciously try to get as much from the soil as possible, in a definition that includes long-term considerations.

On this basis, perhaps, the Indians should eschew the raising of domestic animals, especially hogs and fowl. They do not pay. It could be argued that they permit a more complete utilization of resources, since they feed partly on kitchen refuse and wild flora that would otherwise be largely wasted (but such food constitutes only a small percentage of their diet, the rest mainly corn) and they help to fertilize the soil near the house (although it might be cheaper to buy animal fertilizer from Ladinos than to keep domestic animals). Hogs and the few sheep, goats, and cattle are the only animals kept primarily for revenue. All meat, milk and cheese, and other animal products are purchased; the Indians raise these animals for sale. Except for hogs, these animals add considerably to the total land utiliza-

tion, for they are pastured on land lying fallow that, in the milpa system, would not otherwise be used, and they increase its fertility. Grazing animals are not more popular probably because milpa land (hence pasture) is not plentiful and because the considerable time expended in caring for cattle could earn more money in agriculture. Hogs, on the other hand, are clearly uneconomical to raise. The case of barnyard fowl is different. The corn consumed is returned neither in increase nor in eggs. But it is not a matter of business. Fowl are part of the family and necessary for the prestige of the housewife; they are a food necessity on certain occasions that are difficult to buy; and finally they are a means of insurance—of saving in times when corn is cheap for days when it is scarce and money is needed. One woman said she keeps chickens because she does not like to waste garbage. Nevertheless, in 1941 an Indian with whom we went over accounts in 1937 said the family no longer keep chickens since we had proved that they do not pay. Nor will they have a pig.

Dogs and cats are wanted for their companionship, and dogs to guard the house, and cats to rid the house of small animals. Except that puppies and kittens are occasionally sold, these animals bring no cash returns and they are a considerable expense; they are a consumer item. Horses and mules supply manure, hence increase the fertility of the soil; but they consume more food than they repay in value; indeed, Indian merchants who use them as beasts of burden realize that as compared with human burden-bearers, they eat as much as their value in transportation. Again, the values are not to be separated from a variety of satisfactions. The situation in Panajachel is probably not typical for Guatemala. Where there are wide stretches of land used chiefly for milpa, or useless even for that, the pasturing of animals is doubtless good business; and in communities where barnyard fowl have more room to forage and there is a surplus of corn, chickens and turkeys probably more than earn their keep.

TIME SPENT MARKETING

Table 47 sums up the amount of time spent in buying and selling. The time spent selling local produce is only partly chargeable to its cost, since buying is recreation and, other errands are often combined with visits to markets. This is especially true of time spent in Sololá and of the time of the women who sell produce in the local market where there is a strong element of recreation. Table 48 details the time of women and children in the local market, based on the counts made.

Table 49, summarizing time spent in outside markets, comes from two surveys, with different Indians, and several years apart, plus the innumerable observations of years. The Indians talk about markets, and prices, more than anything else, and merchandising activities are well known. However, the primary data are not all as detailed as table 49 would indicate. Questioning was done in terms of households and general custom. For example, an informant's statement that a certain "whole family" went regularly to Sololá, was true even though part of the family went one week and part another. Thus while it is true that 103 men, 112 women, and 60 children regularly went to Sololá, the number that went on any one Tuesday or Friday is a question. Without a count of Indians on the road for a sample period of time, or some other spot check, the figures in the column headed "Times per year" are based partly on general observations such as that the 82 households regularly patronizing the Sololá market, are regularly represented there 50 times annually (some occasionally going twice weekly), but that the total days are reduced because inclement weather, sickness, and fiesta days keep all of the families away some days, and in cases of compound families, all of the members do not usually go to market at once. The figures for other towns are subject to less error because "whole families" do

not go. The figures for "Hours each time," based on reliable statements and observation, are highly accurate. The totals calculated for "regular" visits are probably accurate to within 10 percent. Those for "irregular" visits on the contrary could be off as much as 30 or 40 percent.

TABLE 48.—*Time spent vending in the local market* [1]

Days	Number of persons		Hours each week	Weeks in year	Number of 9-hour days in year		
	Women	Children			Women	Children	Total
Sunday	[2] 74	[3] 30	5	52	2,138	867	[4] 3,005
Weekdays	[5] 440	[3] 170	1	52	2,542	982	3,524
Total					4,680	1,849	6,529

[1] Not including vendors from other towns.
[2] Number in table 50 reduced by 10 percent for presumed difference in rainy season.
[3] A rough calculation; children accompanying their mothers to the market were not actually counted. (Infants are not included in the table.)
[4] Assuming that the single Sunday market counted (table 50) was typical. The average of 5 hours spent in this market is based on the observation that the market is busy for that period; it is assumed the women who stay longer or less long balance each other.
[5] The total in table 45 is 443. By oversight, no count was made at 2 p.m. One may safely interpolate the average of vendors at 1 p.m. and 3 p.m., to bring the total to 489. With a reduction of 10 percent to correct for the fact that the counts were made in the dry season (when with more merchandise and less sickness there is presumably more selling) the result is 440.

TABLE 49.—*Time devoted to visiting outside markets*

a. REGULAR VISITS

Market	Number in groups			Times per year	Hours each time	Number of 9-hour days in year			
	Men	Women	Children			Men	Women	Children	Total
Sololá	103	112	60	35	5	2,003	2,178	1,166	5,347
San Andrés	9	13	9	30	5	150	217	150	517
San Lucas	11			20	8	196			196
Patulul-Chicacao	4			12	[1] 56	149			149
Tecpán	22			15	[1] 40	733			733
Patzún	8			12	[1] 40	213			213
Guatemala	13	1		10	[1] 56	404	31		435
Quezaltenango	3			10	[1] 80	133			133
Total						3,981	2,426	1,316	7,723

b. IRREGULAR VISITS [2]

Market	Number in groups			Times per year	Hours each time	Number of 9-hour days in year			
	Men	Women	Children			Men	Women	Children	Total
Sololá [3]	151	160	87	10	5	839	889	483	2,211
San Andrés	70	100	60	2	5	78	111	67	256
San Lucas	40			2	8	71			71
Patulul-Chicacao	10			2	[1] 56	62			62
Tecpán	20			2	[1] 40	89			89
Patzún	8	8	6	2	[1] 40	36	36	27	99
Guatemala	30			3	[1] 56	280			280
Quezaltenango	10			2	[1] 80	89			89
Total						1,544	1,036	577	3,157

[1] Half of this time is discounted when the calculation is made, since it represents sleeping-eating time on the road. In the case of Guatemala City doubtless some of the remaining time is "wasted" and should perhaps be assigned to recreation; but it is included here.
[2] Estimates, especially shaky for Sololá and San Andrés.
[3] See note on p. 126.

TABLE 47.—*Summary of time devoted to marketing*

Type of marketing	Number of 9-hour days in year			
	Men	Women	Children	Total
Vending in the local market (table 48)		4,680	1,849	6,529
Regular visits to outside markets (table 49a)	3,981	2,426	1,316	7,723
Irregular visits to outside markets (table 49b)	1,544	1,036	577	3,157
Additional for buying in local market, chiefly Sundays [1]		809	347	1,156
Vending at hotels, piers, and homes [2]		393	185	578
Buying in stores, etc., during the week when not incidental to market visiting [3]	80	436	436	952
Total	5,605	9,780	4,710	20,095

[1] Assuming that each of the households not represented in the local Sunday market sends a woman, who takes 2 hours weekly, to buy there. (70 women, each 104 hours annually; 30 children, the same.)
[2] Calculating that 17 women and 8 children each spend about 4 hours weekly in such selling.
[3] Figured on the basis that the average man-of-the-house spends about 5 hours a year and that women and children spend 25 hours per year per household, evenly divided between them.

CONSUMER GOODS

Although by far the greater part of goods consumed, especially materials for food and clothing, and all utensils, are purchased from outside the community, about a third of all time devoted to production is devoted directly to consumption goods. Prices and purchase are thus of paramount concern; but the final processing of purchased foodstuffs, textile materials, and the like is done at home, and a few important items such as houses and firewood are almost entirely home-produced. Therefore this section describes both buying and making.

BUYING FOR USE

In a specialized community like Panajachel, which does not produce more than a few of the necessities of life, shopping is a very important part of daily, or weekly, life. In general, Panajacheleños, like members of other specialized communities, do not buy from each other, since they all produce about the same things. For this reason retail buying and selling tends to be consummated in markets where Indians of different communities gather to exchange goods. Nevertheless, the Panajachel Indians procure their necessities in several other ways:

Very occasionally Indians buy from each other at home; and Panajachel merchants sometimes sell house to house their merchandise from other towns.[111] Much more important, Ladinos and Indians from other towns very frequently sell their wares from house to house. Thus almost daily Santa Catarina Indians sell fish and crabs at the houses;[112] many of them regularly spend early Sunday mornings at this pursuit, before going to the local market.[113] Ladino or Sololateco pork butchers or their wives frequently sell from

house to house their lard, cracklings, and so on.[114] There are other regular vendors like the woman from San Jorge who in 1936 came every 3 days to sell cooked foods,[115] and many more who came sporadically.[116]

Lumber is regularly purchased on the road into town from Indian sawyers of Concepción, Patanatic, and especially Chichicastenango. (Lumber and thatch are also frequently "ordered" in advance.) Furniture is also occasionally bought on the road from the backs of merchants traveling through town, particularly by Ladinos. Indians usually wait to buy such items in the large markets that come a few times during the year, when the selection is best and the price presumably less.

More important is buying in the Ladino-owned stores. There were in 1936 three fairly large general stores in Panajachel, and a number of smaller ones (map 3), as well as several taverns, two pharmacies, and three beef-butcher shops, two of them Indian-owned. They cater to both Indian and Ladino trade, and to people of other towns passing through or coming in to market. Sololá has a number of large stores of all kinds

---

[111] For instance, Rosales noted on March 16, 1937, that the merchant who buys cheese on the coast was selling it house to house, including Ladino houses. On February 21, 1937, he also noted Indians selling huskcherries that had grown where their corn had been harvested.

[112] Rosales noted them frequently in his diary, and they often came to our house. One reason is that fishing was illegal during the period of study and the fish had to be sold surreptitiously. Another is that fish caught at night must be sold the next day even if it is not a large market day. Some Catarinecos also sell house to house in Sololá if unsuccessful in Panajachel. Occasionally they bring other things besides fish and crabs—tomatoes and eggs, for example. One Friday Rosales noted one who stopped on the way to the Sololá market to sell some corn "because his load was too heavy and would keep him from reaching Sololá until too late."

[113] The reason for this seems to be a wish to avoid paying the market tax. As one expressed it, the tax would buy him a pound of corn.

[114] On October 27, 1936, a Sololateca offered lard from pigs butchered at her *monte* home. She said that on a previous trip she had taken orders for lard, but that now some of the people had no money and she had had to extend credit. She promised to bring pork the next Saturday for the tamales of All Saints' Day, and to sell it 1 cent a pound under what the local butchers charged. On February 20, 1937, the woman came with pork, and at Rosales' house asked to heat her breakfast. While she ate, the town patrol came to take her to the *juzgado* to show her license. They let her finish her breakfast, and she had told Rosales that this was the work of a Ladina competitor angry because she was being undersold. She said she sold sausages to a Ladina on the road and she must have told her competitor. Or possibly, she thought, her accuser might be another Sololateca in the same business who followed her to Panajachel. She said that she came to Panajachel because in Sololá there are nine vendors, Indian and Ladino. She also claimed to have all the necessary papers but to have left them at home.

Competition sometimes is apparently bitter. On August 3, 1936, Rosales reported that an Indian woman selling beef belly had told him that she would quit her business. She explained that a Ladina had started in the same business, and that when they had met on the road that day, this Ladina angrily told her that if she continued selling from house to house, she would have her bewitched. The woman added that she was already bewitched since her stomach was growling and would soon burst open.

[115] She reported to Rosales that she spends all her time on the business: each day she buys enough corn, and in the afternoon and part of the evening she grinds and cooks. Early in the morning she sells to the Indian travelers at the lake ports; they know her and await her. What is left over she sells house to house. She gives credit when she must, and is paid little by little.

Another day she sold Rosales some tamales-with-pork. Breaking them, he saw that the meat was spoiled, and he gave them back. She ate them, said they were perfectly good and that it was a sin to give them back. She went away angry.

[116] Momostenango blanket sellers; Maxeños with pitch wood or spices and *panela* or dry goods; Indians from Cerro de Oro with corn, reed mats, or coast fruit; Concepcioneros with baskets or grass for roofs; Nahualeños with grinding stones, have all been noted. In addition, Rosales reports that on various days a poor Ladina neighbor came with a chicken; a Sololateca offered 4 pounds of onion seed; a Ladino brought a stem of bananas; another tried to sell a gun, and still another a cow; and that a Catarineco came offering his land for sale.

where the people of Panajachel also buy frequently. The general stores carry a great variety of staples. Some necessities, like kerosene and such hardware as machetes, hoes, etc., can be bought no other place. Other items such as dry goods, cotton, silk and wool yarns, straw hats, dishes and cutlery, and such food staples as coffee, lard, *panela*, sugar, chocolate, bread, maize, beans, chile, spices, and salt are found both in the stores and in the market place. Some items such as furniture, pottery, baskets, mats, pitch wood, raw cotton, fruit, vegetables, and fowl, etc., are not usually stocked by the stores.

Prices in the stores tend to be fixed, but bargaining is usually possible. They tend also to be higher than in the market place, often on such important items as corn from 25 to 50 percent higher.[117] Panajachel Indians never buy large quantities of commodities in the stores. If they wish to stock up on corn, *panela*, or sugar, for example, they do so when they can buy more cheaply in the market place. In fact, the stores sell such commodities mainly to poor people who buy from day to day as they get a few cents. Typically store purchases amount to a few cents. Thus an Indian buys a penny's worth of *panela* at one store because "there they give a good portion for a penny," a penny's worth of kerosene in another store because "they give more for the money," and a half-pound of meat (2½ cents). It costs more to buy in stores and in such quantities; yet probably most Indian families do it some of the time, and a few do it regularly.

The several Ladino bakers in town sell their goods through the stores. Indians who have bread for breakfast usually patronize them, and considerable quantities are bought for ceremonial gifts and religious rituals. For Holy Week, when everybody consumes much bread, the bakers begin long in advance, and others who know the trade (including some Indians) also bake. Frequently Indians and Ladinos both buy the materials (flour, eggs, lard, etc.) and pay the bakers to make their bread.

Liquor, for sale only at Government-licensed dispensaries, is sold by the *barril*, the demijohn (a half *barril*, 11 "bottles"), the "bottle," (which, I believe, is 24 ounces of liquid), in sealed *litres*,

---

117 There are exceptions, of course. Very often prices on dry goods seem higher in the market than in the store; but of course an experienced native bargainer may do better than an outsider.

half *litres*, quarter *litres*, and eighth *litres*. The larger quantities are usually bought in Sololá. In 1936 and 1937 it was possible to buy liquor by the glass at the counter. After that only sealed *litres*, half, quarter, and eighth *litres*, could be sold legally, to be drunk off the premises. Two kinds of liquor are sold: *olla* (distilled in pottery vessels) and *alambique*, a cheaper grade distilled in copper kettles; the Indians usually buy the latter. It is not impossible privately to buy illicit liquor which is not only cheaper but being olla, better. The stores and taverns also sell beer and soft drinks, which are occasionally bought by the Indians.

The butcher shops sell only beef. Each is open 3 or 4 days of the week, or until the current animal is sold. Although the butchers try to alternate, there are times when for a day or two one would have to go to Sololá to buy meat. Pork and mutton are sold in the market place on market days. Several Ladinos and Indians sell the milk of their cows, delivering it to customers; it is nowhere regularly for sale. Indians rarely buy milk.

Adobe makers, masons, carpenters, etc., work on order only. Bricks and tiles need to be ordered from artisans in other towns, notably San Andrés. A Ladino blacksmith in Panajachel shoes horses, mends equipment, and makes some articles to order. Two gasoline filling stations in 1936 served mainly the tourists. Indians bought from them gasoline tins, for sale also in stores and from large users of gasoline and kerosene.

MARKET BUYING

Most of the purchases of the Indians are made in the market places that they frequent, especially Sololá on Friday. Sololá has a lively market, with merchants coming from many towns in the highlands and all around the lake. Almost anything is available there, and often at low prices. The Panajachel Sunday market, not more than 10 percent as large as the Sololá Friday market, with its smaller selection and frequently higher prices, is patronized mainly by Ladinos and by Indian families that do not sell in Sololá or other markets. Indians who go to sell in markets farther away, meanwhile take advantage of their opportunities to buy the things there that are cheaper than in Sololá or at home. Thus, for example, lime is bought in Tecpán, corn in Tecpán or Patzún, and so on.

Only women buy in the local market; Panajachel Indian men do not even walk past the vendors, even if they spend all Sunday morning in the adjacent church or on the edges of the market place. Panajacheleños in markets of other towns will buy as well as sell, but if with their wives, the men usually buy the large things, leaving small food purchases to the wife.

Traveling merchants are often to be found in the Panajachel market place on days other than Sunday. When women come to market to sell, they therefore have the opportunity almost any day of the week to buy some of their needs in the market as well as the stores and meat markets. It is thus impossible to separate time spent buying from that spent selling, although one may estimate roughly (table 47) time devoted to purchasing goods when not connected with selling.

Most commodities the Indians need can be bought at one time or other in one or another of the nearby markets. Large fiesta markets display the whole variety at once; in ordinary markets, many of the less common commodities are likely to be absent on a particular day, for the variety and quantity change from week to week. Thus for a while in December of 1936 no Atitecos brought to the local market their usual tropical fruits, which were therefore simply unavailable; they were back the next month with tomatoes, bananas, plantains, and so on. Similarly, one Sunday no Maxeños came as usual with pitch pine (due to the Chichicastenango titular fiesta); the next week one returned, and there was a panic to buy. Two months later an Indian from Cubulco brought a more favored variety and the Maxeños were deserted. Some weeks there are no merchants with thread and yarn, or there are no mats in the market, or no corn, and so on; while at other times there is a surfeit. The following list of commodities noted in one Sunday market of Panajachel (April 5, 1936), therefore includes items not frequently sold and excludes some that are often sold:

Staples:
 Corn.
 Beans.
 Dry chile.
 Salt.
 Panela.
 Coffee beans.
 Ground coffee.
 Bread.

Staples—Continued
 Rice.
 Sugar.
Vegetables:
 Onions.
 Garlic.
 Tomatoes.
 Huskcherries.
 Potatoes.

Vegetables—Continued
 Green beans.
 Carrots.
 Cabbage.
 Radishes.
 Sweetpotatoes.
 Lettuce.
 Green peppers.
 Turnips.
 Squash *(guicoy).*
 Indigo.
 Swiss chard.
 Cintula.
 Horsebeans.
Fruit:
 Oranges.
 Limas.
 Limes.
 Avocados.
 Granadillas.
 Bananas.
 Pig-bananas.
 Plantains.
 Vegetable pears.
 Anonas.
 White sapodillas.
 Pepinos.
 Papayas.
 Pataxtes.
 Coyoles.
 Melocotones.
Spices, etc.:
 Anotto.
 Cinnamon.
 Cacao.
 Pepper.
 Ginger.
 Barley.
 Anise.
 Orégano.
 Balsamito seed.
 Pimienta gorda.
 Linseed.
 Jabilla.
 Cloves.
 Alusema.
 Sesame.
 Pepitoria.
Dry goods:
 Yard goods.
 Notions.

Dry goods—Continued
 Dishes.
 Cutlery.
 Trinkets.
 Cotton yarns.
 Raw cotton.
 Fans.
 Rush mats.
 Reed mats.
 Hammocks.
 Rope.
 Wooden combs.
 Hats.
 Sandals.
 Incense.
 Copal.
 Cigars.
 Cigarettes.
 Matches.
 Inner-tube bands.
 Tin lamps.
 Tin pitchers.
 Pottery
  (small articles).
 Pitch wood.
 Cornhusks.
Miscellaneous:
 Eggs.
 Chickens.
 Dried fish.
 Lake fish.
 Dried shrimp.
 Pork.
 Blood sausage.
 Lard.
 Lard cracklings.
 Coffee (beverage).
 Corn gruel.
 Tamales.
 Cookies *(rosquitos).*
 Taffy candy.
 Peanuts.
 Cold drinks.
 Rice-and-milk.
 Flowers.
 Starch.
 Cross-sapodilla seed.
 Sugarcane.
 Chilacayote seed.
 Pataxte seed.
 Ayote seed.

These items are brought in different combinations by the vendors, patterns varying with the towns from which they come. McBryde's new publication (1947), an exhaustive study of productive specialties, trade routes, and markets, describes what vendors from various towns of the region usually carry. Suffice it to say here that in the Panajachel market there are, in general, two kinds of vendors: those who bring the produce of their own towns [118] or from some one other place,[119] and those who have "stores" containing a limited variety of goods from various places. There are two kinds of "stores" that come to the local market: One run by Maxeños, has salt, chile, a variety of spices, cigars, cigarettes, matches; often *panela*, peanuts, shrimp, and raw cotton; occasionally straw hats, cookies, and other things. The other is larger, usually set up in a canvas booth, with yard goods (cheap cotton and silk prints); clothing such as shirts, trousers, undergarments, socks, handkerchiefs, Indian-woven textiles and garments (partly for the tourist trade); pins, needles, thread, buttons, hooks-and-eyes, combs, mirrors, etc.; cotton, wool, and silk yarns; enamelware dishes and utensils, china, and occasionally glassware; cheap table "silver," trinkets and cheap jewelry; often chewing gum, cigarettes and matches, flashlights, batteries and bulbs, and so on. Some owners of these larger stores are also Maxeños; others are somewhat Ladinoized Indians from Totonicapán, San Cristóbal, or Quezaltenango.

TABLE 50.—*Vendors in the Panajachel market*

Origin of seller	Sunday			Weekdays						
	Total	Men	Women	Total, 47 days	8 Mondays	8 Tuesdays	8 Wednesdays	8 Thursdays	8 Fridays	7 Saturdays
Panajachel, total	82	----	82	443	48	89	66	86	122	32
Outsiders, total	250	99	151	253	18	20	38	76	26	75
Sololá	49	16	33	10	2	3	----	----	3	2
Chichicastenango	30	23	7	34	3	----	4	11	3	13
Totonicapán	9	9	----	3	1	----	----	----	1	----
San Andrés	14	3	11	79	7	7	20	15	16	14
Tecpán	27	21	6	2	----	----	----	----	2	----
Patzún	----	----	----	19	----	2	12	3	----	2
Atitlán	13	13	----	95	3	7	----	38	4	43
Santa Catarina	2	1	1	2	----	1	----	----	----	1
San Antonio	4	4	----	1	1	----	----	----	----	----
San Lucas	----	----	----	2	----	----	----	1	1	----
Cerro de Oro	----	----	----	4	----	----	----	----	4	----
Patanatic	11	----	11	2	1	----	1	----	----	----
Santa Cruz la Laguna	2	2	----	----	----	----	----	----	----	----
Tzununá	2	2	----	----	----	----	----	----	----	----
San Pablo la Laguna	4	4	----	----	----	----	----	----	----	----
Santa Lucía Utatlán	1	1	----	----	----	----	----	----	----	----

Compared with those at Sololá, Tecpán, or Chichicastenango, the Panajachel market never has a great number of vendors. On weekdays from two or three to a dozen outside merchants were counted (table 50), and at the height of the Sunday market, 168.[120] During the period of market counts, the following items were brought for sale:

Sololá	Corn, pork products, eggs, *panela*, coffee beans, potatoes, vegetables, fruit, horsebeans, rice-and-milk, wooden toys, "dry-goods store."
Chichicastenango	Corn, horsebeans, potatoes, eggs, bananas, "spice-store," "dry-goods store," pitch wood.
Totonicapán	Corn, horsebeans, potatoes, eggs, leather goods, pottery, spices.
Santa Lucía U	Bread.
Tecpán	Corn, *rosquitos*, pitch wood, "dry-goods" store.
San Andrés	Corn, beans, horsebeans, vegetable pears, chickens, eggs, tamales, cornhusks.
Patanatic	Corn, sandals.
Santa Catarina	Corn, eggs, tomatoes, *chilacayote* points, pig-bananas.
San Antonio	Corn, tomatoes.
San Lucas	Tomatoes.
Cerro de Oro	Tomatoes, rush mats, beans, papayas.
Atitlán	Tomatoes, coast and citrus fruit, green peppers, coffee beans, turnips, lake fish, rush mats.
San Pablo	Tomatoes, limas, pitch wood, hammocks, rope.
Tzununá	Tomatoes, citrus fruits, sugarcane.
Santa Cruz	Limas, white sapodillas.

PRICES

Official data on prices during the period of study include relatively few of the many items that the Indians of Panajachel produce, buy, and use; and are reliable only for prices prevailing in Guatemala City. Where there is a geographical break-down it goes only to Departamentos, not *municipios*. Reports on prices collected in each town cannot be very accurate, and there is probably justification for not publishing them. Nor can local officials asked to report prices be blamed, since prices of many items vary considerably from day to day and from vendor to vendor on the same day, fixed in particular cases by bargaining. It is therefore difficult to say what "the price" of many a commodity is. Frequently the only

---

[118] Thus, Maxeños with pitch wood; Tepanecos and Andresanos with corn and beans; Catarinecos with rush mats, fish, and crabs; Pableños with hammocks and rope; Sololatecos with vegetables; Cruzeños with citrus and other fruit; Santa Lucía Indians with bread and cookies (*rosquitos*); and so on. The classification is not, of course, perfect, for example, Atitecos who bring fruit from the coast also bring fish from home.

[119] For example, Maxeños with lime from Santa Apolonia or pottery from Totonicapán, and Atitecos with fruit from the coast.

[120] The Sunday of the count happened to be Palm Sunday, which in some towns calls up an extraordinarily large market; however, the Panajachel market that day appeared to be typical of most of the others observed.

satisfactory means of determining the price of an item is to interview a sample of the purchasers and to calculate the average of what they paid. Nobody has done this. Consequently, it is not possible to report in detail on prices and their fluctuations. All that I am able to do, from having lived and purchased in Panajachel over the course of three seasons, from having observed and talked to people who are exceedingly price conscious, and from having taken detailed statements from two excellent informants, is give an idea of average prices and their approximate limits.

In the long run it is in the competitive public market that prices are fixed. The stores receive higher prices for many items than do the market vendors, but the premium must of course be limited and, hence, store prices and fluctuations are also determined in the public market.

The general market custom is for the seller to name a price higher than he expects to receive, and to reduce it if necessary after an interval of haggling. A travel-book notion that this method is pursued because the people enjoy it is exaggerated. Actually, some things are never bargained for: such commodities as salt, sugar, lime, bread, sweets, cold drinks, fresh meats, matches, cigarettes, cigars, etc., have fixed prices, at least over a long period of time; haggling over them would probably not amuse anybody. On the other hand, fruits, vegetables, and chickens are probably always bargained for, the reason being that no two comparable items are equivalent in quality and size. Nor is it true, as one writer has suggested, that the Indian purchaser asks the price and if not satisfied walks away without more ado (Bunzel, 1938, ms.).[121] What frequently happens is that the purchaser first examines the quality of

the goods of the various merchants, the better to evaluate the reasonableness of the first price asked, and thus may be seen to walk away from vendors without bargaining. But when ready to buy, the purchaser does offer less than the vendor's first price, and in anticipation the vendor asks more to begin with than he is ready to take. Bargaining has a genuine commercial function with respect to commodities that cannot have fixed values: only by the bargaining experiences of the particular market day can the buyers and sellers determine how much they are worth. So values are fixed for a given time and place.

The long-time tendency is to sell more and more things by weight. Years ago, according to the Indians, many more commodities were sold by rough measure; even meat, for example. The units of weight are the *quintal*, or hundredweight, the *arroba* of 25 pounds, the *almul* of 12 or 12½ pounds, the pound, ounce, and half ounce. The Government apparently succeeds in its effort to control merchandising by means of full-weight laws; only occasional complaints are heard. Weighing is done by means of a balance with two baskets and a wooden or metal cross bar, held in the hand by a string from the center. Metal weights are most frequently used, but stones are sometimes substituted. Among the articles sold by weight in the market in 1936 and 1937 were:

Corn.	Prepared pork ribs.	*Chichipate.*
Beans.	Alligator.	*Cintula.*
Dry peppers.	Dried shrimp.	Anise.
Coffee beans.	Dried fish.	*Anotto.*
Sugar.	Sweet cassava.	Pepper.
Rice.	Sweetpotatoes.	Peanuts.
Lime.	Potatoes.	Beeswax.
Meat.	Tomatoes.	Raw cotton.
Lard.	Huskcherries.	Incense.
Pressed cracklings.		

There are no standard dry measures; small baskets are used, or frequently the cover of a jar, which is piled high with an article such as green beans. The liquid measure (for honey) is the bottle of about 24 ounces, and for beverages the glass, gourd, or enamel cup. Among articles sold by the measure are:

Ground coffee.	Mushrooms	*Atole.*
Squash seed.	Nances.	*Pinole.*
Garlic cloves.	Small Spanish	Coffee (beverage).
Peas.	plums.	Cold drinks.
Green beans.	Dried Spanish	
Lard cracklings.	plums.	
Tiny lake fish.	Honey.	

---

[121] Bargaining is not confined to the market. House-to-house vendors, artisans, even many storekeepers, follow the practice. Rosales noted one day that it took 2 hours for a local Indian to reach an agreement about the price with a Catarineco who came to buy the fruit of a *jocote* tree. He also reports that one Sunday morning a local Indian on the way to market met some Sololatecos who wanted to buy onions by the *tablón*. He took them home; at noon they were still bargaining, and finally nothing came of it.

A telling comment of Rosales' one day, about the question of bargaining, followed a statement that corn in the Sunday market was scarce and expensive. He adds that "The merchants became angry when the people tried to bargain with them; that is how it is when there isn't much of a needed commodity."

More amusing is an experience of Rosales' that could be matched by many of our own. He writes, "I met some Totonicapeños with tables and chairs, on their way to Guatemala; I asked the price of a table, and the eldest answered $1.25. I said that I did not want to bargain because I was in a hurry, and that it also took too much of their time to bargain, and that they would do better to ask fixed prices. He then said that he would sell the table for 60 cents, but when I offered him 50, he readily agreed."

Most commodities are, however, sold by the piece, by the dozen, by the bunch, or, so many for a cent. Among articles sold by the piece (so much each) are:

Bread (rolls).	Sea fish (also	Cross-sapodillas.
Chocolate (tab-	weighed).	Plantains.
lets).	Sausages.	Petaxtes.
Soap.	Fowl.	*Toronjas.*
Cigars.	Eggs.	*Cidras.*
Candles.	Squash.	Sapodilla plums.
Grinding stones.	Cabbages.	Melocotones.
Tamales-with-	Kohlrabi.	Papayas.
beans.	Pineapples.	Cocoanuts.
Tamales-with-	Large mangos.	Pears.
pork.	Watermelons.	
T toposte.	Sugarcane.	

Produce sold so many for a cent (or half cent) are:

Green peppers.	Coyoles.	Passion-flower
Tortillas (of all	White sapodillas.	fruit.
kinds).	Rose-apples.	Cuchinas.
Oranges.	Avocados.	Vegetable pears.
Sour oranges.	Bananas.	*Pepinos.*
Limas.	Maicenas.	*Cuajilotes.*
Limes.	Spanish plums.	Peaches.
Apples.	Mangos.	Prickly pears.
Guavas.		*Membrillos.*

Commodities sold by the bunch—so much a bunch, or so many bunches for a cent, are:

Onions.	Radishes.	Indigo branches.
Saltwort.	Mint.	Fodder grass.
Vegetable-pear	Coriander.	Straw (thatch).
shoots.	Rue.	*Zacatinta* (dye
Potato shoots.	Chenopodium.	plant).
Turnips.	Borage.	Pitch wood.
Carrots.	"Lime tea" herb.	

Articles sold by the dozen include carrots, turnips, cabbages (wholesale), cucumbers, eggs (to bakers), small lake fish, roses, and other flowers. Crabs are sold in fours. *Panela* is sold wholesale by the *mancuerna* of two large balls, or by the ball, or the *tapa* (half ball); retail by the *tapa*, or in small pieces by the penny's worth. Outside the market, firewood and fodder are bought by the load, bees by the hive (hive and all), rabbits and live pigeons by the pair.

It may be taken for granted that prices change over the course of time. It is a tradition among the Indians that "long ago" times were better because there was more money and because buying prices were lower and selling prices higher:

When, in the last century, silver money was used, a man with a peso felt rich. One could with a peso or two go to a fiesta and buy enough mesh bags, ropes, small bags, a length or two of woolen yard goods to make *gabanes*, baskets, gourds, pots and dishes, cookies, and various sweets, and still have enough left to spend a night or two drinking and dancing (for a large gourdful of *chicha* cost but an eighth *real*, and two or three intoxicated the strongest man). Even if one wished to bring home a calf, which cost at most a peso, the entire fiesta would take only 3 or 4 pesos; the richest needed no more than 10 pesos to go to the fair. Four rolls (bread) cost a quarter of a *real;* a piece of meat 8 inches long and 2 or 3 inches thick cost an eighth of a *real;* sausages cost a quarter of a *real* a yard. The finest straw hats were a *real*, or at most 2. A bottle of liquor cost a *real*. Corn was sold in measures of 12 or 15 pounds for a half-*real* or, when it was most expensive, for one *real*. [In terms of today's Quetzal currency, the peso was worth 1⅔ cents; the *real* was an eighth of a peso.] At the same time, laborers earned a *real* or a *real* and a half daily, plus food. Large onions sold at 2 or 3 *reales* a hundred; oranges and *limas* were a *real* and a half a hundred.

If one should take this information at its face value, it would be notable that wages were slightly higher than today, while corn and bread were a little cheaper, meat and liquor much cheaper, fruit about the same, and onions much more expensive. Times for the Indians would have been, as the Indians say, considerable better. In any case it is evident that prices in relation to wages or of one commodity in relation to another have varied considerably. In more recent times, it is apparent that world economic conditions have affected local prices. There were times when coffee brought $20 and $30 a hundred pounds, after which, in the lean thirties, the price dropped to $2 and $3. Although specific information is not available, such a change must have had its effect on other prices, as well as on wages.

Reliable information on annual price fluctuations in Panajachel over a period of years is nonexistent. However, such fluctuations in Guatemale City (table 51) were probably reflected—for important staple commodities, at least—in similar variations in the country as a whole, and hence in Panajachel.

Prices of corn, beans, and eggs, and most fruits and vegetables change seasonally; those of meat, sugar, salt, and most dry goods do not. In some cases local prices are affected by the seasons indirectly; thus when corn is high and work scarce in the rainy season, women offer chickens at prices they consider too low. Prices vary also with personal factors. A family in need of money (usually because of sickness or a death) may offer commodities at a low price to sell them quickly. More usually, however, prices are determined by supply and demand in the market. This is true in a general way and over a long period of time; but it is also true in particular markets at particular times, so that, depending on the number of vendors, the price of a commodity frequently drops much below, or soars much above, the general market price. A merchant with a perishable item like bananas or tomatoes is sometimes forced to sell below cost simply because many banana or tomato merchants happen to have come together. I have no way of estimating the effect that such "accidental" factors have in determining general price structures.

Prices of most commodities entering into the economy of Panajachel are listed in Appendix 2 together with some Guatemala City prices. On the pages that follow, only those commodities about whose price there is something to add are discussed.

CORN

Seasonal variations in supply, hence price, are most important. After the harvest, January to July or August, corn is plentiful in the market; at the same time, since many Indians have harvested their own, the demand is light. Therefore, it is sold cheaply, and often it goes a begging. During the rainy season, however, home-stored supplies are gradually consumed, and beginning in August the demand for market corn increases at the same time that smaller quantities are brought to market. The price rises rapidly and considerably. The seasonal change is greater in Panajachel than in the Capital, which draws from a variety of supplying areas. The average monthly price of highland corn in the Guatemala City market from 1935 to 1940 was reported as follows: [122]

TABLE 51.—*Annual average prices in Guatemala City* [1]

Commodity	Price per hundredweight in dollars					
	1935	1936	1937	1938	1939	1940
Corn	1.09	1.09	2.05	1.26	0.94	1.21
Potatoes (best)	2.86	2.40	2.82	2.62	2.29	2.53
Salt	1.75	1.39	1.47	2.01	1.77	1.16
Sugar (white)	3.94	3.75	3.74	3.73	3.70	3.70
Low-refined sugar	2.55	1.83	1.91	2.04	2.98	2.77
Lard	17.64	11.42	15.89	15.86	13.79	11.72
Beans, black	1.58	1.72	2.75	1.82	1.61	2.70
Rice	4.69	3.75	4.52	4.85	3.69	2.89
Coffee (shelled)	4.75	4.69	5.96	4.86	5.17	4.12

[1] Data for years 1935–38 from table 26, pp. 597–598, *Memoria del Ramo de Hacienda y Crédito Público*, 1938 (Guatemala, 1939, a); for 1939–40 from table 57, pp. 728–730, *Memoria . . .*, 1940 (Guatemala, 1941).

[122] *Memorias of Hacienda y Crédito Público*, 1938, p. 598 (Guatemala, 1939 a); 1939, p. 729 (Guatemala, 1940).

January	1.25	July	1.24
February	1.24	August	([1])
March	1.21	September	1.34
April	1.26	October	1.39
May	1.43	November	1.23
June	1.36	December	1.25

[1] In August of 1937 no price is given; corn was apparently not available in the open market. Therefore no average is possible.

The base year of this study, 1936, was a fairly normal year, as compared with 1937, when the price went up extraordinarily. The average annual price in Guatemala City for 6 years was reported as follows:

1935	$1.09	1938	$1.26
1936	1.09	1939	.94
1937	2.05	1940	1.21

There are no comparable data for Panajachel and nearby markets. An idea of how large local variations sometimes become and what a shortage means in Panajachel may be had from the following excerpts from Rosales' 1936 and 1937 diaries: [123]

July 26, 1936: Corn is selling at 84 cents a hundredweight in the local market. It did not sell well, and the merchants had to take back their loads.

September 12, 1936: Indians came from Agua Escondida selling corn at 6 *reales* (0.0125 cent) a pound.

September 13, 1936: Cerro de Oro Indians came with corn at $1.25 a hundred.

September 20, 1936: Cerro de Oro Indians brought corn at 6 *reales* (0.0125 cent) a pound.

December 6, 1936: Corn in the local market is a cent and a half a pound; with the harvest in, this is extraordinarily high.

December 13, 1936: Corn is at a cent and a half in the market, and quantities are small.

January 3, 1937: Corn still sells for 2 pounds for 2½ cents.

February 28, 1937: Corn is at 2 cents a pound when it should be 2 pounds for 1½ cents at this season of the year.

June 16, 1937: Corn is very scarce now. An Indian from Patanatic brought 400 pounds on mules. The local authorities ordered him to sell it for a maximum of 2 cents a pound. The rush to buy, on the part of both Indians and Ladinos, was very great, and in half an hour he was sold out. The Ladinos got more than the Indians, for they pushed in ahead, grabbed the scales, and insisted. Only when the Indians became a little rough, too, did they get any. The merchant was as fair as he could be in applying the rule of first come first served. The Indians were at least considerate with one another about who was first, and then when the corn was almost gone, an agreement was reached to allow a maximum of 2 or 3 pounds to each buyer.

[123] The 1937 corn harvest was poor and there was a serious shortage throughout Guatemala, relieved only in part by imports and sales supervised by the central authorities.

July 3, 1937: The Departmental authorities in Sololá have ordered each town to send for its allotment of corn to sell to the people. Panajachel gets 500 pounds a day, which *mozos* are sent to bring down.

July 5, 1937: The corn is sold in the town hall. Indians are given only 2 pounds apiece, while Ladinos are even waited on twice. Unfair.

July 27, 1937: Yesterday and today much corn from the new harvest on the coast was brought here and sold at 3 cents a pound. It is a good thing, because those who still have supplies from last year were getting 5 cents a pound for it, and more recently (because of Government competition) 3½ cents.

August 5, 1937: There is much corn in the Sololá market, at 3 cents a pound.

August 24, 1937: There is much corn brought here by Sololatecos and Atitecos, who bring it from the coast for sale at 3 cents a pound.

August 27, 1937: There is much corn in the Sololá market, but at 3½ cents.

September 17, 1937: Corn is scarce in the Sololá market, and selling at 3½ cents. This is a great hardship because the poor people cannot afford it at that price.

November 7, 1937: Not much corn in the market today; it still sells for 2 cents a pound, when in other years at this season it is a cent and a half at its highest. In the last hard months of this rainy season a Sololateco who lives here helped the people greatly by bringing corn by the hundredweight from the Capital to sell here at a rather reasonable price, with only a small profit for himself. He is still doing this, and people go to his house when they do not find him in the plaza.

November 14, 1937: There was no corn for sale in the market today, but people bought some from the Sololateco. They say that last Friday in Sololá there was so much corn that the merchants had to return home with some. The reason was that at the height of the market a truck loaded with corn from the Capital drove up. Most people bought corn from the driver, and the price went down. Some who bought from the trucker said that it was to punish the merchants who a short time ago took advantage of them when corn was very scarce: they were overcharged and short-weighted.

November 17, 1937: They say that today two trucks came from Antigua with corn at a reasonable price. One truck remained here, and the other went on to Sololá to sell.

November 18, 1937: I learned that the corn that was brought yesterday was sold at $1.90 a hundredweight. Many Ladinos bought several hundred pounds apiece, and a few Indians bought it by the *arroba* (25 pounds).

The average price of corn in 1936 in Guatemala City was $1.09 a hundredweight. In Panajachel I bought it during the cheapest season in March and April for 83 cents,[124] Rosales' diary indicates that this low price prevailed through July. It then rose until in September it was $1.25 and in

December $1.50. Most likely the average price was a little lower in Panajachel than in Guatemala City, and probably about $1.05 per hundred pounds. However, the Indians for the most part paid more than this, for they usually buy by the pound rather than the hundredweight, and they frequently buy in the stores. I have concluded that on the average in 1936 corn cost the Panajachel Indians 1¼ cents a pound. This is the figure I have used in my various calculations. (It may be noted that there is sometimes a small difference in the price of corn depending on its color and origin. This I have not taken into account.) Judging from the average price recorded for 6 years in Guatemala City ($1.275) the usual worth of corn to the Indians of Panajachel during the period of the study was more—about $1.50 a hundredweight. This is the figure that informants gave as the long-time average in Panajachel.

BEANS

The price of beans varies pretty consistently with that of corn, probably because in the country as a whole corn and beans are grown together, have the same seasons, and probably similar fortunes from year to year. During the 6 years recorded [125] for Guatemala City, the price of beans was about 160 percent that of corn. This proportion varied from month to month as follows (with the price of beans in parentheses):

	Percent	
January	166	($1. 33)
February	175	(1. 41)
March	194	(1. 60)
April	198	(1. 57)
May	207	(1. 45)
June	250	(1. 84)
July	232	(1. 87)
August	[1] 215	(1. 67)
September	219	(1. 63)
October	226	(1. 63)
November	226	(1. 63)
December	178	(1. 42)

[1] Omitting 1937.

and from year to year as follows:

Year		
1935	145	(1. 58)
1936	158	(1. 72)
1937	134	(2. 75)
1938	144	(1. 82)
1939	171	(1. 61)
1940	223	(2. 70)

---

[124] It sold for as little as 75 cents in December 1935. Informants say it sometimes sells for as little as 50 cents.

[125] *Memorias of Hacienda y Crédito Público*, 1938, pp: 599–600 (Guatemala, 1939, a); 1939, p. 729 (Guatemala, 1940).

The price of beans in Guatemala City ranged, during this period, from $1.17 a hundred pounds in February of 1936 to $3.39 in October of 1937. The year 1936 again appears to have been a relatively normal year, and the price of beans below average. For some reason the price of beans in Panajachel in 1936 was considerably lower than that in Guatemala City. Informants consistently gave the average price as about 2 cents a pound. However, I have a note of June 29 (when the price in Guatemala City was about $1.75 a hundred) of a sale at 1 cent a pound; this was, however, probably below the market price, since a woman who needed money was anxious to sell a few pounds.[126] I have another note of September 11 (when the price in Guatemala City was about $2.50) of sales in the market place at the rate of $1.67. September is the month of highest bean prices, so I am inclined to think that the average price was somewhat under $1.50 a hundredweight. Since again the Indians bought in small quantities and frequently in the stores, I have set the value of the beans they used and bought at $1.60. (There are small variations in the price of beans depending on whether they are vine or ground beans, and on color.) The year 1936 was undoubtedly a cheap one for beans, too. Informants say that the general maximum is 4 cents, the minimum 1 cent, and the usual average 2 cents a pound.

If the figures for corn and bean prices in Panajachel for 1936 are correct, it may be of interest to note that whereas in Guatemala City beans cost 70 percent more than corn, in Panajachel in the same year they cost but 28 percent more. Probable reasons for this are, first, that Panajachel grows for its own use a larger proportion of beans to corn than most places, with its irrigated bean gardens, and thus reduces the market demand for beans relative to corn; and, second, that Indians consume a smaller proportion of beans to corn than do Ladinos. In Guatemala City, where the proportion of Ladinos is very great, the demand for beans must be relatively greater.

OTHER FOOD STAPLES

For other food staples, the prices are little different in Panajachel from those prevailing in Guatemala City and the country as a whole. However, most of the Indians of Panajachel (and

some Ladinos as well) pay more for some commodities because they buy in smaller quantities. For example, by buying *panela*, the low-refined sugar, not by the ball or the half-ball but usually by the half-cent's worth, they pay at the rate not of 2 cents a pound, but closer to 3. Likewise, although coffee beans are 5 cents a pound, Panajacheleños sell their own higher quality coffee for more and many buy it by the ounce roasted and ground. In 1936 they actually paid at the rate of 24 cents a pound, when ground coffee in the capital sold for a maximum of 15 cents. Lard, which sold in 1936 for as little as 8 cents a pound in Panajachel, is bought by the ounce for as high as 16 cents. Chocolate by the pound came to about 12 cents; by the tablet, to 16 cents. On the other hand, in some commodities there is little premium to be paid on small quantities; for example, red peppers are a half-cent an ounce, and in Guatemala City appear to have averaged the same by the pound.

Eggs tend to vary in price with three factors. Hens lay little during the rainy season (May to October); just when corn, which is the common feed, is high. So during the rainy months eggs are high. But in the dry season, before Easter, the demand is very great and the price rises. The result is that in Panajachel eggs sell for as little as three-fourths of a cent in January and February, double that in March, and as much as 2 cents in September. The average over the year, informants agreed, is about 1¼ cents. In Guatemala City, as might be expected, they are slightly higher (*El Imparcial*, 1937). (See Appendix 2.)

The prices of bread, honey, and chocolate do not vary in Panajachel during the year. The kind of bread that Indians ordinarily use sells at 1 cent a roll of 1 ounce (before baking), and the larger rolls and loaves used during Holy Week are correspondingly higher. In Guatemala City the price appears to have been the same, but it rose in April of 1937. Honey, which is bought only for Holy Week, was 5 cents a bottle (24 ounces liquid) in Panajachel in 1936. This was cheap, for it is more usually 8 cents and in 1937 it sold all year for 12 cents in Guatemala City.

MEAT AND FISH

The price of beef is normally stationary: 5 cents a pound with bones and 8 cents without, regardless of the cut. Before the study ended, the butchers had begun to charge slightly more for the tender-loin, in demand by hotels. This did not influence the cost of meat to the Indians, who always bought meat with bone, at 5 cents. In 1936 a third butcher opened shop and for a while a competitor tried to run him out of business by cutting the price; but the resultant price war was short and without permanent effect.[127] Pork is sold at 8 cents a pound, with bones.

For years before and during the period of study beef sold at 5 cents and pork at 8. Yet, between 1936 and 1940 in the Department of Sololá, the value of cattle slaughtered varied between 4½ cents and 5¼ cents a pound and of hogs (table 52) between less than 8 cents and almost 9 cents. Cattle butchered in Panajachel come from the Pacific lowlands; I know nothing of specific circumstances influencing their price. But whatever fluctuations there may be were not reflected in Panajachel retail prices of meat or of soap or candles made from the tallow. The price of both pork and of soup made from hog fat also remained constant throughout the period. Not so the price of lard, which appears to have a complicated relationship with that of corn (table 52). In 1935, and until the end of 1936, with the price of corn low, many pigs were well fattened, and lard was cheap. Corn prices then rose, and remained high through 1937; hogs, killed smaller, decreased in number and size and the price of lard soared. In 1938 corn was moderate in price; the number of hogs rose, but presumably because they represented new litters, they were very small and lard continued high. In 1939, with corn cheap, there were a smaller number of fatter hogs and the price of lard dropped. Then in 1940, with corn up but still moderate, hogs were evidently killed leaner

TABLE 52.—*Hogs slaughtered in Sololá*

Year	Number of head [1]	Weight per head [1]	Value per pound [1]	Average price in Guatemala City	
				Lard [1]	Corn [2]
1936	3,574	58	$0.08½	$11.42	$1.09
1937	2,762	40	.08⅘	15.89	2.05
1938	3,299	36	.08	15.86	1.26
1939	2,779	46	.08	13.79	.94
1940	2,910	35	.08⅓	11.72	1.21

[1] Data for years 1936 and 1937 from *Memorias* of the Dept. Agri. (1936, pp. 347–348; 1937, p. 577). Data for years 1938–40 from *Memorias* of *Hacienda y Crédito Público* (1938, p. 593; 1939, p. 695; 1940, p. 724).
[2] Data from table 51.

[127] When one of two butchers took sick 1 day, the other immediately raised his price 1 cent.

than ever but lard was cheaper. These statistics may be very unreliable. That pork (and beef) remain constant in price may indicate an element of inflexible tradition in some prices. That prices of hog-fat soap remained unchanged may be because soap is made of hog fat chiefly when disease renders the animal unfit, for meat or lard; otherwise it is made of beef tallow.

The price of fowl, not sold by weight, is variable. Turkeys on our standards run very small. They range in price from about 60 cents to $1.10; the average may be taken as 75 cents for a 6-pound bird. Chickens for eating run from 15 cents to 25 cents and sometimes 30 cents; informants calculated the average to be 20 cents for a fowl I judged to weigh (dressed) about 2 pounds.

Lake fish are not sold by weight. *Mojarras*, sold whole, probably averaged about 20 cents a pound in 1936. The inch-and-a-half-long fish strung four on a straw sell for four straws for 3 cents. I cannot hazard a standard price for the smaller fish sold by a "measure" consisting of a beer-bottle cap on which the fish are piled high and around. Crabs, sold in bunches of four, were 2 cents a bunch from at least December 1935 to January 1937.

VEGETABLES

Since Panajachel produces most vegetables and herbs, it is necessary to fix their prices not only at home, but in the markets where they are sold, a complex matter, particularly with the important onions (table 53). The price is usually low during the dry months, January to May, and high in the rainy season and through November; but it also varies greatly with the number of vendors in the same market at once. The price of onions sold by the bed, the buyer agreeing to harvest and prepare them, depends on the size of the bed, the size of the onions, and the season. The highest price recorded is $10, for a bed about 40 *varas* (36.7 yards) long, the lowest price, $1.50. For a standard *tablón*, the average price in 1936 was probably about $2.50. Since the *tablón* has about 6,000 onions, this works out to 42 cents a thousand—a saving of 14 cents, or about enough to compensate for the labor of harvesting, trimming, and bunching.

Onion seed (which can be kept for a rise in price) from about $1.50 to $6 a pound. The differences are both seasonal and annual; and the seed produced in and near Panajachel sells for a higher price in Guatemala City than locally. In the spring of 1937 I bought at $3 and sold at a profit within the hour to Indians from Mixco who had come for the purpose. In Guatemala City it brought 4 or 5 dollars. The average price of seed in Panajachel in 1936 may be taken as $2.50 a pound.

TABLE 53.—*Onion prices*

Onion size	Price range	Market price			
		Pana-jachel (per 100)	Sololá (per 1,000)	Tecpán (per 100)	Guate-mala City (per 1,000)
Large	Maximum	$0.15	$1.50	$0.20	$4.00
	Minimum	.06	.60	.06	1.00
	Normal [1]	.11	1.10	.15	2.50
Medium	Maximum	.08	.80	.10	1.75
	Minimum	.03	.30	.03	.50
	Normal [1]	.05	.50	.07	1.30
Small	Maximum	.03	.30	.05	1.00
	Minimum	.01	.10	.01	.15
	Normal [1]	.02	.18	.03	.50
Average	Maximum	.09	.87	.12	2.25
	Minimum	.035	.33	.035	.55
	Normal [1]	.06	.56	.08	1.47

[1] Not "normal" in the technical sense—just the most usual.

The price of garlic varies greatly, depending on the season and year; but it can be stored for a better price. It is about the same in Panajachel, Sololá, and Tecpán; but only in Sololá are the small ones sold (by the measure) in quantities, and to Tecpán whole loads of garlic are not taken. Guatemala City records (as reported in *El Imparcial*, 1937) give prices of potatoes and sweet cassava by the piece rather than the pound. In Panajachel (where they are produced and where they are doubtless cheaper) they average 1 cent and 1½ cents a pound, respectively. Green beans are sold by very variable measures. If as they calculate, producers get from 20 to 30 cents for a large basketful which I judge weighs some 20 pounds, the price varies from a cent to a cent and a half a pound, as compared with the 1937 Guatemala City price of from 4 to 10 cents. Green beans are available in Panajachel only in spring, when garden beans are harvested, and late summer, when cornfield beans from other towns come in; hence the variation in price is not great. Tomatoes in season (February, March) are as low as ½ cent a pound and out of season (as in September) as high as 14 cents a pound. Since the Indians do not buy such things as tomatoes and potatoes when they are high, the average prices may be fixed lower than the mean of the extremes. Husk-cherries are in season when tomatoes are not; thus the two (used alternatively in cooking) are not in competition, and although tomatoes may be preferred, the average price of huskcherries is actually higher.

FRUIT

Fruit prices vary most with the seasons. In April and May, oranges, for example, sell for as much as ½ cent, yet in November 1937, large ones were 15 for 1 cent in the Panajachel market. Likewise, Spanish plums are normally high at 10 to 15 for 1 cent and low at 20 to 35, but in November of 1937, they sold for as little as 60 for 1 cent. The seasons of high and low prices differ for different fruits. Thus peaches, mangos, passion-flower fruit, *membrillos*, and *pitahayas* are most plentiful in July and August; apples and pears from August to October; home-grown bananas in October and November; *limas* from October to January; oranges and Spanish plums from November to January; lowland bananas from January to April; white sapodillas from February to April; and avocados and cross-sapodillas from February to May.

Fruit is frequently bought and sold by the tree; although the price is lower, estimates of the number of fruit are so exact that the labor of harvesting and selling accounts for the difference. Thus, when a Panajacheleño who had failed to sell the harvest of a Spanish plum tree because the buyer would not come near the $3 he asked finally picked and sold the fruit in small quantities locally and in Sololá, he realized just about the $3 he had required.

DOMESTIC PRODUCTION
KINDS OF HOUSES

Each of the 157 households occupies at least 1 house; a few have compounds of as many as 4 or 5 houses and 1 household has 7 and another 8 houses. In all but 35 families, who lived in borrowed [128] houses or houses they had built on borrowed land, the houses (and land) were owned, or destined to be inherited, by their occupants. In 1936, 328 houses were occupied by the 146 families for which I have data on the point.[129] Fifty-two of the 146 families occupied 1 house

[128] The natives use this term or frequently "recomendado" which is otherwise used to refer to articles stored or checked.

[129] Based on a careful "personal examination" survey in 1937, begun by Sr. Rosales and me, and finished by him alone. Dealing as it does with observable phenomena, the data are highly reliable.

each; 42, 2 houses; and 39, 3 houses; only 13 had more than 3. Two-thirds of the houses classified (table 54) have walls of cane frame and mass-adobe and grass-thatch roofs,[130] the kind of house typical of the Indians of Panajachel which I call simply "mass-adobe." In general the wealthier people have the one-out-of-five houses with walls of adobe brick (simply called "adobe" here), but where there are several houses, not more than one or two are likely to be adobe. Smaller structures such as granaries, outhouses, and the like are never adobe.

The variety of house types is greater than indicated in table 54, for there is considerable variation in details. Thus, 94 of the 328 houses have porches (corredores), a characteristic of adobe houses, 68 percent of which have them (as compared with 20 percent of mass-adobe and 8 percent of cane houses). Thus also, 32 of the 328 houses have annexes (called culatas) built onto an outside wall; since more than half of these are built into porches, they tend also to be associated with adobe houses, so that 13 of the 32 annexes are found on the few adobe houses. There are differences also with respect to doors and windows. Most houses have wooden doors, but 99 of the 328 have doors of canes tied together, associated with cane houses (43 percent of which have them, as opposed to 34 percent of mass-adobe and only 9 percent of adobe houses) and in all cases thatched roofs. Where windows exist, they are unglazed and only occasionally are more than holes in the wall. Windows are found in 27 percent of adobe houses, 10 percent of mass-adobe and 5 percent of cane-walled houses; but the total number is only 43 of the 328 houses. All houses are rectangular and almost all consist of only 1 room. The largest house of which measurements are available is 14 by 6 varas,[131] with a height at the center of 6 varas; but this is one of the few divided into 2 rooms. The largest 1-room houses noted are 7 by 6 by 7; 7 varas in fact seems to be their maximum length, and 6 varas the maximum width. The roof ridge is only very rarely as high as 7 varas. The walls do not seem to exceed 3 varas in height. The smallest independent house measured is 3 by 3 by 3, with the wall height 1½ varas. Adobe houses tend to be larger than other kinds.

With two minor exceptions, all Indian houses of Panajachel have gabled roofs (two sheds); if there were more with other types, notably hip roofs, they were not observed.[132] The houses, if not square, are always longer along the roof-ridge axis than they are wide. The doorway is most frequently on one side, but in some cases the front of the house is one of the gable ends. Data on this difference were not systematically collected.

Annexes, most frequently built onto an end of the house (when not on the porch) have single shed roofs. They serve as small bedrooms, occasionally kitchens, storerooms, chicken coops, etc. In one case a sweat bath is annexed to the house in this manner. All told, 41 such annexes were counted in 1937. Of these, 24 had mass-adobe walls, 12 cane walls, and 4 adobe-brick walls. One annex, used as a saint house, was constructed of branches. Except for one roofed with boards, and another with tiles, all were thatched.

Sixteen wall-less structures (galeras) were counted in connection with Indian houses. More important are storehouses for corn. In most cases corn is stored in part of one of the main houses, in an annex, or in a walled portion of the porch. But in 1937 there were 20 cases of separate structures for this purpose, all of cane and thatch. Chicken coops are much more frequently separate structures; of the 70 counted, all were cane and thatch, except 1 of boards, 2 of rocks and muck, and one of loose adobes piled up. The 7 chicken houses that were not separate were built on the porch, or annexed to the building. Only one dog house was noted, but there were two pigpens and two rabbit houses, one of the latter with a wooden floor. There was also one separate bake oven, besides a small one evidently a toy.

The sweat bath is a rectangular structure with rounded corners and roof. Of 113 counted in 1937, 74 were constructed of rubble set in adobe mud, 37 of adobe, 1 of mass-adobe, and 1 one of planks. Only 1 was excavated. In addition, 2 sweat baths were annexed to houses. Separate roofs of thatch (and in one case tiles) are frequently built over the sweat bath for protection

---

[130] The terminology used in the discussion of houses conforms to that of Wauchope, 1938.

[131] The vara is about 33 English inches.

[132] Wauchope (1938, p. 41) says: "The gable roof is the most common form in only one Indian region, the Alta Vera Paz of Guatemala . . ." It is true that in the Lake Atitlán region many towns have houses with hip roofs, but Panajachel certainly does not and Sta. Catarina has both types. I believe that most of the houses in Sololá, Chichicastenango, and other towns to the north have gabled roofs.

from rain. Half a dozen sweat baths in ruins were counted.

Until 1935 or 1936 there were probably no privy outhouses among the Indians; on Government insistence, 89 had been built by 1937, and a number of others were under construction. Of the 89, 29 had walls of mass-adobe, 58 of cane, and 2 of wooden planks. With 1 (tile) exception, all outhouses with roofs were thatched.

TABLE 54.—*Kinds of houses*

Roof	Walls				
	Total	Adobe brick	Mass-adobe	Daubed vertical cane	Bare vertical cane
Corrugated iron	6	4	2		
Tile	2	2			
Thatch	320	60	223	18	19
Total	328	66	225	18	19

HOUSE BUILDING

Houses are built at the expense of the owner with no neighborly help or system of communal labor. For a house of adobe bricks, the owner hires an adobe maker, unless he is one. Men of the family may help the adobe maker, and later the masons, as common laborers; or these may be hired. Roof tile must be ordered and masons hired by the day or on contract to lay adobes, tiles, or bricks (for floors). If it is to have a tile roof, a carpenter is hired to build the roof skeleton, for which the owner buys sawed lumber.

On the other hand, walls of mass-adobe or cane and roofs of thatch require no specialists; the owner himself, assisted by members of his household or by hired labor, or both, does the building. The materials used include unsawed tree trunks and poles, either gathered by the housebuilder or bought from Indians of other towns; cornstalks or canes, gathered or bought locally; grass for thatch, usually bought by the large bunch from Concepcioñeros and Andresanos who bring it to Panajachel; maguey fiber, usually bought; long vines (*bejucos*) which are gathered; earth, water, and pine needles, never bought; and quicklime, always bought. Some lumber is bought from Chichicastenango Indians of Panimaché and from the Totonicapeños who live in Patanatic (of the *municipio* of Panajachel) who bring it to town on Sunday mornings or on special order.

Wauchope has described the building of the

mass-adobe and thatched-roof houses of Panajachel in some detail.[133] Suffice it to say here that after the materials have been collected, and the location and measurements of the house determined, the ground is leveled off and post holes dug with old machetes. The roof posts (or king rods) are set in first, followed by the corner and other posts,[134] the height of the smaller posts determining the pitch of the roof, which is decided by sighting. Posts are of hardwood, preferably *guachipilín*. The ridge pole and wall plates, of pine, cypress, or oak, with the bark left on, are then lashed in the forks of the posts with vines and are allowed to extend about a foot beyond the poles; the posts are permanently wedged and stamped into the ground. The rafters, usually of pine, are lashed at intervals of about a foot to the ridge pole and the wall plates, and extend a foot or more beyond the wall plates. The base of the rafter pole is always at the ridge pole. The roof rods are of cane, placed at intervals of some 8 inches and extending flush with the ridge pole and wall plates. The roof is covered with handful-sized bunches of long grass, bought from Indians of the colder country, or shorter grass growing wild in Panajachel. The thatch extends over the eaves, and is packed in tightly, the bunches overlapping in three or four layers. There is no false ridge pole, but extra thatch is laid transversely over the ridge and tightly fastened down with a cane on each side. The thatch is lashed down with maguey fiber. Several men usually work on the roof at once.

The canes of the wall frame are lashed onto the posts, inside and out, with vines or maguey twine, in pairs. They are placed evenly from 4 to 8 inches apart. The frame is then filled with mud, usually mixed with dry pine needles, and with stones, pieces of brick, and so on. Sometimes the walls are then daubed over with mud, and whitewashed; others are whitewashed without daubing. The walls—even those of the gables—are frequently all built in this manner; but often from the level of the wall plate to the ridge, the gables

[133] Unfortunately the house Wauchope saw built and which he describes in detail (1938, pp. 30–31, 81, 107–8, 124, 140; figs. 12d, 27b, c, 40c, d, f, g, h, 43; pls. 8c, d, 11b, 21c, 28c) is not typical of Panajachel. A locally resident Pedrano was doing the building for himself. The house was built with an A-frame resting on the wallplates and supporting the ridge pole rather than with roof posts, as is usual in Panajachel. Also, the house he saw had notched rather than forked posts; but forked posts are certainly more common.

[134] Besides the roof and corner posts, there are frequently posts between the roof post and each corner post on the ends, and one or two posts in the side walls.

are completed with vertically set canes, sometimes daubed with mud.

The doorway is a rectangle of poles, one side often a post of the house, the door frequently canes lashed together with crosspieces; a wider crosspiece in the center serves as a stationary bar to keep the door in place at night. Wooden doors are made by carpenters. The smaller structures such as chicken coops are more simply made, and with less thatch on the roof; annexes are often made of the same materials as the house, but also, frequently, adobe houses have mass-adobe annexes and mass-adobe houses cane annexes.

Despite the variety both of kinds of houses and special features, and of ways of obtaining various materials, sometimes purchased and sometimes collected in whole or in part, one may draw fairly reliable conclusions on their cost in money and labor (table 55).

Smaller structures are usually made with home-gathered materials or left-over adobes, and this cost is small, and almost entirely in the labor of their owners. A mass-adobe annex to a house probably costs about $2, a cane-wall annex $1.50, and a brick-adobe annex $4. *Galeras* and granaries cannot come to more than about $1 in materials and labor cost, and chicken coops and other animal houses probably require an average of 2 days' work. A sweat bath, even if old stones are re-used, probably costs about a dollar to build.

The various parts of houses have different life spans. The heavy lumber, if of good hardwood, may last as long as 50 years; in one case informants said the lumber was re-used for the houses of three

successive generations of a family and is still in use. If kept in repair, the walls of a mass-adobe house last 25 years or more; reliable information on the point is difficult to obtain, but I have seen houses reputedly older than that. Thatch, on the other hand—even if of good quality and well laid—does not last beyond 18 years; and in one case recorded, where the thatch was in part of the local variety, it had to be replaced after 10 years. Such an item as a cane door has to be replaced after from 1 to 3 years.

TABLE 55.—*Average cost of Indian houses, 1937*

Kind of house	Average costs for each house			
	Materials	Labor		Total
		Materials	Building	
Bare cane, thatch_____	$2. 74	$1. 49	$1. 73	$5. 96
Mud and cane, thatch____	2. 74	1. 49	2. 23	[1] 6. 46
Mass-adobe, thatch [2]___	4. 00	2. 42	2. 66	[3] 9. 08
Adobe brick, thatch_____	[4] 9. 50	. 70	[5] 7. 00	17. 20
Adobe brick, tile [6]____	[7] 16. 00	-----------	[8] 11. 00	27. 00
Adobe brick, "zinc"_____	[9] 60. 50	-----------	[10] 8. 00	68. 50

[1] In the 1 case with complete data, a little under $6.
[2] Based on data in table 56.
[3] Compare with 4 cases where complete data are available:
   (1) House 2 by 3 *varas*, $6.99.
   (2) a little larger, $7.51.
   (3) 4 by 5 *varas*, $10.48.
   (4) a little larger, $11.59.
[4] Includes $6 for adobe bricks.
[5] Includes $6 for 10 man-days of time of a mason, 20 of common labor.
[6] Based on personal experience in building, checked with other information. One general check: in 1941 an Indian required $15 to build a new tile roof, including the carpentry.
[7] Includes $6 for tiles, $1 for additional lime for roof.
[8] Includes both time masonry and carpentry.
[9] In the only case for which information is available, the sheet metal cost $52.50.
[10] Requires less sawed lumber and carpentry than a tile roof.

Adobe brick appears to last indefinitely, with good care; on the other hand, houses with cane walls have a relatively short life, estimated by one

TABLE 56.—*Materials and time used in building a mass-adobe house*

Materials	Cost of materials bought	Time spent collecting materials	Time spent building
Main posts_____	$0.30-$2.16_____	2-6 days; average of 10 cases, 3 days____	}2-3 days; average of 4 cases, 2½ days.
Ridge poles, wall plates_____	Average of 9 cases, $1.20_____	(1 case: gathered in 1 day for small house).	
Rafters_____	$0.33-$0.84; average of 9 cases, $0.65_____	(1 case: gathered in 2 days for small house).	1-2 days; average of 4 cases, 1½ days.
Cane_____	$1.10-$2.08; average of 8 cases, $1.36 (part purchased, part gathered; value of time included).	_____	3-5½ days (3 cases).
Thatch_____	{1 case: $0.66_____	8 days_____	}
		1 case: 4 days_____	}2½-3 days (3 cases).
	{Average of 6 cases, $1.08_____		
Vines_____	No cases_____	1-2 days (3 cases)_____	Included elsewhere.
Maguey fiber_____	$0.10 (1 case)_____	No cases_____	Do.
Nails_____	2 cases: $0.10 each_____		Do.
Lime_____	8 cases: 0 to $0.10; average $0.013_____		(?).
Mud_____	_____		2-6 days (2 cases).
Daubing_____	_____	Included elsewhere_____	1½-2 days (2 cases).
Adobes_____	Average of $6.50, 2 houses_____		
Wood doors_____	2 cases: $0.10 and $0.36_____		
General and miscellaneous_____	_____	2 cases: ½ day each_____	1½-2 days (3 cases).
Total for house_____	$2-$6_____	9-20 days_____	16 days.[1]

[1] Wauchope, 1938, says that 14 man-days were needed to build a small kitchen house in Panajachel (p. 156, n.).

good informant at 8 years. Roof tiles frequently break singly and must be replaced; then when the roof lumber is replaced, after 30 to 40 years, new tiles are generally substituted, although some of the old ones may be used again. Sheet-metal roofing is said never to wear out. Smaller structures, less carefully put together, last only a year or two. On the other hand, sweat baths, if constantly repaired, seem to last a generation.

I do not know how many houses were constructed in 1936, 1937, or any other 1 year. But if one supposes that an adobe house lasts 30 years, a mass-adobe house 20 years, and a cane house 10 years, and if it is assumed that the ratio of the various house types has been remaining constant, then in an average year there must be built 2 or 3 adobe houses, a dozen mass-adobe houses, about four cane houses; plus 3 annexes, 2 or 3 *galeras*, 2 maize storehouses, about 50 chicken coops, and 4 or 5 sweat-bath houses. Further, informants claim that privy pits and houses, which take 8 man-days to make, must be replaced every 1 to 3 years. If such is the case, then the annual expenditure of time on the building of new structures (including the gathering of materials that are not bought) must be between 1,000 and 1,200 man-days in the entire Indian community. Excluding the time of masons and adobe makers, and leaving out privies (which did not appear until later), the total in 1936 was about 700 days. Likewise, the cost of materials bought from outside the community must average some $60 to $70; the value of the other materials is, of course, the value of the time required to gather and prepare them.

Although it is difficult to estimate the time and money expended each year in repairing houses, replacing thatch, and so on, the time can hardly be less than 200 or more than 600 man-days or the cash cost less than $5 or more than $25. The total time consumed in the building and maintenance of house structures, leaving out artisans, was therefore between 900 and 1,300.[135] It may be taken for granted that small structures are built and periodic repairs are almost always made by members of the family; on the other hand, frequently adobe bricks and always adobe brick

[135] The total value of labor, excluding that of artisans, may be averaged at $183.33 a year, of materials, $80. The total of $263.33 may be checked by multiplying by 60 the sum, $3.62, that the men of households 58 and 49 calculated to be their average annual expenditure on houses, leaving out the cost of an outhouse. Using this sampling method, the community total comes to $217.20. Or, perhaps more justly in the case of houses, multiplying the $3.62 by 155/2 (there being 155 economic households) the result is $280.55.

walls are made by hired artisans. In the construction of new houses, the owner and his family always do at least some of the common labor, and probably on the average from two-thirds to three-fourths of it. It is likely, therefore, that in 1936 the householders themselves did from 600 to 900 man-days of work on their own house structures; or the average household devoted from 4 to 6 man-days a year to these purposes. In any one year, a particular family, of course, may spend no time at all, or (if a new house is built) perhaps 20 man-days or more; and in each family the time differs from year to year.

TABLE 57.—*Value of Indian houses, 1937*

Kind	Number	Average cost [1]	Total cost (replacement value)
Bare cane, thatch	19	$5.96	$113.24
Mud and cane, thatch	18	6.46	116.28
Mass-adobe, thatch	223	9.08	2,024.84
Adobe-brick, thatch	60	17.20	1,032.00
Adobe brick, tile	2	27.00	54.00
Adobe brick, "zinc"	4	68.50	274.00
Annexes of mass-adobe	24	2.00	48.00
Annexes of cane	12	1.50	18.00
Annexes of adobe brick	4	4.00	16.00
Galeras	16	1.00	16.00
Granaries	20	1.00	20.00
Chicken coops	70	.33	23.10
Dog houses, pigpens, rabbit houses	5	.33	1.65
Sweat baths	113	1.00	113.00
Total			3,870.11

[1] Based on table 55.

VALUE OF HOUSES

The calculated worth of all Indian-owned houses and house structures when the survey was made, $3,870 (table 57), represents neither the value of the time, since it takes no account of depreciation, nor the cost of the construction which had been incurred years before, but simply the cost of replacement. Of course the Indians do not "set aside" funds for the purpose.

SUPPLIES, FURNISHINGS, AND TOOLS

Except for chests and a few chairs and tables and occasional beds, house furnishings are homemade. Beds, for example, consist of stagings built out from a wall, the legs implanted in the floor, the surface consisting of canes or bought boards laid transversely. Most houses have at least one bed, but many individuals sleep on the floor. Utensils and clothing are hung from nails or wooden pegs or branches with evenly spaced twigs which are implanted in the floor or suspended from the ceiling, or else placed on shelves of board or canes either suspended from the roof or resting on the beams of the house. The fireplace consists of three large stones used as they are found. The permanent fixtures are usually made when the house is built, and repaired and replaced as needed, usually by men. The amount of time consumed in making them is negligible—probably no more than fifty or a hundred days a year in the entire community, or a day or two in any household.

Virtually all utensils and tools are purchased readymade. But some time (also of the men) is consumed in making traps and deadfalls, hafts for hoes and axes, staffs, slingshots, etc. The grinding stones that are bought must be prepared for use by the women; pottery must also be "cured," but this is done incidentally to cooking. Some toys are made by the children, or by their parents, for their use. However, the time consumed in the making of tools, utensils, toys and the like, is again too unimportant to be calculated in detail. One day per household probably covers it.

FIREWOOD

Women frequently gather faggots, but for the chief supply of firewood for the kitchen, men are responsible. In rare cases loads of firewood are bought by the few landless professional "foreign" residents from Indians of the higher country who carry it down to supply the Ladinos. Otherwise every Indian family "makes" its own firewood throughout the year.[136]

If they do not own trees to fell, they either cut trees on the communal land (or collect faggots on anybody's land)[137] or else buy trees from their neighbors for the purpose.[138] A hired laborer may, of course, be given the task. The tree is felled with an ax, the branches cut off with a machete. The trunk is cut into sections and split section by section as needed, unless the tree has been purchased or is far from the house, when all is frequently cut into firewood at once and stored.

Six to eight loads of firewood can be prepared in this way in 1 day by an able-bodied man, unless long cartage distance adds to the time.

The amount of firewood used in a household is usually constant. Informants say that one load a week is standard, but large households and those which feed laborers of course use more than small ones. The fire is fed with three pieces of wood continually pushed closer to the center as they are used, a method both economical and universal. The amount of time used in the cutting and carrying of firewood is easily estimated at about 2,700 days by the 90 percent of the households making their own. This figure neglects the faggots collected by women, for the most part casually while on other errands. It assumes a per family consumption of 60 loads a year, more than half of the total of 9,000 loads collected piecemeal and in the hills.[139] Many of the 2,700 days represent Sunday time. A few poor and landless households are said to be too poor to buy firewood, and depend entirely upon their women to gather faggots along the roadsides and in the woods; a few others buy most or all their firewood from their neighbors, or hire laborers to cut it on their land. But the men of most families cut their own firewood on their own land, devoting from 10 to 30 man-days a year to the purpose.

COOKING AND WASHING

The major share of the work connected with the kitchen, is done by women. Conclusions drawn here (table 58) are based largely on reliable information concerning a household (No. 49) in the middle range of wealth, consisting in 1940 of man, wife, two daughters, 19 and 9 years old, and a 5-year-old son, which is "normal" in household composition. The family is also typical in its mode of life, its members wearing traditional costume and so on. Where there are more than one woman in the house they have more time for pursuits such as weaving, gardening, and selling in the market, and the adult time consumed by kitchen work remains relatively constant.

Water for kitchen uses is carried in pottery jars from the lake, the river, or from the nearest large irrigation ditch, whichever is most convenient. The jars vary in size, the largest of the type used

[136] Most frequently on Sundays, according to information from various informants.

[137] One informant said in 1940 that he usually gets his firewood on the public land of the west hill or else gathers it where he finds it, on private lands. He is a poor Indian.

[138] I have at least two notes indicating that this practice is not uncommon. The informant of No. 24 told me that he sometimes buys a big old *ilamo*, avocado, or cross-sapodilla tree for about 40 cents to cut up into firewood. From such a tree he gets 2 *tareas*, or 16 loads. The work involved, including carrying, comes to 4 days. Rosales bought an old silk-oak tree from a Ladino for 15 cents and agreed not to damage the coffee grove in which it stood. In the felling he damaged a Spanish-plum tree, and he agreed to pay half the value of the harvest; this came to another 15 cents.

[139] Two informants figured that their supplies, one load a week, cost them each a half day weekly. In the three families whose budgets were obtained, the average time spent was 22 man-days a year.

at Panajachel holding about 3 gallons; the smaller jars are used by the children. A woman or girl carries the jar on her head and wades into the lake or river to fill it. At times when the river water is not clean, water is fetched from the lake even if it is far. In the west delta practically nobody uses lake water, for on the one hand the town's system of public fountains is available, while the lake shore is for the most part occupied by Ladino houses; the river and irrigation ditches and several springs are the main sources of water. The average family uses two or three jars of water daily; depending upon the distance, each trip takes from 5 or 10 minutes to a half hour. In household 49, 2 jars of water are used; the grown daughter usually makes 2 trips to the lake, 15 minutes each, in the afternoon before preparing supper. Young girls, using smaller jars, need to make more trips, and are usually slower. Since there are many watering places there is very little loitering and gossiping incidental to this work.

The few dishes and cooking vessels are washed in the nearest irrigation ditch in a matter of a few minutes after each meal. The younger daughter of household 49 does this; but when the whole family is to go to the fields, and are in a hurry, the women do it.

TABLE 58.—*Time devoted to kitchen work, 1936*

Task	Time devoted (by women and girls)			
	Average number of minutes daily, per household		Total number of 9-hour days in community	
	Women	Girls under 14	Women	Girls under 14
Carrying water	25	20	2,660	2,128
Washing dishes	10	15	1,064	1,596
Building fire and cooking	420	90	44,688	9,576
Cleaning house	5	25	532	2,660
Laundering	20		2,128	
Total	480	150	51,072	15,960

The fire is kindled in the morning. In this particular case the family (first the women) usually rise at 5 a. m. (for years by an alarm clock that I gave them), and the fire is kindled immediately. It takes 5 or 10 minutes to get it hot and put on the pot of coffee. Then the *nixtamal* [140] (which was boiled the night before) is washed in a nearby irrigation ditch to remove the lime in which the corn was boiled. This takes 10 minutes.

At least in household 49 some leftovers are then warmed for breakfast, which is ready at 6:30. In actual work to this time about an hour of a woman's time and, perhaps, a half hour of a young girl's are taken. [141]

Normally the woman and children are then left alone. In the particular case there is frequently work in the fields for the wife, so the grown daughter is left in charge of the kitchen. If there is no work in the fields, the wife stays at home and does such additional tasks as sewing and laundering.

Immediately after breakfast, at 7 o'clock, the dishes are done; simultaneously the woman begins to grind the day's corn which in this particular case takes 3 hours, during which time other food, such as beans and meat, are put on the fire and watched, frequently with the help of a child. Tortillas are baked immediately the corn is ground; this takes an hour, after which the cooking ware is washed. Frequently lunch is carried to the fields and all the family gathers there, at noon. Otherwise there is a wait until the workers arrive home at noon. Since breakfast a woman has spent at least 4 hours cooking, assisted by a child who has spent on the average a fifth of that time.

Lunch takes half an hour; if at home, they quickly wash the dishes and the whole family goes to the fields, since there is little cooking to be done in the afternoon. But a woman (in case used, the daughter) must return home at 4 o'clock to fetch water, get the fire going again, put on coffee, and at about 5 o'clock set the supper to heat. Meanwhile, she has also taken a half hour to remove grain from the ears of corn stored in the house, and she sets the pot of *nixtamal* on the fire when she heats the food. Thus by the time supper is served, at 6 o'clock, she has devoted an hour and a half to cooking, which is probably near average.

During supper, the *nixtamal* remains on the fire, which is tended incidentally; it is removed 2 hours after it is set on, by which time the dishes are washed and the cooking day is over. Seven

---

[140] Corn boiled with lime. It is the basis of most corn foods. A description of the cooking techniques in Panajachel will be published later.

[141] One informant said that in his house the *nixtamal* is washed at 6 a. m. and it takes an hour to grind enough for breakfast tortillas at 7 a. m. Then at 11 a. m. his sister grinds again for a half hour to cook tamales for lunch, and repeats the process at 5 p. m. for supper. In this case the *nixtamal* is set to boil at 8 p. m.; the quantity is smaller (since there are but two adults and a child) and it takes only an hour. The whole schedule appears to be later than in the house of Santiago Yach, but the differences in time consumed are relatively small.

hours have been spent by a woman perhaps an hour and a half by a young girl. When two women are present, efficiency may be impaired in that each spends more than the expected fraction of the time, but the figures must be near the average.

The house is swept out in the morning, most frequently by a boy or girl, otherwise by the housewife; the patio by a child or man. This takes longer if a child sweeps; but the average is about 15 minutes a day.

Laundry is done about once a week, almost always in the morning and most frequently on Thursday or Saturday. Monday, Tuesday, and Wednesday are usually busy days in the fields. Thursday is a light day because, frequently, only harvesting for the Friday market, and preparation of the vegetables and fruit, are done. Friday is usually busy, either in the fields or in the market, but Saturday again tends to be lighter in preparation for the Sunday market which almost all women visit. If there is but one woman in the house, on the day that she launders she grinds only enough *nixtamal* for lunch, leaving the rest for an afternoon grinding. Where there are two women, both (using two stones) hurriedly grind in the morning and then go to the river to wash clothing. Or sometimes both go quickly after breakfast and finish the laundry in an hour to come home for the grinding. Or, again, sometimes one of them stays home to cook while the other washes. There is no ironing among the Indians. The average time devoted to laundry is about 2½ hours a week; if children go along, they just play (or take care of younger siblings). I have never seen one seriously washing clothes, which is hard work.

To these ordinary household tasks, therefore, a woman devotes just about 8 hours a day. In some households, less time is spent where man and wife alike go off to work and receive food as part wages. A very few women take their *nixtamal* to be ground in a power mill in town. In the houses of the rich the women have laborers to feed, and two or three women perhaps including a servant may all work in the kitchen. The total figures (table 58) take these differences into account; they do not include time expended in cooking food for religious ceremonies and public fiestas, although they provide for time to cook for home festivals, private gifts, and the like.

CLOTHING

Partly because of the diverse origin of some of the Indians, partly because of continuing changes in fashion, there is a variety of clothing worn by the Indians resident in Panajachel. The garments themselves [141a] briefly may be described as follows:

Men's: The *gabán*, so called, is made of heavy natural-black wool woven in Chichicastenango and bought by the 3-by-¾ *vara* piece in the Sololá market and usually prepared for use by the man who will wear it. He cuts and hems a square hole in the center, then doubles the piece lengthwise and tacks the two ends together on both sides below what become the armholes. It is then ready to slip over the head much like the *huipil* of a woman.

The *rodillera* is a small woolen blanket about a meter long and a half meter wide, usually of fine checks of white and either blue or black. There are two kinds: those made in Chichicastenango or Nahualá are heavy and coarse, and always black; those made in Momostenango and worn typically by the Indians of Tecpán (hence called locally the "Tecpán *rodillera*") are finer, usually blue in color, and often with fine fringe at the ends. No preparation of the *rodillera* is required; it is simply wrapped around the waist to hang like a skirt to the knees.

The *calzón* is a home-woven cotton garment, usually white with fine vertical red stripes. It is woven in two pieces and sewed together by the weaver in the form of drawers. It is a bulky garment, but worn so high at the waist (where its width makes many folds) that it seems very short and, indeed, never shows below the *rodillera* worn over it.

The *calzoncillo* is a white cotton garment that is either bought readymade or sewed at home of factory-woven cloth. It is something between a pair of drawers and a pair of trousers, tends to be form fitting over the legs and reaches down to the middle of the calf.

Trousers of European type are bought in the stores and markets.

Underdrawers of modern type, factory-made, are also bought of merchants and in the stores.

The sash is a long strip of red cotton about 8 inches wide that is wound about the waist and tied in front, the ends tucked in. There are two kinds frequently distinguished as *faja* and *banda*. The first is home-woven in Panajachel, the second made by women in other towns and bought by the local Indians. The *banda* is of lighter quality than the *faja*.

The belt worn around the waist is made of cowhide by leatherworkers of other towns and bought from them by the local Indians. It tends to be an inch and a half wide, with heavy metal holes and a large metal buckle.

The shirt (always of cotton) is of one of three general types. First, there are factory-made shirts that

---

[141a] Their combinations into costumes are discussed on pp. 158-165.

are bought in the stores or from market merchants. Second, there are shirts made by Indians of other towns, such as Chichicastenango, of bought cloth (usually striped) and tailored in poor imitation of the factory models. Lastly, there are the increasingly popular shirts made in San Pedro la Laguna of home-woven cotton cloth, of bright colored with tie-dyed blue stripes that give them their characteristic design. The "San Pedro" shirts are now also made in Atitlán, and there is in Atitlán at least one foot loom that makes shirt cloth of this kind that is hard to distinguish from the belt-loom cloth of the Pedranas.

The *sutes* are home-woven square cloths, red with occasional fine stripes, used as head cloth, or worn around the neck, or carried as kerchiefs. Some Indians also buy factory-made kerchiefs. Some handkerchiefs are also used.

The *caite* is a simple sandal consisting of a leather sole and an instep piece, bound to the foot by a leather thong between the big toe and second toe. A few *caites* of tire-casing soles are used. There are also *sandalias* built more like shoes, straps over the instep and around the back of the foot. Usually both kinds of sandals have a slightly raised heel. Sandals are bought of leatherworkers from other towns who set up shops in the markets. Shoes or boots are worn only as part of the Ladino costume.

Hats are typically of straw. A fine type frequently with a cord for a band is factory-made and bought in the stores. A coarser type, made by the Indians of Chichicastenango, Lemoa, Quiché, and perhaps other towns, of coiled and sewed strips, is bought in the market. These hats, of natural straw color with some black or colored designs, have crowns of various shapes and variously wide brims but those bought by Panajacheleños are usually of one type, medium in both height and width of the brim. Occasionally an Indian owns a factory-made felt hat.

Tailored jackets are worn by a few men.

Women's: The *corte* is a wrap-around skirt that gets this name because it is bought in a length (*corte*). The Panajacheleño *corte* is a heavy solid blue cotton woven especially for Panajachel women in foot looms run by Ladinos in Sololá. It is only a *vara* wide, and must be pieced to give the proper length when worn. It is sewn with either a silk or a cotton embroidery stitch (forming, when the skirt is worn, ¼-inch to ¾-inch stripes around the hips and down the back). When sewn it extends to the lower ankle. It is simply wound tightly about the body, and held together with a sash. The "Totonicapán" *corte*, worn by a few women in Panajachel, is lighter cotton of various colors with tie-dyed stripes made in the Totonicapán-Quezaltenango region on foot looms. It is worn like the Panajacheleño *corte*.

The *huipil* typical of Panajachel is woven by the women on the back-strap loom of natural brown cotton with red vertical stripes. In the area covering the shoulders and arms, breast and back, small purple designs are worked in with cotton or silk.

The *huipil* is woven in three long pieces, which are then sewn together, with breast openings left for nursing. In the center a square for the head is cut out and edged with cotton or silk. Then the garment is doubled and the sides are sewn except for the armholes. This *huipil* comes down to the ankles, but below the waist is entirely covered by the skirt.

The second kind of *huipil* is typical of neighboring San Andres; it is made by some Panajachel women, also on the back-strap loom, or bought from Andresanas. It is made in the same way, but it is shorter, has a white background, and bright-colored cotton designs. The San Lucas *huipil*, worn by one woman, is similar.

The third type is called the Totonicapán *huipil*. Foot-loom-made in the Totonicapán region, it is typical of a large area of western Guatemala where women no longer weave their own *huipiles*. It is shorter than the Panajachel *huipil*, coming down only to the hips. The Panajacheleñas who use them buy them in the market stores.

Ready-made white blouses, or the same garments home-sewn of bought cloth, are occasionally worn.

The sash, red cotton, some with fine colored figures, is locally woven. It runs to 158 inches long and 8 inches wide. Like that of the man, it is wound around the waist and the ends are tucked in. Other sashes, worn with Totonicapán *huipiles* and skirts, are made elsewhere.

Carrying cloths, home-woven of red cotton, usually have fine colored stripes. There are a variety of sizes, all but the smallest woven in two pieces and sewn together with cotton. The larger ones are used to carry babies (slung over the shoulders to the back) and others to set on the head, in a roll, to support a basket being carried. When carrying no basket, the cloth is folded and placed on the head.

The *cinta* is a long (256 inches) narrow (⅝-inch) dark red and navy blue cotton ribbon bought in the market and said to be woven in Totonicapán. It is wound around bunches of hair, then the whole wound about the head.

TEXTILE WORK

Of all the garments used in Panajachel the only ones that are woven locally are men's drawers (*calzones*), sashes of both men and women, head cloths (*sutes*), women's blouses (*huipiles*), and carrying cloths. In addition, men's woolen cloaks (*gabanes*), some men's trousers (*calzoncillos*), and shirts, and women's skirts and some blouses are tailored or sewed in Panajachel. Among the "foreign" Indians in Panajachel in 1936 were a few who wove garments typical of their towns of origin, for the use of their families.

No Panajacheleña spun cotton in 1936, although there was an old Sololateca living in town who did.

Doubtless in years past cotton spinning was practiced in Panajachel; I do not know if any women
still know how to do it but certainly none of them
practice the art. They use the whorl, however,
for twisting thread. Factory-spun cotton is
bought in skeins in the stores or markets. The
first task in weaving is to wind the cotton on a
ball, by use of a wooden winding frame that is
bought.[142] As it is rewound, it is usually
(?) doubled; and then it is twisted with the aid of
a simple spindle. This is a long and tedious
process. The next stage, warping, is done on a
wooden warping frame that is bought. Then the
loom is set up, and the heald prepared. The
woman weaves kneeling on the ground or on a mat
in the patio or corridor, occasionally in the house,
the near end of the loom fastened around her back
with a strap, and the far end tied to a tree or a
pillar of the house. Since not all women who
know how to weave know how to work in the
designs on the women's *huipiles*, a weaver at this
point in the process finds a specialist to complete
her *huipil*. The last step is to cut and sew a
garment that requires it. This in Panajachel
(where the Indians do not use sewing machines)
is a minor task done with a steel needle.

Of the 133 Panajacheleño families, there are 54
in which women engage in textile arts besides
simple sewing and repairing. On 2 others I have
no data, but the remaining 77 apparently have no
women doing this work. On the "foreign" households my information is poorer. Besides the
Sololateca who spun cotton and wove, there was a
Jorgeña weaver and a Pedrana who wove clothing
for herself and her family. The Totonicapán
women do not weave. An Atiteca, a Sololateca,
and a Nahualeña that we knew did not weave.
On most of the others of this class I have no
specific information; but I believe that few if any
of them practice these arts.

In Panajacheleño households (which include a
few "foreign" women) there are 84 women and
girls who twist thread, sew, and weave. Their
age-distribution (table 59) indicates that while
ordinary weaving does not seem to be disappearing
as an art, women who know how to work figures
into *huipiles* are not being replaced as they age.

It is likely (as informants agree) that fewer women
than formerly practice weaving,[143] since changes
in costume render weaving less necessary in the
community as a whole. At the same time, however, women in Santa Catarina, Sololá, and Concepción "take in" Panajachel weaving. In those
towns, where women are far less important in
agriculture than in Panajachel, it is probably
easier for Panajacheleñas to find weavers; also, it
may be cheaper, since the value of a woman's
time is almost certainly less than in Panajachel.

The following account of costs comes from a
weaver who laboriously worked them out with
me. Although I checked the results against other
information, I became convinced of her accuracy
through the following (not isolated) instance,
quoted from field notes:

With the aid of his wife, who was sitting weaving a
huipil, I obtained figures on the cost of making a *huipil*.
Figuring in the material, and figuring the woman's labor
as worth 15 cents a day—as these informants insisted—
I came out to some $4.68 for a completed *huipil*. Without
mentioning this sum, I asked how much the *huipil* would
sell for if occasion arose (a rarity here) and the woman
said $10. I tried to get her down, but she refused to come
lower than $9. I said "Wouldn't you sell it for $5?" and
she blurted out in reply that it cost her 350 pesos to make!
Three hundred and fifty pesos come to $5.86, so I asked her
why she said that when according to our calculations the
total was $4.68. Then she called to my attention that we
had not figured the job of cutting and sewing the neckline
and sewing the *huipil*. The former is a job that only
experts can do, and one must not only pay the woman 50
cents but must ask a formal favor with a large gift of food.
Calculating the value of the food, and adding that and
50 cents to the $4.68, I came out with a total cost for the
huipil of $5.83 just 3 cents short of the 350 pesos that the
woman knew all the time!

TABLE 59.—*Panajacheleño weavers*

Arts practiced	Number of women in approximate age groups				
	Total	Under 20	20–40	40–60	Over 60
Thread twisting only	9	2	3	4	
Thread twisting and sewing [1] only	5	1	4		
Sewing [1] and ordinary weaving only	1				1
Thread twisting, sewing,[1] and ordinary weaving	63	10	31	19	3
All processes, including weaving, in designs	6		1	3	2
Total	84	13	39	26	6

[1] "Sewing" here refers to the specialized sewing required on women's
huipiles, shirts, etc., not ordinary repairing.

---

[142] The technology of weaving in Panajachel need be discussed here only
insofar as it is necessary to explain the economic aspects. Textiles of Panajachel and other communities of Guatemala were studied in 1936 for the
Carnegie Institution of Washington by Dr. Lila M. O'Neale; see O'Neale,
1945.

[143] An informant, who later helped me make the census of weavers, told me
that "only 10 or 12 women weave their own clothes, and 3 or 4 weave for
others." He grossly underestimated, of course, but that emphasizes that the
general impression is that "weaving is no longer practiced."

A woman's carrying cloth 1¼ *varas* (about 1 meter square) takes:

½ pound of white cotton yarn, which cost in 1936_ $0. 16⅔
1 pound of red cotton yarn, which cost in 1936__ . 66⅔
½ ounce of green cotton yarn, which cost in 1936__ . 02
½ ounce of another color cotton yarn, cost in 1936_ . 02

The twisting of the cotton takes about a day for a pound; Toribia did not do this herself, but had a woman do it for 8 cents a pound, the usual rate in 1936. The warping, which she did herself, took her 2 hours.[144] The weaving would take her 4 days, but she usually had another woman do it and this cost her but 25 cents. The sewing is done with the same thread, and takes but a short time. The total cost to her came to about $1.25 plus some 2 hours' work, not counting that incidental to buying and arranging with a weaver to work. Had she done all the work herself, the cost would have been about 87 cents plus nearly 6 days' work. If purchased, such a cloth would cost about $2, so there is some profit even if labor is calculated at the man's rate.

Other carrying cloths vary in cost according to size; since the cotton is the greater part of the cost, and most of the work involved varies directly with the size, there is a close relationship between size and cost.[145] Probably every woman has 1-meter square cloth for carrying large things, including babies; but probably the average size of all such cloths is about 1 *vara* square. One may conclude, therefore, that the average Panajachel woman's carrying cloth takes 70 cents' worth of cotton thread and about 4½ days of labor.

Men's *sutes* are smaller; since the colors are usually only red and green (and not white, which is cheaper) they probably cost some 60 cents in cash and take only about 3½ days of work.[146]

A man's sash takes 12 ounces of red cotton and a half ounce each of green, yellow, and purple (at 2 cents the half ounce). The material thus costs 54 cents. The twisting takes a day, and the warping about 2 hours. The weaving is a matter of

2½ days, but it takes an additional 2 or 3 hours to fix the fringe. Thus, if the woman does all her own work the sash costs her 54 cents and about 4 days of time. Such a sash is worth about $1 as here there is a profit only if a woman's time is valued at less than 11 cents a day. The woman's sash is larger than the man's, and on the average probably costs, as in one case that I have, 70 cents in cotton and 5 days' work. When figures are woven into the sash, in the case of the feminine garment, the cost of silk adds about 5 cents, and probably another half day is required.

Calzones take 12 ounces of white cotton and a pound of red; the cost in cash is thus 92 cents. The labor amounts to almost 7 days.[147] An informant in 1941 told me *calzones* were worth $2.

When shirts for young boys are home-woven and tailored, the cost comes to about 13 cents in cash (for 4 ounces of cotton yarn), and about 2 days' work. The value of the garment is thus about 35 cents.[148]

The cost of *huipiles* has already been mentioned. A *huipil* takes 4 pounds of cotton, which costs $2.66.[149] Twisting the yarn takes 4 days, the warping 1½ days. The ordinary weaver can then weave only the two ends, after which she must find a specialist for the center portion where the figures come. To weave the ends takes 6 days, and it takes another 4½ days for the center. The sewing and embroidery of the neck is also frequently done by the specialist, who then spends another day and a half. The owner of a *huipil* pays the specialist 66 cents in cash, 50 cents for the weaving, and 16 cents for the sewing and fixing of the neckline. But in addition she has to give her 4 pounds of meat (32 cents) and tortillas and tamales requiring 4 pounds of corn (5 cents). If silk is woven into the *huipil* the added cost, in cash for the silk, is about 50 cents. One may say, therefore, that if a woman does all her own work an ordinary *huipil* costs $2.66 in cash and 17½

---

[144] If the warping is given out to another woman, according to this informant, she must not only be paid for the time but must be given 2 penny rolls and a cup of coffee. The woman comes to the house to warp, and the food is customary "to keep the woman from talking." It is a "shame" not to know how to warp.

[145] In 1940 an Indian woman tried to sell me an oversize carrying cloth that she had "made." She said it had taken 2 pounds of red yarn at $1.10 per pound and "much" tie-dyed yarn, which is expensive. She let out the work to a professional who charged her 80 cents. She refused to sell for less than $6.

[146] In 1941 I was told that a *sute* is worth 60 cents, but this is certainly too little.

[147] The husband of this informant, whose clothes are otherwise old-fashioned no longer used home-woven *calzones* in 1937. He bought two *varas* of white cloth for 26 cents, and the tailoring—done by his wife—was a matter of but half a day. He said he liked this kind better because it is finer and "doesn't hurt him." Although more economical than the home-woven kind, the difference is not as great as it sounds because these drawers last no more than half as long as the others. I have heard of this fashion from no other source and am disregarding it.

[148] This is about twice what a young child's shirt costs when bought in the market, but it lasts much longer. The great majority of shirts—and all those for youths and men—are bought.

[149] There is one case of a woman who uses the cheaper white cotton instead of the brown for the background of her *huipil*.

days of work,[150] a silk-figured *huipil* $3.16 in cash and about the same labor.

The Panajachel woman's *corte* requires 8 *varas* of material, which in 1936 cost about $3. It takes about 2 days to prepare it for use. Those that sew with silk use from 50 cent's to a dollar's worth, depending upon the width of the stitch. Seventy-five cents may be taken as average. Silk-sewn *huipiles* also probably take an extra day's work to sew.

A man's *gabán* takes 3 *varas* of woolen cloth, which cost $1 in 1936 (and had come down to 75 cents in 1941). A spool of black thread adds from 6 to 10 cents.[151] It takes a man but 2 hours to half a day to tailor his *gabán* depending on his skill.

Based on this information and that on the variety of costumes in the community it may be concluded that all woven or sewed costumes for the Indian community in 1936 required nearly 9,000 work days. Slightly more than a third of this time was spent by women hired in other towns to do it. Probably in 1936 in Panajachel some 5,760 work days as compared with a little over $4,000 in cash were spent making and repairing garments, buying materials and garments, and, in general, clothing the community. One may conclude that although weaving is a significant occupation of women, and essential to the culture as long as the unique costumes of Panajachel are valued, clothing is primarily an object in the cash economy.

TABLE 60.—*Time consumed in domestic production, 1936*

Domestic production	Total	Man-days per year		
		Men	Women	Children under 14
House building and maintenance	[1] 1,100	1,050	---------	50
House furnishings	[2] 75	65	---------	10
Tools and utensils	155	125	25	5
Firewood	2,000	1,800	---------	[3] 200
Kitchen work (table 58) and laundry	67,032	---------	51,072	15,960
Spinning, weaving, sewing, repairing clothing	5,763	10	5,503	[4] 250
Total	76,125	3,050	56,600	16,475

[1] The average of 900 and 1,300 man-days (p. 147)—the figures excluding artisans.
[2] The average of 50 and 100, the extremes mentioned on p. 148.
[3] For the boys that gather and make firewood; what the women pick up along the paths is not included, since it takes no extra time.
[4] Girls almost exclusively.

[150] Yet an informant in 1941 said a plain *huipil* is worth $3. Cf. the case above (p. 154) referring to a *huipil* with silk.
[151] An informant said that formerly the sewing was done with home-spun maguey fiber.

Table 60 summarizes the time the Indian Community spends in all its tasks of domestic production.

THE LEVEL AND COST OF LIVING

HOUSEHOLD ESTABLISHMENTS

Chart 18 is a guide to a sample of 10 Indian establishments chosen to represent economic differences (the numbers correspond to those in Appendix 3, the smaller the richer).[152] Their description will indicate, together with the descriptions of costume and, especially, diet that follow, the level of material well-being.

No. 3. Yard 40 by 25 feet. A and C were thatched until about 1925 when the roofs were remodeled. Each is 18 by 15 feet, the walls 9 and the roofs 16 feet high. Walls are whitewashed and each house has a carpenter-built door.

A is the kitchen; high on one wall is an 8-inch-square opening to let out smoke. There are two large fireplaces, one in the northwest corner, the other a little to the south. The large cooking pots are on the floor nearby. On north and west walls, about 5 feet high, boards are suspended on which small articles of food are kept. Against the west wall there is a large, low table on which there are dishes. In the southwest corner, both on the floor and suspended, are large old pots kept as remembrance of the owner's first wife. Two beds, of boards resting on large pieces of logs, are in the northwest and southeast corners, heads to east; in first sleep 3, 6, and 7 (the children are illegitimate), and in the second 4, who is a deaf mute. A cornstalk fence separates the second bed from the utensils on the floor.

C is the Saint's house. It has a full ceiling of planed boards nailed over the rafters. Against the north wall is a platform of boards on planted posts on which are three images and some garlic, beans, and coffee of the last harvest. In the northwest corner are several great old pots which once served in ceremonial cooking; in the other corners are wooden boxes of corn, beans, and coffee, and many agricultural tools.

The annex D is the granary in which corn on the ear is stacked. It is 9 by 6 feet, its highest wall 9 feet and its lowest 6 feet high; a wooden door faces the yard. B, a one-pitch-roof structure 6 by 9 feet, is used as a chicken house, with many poles for perches. It has a door of old boards.

E is the newest house, 12 by 15 feet, with a roof 15 feet high, with a carpenter-made door and a ceiling of rough boards resting upon (not nailed to) the rafters. This is the bedroom, and so cluttered that there is hardly room to move in it. One bed, in the southwest corner, a bought one, is not used; the owner said it was his first wife's bed and nobody should use it while he lived. In the northwest corner is a bed of boards set on logs where 1, 2, and 5 sleep. Against the wall near this bed a well-adorned *santo* is on

[152] All 10 families are as "pure Panajacheleño" as there are. All live east of the river; it was convenient to confine the survey to that neighborhood.

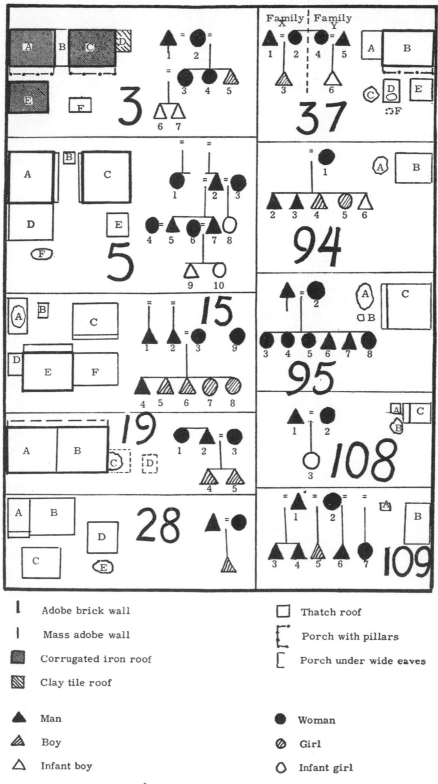

CHART 18.—Guide to description of 10 Panajachel establishments.

a table. In the southeast corner stands a locked chest, and under the bed a smaller one, where the money is supposedly kept. Other chests near the foot of the bed contain clothing and valuables. In the room also are a coffee-pulper, riding saddle, new tools, and hanging from the rafters inside and out are stems of ripening bananas to feed the caged pigeons outside, and ropes, bags, bridles, and the life.

Covering the 7-foot 6 by 9 adobe sweat bath (F) is a thatched roof supported by corner pillars of adobe. Near the fire (always in a corner next to the door), are the vessels used in bathing, and along the walls are wooden benches for the bathers.

Pitchpine torches are used for lighting the houses in the evening.

No. 5. Yard 30 by 45 feet. All three houses have carpenter-made doors. A and C, made at the same time, are each 20 by 18 feet, with 9-foot walls and the roof ridge 20 feet high.

C is the kitchen. Firewood is stacked on the porch in the rainy season. The fireplace in the northeast corner has very large stones and many large pots around it, for many hired hands join a large family to be fed. There are two large grinding stones besides the smaller ones for coffee, etc. In the center is suspended a large shelf for foodstuffs; to the north, a smaller one for tortillas. On the walls are more shelves; but the dishes are in two large baskets on the floor near the fire. Strung on a line are many cross-sapodilla seeds, drying for later sale. In the southeast and northeast corners are beds of boards on implanted posts, shielded from the door and the fire by large mats. On the walls above clothing hangs on lines; at the head of each bed is a wooden chest, and under each, garlic is stacked, waiting to be braided. In the first sleep 2, 3, and 8; in the second, 6, 7, 9, and 10.

A is the Saint's house, where in the center of the north wall are three *santos* on a small table on a platform of canes supported by implanted posts. The whole is adorned with flowers, and before the tableau stands a small table with flowers and candles. On the floor of the house four and five make their bed. In the corners of the house are agricultural tools, and on the floor the huge pots used years ago to cook ritual foods. On a wall hang several large mats used to dry coffee. Along two walls are benches. On the porch is a cane-walled enclosure in which ears of corn are stacked.

D is an old house, 18 by 15 feet, with 7- or 8-foot walls and a roof ridge 18 feet high, which is used both as kitchen and bedroom by the elderly woman, 1. On the floor near the fire, in the southeast corner, are her old grinding stone and a few old pots. The bed, in the northwest corner, is of cornstalks supported by implanted posts. Clothing is hung on a line overhead.

The sweat bath (F) is 7 to 8 feet long and 6 feet wide and high, with a 3 foot opening. Near the fireplace are large pots, and in the center a large bowl used to mix hot and cold water and bathe the children. Boards set on stones along the sides serve as benches.

E is the granary, 9 by 4 feet, with a door of canes, in which are stacked ears of corn. The chicken house (B) has a board for a door, and canes which serve as perches.

No. 15. Yard 30 by 30 feet. C is a kitchen (18 by 30 feet, 7- or 8-foot walls, and roof 18 feet high) with firewood stacked on the porch to one side of a home-made door of wood. A larger fireplace is in the northwest corner (for large vessels of corn, etc.); a smaller one is nearby (for coffee, beans, etc.). Cooking pots are on the floor near the west wall. A set of three cornstalk shelves fastened to four embedded posts near the door holds (top shelf) new pots, sweets to be kept from the children, and dishes; and (bottom shelf) foodstuffs used daily. There is at the south wall a small table, and in the wall embedded wooden pegs on which old cooking pots are hung. On the floor sleeps the servant (9).

E is a bedroom and reception room, 20 by 15 feet with 9-foot walls and the roof 18 feet high, with a large bought door and a ceiling, formed by canes tied to the rafters, which extends to the porch, and on which (outside) corn is stored. Unlike other houses which have simple tamped-down earth floors, this one has a base of stones covered with leveled-off clay which, dried, gives a hard smooth surface. Bought beds are in the corners, northeast (for 2 and 6), northwest (for 3, 7, and 8), and southeast (for 4 and 5); mats are suspended over them to form canopies. Across the center of the house, north to south, is a hammock for daytime rest. Between the beds on the north wall is a large chest containing clothing, which is also strung on lines across corners. On the west wall is a locked cupboard with valuables. There are several chairs.

F is a new house (technically an annex), the outside walls smoothed off as if plastered, 18 by 13 feet with 7- or 8-foot walls, and a roof 16 feet high. There is a home-made door of wood, and a wood-shuttered window-opening 1½ feet square. The floor is like that of E. Not yet in use, this house will be a storeroom for tools, produce, etc.

D is made of lumber left over when E was finished. This annex is 9 by 6 feet, and 9 feet high, with a crude wood door, and has the bed of the deaf-mute half-brother (1) along the north wall, a bed of boards resting on wooden "horses." He hangs his clothing on a line across the room and keeps valuables in a chest under his bed. He uses no light at night, though kerosene is burned in the other rooms.

The chicken house (B) is 6 by 4 feet, and 6 feet high, with a 1½-foot door and cane perches. The sweat bath is new, 9 by 7 feet and a little over 5 feet at its greatest height, covered with a raised thatched roof, and with benches along all the walls.

No. 19. Yard 42 by 36 plus a flower garden 30 by 6 feet. A and B are two rooms of a single house, 40 by 18 feet with 7- or 8-foot walls and the roof almost 18 feet high. The pillars of the porch are on bases of cut stone and on it are flowers in tins. The adobe partition completely divides the house, and each room has only its outside (bought) door. The house was begun in 1930; in 1936 it was not considered finished because a *tepanco* (boards or canes over the rafters) was planned.

A is the kitchen, with fireplace in the northeast corner, a second fire nearby, and all pots and dishes on the floor against the surrounding walls. There are beds of boards on planted posts, one in the northwest corner for 2, 3, and 5; the other (southwest corner) for 1 and 4. At the head of each bed is a wooden chest. Clothes are on lines across the corners. Along the south wall are large piles of garlic waiting to be braided.

B is for *santos* and storage. A large table opposite the door has on it a painted wood cross; it and the table are covered with flowers. Along the north wall is a bench for visitors and along the south wall sacks of corn, beans, and coffee (for in this house supplies are bought weekly instead of in small quantities daily). The agricultural tools are also kept in this room.

The sweat bath (C) is annexed; it is 6 by 7 feet, but around it is built a 9 by 9 house 9 feet high. Inside the bath are the pottery vessels used in bathing and there are benches along three walls. The chicken house (D) is 6 by 7 feet and 4 or 5 feet high, with a cane door, and poles for perches.

Except in heavy rains, firewood in quantity is stacked in the yard and covered with thatch. The house is illuminated with kerosene (most of the time) and pitch pine.

No. 28. Yard 24 by 18 feet; under an orange tree at one edge there is a bench for occasional dining.

B, the 8-year-old kitchen house, is 18 by 15 feet with an 18-foot roof and 5-foot walls; the doorway (fitted with a hinged door) is so low that one must stoop to pass through. The fireplace is in the southeast corner; a second fire is occasionally made nearby. A high table of canes supported by implanted posts holds pots, dishes, and the basket of tortillas. A branch implanted near the fire has drinking cups and gourds hanging on its twigs. There are some dishes of china. The grinding stone leans against the wall nearby. The north side of the house is used to store corn. Because this kitchen house is dark, food is carried to the Saint's house where the family dines.

The annex A is 15 by 9 feet, with 6-foot walls and a 10-foot roof, and has on the west wall a bed of boards on posts in which sleep the three members of the family. On the north wall is a chest on a low table, in which documents and valuables are kept. Above the head of the bed hang a rifle and a machete, and at the south end of the room a line runs the whole width; on it clothing of the whole family hangs. Under the bed is garlic to be braided. Tools are hung on the porch.

The Saint's house (D), built in 1931, is 12 by 12, the walls under 5 feet and the roof 9 or 10 feet high. It has a hinged wooden door. The floor is covered with pine needles. The saints are on a table against the north wall, adorned with flowers. On another table before it, the shaman performs his rituals. Benches line the walls.

C is the oldest house (12 years in 1936) and decrepit, with a door of canes, used only to keep adobes and other materials with which to build a new house. The house is 15 by 12 feet, walls 6 feet, and roof 15 feet high.

Kerosene (and candles before the Saints) furnish illumination.

The house belongs to family X; the two families have separate kitchens and constitute economically different households. Y therefore simply rooms here. (1 and 5 happen to be cousins.)

No. 37. Yard 18 by 18 feet, parts planted with flowers.

B is both bedroom and reception room. A house 2 years old, 20 by 15 feet with 9-foot walls and roof 18 feet high,

has porch pillars based on cut-stone, a spacious wooden door made to slide open, and two windows (front and back) fitted with sliding wood panels. The house was originally built when 1 led the masked dancers at the titular fiesta and had to receive his companions. There are two bought beds, one in the northwest and one in the southwest corner, in each of which sleeps one of the families. Next to each bed is a wooden chest for clothes; other clothing hangs over the foot of each bed. On the walls are pictures from magazines and newspapers.

A is a 12- by 9-foot annex of 12-foot walls of board and cane with a wooden hinged door, built shortly after the house and used as a storeroom for large pots, tools, boxes, etc.

E, 9 by 9 feet with 6-foot walls and a 12-foot roof ridge, is the 8-year old kitchen house used by family X. The outside front wall is plastered to present a smooth surface. There is a hinged wood door, and on the porch a bench. The fire is in the center of the west wall, with pots on either side; dishes are in a basket on the floor or hung from wooden pegs in the wall. Suspended in the center of the room is a 3- by 1½-foot shelf for food. There are several stools on which members of the family sit while eating.

The adobe oven (D) is enclosed in a house with walls 4½ feet high and roof 9 feet high. The part not occupied by the oven (6 by 6 feet) is used by family Y as a kitchen. It has a door of canes. The fire is in the southwest corner. No rent is paid, but when necessary 5 works for 1 in his fields. The sweatbath (6 by 6 feet) and privy are used by both families. Family X uses kerosene exclusively for light at night.

No. 94. Yard, 23 by 23 feet, surrounded by a cane fence.

B is 15 by 12 feet, walls 6 feet and roof 12 feet high, with a door of canes. Near the fireplace, in the northwest corner, are three kinds of shelves: a 2-shelf cupboard of cornstalks for dishes and small pots, a board shelf supported by pegs in the wall, and another suspended from the rafters. The latter two have food on them. Large pots and grinding stones are on the floor. In a bed 7 by 4½ feet of boards on posts set in the floor in the southeast corner sleeps 1, 3, 4, 5, and 6. In a small bed of the same kind in the southwest corner 1 sleeps alone. At the foot of this bed is a locked wood chest of documents. On the south wall hangs a paper carton with clothes of the older boys. Tools are in the northeast corner and hung on the walls. In the northeast corner, canes over the rafters hold garlic to be braided. The only light used in the house is that of the fire.

In the 6 by 7 and 4-foot high sweat bath (A) there are no vessels. Pots from the kitchen are brought for bathing.

No. 95. Yard, 30 by 30 feet, with many flowers and 2 beehives. A second house (for saints and ritual activities) had collapsed shortly before 1936; materials for a new one were being collected, and meanwhile the *santos* were kept on the porch of C, and taken in at night. ("It would be wrong to keep them in the kitchen in the day or outside at night.")

The house, 18 by 18 feet, with the roof ridge 15 feet from the floor, and the walls a little over 6 feet high, is 12 years old. It is of whitewashed mass-adobe, with a thatch roof. The doorway, center of north wall, is 5½ feet high and 2 feet wide, with a door of canes.

The fireplace is in the southeast corner, with a load of firewood nearby. At the base of east and south walls are cooking pots, grinding stone, and a jar of water. There is a table of boards over crosspieces supported by posts implanted in ground, on which are kept dishes and food-stuffs. Nearby are several shelves on pegs in the walls, with additional ones hung from the rafters with cords, in the middle of which are strung gourd bowls.

There are no beds in the house: the family sleeps on mats on the floor; 6 and 7 sleep in the northeast corner, 8 with 5 in the southwest corner, and parents with 3 in the northwest corner. Blanket and clothing are hung over each of the three sleeping places on a line. Several old wooden chests are on the floor. There is an ax against the wall near the fire, and hoes and machetes are kept in other corners of the house. Several worn-out machetes hang by a rope, with some ox horns from which containers to carry water to the fields can be made.

Pitch-wood torches are used as much as kerosene lamps for lighting the house.

The sweat bath (A) is 6 by 9 feet; the privy (B), a doorless structure of canes with a one-pitch thatch roof, is about 2 by 2 feet and 6 feet high.

No. 108. No yard. The house, 8 by 8 feet, with an 8-foot roof and 4-foot walls, is of mass-adobe and thatch. The porch, about 3 feet wide, has three posts supporting the eaves. The door is carpenter-made of old wood. The house is in poor condition, the roof patched with leaves in several places.

The fireplace is in the northeast corner of the house, and the pots stand near it. On the walls are a board, hung as a shelf where foodstuffs can be stored, and a few bats, old gourds, weaving sticks, and bunches of medicinal plants. In 1936 there was no bed; the family slept on a mat on the floor, all together with but one blanket. There are two or three small stools and a small wooden chest. Clothing hangs on lines tied to the walls.

On the porch are usually kept firewood, the man's carrying frame and hoes, axes, and machetes. Sticks used in planting and weeding truck gardens are stuck into the thatch of the roof, in the house, and on the porch.

A, a chicken coop of old canes with old boards laid on for a roof, is about 4 by 4 by 4 feet. The sweat bath (B), about 6 feet in each dimension, was in disrepair in 1936. Inside, beside the fireplace, are wooden benches.

No. 109. No yard. The mass-adobe house, 16 by 10 feet with 5-foot walls and 16-foot roof ridge, is 8 years old. The walls are whitewashed according to Public Health regulations; there is a door of canes. This was the only house described in which there was a glass window: a pane about 8 inches square set into the north wall.

Near B, another house of the same type and material, 7 by 13 feet, was being constructed to serve as a bedroom. A is a chicken coop, 3 by 4 feet, of thatched mass-adobe; besides a few chickens, it contains accumulated excrement to be used or sold as fertilizer.

The small fireplace is in the southwest corner of the house. Above it hangs a twigged branch with enamelware drinking cups and pottery pitchers. There is also a wooden shelf on the wall for the gourd in which tortillas are kept. Along the south wall are the grinding stone and earthenware pots used in the kitchen; pots less frequently used are kept outside.

A bed of three boards resting on four implanted posts replaced (in 1936) the mats which the family formerly slept on. The bed is covered with a mat and a blanket; clothing serves for a pillow. Beans, garlic, and onions are stored under the bed.

The only piece of furniture besides the bed is a smoke-blackened wooden chest in which papers and documents are kept. In the northwest corner of the house, two ropes strung across hold a second blanket, a mesh bag, and a small bag, some ropes and tumplines. Below them are axes, hoes, machetes, and a carrying frame.

Except for the fire and occasional pitch-wood torch, there is no regular means of lighting the house.

COSTUMES

The individual garments made and purchased by Panajachel Indians are combined into various costumes:

Men's and boys':

(1) The "old fashioned" costume consists of a *calzon* covered by a *gabán* and then a Nahualá *rodillera,* all fastened with a home-woven sash and with a leather belt. An extra *rodillera* is hung over the shoulders by men who have attained a certain grade in the politico-religious hierarchy. A hat is worn on the head, but a *sute* is substituted on formal occasions. The feet are bare or with *caites*.

(2) The "newer" costume substitutes a shirt for the *gabán,* but otherwise the costume is the same.

(3) The "modern" costume consists of a shirt and *calzoncillo* covered by a Nahualá *rodillera* and bound with a sash, either home-woven or purchased, and a leather belt. The rest of the costume is the same. In two cases no belt is worn. In one case a Chichicastenango *rodillera* is substituted for that from Nahualá.

(4) The "fashionable" costume is the same except that the *rodillera* is of the blue Tecpán type, frequently with white borders and open work at the ends. A bought kerchief is frequently worn around the neck. San Pedro shirts are especially popular with this costume. In one case the sash is omitted and the belt performs a more important function.

(5) The "city" costume, worn especially by men who have been in military service, and some boys, and which is typical of Indians of communities where the regional costume has been lost, consist of shirt, trousers, belt, and sash. In five cases the sash is also discarded and the costume is quite European in type (but neckties and shoes are not worn). The number of wearers shown in table 61 includes "foreign" Indians resident in Panajachel.

(6) Regional costumes of other communities. The costumes of Sololá, San Jorge, and Concepción, if not the same, are enough alike to be treated together. The San Pedro, Atitlán, and Santa Catarina costumes are distinct. The local Indians of Tonicapán and San Andrés wore trousers in 1936 and are included under (5) above. The Ladinos, of course, also wear the "city" costume, but those included in the Indian population also wear shoes and other appurtenances and should be treated separately.

Women's and girls':

(7) The "simple" Panajachel costume consists of the Panajachel *huipil*, *corte* without silk, and sash without figures. One woman wears this costume but has substituted a *huipil* of San Lucas for that of Panajachel. The hairdress is the bought ribbon. The women use the locally woven carrying cloth. Rarely, they wear *caites* on journeys.

(8) The "silk" Panajachel costume is the same except that silk figures are woven into the *huipil* and silk is used to sew the *huipil* and the *corte*.

(9) The "elaborate" Panajachel costume is the same, but in addition to the silk in the *huipil* and *corte*, it has figures (of silk) woven into the ends of the sash.

(10) The "San Andrés" costume worn by women of Panajachel, as well as those from San Andrés and some of the women in San Andrés, consists of the San Andrés *huipil*, Totonicapán skirt, and in most local cases the plain Panajachel sash. The local carrying cloths and hairdress are used.

(11) The "Totonicapán" costume consists of the "Totonicapán" *huipil* and *corte* and a bought sash. It corresponds to the "city" costume of Indian men, and may best be described, in the whole region, as a generalized Indian costume. It is worn in Panajachel not only by the resident Totonicapeñas but by some Panajacheleñas. Bought carrying cloths are usually used with this costume.

(12) Costumes of other Indian towns: Again Sololá, San Jorge, and Concepción costumes may be considered one. The Atitlán, San Pedro, and Nahualá costumes are distinctive. The San Andrés and Totonicapán women wear costumes included under (10) and (11) above; the San Andrés women wear Totonicapán shirts and a sash the origin of which I am not sure. The Ladina costume consists, of course, of European-type dresses, shoes, etc., and is worn in Panajachel only by a Ladina married into the Indian community, and her daughter, and the daughter of a Totonicapeño and an Antoñera who wears Totonicapán clothes.

The number of various garments used in Panajachel is calculated on the basis of a census of costumes used (table 61). It will be noted that

I have no positive information on what costume 190 persons wear. In addition six youngsters are not included because I do not know even their sex. However, knowledge of general patterns and who the people are make possible good guesses as to the costumes of most of the people passed over by the survey (usually children). Table 62 is the result of careful and conservative family-by-family analysis. The infant costume presents a special problem. Until about the age of 4, a child is dressed in odds and ends, and cast-off and remade clothing, probably taking no more than a day's time a year, or more than 20 or 30 cents for occasional diaper cloth and shirts. The baptismal garments hardly raise that figure and are presented by the godparents, usually Ladinos. Probably about 25 of the 54 boys and girls whose costume cannot be safely guessed at were also under 4 in 1936 (exact information on ages is hard to get.)

TABLE 61.—*Costumes*

a. MEN'S AND BOYS' COSTUMES

Costume	Number of cases known		
	Total	Men	Boys
(1) "Old fashion"	21	21	
(2) "Newer"	23	23	
(3) "Modern":			
Normal	84	74	10
Beltless	2	2	
Chichicastenango *rodillera*	1	1	
(4) "Fashionable":			
Normal	78	65	13
Sashless	1	1	
(5) "City":			
Normal	33	31	2
Sashless	9	5	4
(6) Sololá and Concepción	22	20	2
Atitlán	1	1	
Santa Catarina	1	1	
San Pedro	2	2	
Ladino	5	3	2
No information	107	5	102
Total	390	255	135

b. WOMEN'S AND GIRLS' COSTUMES

Costume	Number of cases known		
	Total	Men	Boys
(7) Simple Panajachel:			
Normal	141	128	13
With S. Lucas *huipil*	1	1	
(8) Silk Panajachel	15	13	2
(9) Elaborate Panajachel	46	34	12
(10) San Andrés variation	24	21	3
(11) Totonicapán	25	24	1
(12) Sololá and Concepción	44	37	7
Atitlán	3	2	1
Nahualá	1	1	
San Pedro	3	1	2
Ladino	3	2	1
No information	78	8	70
Total	384	272	112

There remain four men, three women, and thirty-odd boys and girls whose costume I cannot guess; to complete the picture, I simply add a numerically proportionate amount to costume costs to take account of these unknowns. Then combining tables 61 and 62 and including 24 of the "still unknowns" of table 62 in the infant's costume classification, it is possible to calculate the number of garments of different kinds worn by Panajachel Indians in 1936 and the amount of time and money that they cost (table 63). Data on the length of time a garment lasts, or number bought in a year, come from household budgets (described below) and miscellaneous information. The prices of items not made in Panajachel are from the price list, Appendix 2.

TABLE 62.—*Probable costumes of those on whom census information is lacking*

Probable costumes	Men	Boys	Women	Girls	Sex un-known
Infants' costume	--------	41	--------	29	6
(3) "Modern" normal	--------	13			
(4) "Fashionable" normal	1	10	--------		
(7) Simple Panajachel normal	--------	--------	5	18	
(9) Elaborate Panajachel	--------	--------		3	--------
(10) San Andrés variation	--------	--------		1	
(11) Totonicapán	--------	--------		2	
(12) Sololá and Concepción	--------	--------		1	
Still unknown	4	38	3	16	--------
Total	5	102	8	70	6

Individual garments of "foreign" Indians are not itemized except for trousers, shirts, belts, Totonicapán garments, and the San Andrés *huipil* which are also worn by Panajacheleños. Information is too incomplete to itemize costs of Sololá, Concepción, Atitlán, Santa Catarina, and Ladino costumes, and the San Pedro costume except for the woman's (Totonicapán) shirt, and the San Andrés sash. To complete table 63, the cost of these costumes was roughly calculated from knowledge of costs of the Panajachel garments (table 64) in the following manner: The Sololá-Concepción male attire consists of long home-woven *calzones* and shirt, a Nahualá or Chichicastenango *rodillera* and a woolen jacket. In addition the men carry woolen bags that they make (and that Panajachel Indians use only rarely). The cash cost is probably slightly less than that of the "old-fashioned" Panajachel costume: the woolen cloth of the jacket is less than that of the *gabán*; the cotton for the shirt costs less than does the bought shirt of Panajachel (especially since

much more spinning is done in Sololá); on the other hand only the Sololá *calzón* takes more material than that of Panajachel. It is therefore probable that the cash cost of the whole Sololá attire is about $4. On the other hand the labor probably comes to twice that of Panajachel. At the Panajachel labor rate, it would be $6. Boys' costumes would then come to about $2.25 plus 12 days' work, or $3.45.

The Sololá-Concepción female attire, on the other hand, is certainly cheaper than the plain Panajachel costume. The shirt and sash are nearly the same, and the *huipil* is much like the man's shirt. The woman's costume would take but $6 in material and about 20 days' time (or if the cotton is spun rather than bought, less cash and more time) for a total of $8. The girl's costume would cost $3.60 and 12 days' time, or $4.80.

The Ladino costume values are almost pure guesses, based only on general knowledge; these costumes are assumed to be bought for cash, although there are tailors and dressmakers in the Ladino community.

The figures for the clothing of persons on whom there is no costume information were obtained by adding 4/255, 26/80, 3/272, and 4/67 to the totals of the figures—excluding the unknowns and infants for the men's, boys', women's, and girls' garments respectively. From the total of 8,937 9-hour days (table 63) of time consumed in the preparation of clothing in 1936 must be subtracted some number of days of work that Indians outside the community actually did. First there is the work on Panajacheleño textiles let out to Indian women of other towns, 3,000 man-days or $180 (calculated at 6 cents a day, since women's time is worth less in the towns where the work is done than in Panajachel). Second, probably 350 of the 468 days reported in table 63 as time devoted to "foreign" costumes were actually spent by people outside of Panajachel. Since ready-made clothing is more expensive than time-plus-materials, these 350 days to be subtracted should probably be translated into $40 spent outside the community. Finally, to the cost of clothing must be added that of repairing. One may guess that in each household a total of about a day, at odd moments, is devoted to sewing and patching, and that a spool of thread is used by each, for a total

TABLE 63.—*Cost of clothing*

a. MEN'S CLOTHING

Item	Number using	Average number per year each	Total number items in year	Cost per item		Total cost	
				Cash for materials or items	Labor in hours	Cash for materials or items	Number of 9-hour days
Gabán	21	1	21	$1.08	3	$22.68	7
Nahualá or Chichicastenango *rodillera*	121	1	121	1.00		121.00	
Tecpán *rodillera*	67	1	67	1.75		117.25	
Home-woven *calzón*	43	1	43	.92	63	39.56	301
Bought-cloth *calzón*	1	2	2	.26	4½	.52	1
Home-sewn *calzoncillo*	12	3	36	.26	4½	9.36	18
Bought *calzoncillo*	144	3	432	.40		172.80	
Trousers	36	1½	54	1.00		54.00	
Underdrawers	12	2	24	.25		6.00	
Home-woven sash	128	2 4/7	37	.50	36	18.50	148
Bought sash	90	½	45	.20		9.00	
Leather belt	222	⅓	74	.25		18.50	
Factory or factory-cloth shirt	178	3	534	.32		170.88	
San Pedro shirt	25	1	25	1.25		31.25	
Sute	50	½	25	.60	22½	15.00	63
Kerchief	150	4	600	.10		60.00	
Sandals, *caites*	240	2½	600	.20		120.00	
Sandals, high	5	2	10	.60		6.00	
Factory hat	90	2	180	.30		54.00	
Indian-made hat	160	2	320	.18		57.60	
Handbag	30	⅓	10	.15		1.50	
Coat	70	½	35	1.00		35.00	
Mirrors	150	1	150	.12½		18.75	
Combs	150	1	150	.07		10.50	
Sololá costume	20			4.00	180	80.00	400
Atitlán costume	1			3.00	135	3.00	15
Santa Catarina costume	1			4.00	160	4.00	18
San Pedro costume	2			4.00	150	8.00	33
Ladino costume	3			18.00		54.00	
Subtotal						1,318.65	1,004
No information	4					21.11	157
Total						1,339.76	1,161

b. BOYS' CLOTHING

Item	Number using	Average number per year each	Total number items in year	Cash for materials or items	Labor in hours	Cash for materials or items	Number of 9-hour days
Nahualá or Chichicastenango *rodillera*	23	1	23	$0.75		$17.25	
Tecpán *rodillera*	23	1	23	1.40		32.20	
Home-sewn *calzoncillo*	2	3	6	.15	4	.90	3
Bought *calzoncillo*	46	3	138	.25		34.50	
Trousers	6	1½	9	.60		5.40	
Under drawers	2	2	4	.15		.60	
Home-woven sash	25	2 4/7	7	.30	22	2.10	17
Bought sash	23	½	12	.08		.95	
Leather belt	52	⅓	17	.15		2.55	
Home-woven shirt	10	1	10	.13	18	1.30	20
Factory or factory-cloth shirt	37	3	111	.16		17.76	
S. Pedro shirt	5	1	5	.60		3.00	
Kerchief	50	2	100	.05		5.00	
Sandals, *caites*	40	2	80	.15		12.00	
Factory hat	10	2	20	.30		6.00	
Indian-made hat	80	2	160	.10		16.00	
Combs	10	1	10	.07		.70	
Infants' clothes	55			.25	9	13.75	55
Sololá costume	2			2.25	108	4.50	24
Ladino costume	2			8.00		16.00	
Subtotal						192.47	119
No information	26					58.08	29
Total						250.55	148

c. WOMEN'S CLOTHING

Item	Number using	Average number per year each	Total number items in year	Cash for materials or items	Labor in hours	Cash for materials or items	Number of 9-hour days
Plain Panajachel *corte*	128	1	128	$3.00	18	$384.00	256
Panajachel *corte* with silk	47	1	47	3.75	27	176.25	141
Totonicapán *corte*	46	1	46	2.00		92.00	
Panajachel *huipil*, no silk	133	1	133	2.66	157½	353.78	2,327
Panajachel *huipil* with silk	47	1	47	3.16	157½	148.52	822
S. Andrés *huipil*	21	1	21	1.25	120	26.25	280
S. Lucas *huipil*	1	1	1	1.25	120	1.25	13
Totonicapán *huipil*	18	1½	27	1.25		33.75	
Bought blouse	6	2	12	.50		6.00	
Plain Panajachel sash	162	⅔	108	.70	45	75.60	540
Panajachel sash with figures	34	⅔	23	.75	54	17.25	138
Totonicapán sash	24	⅔	16	.40		6.40	
Panajachel carrying cloth	245	1	245	.70	40½	171.50	1,102
Totonicapán carrying cloth	24	2	48	.50		24.00	
Panajachel head band	190	1	190	.12		22.80	
Totonicapán head band	79	2	158	.20		31.60	
Servilletas (cloths)	150	1	150	.20		30.00	
Necklaces	50	1	50	.25		12.50	

TABLE 63.—*Cost of clothing*—Continued

c. WOMEN'S CLOTHING—Continued

Item	Number using	Average number per year each	Total number items in year	Cost per item		Total cost	
				Cash for materials or items	Labor in hours	Cash for materials or items	Number of 9-hour days
Sandals, *caites*	25	5	125	$.18		$22.50	
Rings	200	1	200	.10		20.00	
Earrings	50	1	50	.10		5.00	
Combs	269	⅔	179	.02		3.58	
Sololá-Concepción costume	37			6.00	180	222.00	740
Atitlán costume	2			4.75	160	9.50	35
Nahualá costume	1			7.00	270	7.00	30
S. Andrés sash	6			.70	45	4.20	30
Huipil and sash of S. Pedro	1			1.20	60	1.20	7
Ladino costume	2			15.00		30.00	
Subtotal						1,938.43	6,461
No information	3					20.81	71
Total						1,959.24	6,532

d. GIRLS' CLOTHING

Item	Number using	Average number per year each	Total number items in year	Cash for materials or items	Labor in hours	Cash for materials or items	Number of 9-hour days
Plain Panajachel *corte*	13	1	13	$1.80	11	$23.40	16
Panajachel *corte* with silk	17	1	17	2.25	16	38.25	30
Totonicapán *corte*	9	1	9	1.20		10.80	
Panajachel *huipil*, no silk	31	1	31	1.60	95	49.60	327
Panajachel *huipil* with silk	14	1	14	1.90	95	26.60	148
S. Andrés *huipil*	4	1	4	.75	72	3.00	32
Totonicapán *huipil*	2	1½	3	.75		2.25	
Bought blouse	1	2	2	.30		.60	
Plain Panajachel sash	36	⅔	24	.42	27	10.08	72
Panajachel sash with figures	15	⅔	10	.45	32	4.50	36
Totonicapán sash	3	⅔	2	.25		.50	
Panajachel carrying cloth	80	1	80	.42	24	33.60	213
Totonicapán carrying cloth	3	1	3	.35		1.05	
Panajachel head band	50	1	50	.08		4.00	
Totonicapán head band	20	2	40	.12		4.80	
Servilletas (cloths)	10	1	10	.15		1.50	
Earrings	5	1	5	.10		.50	
Combs	40	⅔	26	.02		.52	
Infants' clothes	45			.25	9	11.25	45
Sololá-Concepción costume	8			3.60	108	28.80	96
Atitlán costume	1			2.85	96	2.85	11
S. Andrés sash	1			.42	27	.42	3
Huipil and sash of S. Pedro	2			.72	36	1.44	8
Ladino costume	1			8.00		8.00	
Subtotal						268.31	1,037
No information	4					15.20	59
Total						283.51	1,096
Grand total of *a, b, c, d*						3,833.06	8,937

TABLE 63.—*Continued*

e. SUMMARY

Item	Cost in year		
	Total	Within community (value of labor) [1]	Bought outside
Men's (table 63*a*)	$1,455.86	$116.10	$1,339.76
Boys' (table 63*b*)	265.35	14.80	250.55
Women's (table 63*c*)	2,612.44	653.20	1,959.24
Girls' (table 63*d*)	393.11	109.60	283.51
Total	4,726.76	893.70	3,833.06

[1] Calculated at 10 cents a day.

TABLE 64.—*Average cost of annual costuming*

Costume	Adult	Child
Male:		
"Old fashioned"	$4.53+9⅔ days=$5.50 [1]	
"Newer"	$4.50+9⅓ days=$5.43	
"Modern" (normal)	$4.72+1⅙ days=$4.83	$2.49+⅔ day=$2.56.
"Fashionable" (normal).	$6.27	$3.09.
"City" (normal)	$4.62	$2.79.
Average cost (unweighted).	$5.33	$2.81.
Female:		
"Simple Panajachel" (normal).	$7.28+27⅓ days=$10.01	$4.25+16 4/6 days=$5.90.
"Silk Panajachel"	$8.53+28⅓ days=$11.36	$5.00+17 days=$6.70.
"Elaborate Panajachel."	$8.56+29 days=$11.46	$5.02+17⅓ days=$6.75.
"San Andrés Variation."	$5.87+23⅙ days=$8.18	$3.40+13⅚ days=$4.78.
"Totonicapán"	$5.67	$3.04.
Average cost (unweighted).	$9.34	$5.44.

[1] Calculating the day as worth 10 cents.

of 157 days of work and $12.56 in cash. (Equipment will be accounted for below.)

Thus, all told, the totals of table 63 should probably read:

Total cost of clothing_____ $4, 640. 02
Value of labor within the community, 5,763
    days at 10 cents_____ 574. 40
Materials and items bought outside the com-
    munity_____ 4, 065. 62

FOOD

Data on the consumption of food in the community is based on three kinds of information: (1) Annual family budgets worked out with four families, two of them very complete and reliable; the third reliable but complete only for food and utensils; and the fourth (from the wealthiest family), neither complete nor highly reliable, useful only as a check and for some comparisons. The data are given in table 65. (2) A very careful 7-day account of the actual consumption of a sample of six Panajachel families in the winter of 1944, made as a part of a more general food survey of the Carnegie Institution of Washington (1944, pp. 176-177), under my direction (Goubaud, 1946). Juan Rosales collected the data in Panajachel. The results were turned over in 1945 to the National Indianist Institute of Guatemala directed by the late Antonio Goubaud Carrera, who had also been field director of the survey. In turn the data were tabulated by the Food and Agricultural Organization of the United Nations, who made available to me the results as shown in table 66. Since only 1 week is involved, the results are useful only as they supplement and check the material otherwise collected to permit calculations for the entire year. The three families supplying reliable data in terms of household budgets are all included in the 7-day study.[153] (3) A variety of general information on seasonal differences, on ceremonial and other uses of food, and the like.

THE SAMPLE FAMILIES

Family No. 58 consisting in 1936 of father, mother, five sons, the eldest with wife and infant daughter, the others 18, 14, 4, and 2 years of age,

respectively, was well above average size. The father, of pure Panajachel stock, as far as can be determined, has lived in Panajachel all his life, and is in most respects a typical Indian.[154] When he was a boy he went to school and served the local priest and learned to read and write. The mother, daughter of a Panajacheleño and a Concepcioñera who was in 1936 a widowed midwife, was born and raised in Panajachel, wore the local costume, partook of the local customs, and with her husband went through public and religious offices. The eldest son spent a period in military service in Sololá after having learned to read and write in the local school. He brought back with him European-type trousers and a Totonicapeña wife raised in Concepción, where her father plied a trade. She wears Totonicapán clothing, and like other Totonicapeños is Ladinoized in certain respects; for example, she speaks Spanish quite well, does not know how to weave, and uses frying techniques in cooking.

Family No. 49 consisted in 1936 of the father [155] and mother and two daughters, aged 15 and 5, of old Panajacheleño stock, and old fashioned and "typical" in most respects.

Family No. 37 consisted in 1936 of man and wife and 10-year-old son. (Four children had died in infancy.) The man comes of a pure Panajacheleño family, as nearly as can be determined; the wife, however, is a daughter of family 55, of mixed ancestry.[156] The family in most respects is culturally typical; but Mariano may be said to be a "go-getter," and within the culture, extraordinarily enterprising and "progressive." He is one of two Indians owning canoes, and ambitious to own an outboard motor for his dugout. He is the only one who has built a bake-oven; one of two who make fish nets; the only organizer of a marimba band. It was he who brought about a revival of the Conquista dance in Panajachel. But he enters fully into normal Indian social life, and evidences no desire to go beyond it. Since Mariano is something of an individualist it is probable that the diet in his home is not quite typical; and indeed some differences are apparent.

---

[153] All of the figures in table 65 are printed as they were calculated from the original 1936 data. When the 1944 data became available, I compared notes where possible and became convinced that the original figures are highly reliable. Family compositions had changed, so that any exact comparison is impossible; but I am unable to find contradictions in the two sets of evidence. Therefore I continued to use the fuller 1936 data as the primary basis of the calculations for table 65.

[154] In 1940 he and his family became the first Panajacheleño converts to Protestantism. Relatives in Guatemala City had been converted earlier and may have influenced the family, but at least Bonifacio and his eldest son had for a long time been interested in the new faith.

[155] Santiago became my best informant before this study was finished, but the data referred to in this chapter were for the most part taken from him by Sr. Rosales, 1937.

[156] Supra, pp. 75-79.

Family No. 1 consisted in 1936 of man and wife, five sons—11 to 32 years of age—and two daughters, 27 and 16 years old. The family, pure Panajacheleño, tends to be old-fashioned in most respects. The man's father was probably well-to-do and he inherited a fair portion; but he has since acquired very much more land and was in 1936 by far the largest landholder. He is generally believed to be the richest Indian in Panajachel, and no doubt he is.

Families 58 and 49 were interviewed at length over the course of several weeks each, the time being devoted almost exclusively to their household finances. The wife as well as the husband was present during most of the interviews. In the case of family 37 only the husband was interviewed, during days when he guarded the church as sacristan. Only the head of family 1 was interviewed on this subject, and not at great length. An elaborate series of schedules had been worked out, and they were filled in (and revised) with each of the families. The food schedules included lists of all commodities, as specifically as possible, with spaces for the quantities consumed daily, weekly, or monthly; variations seasonally or for holiday periods; total annual consumption; the source of the commodity (home-grown or purchased); the average price; and the total annual value. Clothing and utensils and other schedules varied slightly to suit the necessities of the case. Table 65 summarizes the results for the three families for which information is most complete. The values of the quantities consumed are calculated on the basis of prices listed in Appendix 2, which are not always the same as those given by the three families.

Although a fuller sampling would be desirable, a fair picture of the cost of living in Panajachel may be had from the information available; first, because the three informants are unusually conscientious and reliable and desired themselves to discover where their money goes, and second because the variations in most items of expenditure do not appear to be very great in the Indian community. It seems likely that the method used is more reliable in Panajachel than it would be in an American farm community, for the Indians tend to buy at regular intervals, and in about the same quantities, and it is not difficult for them to keep track of the amounts of various commodities that they use. Since the Indians are very money-

minded, and price-conscious, and are accustomed to keeping accounts mentally, they make excellent informants in these matters.

COMMUNITY TOTALS

For the figures in table 67, heavy reliance is had on the information supplied by the three sample families. It would therefore seem useful to weight members of the families by sex and age (as was done with the 7-day food count). In studies in the United States the proportions consumed by persons of the two sexes and various ages have been worked out on the basis of the value of food consumed,[157] but the scale cannot be applied to Panajachel because consumption differences are certainly distinct; the use of high-priced milk in the United States, for example, raises the relative value of a child's diet far beyond what it must be in Panajachel. On the other hand, I know too little of the differences in diet within the Panajachel family to hazard setting up a comparable scale.

For the purpose of determining the consumption of the community as a whole, the selection of families 37, 49, and 58 is not too fortunate, since they are all above the middle of the wealth scale (66–67). Yet they surely represent something near the norm of families with land. The large size of family 58 makes it poorer than its amount of land would indicate, while the other two, lower in the scale of land controlled, are under the average in size. No. 58 is economically stable (owning and controlling the same land) while No. 49 was once richer, since it owns more land than it controls, and No. 37 poorer. All three families have dogs; No. 58 also has a cat and two sheep; Nos. 58 and 37, chickens. The three families are primarily agricultural; the man in No. 58 butchers pigs, in No. 49 he is a caponizer, and in No. 37 he is an occasional baker, he makes nets, has a canoe, and plays the marimba. The wife in No. 58 does ordinary weaving; the women of No. 49 only twist thread for the family's clothing, and the wife of No. 37 does no work in textiles. Among the three families are found all the common types of house (one cane and thatch, 4 mass-adobe and thatch, one adobe brick and thatch) in about the proper proportions, and all of the common types of clothing (2 "old fashioned," 1 "modern," 1 "elaborate," 1 "city" male costume, and 3 "plain

---

[157] See, for example, Stiebeling and Phipard, 1939, table 2, p. 7.

TABLE 65.—*Consumption of food in 3 families*

Item	Family 58			Family 49			Family 37		
	Quantity	Value	Percent	Quantity	Value	Percent	Quantity	Value	Percent
(1) Corn, pounds	3,900	$19.50 29.25B	31.8	1,642	$6.90 13.62B	25.3	766.5	$1.50 8.08B	14.9
(2) Lime for food, pounds	260	1.30B		60	.30B		96	.48B	
(3) Black beans, pounds	390	1.38 4.86B	4.0	144	1.36 .95B	3.3	150	.24 2.16B	3.6
(4) White beans, pounds				20	.40B		3	.06B .25B	
(5) Dry red peppers, pounds	13	1.04B	.9	5.1	.41B	2.0	10	.80B	1.9
(6) Green peppers, pounds	2.5	.40		7.5	1.21		3.12	.25	
(7) Coffee beans, pounds	208	5.20 5.20B		52	1.50 1.10B		50	2.50	
(8) Low-refined sugar, 3-pound *tapas*	156	12.48B	15.1	52	4.10B	9.2	43	3.44B	9.7
(9) White sugar, pounds	8	.40B		8.5	.42B		6	.30B	
(10) Chocolate, ounce tablets	56	.57B		48	.48B		39	.35B	
(11) Bread, 1-ounce rolls	816	8.18B	5.4	438	4.39B	5.5	506	5.05B	7.6
(12) Honey, 24-ounce bottles	5	.25B		3	.15B		3	.15B	
(13) Anotta, ounces	12	.81B		2	.18B		5	.48B	
(14) Anise seed, ounces				2	.03B		6	.01B	
(15) Pepper *de castilla*, ounces	(?)	(?)		.5	.01B		.5	.01B	
(16) Pepper *de chiapa*, ounces	(?)	(?)		.5	.01B		.5	.01B	
(17) Ginger, amount in cents	(?)	(?)	.7		.02B	1.1		.02B	1.9
(18) *Cordoncillo*, in cents	(?)	(?)			.01B			.01B	
(19) Squash (*ayote*) seed, in cents		.12			.29			.25B	
(20) Squash (*chilacayote*) seed, in cents		.12			.32B			.50B	
(21) Chickens, 2-pound units	9	1.80	1.1	1	.20B	.2	4	.80	1.2
(22) Eggs, units 1¾ ounces	936	4.50 7.20B	7.4	260	3.25B	4.0	120	1.50	2.2
(23) Lake fish, amount in cents		5.20B	3.6		1.80B	2.4		4.50	7.4
(24) Crabs, bunches of 4	20	.40B		7	.14B		24	.48	
(25) Sea fish, dried, pounds	3	.60B		6	1.20B		7	1.40B	
(26) Alligator meat, pounds	2	.30B	.2	9	.14B	1.6	156	2.44B	5.7
(27) Shrimp, dried, ounces									
(28) Beef-with-bone, pounds	386	19.30B		421	21.05B		115	5.75B	
(29) Pork-with-bone, pounds	36	2.88B		12	.96B		17	1.36B	
(30) Pork sausages, 1-ounce unit	416	4.16B	23.0	108	1.08B	30.7	100	1.00B	17.3
(31) Pork-blood sausage, 8-ounce unit				18	.54B			3.00B	
(32) Lard cracklings, cents					.48B				
(33) Lard, pounds	82	9.84B		9	1.08B		5	.60B	
(34) Tomatoes, pounds	104	1.04B	.8	24	.24	.6	64	.64B	1.48
(35) Huskcherries, pounds	10	.15		16	.18 .06B		48	.36 .36B	
(36) Potatoes, pounds	12	.18B		26	.39B		64	.96B	
(37) Sweetpotatoes, pounds	12	.12		24	.24		150	1.50	
(38) Sweet cassava, pounds	26	.26		10	.10		25	.25	
(39) Squash (*ayote*), units	12	.09		68	.52		8	.06B	
(40) Squash (*chilacayote*), units	3	.09							
(41) Green onions, units	780	.39		1,950	.97		1,500	.75	
(42) Garlic, 60-head bunches	2	.10		6	.24		6	.24	
(43) Cabbages, 2-pound units	15	.15		156	1.56		25	.25	
(44) Carrots, dozens	4	.02							
(45) Turnips, dozens	10	.05							
(46) Green beans	20	.25		40	.51		80	1.00	
(47) Swiss chard, bunches	20	.20							
(48) Cucumbers, 3-ounce units	48	.50							
(49) Mulberry herb, 1-pound bunch	104	.52	2.0	60	.06 .24B	8.3	24	.12B	11.02
(50) Amaranth, pound bunches	8	.08		24	.24		50	.50	
(51) *Chipilín* herb, bunches				14	.10		12	.06	
(52) Cintula, ounces	(?)	(?)		1	.04B .01B		1	.06B .01B	
(53) *Chichipate*, ounces	(?)	(?)		1	.01B		1	.01B	
(54) "Lime tea," amount in cents	(?)	(?)			.02				
(55) Rue, amount in cents	(?)	(?)			.02				
(56) Coriander, bunches of 5	(?)	(?)		6	.03		50	.25	
(57) "7 shirts" herb, units	(?)	(?)			.06				
(58) Col, 12-ounce bunch				24	.24B			.25	
(59) Other herbs, amount in cents	(?)	(?)			.48			.25B	
(60) Vegetable pears, units		.06			.69			.25 .75B	
(61) Avocados, 5-ounce units	61	.20		90	.30		150	.50	
(62) Oranges, 4-ounce units	160	.40		360	.90		160	.20	
(63) Sour oranges, 2-ounce units	216	.20		464	.42		552	.50	
(64) Limas, 3-ounce units	155	.26		229	.38		576	.96	
(65) Limes, 1-ounce units	350	.35		80	.08B		250	.25	
(66) Cross-sapodilla, 6-ounce unit	200	.50	3.5	72	.10 .08B	5.1	200	.50	10.6
(67) White sapodilla, 5-ounce unit				40	.08B		50	.10B	
(68) Spanish plums, 1-ounce units	400	.20		400	.24		1,440	.96	
(69) Papayas, 1½-pound units	98	.98		15	.03B .15				
(70) *Granadillas*, 2-ounce units	296	.30							
(71) *Cuajilote*, units	25	.10							
(72) Peaches, 2-ounce units	72	.06B		96	.12B		280	.35B	
(73) Bananas of coast, 4-ounce units	400	1.00B					800	2.00B	

(This group continues on p. 166.)

TABLE 65.—*Consumption of food in 3 families*—Continued

Item	Family 58			Family 49			Family 37		
	Quantity	Value	Percent	Quantity	Value	Percent	Quantity	Value	Percent
(This group continued from p. 165)									
(74) Local bananas, 10-pound stem				8	$0.56				
(75) Plantains, 8-ounce units	90	$0.68B							
(76) Prickly pears, units	36	.09B		28	.07B		48	$0.12B	
(77) Custard-apples, units	30	.10B		27	.09B		72	.24B	
(78) *Coyoles*, units	16	.02B							
(79) Mangoes, 4-ounce units				140	.28		250	.50B	
(80) *Melocotones*, units					.06B				
(81) *Pepinos*, 3-ounce units				224	.32				
(82) Candy (*bocadillos*), amount in cents		.15B			.24B				
(83) Candy (*caramelos*), amount in cents		.20B							
(84) Toasted horsebeans, amount in hundredweight			.4			.68		.18B	2.57
(85) Cookies (*rosquitas*), amount in cents					.12B			.28B	
(86) Fresh-corn tortillas, amount in cents					.20B			1.28B	
(87) Rice-with-milk, 8-ounce units	25	.25B		.4			.88		
Total		157.53	100.0		82.15	100.0		67.73	100.0
Produced		39.54	25.1		21.17	25.8		21.30	31.4
Bought		117.99	74.9		60.98	74.2		46.43	68.6

TABLE 66.[1]—*Seven-day food intake (1944) of 6 families (in net grams)*

Items	Food intake of families according to wealth as indicated by order of numbers					
	13 (3)[2]	15 (10.9)	37 (3.9)	49 (6)	58 (5)	106a (6.3)
(1) Corn	17,000	34,659	10,492	21,377	26,637	20,200
(3) Beans, black	630	5,424	1,009	920	3,600	767
(5) Dry peppers	8	19	5	15	5	7
(6) Green peppers	15	28			168	106
(8) *Panela*	825	3,700	1,335	1,577	2,750	1,100
(9) White sugar	120	440	30			
(10) Chocolate						245
(11) Bread (sweet rolls)	980	1,455	660	648		540
Bread, white		130	324		84	
(13) *Anotta*		42		91		
(21) Widgeon			720			
(22) Eggs	235	1,269	188	329	470	611
(23) Lake fish				57	100	
(25) Sea fish			240			
(26) Alligator meat	200					
(28) Beef	660	4,778	910	660	1,036	302
(29) Pork			60			
(30) Pork sausage	90				460	570
(32) Lard cracklings	180	118		90	120	93
(33) Lard	14	50	20		60	185
(34) Tomatoes	875	2,200	1,200	910	420	425
(35) *Miltomate*			15			
(36) Potatoes, white	85	800			807	240
(37) Potatoes, sweet	240					
(39) *Ayote*				1,840		
(41) Onions	350	930	300	450	450	400
(42) Garlic	42	24				100
(43) Cabbages	60	2,310		1,380		100
(46) Green beans				460		405
(50) Amaranth	360	2,300		920		480
(51) *Chipilin*	115		180			
(56) Coriander	10	30	16	5	10	
(59) Hierba blanca				1,840		
Epazote		30	24	10	40	16
Patoxte		180				
(60) Vegetable pears		348	25			
(61) Avocados		360	460	360		720
(62) Sweet oranges	830	9,940	560			
(63) Sour oranges			30			
(64) Limas		12,740	300	140		
(65) Limes	20	500	10			
(66) Cross-sapodilla		50	120			
(67) Spanish plums		432				
(74) Bananas, local	550	3,190	440			
Milk	1,500	1,125				
Cheese, fresh						30
Garbanzos			907			
Habas, fresh						500
Corn, green				454		
Pineapple juice			40			
Rice	60		120			75
Melchocha		240				

[1] From tabulations supplied by Miss Emma Reh, of Instituto de Nutricion de Centro America y Panamá.
[2] Numbers in parentheses indicate the number of people who partook of the family food during the week, subtracting fractions for meals missed and adding fractions for guests.

Panajachel," 1 "Panajachel with silk," 1 "San Andrés Variation," and 1 "Totonicapán" female costume).

Family 49 is most normal or typical socially and representative of the conservative families of the community; family 58 has a foreign and Ladinoized element, representing in that respect many Panajacheleño families; and family 37 is representative of the younger, progressive, and ambitious family that is still otherwise purely Indian in its way of life. Discounting a bit for above-average wealth, the three together appear to add up, roughly, to the Panajachel community. I propose to add them up, make allowances, use what checks are available, and so judge consumption in the whole community.

The population of the three families in 1936 was as follows:

Group	Number of persons			Total
	Family 58	Family 49	Family 37	
Men	3	1	1	5
Women	2	2	1	5
Children, 4–15	2	1	1	4
Infants	2			2
Total	9	4	3	16

The total of 16 represents 1/48.75 of the total population (table 3); the 5 adult men are 1/51, the women 1/54.4, the children 1/36.75, and the infants 1/53 of the totals in their respective classes. The average of the fractions in the four groups is 1/48.8; virtually the same as that of the total. The three households represent, of course, but 1/52.3 of the 157 in the community, but family 58 is so large that the people represented in the sample are more than that. The fraction (roughly 1/49) is that large because in the sample there is a disproportionate number of children 4 to 15 years of age; however, these are 4, 5, 10, and 14 years old, respectively, an apparently normal distribution, and I see no reason for giving greater or less weight to the group. Therefore when there seems no reason not to do so, I propose to multiply by 49 what these three families consume of those things wherein the number of individuals is the important fact and use that figure as a basis for judging the consumption of such items in the entire community. Each item will be individually considered, however, and the various factors weighed. Likewise, when I have data of only two of the three families, I shall use a similar calculation and multiply by 60 if the information is on the consumption of families 58 and 49, and 111 if it is on families 49 and 37.

The major difficulty for which I have no solution is the application of the Panajacheleño standard of living to the foreign Indian families resident in Panajachel; in fact, except for those of the one foreign family in the 7-day study, I have no good data on their food consumption.

(1)[158] *Corn.*[159]—Corn occupies by far the most important place in the diet. Fresh corn on the cob is roasted and also made into gruel; but the ripe corn, either toasted and ground and made into gruels or, most importantly, boiled with lime or ash and then ground and made into tortillas, tamales, and various gruels, and combined with other ingredients, is the basic food. Corn is important not only in the kitchen, but it is a festival and gift food, and it is the chief feed of fowl and pigs.

Since it is the breadstuff, and a cheap food, the poorer families use more corn relative to other foods than do richer families. The figures for family 58 include corn fed to chickens (there were no pigs) so the first adjustment of the figures for table 67 subtracts 480 pounds from the No. 58 corn total.

Families 49 and 58 consumed corn evidently in proportion to family size while No. 37 consumed little more than half as much; the man is said not to be fond of tortillas (and can afford substitutions better than the others) and this may be the reason;

but it is also possible that he underestimated his consumption. Family 58 calculated on the basis of 12 pounds daily (including chickens), No. 49 on 4¼ pounds, and No. 37 on only 2 pounds. Another informant in the middle of the wealth scale, with a family of two men, one woman, and two young children, said they used 5 pounds daily, which is in proportion to that used by Nos. 58 and 49. Family 1 reported using 25 pounds daily (but they have many chickens and a pig and, besides, feed many laborers). It must be concluded that family 37 uses abnormally little corn. An upward adjustment of the total figure by about 15,000 pounds for the whole community probably takes care both of this peculiarity and the skewness of the sample; the correction is not so great that it eliminates the possibility that other families may be atypical in the direction of No. 37.

Corn used in fiestas and gifts for the most part replaces corn used in the home, since customarily ceremonial food is sent to the houses of those who are supposed to receive it. Yet, doubtless when such food is available, more than the normal amount is consumed. According to my calculations, 4,387 pounds of corn are used in the calendrical fiestas by the officials. It does not seem unreasonable to suppose that 1,000 pounds of this is extra consumption. Food gifts for baptisms, favors, etc., are less likely to add to total consumption, and I shall leave them out of account.

In addition, corn fed to paid laborers from outside the community must be added. It has been calculated that 300 man-days of such labor are so employed by the Indians, and the laborers given food. Since many of these days are in milpa-harvest work, when festival spirit prevails, doubtless something like 400 pounds of corn would have to be added to the total consumption. On the other hand, local Indians who work for Ladinos are only rarely paid in food, and I imagine that, although 7,500 man-days are put in for outsiders, this factor does no more than about balance the other. The only additional disturbing factor that I can think of that enters into the consumption of corn is that people on long trips and in market visits, sometimes buy corn foods; usually, however, they take their food with them, and I doubt if the total consumption in the community is affected.

(2) *Lime.*—Lime is used in softening corn for grinding, and the quantities of corn and lime should be in some proportion. Actually, however,

[158] The numbers of the items correspond to the numbers of table 67.
[159] A full discussion of the preparation of food appears in my microfilmed notes, pp 250-329.

TABLE 67.—*Food consumption* [1]

a. STAPLES

Item	Quantity (total of sample)	Estimated total in community [2]	Value		
			Produced in community [3]	Bought outside	Total
(1) Corn	6,308.5 pounds	314,718 pounds	$2,051.00	$1,882.97	$3,933.97
(2) Lime (food)	416 pounds	5,200 pounds		26.00	26.00
(3) Beans, black	684 pounds	34,702 pounds [4]	301.95	253.28	555.23
(4) Beans, white	23 pounds	1,130 pounds	8.00	14.60	22.60
(5) Dry peppers	28⅛ pounds	1,540 pounds		123.20	123.20
(6) Green peppers	13⅛ pounds	483 pounds	77.28		77.28
Salt	(?)	9,645 pounds		144.67	144.67
(7) Coffee	310 pounds	12,780 pounds	418.32	610.80	1,029.12
(8) Low refined sugar	753 pounds	37,993 pounds		1,013.11	1,013.11
(9) White sugar	22½ pounds	1,227 pounds		56.35	56.35
(10) Chocolate	140 ounces	526 pounds		84.10	84.10
(11) Bread	1,762 ounces	5,646 pounds		903.38	903.38
(12) Honey	11 bottles	559 bottles	1.00	26.95	27.95
(13) Anotta	16½	800 ounces		72.00	72.00
(14) Anise seed	2⅔ ounces	140 ounces		2.10	2.10
(15) Pepper *de castilla*	1 ounce	111 ounces [5]		2.22	2.22
(16) Pepper *de chiapa*	1 ounce	111 ounces [5]		2.22	2.22
(17) Ginger	4 cents [6]	$4.44 [5]		4.44	4.44
(18) *Cordoncillo*	2 cents [6]	$2.22 [5]		2.22	2.22
(19) *Ayote* seed	66 cents [6]	$29.09	19.09	10.00	29.09
(20) *Chilacayote* seed	94 cents [6]	$41.46	21.46	20.00	41.46
Total			2,898.10	5,254.61	8,152.71

b. POULTRY, EGGS, MEAT, MEAT PRODUCTS, AND FISH

(21) Chickens	14	724	$30.00	$114.80	$144.80
Turkeys		23		13.80	13.80
(22) Eggs	1,316	64,484	112.50	693.55	806.05
(23) Lake fish	$11.50 [5]	$438.50	12.00	426.50	438.50
(24) Crabs	204	6,996	4.00	30.98	34.98
(25) Sea fish	16 pounds	884		176.80	176.80
(26) Alligator meat	2 pounds	118 pounds		29.50	29.50
(27) Shrimp (dry)	165 ounces	8,085 ounces		126.32	126.32
(28) Beef	922 pounds	45,223 pounds		2,261.15	2,261.15
(29) Pork	65 pounds	3,185 pounds		254.80	254.80
(30) Pork sausage	624 units	30,576 units		305.76	305.76
(31) Blood sausage	18 units of 8 ounces each	822 units		24.66	24.66
Loganiza		$25.00 [6]		25.00	25.00
(32) Lard cracklings	$3.48 [6]	$170.52 [5]		170.52	170.52
Prepared pork ribs		$60.00		60.00	60.00
(33) Lard	96 pounds	2,707 pounds		324.84	324.84
Wild game			30.00		20.00
Total			188.50	5,038.98	5,227.48

c. VEGETABLES AND HERBS

(34) Tomatoes	192 pounds	8,608 pounds	$1.00	$85.08	$86.08
(35) Huskcherries	74 pounds	3,026 pounds	45.39		45.39
(36) Potatoes	102 pounds	4,998 pounds		124.95	124.95
(37) Sweetpotatoes	186 pounds	5,714 pounds	57.14		57.14
(38) Sweet cassava	61 pounds	2,689 pounds	26.89		26.89
(39) Squash (*ayote*)	44 units	2,156 pounds	32.34		32.34
(40) Squash (*chilacayote*)	3 units	247 pounds	7.41		7.41
(41) Onions	4,230 pounds	227,270 pounds	113.63		113.63
(42) Garlic	840 heads	44,160 heads	36.80		36.80
(43) Cabbages	196 heads	12,000 heads	120.00		120.00
(44) Carrots	48	1,852	.77		.77
(45) Turnips	120	4,680	1.95		1.95
(46) Green beans	140 pounds	8,860 pounds	50.75	60.00	110.75
(47) Swiss chard	20 bunches	780 bunches	7.80		7.80
(48) Cucumbers	50	450	4.50		4.50
(49) Mulberry	188 pounds	10,212 pounds			51.06
(50) Amaranth	82 pounds	5,018 pounds			50.18
(51) *Chipilin*	26 pounds	1,974 pounds			19.74
(52) Cintula	2 ounces	222 ounces [5]			1.66
(53) *Chichipate*	2 ounces	222 ounces [5]	40.50	251.96	2.22
(54) "Lime tea"	2 cents [6]	$2.22 [5]			2.22
(55) Rue	2 cents [6]	$2.22 [5]			2.22
(56) Coriander	280 plants	21,080 plants [5]			21.08
(57) "7-shirts" herb	12 plants	1,332 plants [5]			6.66
(58) Col	18 pounds	1,998 pounds [5]			26.64
(59) Other herbs	98 cents [5]	$108.78 [5]			108.78
Total			546.87	521.99	1,068.86

[1] See footnotes at end of table.

TABLE 67.—*Food consumption*—Continued

d. FRUITS AND REFRESHMENTS

Item	Quantity (total of sample)	Estimated total in community [2]	Value		
			Produced in community [3]	Bought outside	Total
(60) Vegetable pears	$1.75 [6]	$85.75	$85.75		$85.75
(61) Avocados	300	13,200	44.00		44.00
(62) Sweet oranges	680	29,988	74.97		74.97
(63) Sour oranges	1,232	54,368	21.00	$28.43	49.43
(64) Limas	960	42,340	52.50	18.06	70.56
(65) Limes	680	30,020	30.02		30.02
(66) Cross-sapodilla	472	11,828	39.43		39.43
(67) White sapodilla	90	4,010	8.02		8.02
(68) Spanish plums	2,245	99,005	49.50		49.50
(69) Papayas	113	2,037	8.80	11.57	20.37
(70) Granadilla	300	4,700	2.20	2.70	4.70
(71) *Cuajilotes*	25	1,100	1.00	3.40	4.40
(72) Peaches	448	21,952	6.30	11.90	18.29
(73) Bananas (of the coast)	1,200	28,800		72.00	72.00
(74) Bananas (local)	8 stems	352 stems	24.64		24.64
(75) Plantains	90	410		3.07	3.07
(76) Prickly-pear	112	5,488		13.72	13.72
(77) Custard-apple	129	6,321		21.07	21.07
(78) *Coyoles*	16	784		.98	.98
(79) Mangoes	390	17,110	34.22		34.22
Nances	28 cents [5]	$21.08	1.00	20.08	21.08
(80) *Melocotones*	6 cents [5]	$2.09	2.09		2.09
(81) *Pepinos*	22	9,025	13.54		13.54
(82) Candy (*bocadillos*)	39 cents [5]	$19.11		19.11	19.11
(83) Candy (*caramelos*)	20 cents [5]	$9.80		9.80	9.80
(84) Toasted horsebeans	18 cents [5]	$8.82		8.82	8.82
(85) Cookies (*rosquitas*)	20 ounces	580 ounces		2.90	2.90
(86) Fresh corn *tortillas*	$1.48 [5]	$22.50		22.50	22.50
(87) Rice and milk	25 glasses	1,225 glasses		2.25	2.25
Total			498.78	272.45	771.23

e. SUMMARY

Item	Value		
	Produced in community	Bought outside	Total
Staples	$2,898.10	$5,254.61	$8,152.71
Poultry, eggs, meat products and fish	188.50	5,038.98	5,227.48
Vegetables and herbs	546.87	521.99	1,068.86
Fruit and refreshment	498.78	272.45	771.23
Total	4,132.25	11,088.03	15,220.28

[2] Total of previous column, times 49 (unless otherwise indicated), the result corrected as indicated in text.
[3] When a sufficient amount is grown within the community, all is put in this column, in spite of the fact that an individual may buy what is actually produced elsewhere, in a market. This may occur even with onions when the individual does not happen to grow them.
[4] Includes red beans, sometimes substituted but not important.
[5] Multiplied by 111 instead of 49.
[6] Quantity not known; information given in money value, and price not known.

No. 58 reports using corn and lime in a ratio of 15 to 1; No. 49, almost 27 to 1; No. 37, a little less than 8 to 1; and No. 1, 7 to 1. A difficulty is that lime is used for other than cooking purposes, and I suspect that this has caused some confusion. An informant discussing fiesta needs said that for 150 pounds of corn, a half pound of lime is used—a ratio of 300 to 1, which seems impossible. Rosales reports that in general ⅟₁₅ of ½ pound of lime is cooked with 3 pounds of corn—ratio of 90 to 1 (corn to lime). It seems to me most likely, on the basis of these contradictions, that the proportion may be something like 60 to 1, and if that is the case, 5,200 pounds were used in 1936.

(*3, 4*) *Beans.*—Black beans are commonly cooked, typically without fat, as part of the daily diet. Red beans are very occasionally substituted, and white beans are used almost exclusively for certain holidays. Beans must be considered a semiluxury food; if corn is the bread, beans are the butter. A richer family certainly tends to use more beans than a poorer family, relative to family size and to corn; but the difference is not as sharp as in the cases of more expensive foods. Although it might be expected therefore that the three families are a little high in their use of beans, other data (e. g., that of 1941) induce me to forego a correction, except to add 1,186 pounds of black beans and 187 pounds of white beans which are served in ceremonies, probably all in addition to normal consumption.

(5, 6) Peppers.—A number of varieties of dried red peppers, and, to a much lesser degree, of fresh, green peppers, are the most important condiment in the diet. They are ground and eaten with salt and tortillas, and are used in or with most cooked foods. Tastes differ considerably and the consumption of peppers probably varies without respect to wealth. I see no reason why the small sample should not reflect the variety reasonably well. In ceremonies perhaps 24 of the 40 ounces of chile used throughout the year represent additional consumption, since it goes with beans, meat, and fowl that are not frequently eaten in quantities. The sample is faulty with respect to the use of red peppers versus green peppers. All three families grew green peppers and doubtless ate them in larger proportion than did many others, especially the landless Indians. Green peppers are twice as expensive as red. Therefore, it is necessary to transfer about a fourth of the green pepper to red pepper.

Salt.—By an oversight, salt was left out of the consumption schedule and, curiously, the omission was never called to my attention while in the field. I therefore have no direct data on how much is consumed. The only hint that I have is that for the ceremonies a pound of salt is bought for every pound of chile, and I shall simply apply this ratio to the community.

(7) Coffee.—The consumption of coffee is Panajachel is remarkably high. In many families it is the only daily beverage, atole not being used, and it is drunk with each meal by adult and child alike. Even where atole is still made, coffee is by far the leading beverage. Family 58 probably drinks more coffee than is normal, and allowance must be made for this in using the sample, but the other two families are probably representative. Many of the poorer families, unlike those of the sample, buy their coffee roasted and ground, daily, by the ounce. This is much more expensive; I am assuming that one-eighth of all coffee consumed is so purchased. Since poor people are the chief purchasers of coffee bought this way, it is likely that they use less coffee than the families of the sample. In the cases of two such families I find, indeed, that they buy but an ounce (each) daily, which is about half the consumption of the sample families.

Therefore I am lowering the total of coffee consumed by another one-twelfth. Most Indians who grow coffee use some of it in their kitchens, although many producers sell their coffee and buy cheaper grades for consumption. I am assuming on the basis of knowledge of the number of coffee growers and the information in the sample, that 60 percent of the bean coffee used is home grown. Coffee is not used in the ceremonies.

(8) Low-refined sugar (panela).—*Panela* is used in certain desserts, especially those made with squash, and in the ceremonies to help sweeten chocolate, but it is consumed chiefly with coffee, so the two items tend to have a fixed ratio which in the three families is 1 to 2.25, 1 to 3, and 1 to 2.58, respectively. The ratio of 1 to 3 is probably most typical of conservative Indians; family No. 1 also so reports the use of coffee and *panela*. I therefore think that the sample is probably a little low, and if the total it indicates were raised by a thousand pounds it would come near to being three times the total of coffee consumed. The 96 pounds of *panela* used in the ceremonies must also be added as extra.

(9, 10) White sugar, chocolate.—White sugar is consumed exclusively, as far as I know, with chocolate, and the two may best be considered together. They are normally used only during Holy Week; but they are also consumed by the officials in ceremonies and at any time when brought as gifts. The ratio of chocolate to sugar in the three families are 1 to 2.25, 1 to 2.83, and 1 to 2.74. It may be noted that family 58 evidently uses less sweetening in both coffee and chocolate than do the others. Family No. 1 buys neither chocolate nor sugar, for it receives at least what it needs in the form of gifts from others. The only comparison I have [160] comes from the sugar and chocolate used in the rituals; and here the ratio is given as 1 part chocolate to 2.24 parts sweetening (six-sevenths *panela*, one-seventh sugar). If this information is correct, then probably 49 and 37 are atypical or mistaken. I have no way of telling, however, which of the two items, sugar or chocolate, should be raised or lowered so I give both as shown by the sample. However, the 13 pounds of sugar and the 800 ounces of chocolate used ceremonially must be added. Sugar and chocolate (in tablet form) together with bread, are the most common gifts

[160] Evidently family F106 a (Totonicapeños) in the 1944 sample week were using *panela* with their chocolate, which Panajacheleños do not do.

among the Indians. Gifts are brought when favors are asked or services (from weaving garments to baptizing a child) done. This fact interferes with the calculation of the total, for the informants of the sample included only what they thought they had actually purchased and consumed. Some of the sugar and chocolate received as gifts doubtless was passed on to others as gifts, but some (as in the case of family No. 1) was certainly consumed and must be added to the total. It happens that family 58 gave away no chocolate or sugar in 1936, however, and that family 49 gave but 2 ounces of chocolate and a half pound of sugar. (I have no information on the point from 37 so that the sample gives little guidance.) One can guess, however, that some 200 gifts were exchanged among the Indians (Ladinos do not give such gifts, certainly not to Indians); that on the average they consisted of 10 ounces of bread, three-fourths pound of sugar, and 5 ounces of chocolate; and that half the sugar and chocolate (and all the bread) changed hands twice before being consumed. The totals are therefore raised by 112 pounds of sugar and 750 ounces of chocolate.

(11) Bread.—Bread, usually in the form of 1-ounce sweet rolls (made with lard, eggs, sugar, salt, wheat flour, and yeast) is frequently eaten for breakfast instead of corn food; it is also an important ceremonial and gift food and is eaten in large quantities, with honey, during Holy Week.[161] The Holy Week bread is frequently richer (especially in eggs) and usually comes in large loaves or in rolls larger than usual. Some Indians have their Holy Week bread made to order. The daily use of bread varies with wealth, and the sample is consistent in this respect. I should subtract some bread to correct the sample for the above-average-wealth consumers; but the sample families all live east of the river, where bread is more difficult to buy; and this fact compensates. To the total, however, must be added some 2,000 of the 2,785 ounces distributed at ceremonies, and another 2,000 that (according to the guess above) were distributed as gifts. The Holy Week bread that is made to order (of purchased materials) probably comes out slightly cheaper than purchased bread; but since this bread

is somewhat more expensive than the ordinary, it may all be averaged at a cent an ounce, the usual price.

(12) Honey.—Honey is bought, as far as I know, only for Holy Week. The little honey produced locally, however, is probably eaten also at other times. Since the sample families kept no bees, local Indian production should be added to the total indicated by the sample.

(13–20) Spices.—After peppers, the most important spice is *anotta*, used in coloring sauces and meats. The difference among the sample families in the use of *anotta* is striking, but I do not know enough to account for it; it does not seem proportional, in the sample including family 1, to the use of meat and fowl. Using the information as given, the resulting total appears high; but since family 1 alone reports using 144 ounces a year, it may not be. The use of anise seed appears also to be highly irregular. Family 58 uses none at all (neither does family 1). The other two of the sample consumed quite different quantities. Though doubtless others besides No. 58 use no anise, there is no reason to think that these are all large families, so the total indicated by the sample must be raised. Family 58 reports nothing on the use of ground pepper, ginger, and *cordoncillo, cintula, chíchípate,* "lime tea," and rice but since I failed to ask about them, they may actually have been used. The formula factor 49 cannot therefore be used in this case and, instead, the total of the 2 families reported is multiplied by 111. Squash seed is used in some foods by all the sample families; but poor families who do not have their own cornfields (in which squash is produced) probably use less than the sample families (despite that No. 37 bought all his squash seed and No. 49 part of his) and a correction should be made.

(21) Chickens.—Chickens are used as food in the home almost exclusively on very special occasions, such as an after-birth festival; they are also cooked for sick persons and lying-in mothers. The differences in the sample represent in part accidents of circumstances, but the large number used by family 37 probably reflects its atypicality and relative wealth. Family No. 1 also reported using 36 chickens in 1936. However, the sample is probably representative enough to be used in calculating the community total. In addition, chickens (as well as turkeys, which are not used

---

[161] A week before Good Friday (1937) the largest local bakery already had a stock of $400 worth of bread for Holy Week. The owner said it would remain fresh because of the quantity of eggs and lard in it. The baker opined that even the poorest Indians buy three or four dollars' worth of bread for Holy Week, for themselves and for gifts.

domestically) are important in the officials' cere-monies, and the 38 chickens and 23 turkeys used in a year must be added.

(22) *Hens' eggs.*—These are part of the normal diet, but the differences probably depend partly on taste, partly on wealth. That family 58 uses so many is probably to be attributed to city-cultivated taste. Why No. 39 uses so few eggs I do not know. Family No. 1 reports using 3 dozen a week. Since two of the three families of the sample kept fowl, it is close enough to being representative to require no correction.

(23–27) *Fish and sea food.*—Lake fish and crabs are eaten during the year. They are usually bought, but occasionally caught for home use. The sample in this case is bad because No. 37 is one of the few local Indians who do considerable fishing. The result is that his consumption of fish and crabs is far out of proportion to that of the others. A correction must be made. Dried sea fish and alligator meat are bought only for Holy Week (the prohibition against meat during Lent or on Friday is not kept, if known). The quantity bought, to judge from the sample, probably depends partly on taste, chiefly on wealth. Family 1 reports buying 25 pounds of sea fish and 15 pounds of alligator, 8 times as much as the poor family 58 of comparable size. The sample is therefore defective, since it is accident that the largest family happens to be poor, and the total quantities must be raised. The use of shrimp, which is bought at any time of the year, is probably a matter of taste. Family 58 uses none, 49 a very small quantity, and 37 much; No. 1 uses none. It is as probable as not that the sample is representative of the distribution of tastes.

(28–32) *Beef.*—Beef is by far the favorite meat, and the only one used (although in a minor way in recent times) in ceremonial cooking. It is bought in small quantities, bone and meat, and usually cooked in soup. Pork is more expensive than beef, and is used most usually in tamales. Of the three sample families, No. 39 eats the highest percentage of pork to beef. Family 1 reports using 104 pounds of pork to 468 pounds of beef, an even higher percentage. At the opposite extreme is family 49, using 35 times as much beef as pork. I cannot explain why family 37 uses relatively so little meat (even its high fish and sea-food consumption cannot account for it); but, again, there seems no reason not to accept the

sample. To the total must be added only 45 pounds of beef used in ceremonies. Sausages of pork meat seem to be bought by all families more than is fresh pork; in the sample, those eating less than their share of fresh meat seem to eat more sausage (so, too, the rich and large No. 1 family which consumes only 572 pounds of fresh meat in a year, bought almost $15 worth of various preserved meats). Pork-blood sausages are evidently much less popular, only 49 and 1 reporting their use. Only the latter reported also the consumption of *longaniza*, another kind of pork sausage; but on the basis of the $2.40 worth he bought, one can guess that the Indian community probably consumed it to the value of some $25. Three kinds of lard cracklings are obtainable, *piñas*, *chicharrones*, and pressed *chicharrones*. The last-mentioned have the fat squeezed out in some special press, and are cheaper and less nourishing. Families 37 and 49 reported consumption of only *piñas* and *chicharrones*, but family No. 1 bought, in addition to $7.80 worth of these, 10 pounds of pressed *chicharrones*. Cracklings are bought usually as "snacks" in the market place, and doubt-less the man of family 37 bought so many because he is a frequent merchant, and a person who likes "snacks." Family No. 1 has sons whose pockets probably jingle with loose change. I think that the total derived from the sample is, however, probably fair. Family 1 is the only reporter of the use of prepared pork ribs; this family's $6 worth probably can be translated into $60 in the whole community.

(33) *Lard.*—Lard is used much more typically by Ladinos than by Indians, both for frying and the cooking of beans. Family 58 clearly shows outside influence in its use of lard, and allowance is to be made for that in calculating the total lard consumption.

(34, 35) *Tomatoes, huskcherries.*—Tomatoes, or instead the small wild huskcherries, are very important in the diet, cooked, and especially with meats. Why No. 37 reports the consumption of so much tomato in comparison with the other two families I cannot explain, although it may be noted that his family's diet is heavily weighted on the side of vegetables and fruit. Even the large, rich No. 1 family, which also feeds laborers, consumed a little less (60 pounds of tomatoes, 40 pounds of huskcherries). I am inclined to think

No. 37 atypical or mistaken, and to make a correction in reaching a total for the community.

(36–38) Potatoes.—Potatoes are used chiefly as one of the ingredients in soup. Sweetpotatoes are a dessert, boiled with no added sweetening. How sweet cassava is cooked I do not know except that it is used as a vegetable. Again it appears that family 37 is exceptional in its consumption of potatoes and especially sweetpotatoes (even family 1 reported using a little less potatoes, a third the sweetpotatoes, and only the same cassava). But probably family 58's consumption of these foods is abnormally low, and I am making a downward correction for the total only of sweetpotatoes. However, a further downward correction is required for both sweetpotatoes and cassava because the sample families all produce them and probably eat more than nonproducers do.

(39, 40) Squash.—This vegetable is cooked into desserts, and seems to be a rarity in the diet despite the fact that it is grown in Panajachel. In comparison with the others, family 49 consumes a great many *ayotes* (but family No. 1 reported that it consumed 1,200 *ayotes* and 200 *chilacayotes*, all that it produced). On the other hand, family 58 could have consumed more of its production while 37 had to buy what it ate. If the information is correct it appears that the determinant is individual preference. I think that probably the number of *chilacayotes* should be raised, since the three families happened to consume very few, but otherwise I see no reason to believe that the sample gives a false picture. I cannot think that the figures of family 1 are reliable.

(41, 42) Condiments.—Although not in proportion to their place in the productive economy of Panajachel, onions and garlic are important condiments, cooked especially with meats and sauces. I do not know why family No. 58 reports such small consumption in comparison with the others. I doubt if the others have overestimated (family No. 1 reports consuming a whole *tablón* of onions and 75 pounds of garlic) and am inclined to think that family 58 either undercalculated or is atypical in this respect. Since it has a large weight in the sample, the totals should be raised.

(43–48) Common vegetables.—The common vegetables most consumed in Panajachel appear to be cabbages and green beans, which like all greens and herbs are cooked together with other ingredients. All three families, and almost surely every Pana-

jachel family, eat these vegetables. On the other hand only family 58, with its city influence, also cooked other vegetables. That of course explains why this family ate less cabbage and green beans than might be expected: its vegetable diet was more varied. Since family 58 is large, this atypicality (as I think it is) must be corrected; for the total consumption of cabbage and green beans is greater, and that of carrots, turnips, and swiss chard smaller than the sample would indicate. The cucumber picture is quite false, for family 58 was one of very few who grew and ate cucumbers. The total here requires a large correction. At the same time account must be taken of the fact that the sample families are all vegetable growers. Differences in taste are indicated by the No. 49 emphasis on cabbage and the No. 37 emphasis on green beans, but such differences are doubtless representative.

(49–59) Other vegetables.—Of the less common vegetables, the "mulberry" herb, amaranth, and *chipilín* herb are the most consumed. Family 58 eats less of these than one would expect, perhaps again because of the variety of vegetables used in that house. It used no *chipilín* at all in 1936. Again corrections must be made. For all of the remaining herbs I have no information from family 58, and again must change the multiplication factor from 49 to 111. I do not know how col, rue, coriander, and the "7-shirts" herb are used in the kitchen. Rue, at least, is used medicinally. Coriander is used especially with meat and is given away by the beef butchers. Again it is a mystery why No. 37 reported using so much, and I think it wise to correct the total on that account.

(60) Vegetable pears.—This fruit appears to be consumed in surprisingly small quantities, considering their general importance in the region. They are used in cooking in various ways, playing the part of a vegetable rather than a fruit.

(61–82) Fruit.—Fruit is eaten raw, for the most part, and not as parts of regular meals. It may be considered refreshment. In general the fruit that is bought is eaten more by the wealthy than the poor, so that, for example, prickly pears, custard apples, and peaches (which were bought by the sample families) are consumed progressively more by families 58, 49, and 37. On the other hand, the question of taste and custom enters in the use of such fruit as plantains (which are fried) exclu-

sively by family 58, which has more Ladino-like tastes and techniques; in this case, a sharp correction of the total must be made. A correction must be made for "imported" bananas, too, for Nos. 58 and 37 seem to be wildly extravagant in their use. There is little to be said of the fruit locally produced; it is difficult to rely on any figures, since children, especially, are apt to pick a fruit to eat whenever they please. Obviously also, what is consumed depends in part on what an individual family happens to produce. I could go through my fruit census and make corrections of the sample on this basis, but considering the vagueness of the figures, I think it not worth while; the families of the sample, at any rate, are fairly representative of fruit-tree owners. A general correction should be made for all locally produced fruits, however, to take account of the 18 percent of the families who own no land or fruit trees and who doubtless eat less of these fruits grown by the sample families. I have taken off roughly 10 percent to account for this difference, and in special cases (such as those of the granadilla and papaya), when I know that the fruit is more rarely grown than the sample would indicate, I have made special corrections.

(83–88) *Sweets.*—Lard cracklings have already been mentioned as favorite "snacks," and it has been noted that fruit is eaten outside of meal hours as a refreshment. In addition, candies are bought in the stores and toasted horsebeans and cookies in the market place. Peanuts are also bought in the market, but were left out of the original schedule as must have been other miscellaneous sweets, such as candied popcorn that is occasionally found in the market. Certainly some Indians also drink the cold beverages to be bought, but none of the sample families did. The rice-with-milk beverage is a Ladino favorite, and indicates again that family 58 is not typically Indian. Correction must be made in this case as in those of cookies and fresh-corn tortillas wherein again the No. 37 family shows its liking for snacks and sweets.

In summary (table 67, *e*) it is seen that, according to my calculation, the community as a whole consumed $15,255.35 worth of food in 1936. About 26 percent of this was produced within the community and 74 percent outside. Clearly, Panajachel does not produce what it consumes, nor consume what it produces. An examination of the proportions of different kinds of food consumed makes it equally apparent that if the data and calculations are anywhere near correct, the Indian diet is by no means confined to, nor the dollar spent on, corn, beans, and chile.

EQUIPMENT

General information on equipment owned by the Indians was obtained from many sources, including simple observation. Dependence for the quantitative statements of table 68 is had chiefly on the sample of three families referred to above. Table 68, *a* estimates the value of all equipment owned by Panajachel Indians at a point in time in 1936. It excludes supplies of a transient nature, such as soap, kerosene, and firewood. The method pursued in arriving at the conclusion of the second last column is essentially that used to determine quantities of food consumed. With the information of the sample judged in the knowledge of its peculiarities and tempered by common sense and general knowledge of the community, it is possible to reach conclusions that seem sound.

It will be noted that, either because the families were not asked about them, or because they did not use them, some items used in Panajachel were not reported by the sample families. I know that some people have shotguns and flashlights, many use bought brooms (a bunch of branches serves otherwise), a few have hammocks—to rest, not sleep, in—china and pottery cups, forks and knives; I am sure that most, if not all, households own liquor glasses, and the wooden troughs that are placed around the grinding stone. For all such items general knowledge had to take the place of special data, but the results cannot be far off.

It will be noted, also, that the three families differed somewhat in their judgments of how long certain objects are used before they need to be replaced. Thus a table lasts family 49 15 years, family 37 only 10; a kind of chair lasts family 58 3 years; the others, 5; and so on. This is to be expected, and I have tended to average the estimates in drawing conclusions (except where information is apparently wrong, as in the case of family 37's report that a tump-strap lasts him only a year). Some of the differences reflect differences in the kind of use the articles get. For example, there is a nice (if rare) consistency in the statement that three tin lamps last 3 years, two last 2 years, and one lasts but 1 year. Some of the differences are not simply variations of opinion. Thus, the reason No. 58's one machete lasts but 2 years is that four people use it; No. 37, on the other hand, preserves his for 5 years because not only does he alone use it, but he has occupations that do not require his machete.

A number of things owned by the Indians have doubtless escaped my list.[162] The carpenters and butchers, for example, have their kits of tools; and there are always odd objects that people acquire. The last items of table 68, a indicate what one rather abnormal person (in this respect) has collected. The man of family 37 was once interested in learning carpentry, and the mason's trade; he (with other youths) owned a marimba in 1936; he is one of two Indians with a canoe; and he is the only Holy Week baker among the Indians. The $3,000-odd worth of goods listed in the table may be said to be a community minimum (if my calculations are near to being correct). Of course no account is taken of depreciation, which would be nearly impossible to calculate accurately; but the sum (as in the case of houses, above) is the replacement value of the property.

Finally, it may be noted that, as one would expect, some items such as cooking utensils and dishes are more numerous in larger families, while the numbers of others vary with wealth (as in the case of furniture, blankets, and mats) and still others, such as weaving equipment, with the special occupations of the householders. In general, however, there is uniformity as one goes from house to house. A weathy family has little more variety, and few more objects of a kind, than has a poor family; and there is a basic homogeneity in the kinds of things owned by the Indians of the community.

Table 68, b shows how much money the Indians probably spent in 1936 on the objects listed in table 68, a and, in addition, on certain supplies. The conclusions are drawn on the basis of the same data, and by the same method. The reports

of expenditures of the sample families are the average annual expenditures for the various items, respectively, but of course the sum of the average annual expenditures of all of the families of the community tend to be the same as the total community expenditure in any one year.

TABLE 68.—*Household furnishings and supplies, and tools*
a. VALUE

Item	Prorated number in year			Number in community [1]	Total value of property in community
	Family 58	Family 49	Family 37		
Flashlights				20	$15.00
Brooms				100	3.50
(93) Tin lamps	²3/3	1	2/2	250	20.00
(94) Tables		1/15	1/10	100	22.00
(95) Chairs	2/3,3/1½	2/5	8/5	600	60.00
(96) Dish chests	(?)		1	20	5.00
(97) Chests	(?)	1/4, 1/10	1/5, 1/15	300	150.00
(98) Beds			1/20	30	30.00
(99) Bed boards	(?)	8/20		240	18.00
(100) Mats	2	2	9	500	200.00
(101) Blankets	2/2	2/5	3/10	350	437.50
Hammocks				25	12.50
(102) Towels	1			10	2.00
(103) Padlocks	1/5			20	1.60
(104) Religious pictures			(?)	100	10.00
(105) Cooking pots	30	13	(?)	1,500	375.00
(106) Water jars	1/2	3/4	2/2	300	45.00
(107) Pottery pitchers	(?)	2	(?)	300	15.00
(108) Pottery bowls	(?)	4	(?)	400	32.00
China cups				25	5.00
(109) Enamelware cups	12/2	5/15	(?)	500	60.00
Pottery cups				200	4.00
(110) Enamelware plates	5/3	4/13	(?)	400	44.00
Kitchen knives				40	10.00
Table knives				20	2.40
(111) Spoons	8/5	3/7	(?)	300	21.00
Forks				50	3.50
Liquor glasses	(?)	(?)	(?)	150	15.00
(112) Bottles	(?)	6/16	(?)	400	4.00
(113) Calabashes	(?)	9/3	80/10	200	10.00
(114) Grinding stones	3/25	5/30	(?)	500	450.00
Grinding troughs	(?)	(?)	(?)	200	20.00
(115) Gasoline tins		1/3		50	6.00
(116) Baskets	3	3	3	300	13.50
(117) Tin basins	2	1/4	2	200	27.00
(118) Tump straps	2/7	1/15	1	200	26.00
(119) Ropes	3/1½	1/3	1	250	10.00
(120) Measuring cords	1/6	(?)		75	11.25
(121) Mesh bags	2/4	1/5	1, 1/2	250	37.50
(122) Carrying frames	1/5	(?)	1	150	24.00
(123) Machetes	1/2	2/6	1/5	200	120.00
(124) Axheads	1/15	1/6	1/20	140	161.00
(125) Hoe blades	3/2	4/4	¼	400	200.00
(126) Pickax heads	1/4			40	34.00
(127) Sickles	2/6	1/4		125	18.75
(128) Files		1		50	7.50
Shotguns			(?)	15	15.00
(129) Needles	15	36	(?)	400	4.00
(130) Warpers	1/20			60	19.80
(131) Spindles	6/2	3/3		500	7.50
(132) Looms	1/30			75	30.00
(133) Scissors	2/5	1/6	1/10	200	40.00
(134) Pencils	4	2	2	100	4.00
(135) Pen points	2			5	.25
(136) Tablets of paper	4			5	1.25
(137) Bottles of ink	1			5	.50
(138) Canoes			1/3½	2	70.00
(139) Oars (paddles)			(?)	(?)	1.00
(140) Sails				2	.35
(141) Marimbas			1/(?)	1	2.75
(142) Cloth for marimbas			1/(?)	1	.25
(143) Cover for marimba			1/(?)	1	.25
(144) Canvas sacks			1	10	2.00
(145) Barber's razors			1/10	4	1.80
(146) Hammers			1/20	10	2.00
(147) Saws			1/10	10	6.00
(148) Trowels			1/8	8	2.00
(149) Mason's plummets			1/20	8	3.20
(150) Bread pans			(?)/8	4	.35
(151) Baking sheets			(?)/8	2	.70
(152) Baker's shovels			(?)/8	2	.40
(153) Baker's mixing troughs			(?) (?)	1	.25
Total					3,015.10

See footnotes at end of table.

---

[162] Expenditures for toys, for example, are not included. The few used are almost always home-made, of plant parts. In 1937 a 12-year-old girl came with a load on her back that had the form of a baby. When asked how the "baby" was, she replied, laughing, that it was a piece of log with a rag around it for a skirt and a *gorra* (stocking cap), that she had made, over the top. A girl of 18 was present and said she had done the same when young and that her younger sister also carried a stick for a baby. However, she added that she still had a doll that her father had once bought her for 80 cents. Other Indians remarked on toys seen at our house and showed interest in buying similar ones, but the amount of money annually spent on such things cannot be more than a few dollars.

TABLE 68.—*Household furnishings and supplies, and tools*—
Continued

b. CONSUMPTION

Item	Value of quantity used			Estimated total in the community [1]
	Family 58	Family 49	Family 37	
(88) Firewood, produced	$4.16	$3.84	$3.00	[3] $450.00
Firewood, bought				60.00
(89) Pitch pine	.26	1.30	.50	100.94
(90) Kerosene	3.65	.36	2.00	294.49
(91) Matches	.54	.48	.45	72.03
Flashlight batteries				2.00
(92) Soap	5.20	1.44	2.50	447.86
(93) Tin lamps	.08	.08	.02½	9.06
(94) Tables		.01½	.10	2.00
(95) Chairs	.11	.05	.20	5.00
(96) Dish chests	(?)		.02	2.00
(97) Chests	(?)	.07½	.06	3.50
(98) Beds			.04	2.00
(99) Bed boards	(?)	.03		2.00
(100) Mats	.40	.46	2.17	75.00
(101) Blankets	1.25	.51	.43	100.00
Hammocks				1.00
(102) Towels	.20			2.00
(103) Padlocks	.01½			.30
(104) Religious pictures			.02	1.00
(105) Cooking pots	.90	.38	(?)	80.00
(106) Water jars	.05	.14	.21	10.00
(107) Pottery pitchers	(?)	.05	(?)	7.50
(108) Pottery bowls	(?)	.06	(?)	6.00
China cups				.50
(109) Enamelware cups	.43	.05	(?)	5.00
Pottery cups				.40
(110) Enamelware plates	.19	.03½	(?)	3.00
Kitchen knives				.50
Table knives				.25
(111) Spoons	.10	.03	(?)	5.00
Forks				.40
Liquor glasses	(?)	(?)	(?)	1.20
(112) Bottles	(?)	.04	(?)	2.00
(113) Calabashes	(?)	.01½	.04	4.00
(114) Grinding stones	.11	.16	(?)	20.00
Grinding stone troughs	(?)	(?)	(?)	2.00
(115) Gasoline tins		.04		.60
(116) Baskets	.24	.23	.33	39.20
(117) Tin basins	.30	.15	.33	38.22
(118) Tump straps	.04	.01	.10	2.50
(119) Ropes	.08	.06	.30	12.50
(120) Measuring cords	.02½	(?)		1.50
(121) Mesh bags	.03	.02	.12	7.00
(122) Carrying frames	.03	(?)		2.50
(123) Machetes	.20½	.18½	.06	20.00
(124) Axheads	.07	.17	.09	15.00
(125) Hoe blades	.73	.47	.19	68.00
(126) Pickax heads	.19			4.00
(127) Sickles	.05	.02½		3.75
(128) Files		.15		2.00
(129) Needles	.15	.36	(?)	20.00
(130) Warpers	.01			.70
(131) Spindles	.03	.01		2.00
(132) Looms	.01			.70
(133) Scissors	.08	.02½	.02½	5.00
(134) Pencils	.16	.08	.10	5.00
(135) Pen points	.02			.10
(136) Tablets of paper	1.00			2.00
(137) Bottles of ink	.10			.50
(138–153) (see table 68, a)			14.97	29.00
Total	21.19½	11.58½	28.38	2,061.70
Total produced	4.16	3.84	3.00	450.00
Total bought	17.03½	7.64	25.38	1,611.70

[1] As calculated from the sample and corrected to take account of other information.
[2] A simple digit indicates the number reported purchased in a year. Where there is a fraction, the numerator indicates the number possessed, the denominator, the number of years each one lasts. From the table it is not possible to tell how many of an item a family possesses if that item lasts less than a year; thus, a family buying 30 cooking pots in a year might (as far as the table shows) have from 1 to 30 at any one time.
[3] This is the only item of the table not purchased outside the community.

Firewood has already been discussed; it is now assumed that the 15 or 16 families buying most of their firewood spend about $55 a year for it, and

another $5 is paid for trees by other Indians. Pitch pine is used to kindle the fire, but it is used also to light the house and, more rarely, the wayfarer's path; almost all homes also use tin kerosene lamps both in the kitchen and on the road. It may be noticed that families 58 and 37 reported using kerosene (for illumination) almost exclusively, and only family 49 lights the kitchen with pitch pine (but uses kerosene for night traveling). The use of kerosene raises the cost of living, and in the case of family 58 is probably an extravagance that accompanies its more citylike ways. As far as I know, candles are never used for lighting. Together with incense, they are used ritually. The matches included in table 68, b were used to light cigarettes and cigars, and candles and incense, as well as the kitchen fire; but the consumption of matches for these other purposes is minimal, for embers of the fire are used more frequently than are matches.

The total community expenditure, including that for firewood, for kitchen and laundry supplies, is seen to be $1,417.32. In comparison, the cost of furnishings and utensils comes to $352.61; that of tools connected chiefly with agriculture and marketing, $216.77; weaving and sewing equipment cost $28.40 (which might well be added to the cost of clothing). According to the table, only $7.60 was spent on writing equipment. Family 58 has three literate members who like to write letters. There are few others in the community, but letters are occasionally written for illiterates by literate friends, and paper is furnished by the letter writer. I have no specific information on the school expenses of pupils, but I doubt that any exist. The few supplies and books are, I believe, furnished by the central Government.

Differences among the three sample families are not very great, if one leaves out of account No. 37's prorated expenses for technical equipment. Most of the expenses listed do not increase proportionally with the increase in the size of the family. Soap, firewood, blankets, and dishes are the most striking exceptions, and they account in large part for differences in the expenditures of the three families. Family 37's higher expenses, if his reporting is correct, probably reflect in part a higher standard of living with greater per capita wealth, and in part his progressiveness and variety of business interests.

CEREMONIAL, FESTIVE, AND MISCELLANEOUS EXPENSES

Table 69 itemizes a variety of miscellaneous expenses in all of which liquor is an important item. The table is readable in two ways: to see how much liquor, incense, candles, etc., are used in the community, and how much is spent on religion and on life-crisis occasions, etc. It is notable that the alcoholic-intoxicants budget is far greater than the housing budget, and the amount of money spent on liquor is about a fourth of that spent on clothing; it is more than that for any item of food excepting corn or meat; and it is almost as much as is spent on all tools and household utensils and supplies. The consumption of incense, candles, and rockets is considerable but hardly comparable to that of liquor. It is also notable that pharmacy-bought drugs (including some attention by the pharmacist) represent more important expenditures than the use of shamans and their curing rituals.

In calculating the expenditures included in table 69, the use of the sample had definite limitations, since many of the expenses are special and extraordinary and not routine for particular families. Other data were available, however, and the total expenditures calculated are based on considerable variety of them.

Public rituals are those of the cult of the saints, organized and paid for by the holders of office in the political-religious organization of the Panajacheleño Indian community. These officials are required by custom to perform ceremonies in connection with their offices, and these ceremonies require rather fixed expenditures of food, liquor, candles, incense, rockets, etc., that vary little from year to year (though in the course of a generation may change considerably).[163] Table 70 classifies these expenditures by the occasions and by the officials making them.[164] It is seen that in any one year the expense is frequently entailed both

[163] It is frequently said that the ceremonies are relatively inexpensive nowadays—that formerly much more food and liquor, etc., were required. On the other hand it is recalled that liquor was so much cheaper, and money so much more plentiful, a generation ago that the hardships of officials are now greater than they were.

[164] These expenses are as of 1936, although some of the data were collected later. In 1938, 1939, and 1940 an additional expense was borne by a group of families who organized a dance for the titular fiesta. The leader of the dance itemized its cost, with me, and we found it came to $85.30 each year, distributed evenly along 18 dancers. The cost to the community was greater than this, however, for at each of the 20-odd houses where they danced, the dancers were given 50 cents (which could be applied to the cost of the dance) and a bottle of liquor. An informant said, in 1941, that the dance would probably not be undertaken again because the public objects to the added expense of the fiesta.

TABLE 69.—*Ceremonial, fiesta, and miscellaneous expenses, 1936*

Item	Sample expenditures			Estimated totals in the community												Total		
	Family 58	Family 49	Family 37	Cult of the Saints			Life cycle				Sickness	Miscellaneous[1] Shaman rituals	Gifts and favors	Other (secular drinking)	Within community	Outside community	Total
				Public rituals	Private rituals	Private participation	Births	Baptisms	Marriages	Deaths							
Food				$149.80	$3.00	$50	$35.00	$30.00	$25.00		$25		$2	$45.00			$364.80
Liquor	$2.00	$8.76	$4.43	309.92	50.00	150	95.00	30.00	50.00	$270.00	75		6	5.00	$150	$1,190.92	1,190.92
Incense	2.16	1.40	.08	10.86	6.00						10	2.60	1			30.46	30.46
Candles		2.18	.72	14.42	8.00	3					50	45.00	5			125.42	125.42
Rockets				49.17	3.20											52.37	52.37
Drum—flageolet				15.20	.40										$15.60		15.60
Marimba				6.00												6.00	6.00
Band				8.00												8.00	8.00
Priest—fees				10.00					15.00							25.00	25.00
Priest—food				1.00												1.00	1.00
Special clothing				5.00					6.00	54.50						5.50	65.50
Shaman fees												100	10		87.00	23.00	110.00
Midwife fees							45.00								40.00	5.00	45.00
Drugs	2.50	4.20	(?)				3.00				300					303.00	303.00
Coffins										61.50						61.50	61.50
Government fees				(?)						6.63						6.63	6.63
Miscellaneous				2.50						[2]25.00	[3]3.50				30.50	.50	31.00
Unknown				3.00													3.00
Total				584.87	70.60	203	178.00	81.00	100.00	443.73	560	24	50.00	150			2,445.20
Family No. 58				.66	.16		[4].83	[4].35		[4].55			.33				
Family No. 59				.75			[4].58	[4].14		[4]1.72			.15				

[1] Table 71.
[2] Cash given to girl's parents and usually used for her wardrobe.
[3] Fee for ringing church bell; ultimate destiny of money unknown.
[4] Annual average.

by the outgoing and the incoming officials, but since the incoming officials one year are the outgoing officials the next, the expenses are carried by the same groups of men (or families) over periods ranging from one year to about 15 months. A limited number of individuals obviously bear the burden of the costs of public ritual to the community,[165] but the individuals change from year to year so that in the long run the expenses are distributed among all. It may be noted, too, that certain officials spend much more than others, and since these are generally chosen from the ranks of the more wealthy, the costs tend to be distributed according to "ability to pay." Table 71, the conclusions of which are included in table 69, shows how these public-ritual costs are divided among the various items consumed. The foodstuffs have already been mentioned and accounted for, and they, of course, replace in some degree food that would be consumed anyway. The liquor, candles, incense, music, priest's fees, etc., are extra expenses to the community. Tables 70 and 71 are based on special information on the politico-religious organization and detailed calculations of a veteran of the system, and are probably at least 90 percent accurate. At least one item I know to be lacking. On one occasion the *cofradia* has to pay a license fee to have a *zarabanda* and sell liquor, and I do not know the amount of the fee.

"Private" rituals consist of harvest rites and the lighting of candles to saints. A number of the homes have private altars, and on certain days candles and incense are burned at them, either by the owners or by other Indians. Candles and incense are also burned to saints elsewhere when the Indians visit out-of-town fiestas and, occasionally, in the local church. The cost of such ritual is very little, however, and almost $15 of the $70.60 total shown in table 69 represents expenses

incurred by one man who has in his house a saint whose day (San Juan Bautista) he celebrates publicly, spending about $8 on liquor alone and $3.20 on musicians. When people go to fiestas in other towns, even if primarily on business, they frequently pay devotion to the saint there, and they also frequently drink. In the harvest rituals (for the corn harvest only) liquor also frequently plays a small part.

The items included under "private participation" in fiestas of the cult of the saints have reference to the celebration of persons not in the organization carrying out the rituals. Most of the populace buy food and refreshment in the plaza, especially during the titular fiesta, and of course a great many men and many women drink in taverns and *zarabandas*. Women especially join the processions with candles.

The calculation of the amount spent on births is based on the supposition that 70 (42 male, 28 female) live births and 4 stillbirths occurred in the Indian community in 1936. The midwife's fee has already been discussed. The items for food and liquor are chiefly for that given the midwife at the time of the birth and in the subsequent ceremony. The calculation may be checked against an informant's independent estimate that a birth usually costs $2.50.

It is assumed that there were about 65 baptisms of Indian children in 1936, but that Ladinos acted as godparents (hence paid the priest and bough the garments) in 40 of those cases. In all cases, Indians supplied food-gifts and liquor. Subsequent gifts to the godparents are not here included. (The priest's fee for a baptism is 60 cents.)

From 1922 to 1937 there were 15 cases of Indian marriages in the legal religious sense. There was none in 1936, and I have left out of consideration the costs additional to those of an ordinary mating. According to my records, there were seven customary matings between May 1936 (when the household census was made) and September 1937, when changes were first recorded. One may therefore suppose that there were five such unions in 1936. Some of these were first marriages, others second, and of course the expenses differ. I do not have information on what was spent in these specific cases, and judge the total on the basis of information on a number of other cases. Liquor is consumed by the representatives of the young

[165] It is seen in the table that a relatively small sum comes from general contributions. An informant (1941) explained that the seeking of contributions is illegal (and Rosales noted in 1936 that it was illegal but that the *principales* obtained special permission from the authorities to solicit) and done among Indians on the quiet—that formerly Ladinos were asked for money, but now they would complain to the authorities. For the titular fiesta each married man is expected to give 33 cents if he has not yet reached the stage of being a *cofrade*, and 50 cents if he has. Widows who have done services with their husbands give 16 cents. (In some households more than one man or woman thus contributes.) Office holders are exempt. For the Holy Week mass each household gives 5 cents and some Ladinos also contribute. When the image of the Christ Child is taken from house to house on Epiphany, from 1 to 3 cents (rarely more) is contributed by Indian families whose members hold no office—and the office holders serve liquor. Masses other than those of Holy Week, the titular fiesta (San Francisco Caracciola) on June 4, are paid for by Ladinos who arrange them.

pair from the night of the first asking through the period of courtship when gifts of food are delivered by the family of the boy and when an agreed sum of money is turned over—to be used, generally, for the bride's trousseau.

Of the Indian deaths in 1936 there were 39 registered—14 infants, 12 children, and 13 adults. The cost of the death varies with age something like the following:

	Infant	Child	Adult
Coffin	$0.75	$1.00	$3.00
Clothing	.25	1.00	3.00
Liquor	3.00	6.00	12.00
Candles	.50	1.00	2.00
Incense	.05	.10	.10
Total	4.55	9.10	20.10

with the cost of having the church bells rung (almost always done, for 10 cents) and the charge

TABLE 70.—*Expenditures of officials for rituals*

Official	Occasion	Amount	Total expenditures	
			Per person	Total
Each of 2 fiscales	New Year's	$1.60	$1.60	$3.20
Each of 2 sacristans	do	5.70	5.70	11.40
Alcalde	Epiphany	.40	9.31	9.31
	Mar. 15	5.27		
	Palm Sunday	.47		
	San Buenaventura	3.17		
Each of 4 regidores	Palm Sunday	.47	3.64	14.56
	San Buenaventura	3.17		
Each of 4 mayores	Good Friday	.40	.40	1.60
All alguaciles	Mar. 15	1.00		1.00
	do	.10		
Outgoing cofrade and each of 3 mayordomos of cofrade San Francisco.	Day of the Cross	7.67	25.05	100.20
	San Francisco Caracciola	6.56		
	San Joaquín	.13		
	San Francisco de Asis	6.09		
	Octave of San Francisco de Asis	4.50		
	San Joaquín	3.48		
Incoming cofrade of cofrade San Francisco	San Nicolas	22.74	36.92	36.92
	Octave of San Francisco de Asis	6.73		
	All Souls'	3.97		
Each of 3 incoming mayordomos of San Francisco	Octave of San Francisco de Asis	6.73	10.70	32.10
	All Souls'	3.97		
	First Friday of Lent	7.06		
Outgoing cofrade and each of 2 mayordomos of cofrade Sacramento.	Mar. 15	.10	14.27	42.81
	Holy Saturday	.21		
	Corpus Christi	6.90		
	Holy Saturday	2.10		
	Ascension	22.74		
Incoming cofrade of cofrade Sacramento	Corpus Christi	9.00	55.81	55.81
	Octave of Corpus Christi	7.42		
	San Francisco de Asis	9.53		
	All Souls'	5.02		
	Corpus Christi	9.00		
Each of 2 incoming mayordomos of Sacramento	Octave of Corpus Christi	7.42	30.97	61.94
	San Francisco de Asis	9.53		
	All Souls'	5.02		
	Epiphany	5.63		
Outgoing cofrade of cofrade Santa Cruz	Mar. 15	.10	6.34	6.34
	Holy Saturday	.21		
	Day of the Cross	.40		
	Epiphany	5.63		
	Mar. 15	.09		
Each of 2 outgoing mayordomos of cofrade Santa Cruz	Holy Saturday	.21	6.73	13.46
	Easter Sunday	.40		
	Day of the Cross	.40		
	Holy Saturday	2.90		
Incoming cofrade of cofrade Santa Cruz	Day of the Cross	7.12	15.66	15.66
	Christmas	5.64		
Each of 2 incoming mayordomos of cofrade Santa Cruz	Day of the Cross	7.12	12.76	25.52
	Christmas	5.64		
	Second Friday of Lent	5.55		
Outgoing cofrade and each of 2 mayordomos of cofrade San Nicolas.	Mar. 15	.10	6.24	18.72
	San Joaquín	.18		
	San Nicolas	.41		
Incoming cofrade of cofrade San Nicolas	San Joaquín	4.68	10.34	10.34
	San Nicolas	5.66		
Each of 2 incoming mayordomos of cofrade San Nicolas	do	5.66	5.66	11.32
All high officials and principales	Epiphany	12.00		62.00
	Corpus Christi	50.00		
Principales (12)	San Isidro	2.93		2.93
Cross-planters (principales)	Lazarus Sunday	1.20		2.80
	Good Friday	1.60		
"Negrito" dancers	Corpus Christi	5.00		5.00
Rocket burners	Day of the Cross	1.60		4.80
	San Francisco Caracciola	3.20		
General public (no officials)	Epiphany	3.00		35.13
	Holy Week	3.50		
	San Francisco de Asis	28.63		
Total				584.87

for using the cemetery and getting the official registration ($0.17) remaining constant. An informant calculated the cost of a funeral at $16.67. The greatest cost is always that of the liquor consumed by the mourners and those who help open the grave, etc., and the official in charge.[166] The few cents buried with the body in at least some cases are not included. Nor is the cost of protracted drinking that frequently follows a death; this cost is attributed to "secular" drinking.

The cost of sickness—not including the value of the time lost, which will be calculated in the next chapter—is seen to be considerable. These figures are less authentic than the foregoing because I have no independent data on the number of the sick during a year. However, the number of cases of local shamans and curers has already been calculated, and one can judge the cost of drugs from the data of the sample families, so that a calculation can be made without knowing the total number of cases of all kinds of sickness in a year.[167] The liquor, incense, and candles referred to is chiefly that consumed by the shamans in their divinations and rituals; but food and liquor are sometimes brought to the patient by friends and relatives.

The other shamanistic rituals are those for finding lost articles, getting luck for a business venture, and so on. Twenty cases in a year seems a good guess, though it is not more than a guess.

To ask for a wife for one's son, or a godparent for one's child; or to ask for a loan of money, even with land as security, or that a document or a bargain be witnessed or a letter written—to ask any "favor" it is customary to accompany the request with a gift of food, and sometimes liquor. Most of these gifts have already been included in such items as marriage, baptism, etc., but the residue is accounted for under "gifts and favors." Likewise there are here included the periodic gifts to godparents, usually presented during certain festivals, and the occasional gifts of food to relatives and friends. The calculation of the value

---

[166] In 1941 an informant described a funeral whose participants are usually sober people. Both men and women drank. By the time the funeral procession began, 3 rounds of liquor had already been passed among the twenty-odd relatives and friends; a liter was taken to the cemetery and consumed; and back at the house another 2 liters were drunk before the visitors left for the night. The next morning 11 persons did away with 3 liters more, and of course on the following day there was hangover to be cured with more liquor. In this case the drinking did not long continue partly because the men are not "drinkers" and partly because the deceased was a very old widow and there appeared to be no great grief involved.

[167] The shaman's fee is calculated at 50 cents a "treatment." I have cases where it is less (when it is explained that the shaman was a "friend" and wouldn't charge much) and one case in which a Ladino "doctor" of another town charged a woman $15 (and still she died). Nonshaman curers take no cash fees.

TABLE 71.—*Expenditures for public rituals*

Occasion	Expenditures						
	Total	Food	Liquor	Incense	Candles	Rockets	Other
New Year's	$14.60	$3.40	$11.20				
Epiphany	32.29	6.30	20.16	$0.33	$0.50	$1.60	¹ $3.40
First Friday of Lent	21.18	6.11	12.24	.33	.50	1.60	² .40
Second Friday of Lent	16.65	5.87	8.16	.52	.50	1.60	
March 15	7.55	1.30	4.00	.03	.02	.80	³ 1.40
Lazarus Sunday	1.20		1.20				
Palm Sunday	2.35		1.60	.35	.40		
Good Friday	3.20		3.20				
Holy Saturday	9.76		4.80	.74	1.20	.52	⁴ 2.50
Easter Sunday	.80		.80				
Day of the Cross	54.84	22.34	24.24	.66	1.00	2.40	⁵ 4.20
San Isidro	2.93			.33	.60	1.60	³ .40
Ascension	22.74	5.87	12.24	.33	.50	.80	⁶ 3.00
San Francisco Caracciola	29.44	8.21	12.24	.99	1.10	3.20	⁷ 3.70
Corpus Christi	102.70	15.96	74.48	.66	1.00	4.00	⁶ 6.60
Octave of Corpus Christi	22.26	5.59	12.24	.33	.50	2.40	⁸ 1.20
San Buenaventura	15.85	4.13	8.16	.66	.50	1.60	². 80
San Joaquín	9.22		8.00	.30	.40	.52	
San Nicolas	40.95	15.16	20.80	.66	1.00	2.53	². 80
San Francisco de Asis	81.58	21.81	25.28	1.99	2.20	12.80	⁹ 17.50
Octave of San Francisco de Asis	44.92	16.46	20.40	.66	1.00	4.80	¹ 1.60
All Souls'	30.94	5.76	16.32	.66	1.00	4.80	² 2.40
Christmas	16.92	5.53	8.16	.33	.50	1.60	². 80
Total	584.87	149.80	309.92	10.86	14.42	49.17	50.70

¹ $0.40 to drum-flageolet players; destiny of $3 (public contributions) not known to me.
² To drum-flageolet players.
³ $0.40 to drum-flageolet players; $1 for purchase of drum by new *alguaciles* from old *alguaciles*.
⁴ $2 the Priest's fee; $0.50 for the Priest's breakfast.
⁵ $3 for hire of a marimba band, $1.20 for drum-flageolet players.
⁶ Hire of a marimba band.
⁷ $2 the priest's fee; $0.50 for the priest's breakfast; $1.20 for drum-flageolet players.
⁸ $5 (estimated) for purchase and rental of clothing by "Negrito" dancers; $1.60 for drum-flageolet players.
⁹ $6 the priest's fee; $8 for hire of a band; $1, rental of house; $0.50, hiring of a cook for the band; and $2 for drum-flageolet players.

of the gifts is based partly on the sample and partly on independent knowledge of the gift-giving occasions (something like 200 gifts are probably exchanged annually) and the content of such gifts (on an average, 10 cents bread, 3¾ cents sugar, and 5 cents chocolate; or about 35 cents worth of corn and meat foods).

When, because of a funeral, a ritual, or a fiesta, the Indians drink, they frequently keep on drinking for several days.[168] It is difficult to draw a line between drinking in purely secular contexts and this "aftermath" drinking, for men who like to drink seek any occasion and of course take advantage of times when drinking is socially most expectable. It is rather rare for Indians to drink when occasion demands. Nevertheless, ordinary drinking is common enough to be economically important. People who like liquor (and of course some like it better than others) succumb when they go to markets out of town and especially when they visit fiestas,[169] when there is emotional disturbance,[170] or, less frequently, simply when friends meet and one invites the other to a drink. It is certain that some men consume, besides that in rituals, as much as 20 bottles (worth $20 or more by the glass) a year. Excepting the Protestant converts, there are no teetotalers. Every man probably drinks three or four times a year and may drink oftener. An informant listed 19 men as "heavy" drinkers (those who, when they drink, keep drinking for a week or longer). All except three of these men were relatively wealthy,

all except two were old *principales*, and four were shamans, and it is evident that men become drinkers partly because of long and habitual ritual use of liquor. According to the same informant, there once were women "drinkers" as well, but, "Women nowadays are ashamed to drink; those who do not drink speak ill of them when they do. Female *mayordomos*, when they receive their year, are forced to drink, and then they keep on drinking for 2 days."

PERSONAL EXPENSES, TAXES, ETC.

Table 72 concludes the inventory of expenditures supposedly incurred by the Indian community in 1936 with items of a personal and legal nature. The item of secular drinking in table 71 is also a personal expenditure, of course, but, as has been seen, liquor has many other uses. Most men smoke in moderation, and women will smoke occasionally, but rarely if ever buy tobacco. Men smoke both cigarettes and cigars (and very rarely pipes made in other towns) but the older men usually buy cigars, the younger men cigarettes. The small amount of tobacco used by the No. 58 family in 1936 was a reflection of its tendency towards Protestantism, since the missionaries discourage the use of tobacco as well as liquor, and in later years none at all was used. In 1936 the only smoker was the head of the family.

Photographs are occasionally made for the Indians by traveling photographers at festivals. Only men and boys have their hair cut, and almost always by barbers. The local Indian barber is less patronized than the outside Indian barbers who come on market day and who are found in Sololá.

Every man between the ages of 18 and 60 is required to work on the highway for 2 weeks (12 days) each year; instead of working he may pay the sum of $2. It could be determined from local treasury records how many men worked and how many paid in 1936, but this was not done. The fixed rate of $1 for 6 days happens to be the prevailing labor rate in Panajachel, so that one who works for others finds it economically as easy to pay as to work. The wealthier Indians prefer to pay, since they are able to and find it more profitable to spend the time on their own lands; the poorer people more frequently work, partly because a dollar in cash (the work is divided into semesters) is often more than the liquid assets

---

[168] The following seems typical: The man who became Indian Alcalde in 1941 is not a "drinker." Yet when he assumed office he of course drank at the ceremony at his house. When the guests left (he says) "I stayed at home until about 5 p. m., then met the other two *regidores* in the *juzgado*. We contributed 8 cents apiece and went to the store to drink a fourth liter. Then we went to my house and drank half the liquor remaining from the ceremony. I was pretty drunk, but had a little supper, and the next morning had hangover [locally a sickness that must be cured with a drink] and took one drink. At about 8 o'clock the other *regidores* arrived and we finished the other half of the left-over liquor and went to the *juzgado*. One of the *regidores* then invited us to drink, and he bought a half-liter; the other then bought a quarter-liter and then, drunk, we went to our homes. The next morning I had hangover and sent for liquor. After breakfast I went to the *juzgado*; it was not my week, but the *regidor* suggested that I come and, besides, I had to end my hangover. I returned home early and went to bed."

[169] A very poor Indian and his wife and 12-year-old daughter reported on their return from a selling trip to Patzún that they had spent about $1 on liquor there, "all because the husband likes to drink." (He became drunk, the wife less so; even the girl drank some.)

[170] A Panajacheleño plantation worker had been widowed recently and left with three children. He was lonesome and sought the 16-year-old daughter of a fellow worker for a wife. She accepted (he said) but her father refused. Thinking to win him with liquor, he drew $2 from his employer and went to Sololá where he bought four bottles. On his return he "began thinking about my late wife and also my late mother and took a drink." When we found him on the road he had only a half bottle left, but he explained that one bottle had been stolen in the night. (The stolen bottle seemed to be his and his brother's chief concern.)

available at one time. Many Indians sometimes work and sometimes pay, depending upon circumstances at the time. No. 49, who frequently does his road work, borrowed the money from me in 1941 because I was paying him more for his time than the standard rate. Frequently laborers will work rather than pay when they work for an employer paying substandard wages. In table 72 I suppose that half of the people work, but take into account the fact that men serving in public office are exempt. This exemption holds also for the *ornato* tax for public works; this tax must be paid in cash by every man in the given age group.

TABLE 72.—*Personal expenses, taxes, etc.*

Item	Sample expenditures			Estimated community total		
	No 58 family	No. 49 family	No. 37 family	Within community	Outside community	Total
Cigars	$0.52	$1.04	$0.15	--------	$90	$90
Cigarettes	--------	--------	2.40	--------	130	130
Photographs	.25	--------	(?)	--------	15	15
Haircuts	2.50	.36	(?)	$2	73	75
Road tax	4.00	2.00	2.00	¹ 160	160	320
Ornato tax	1.50	.50	.50	--------	80	80
Real-estate tax	--------	.60	(?)	--------	75	75
Revenue stamps, stamped paper	(?)	(?)	(?)	--------	3	3
Fines	--------	--------	--------	¹ 100	50	150
Interest	--------	--------	--------	5	15	20
Total	8.77	4.50	5.05	267	691	958

¹ Value of time.

The real estate tax is popularly called the three-per-thousand. I am not sure, but I believe the rate is actually higher. Most landholders do not pay this tax because their land titles are not legally registered with the higher authorities.

Most documents must be written on Government-stamped paper; in addition, every person over 18 is supposed to buy the 10-cent stamp for his or her *cédula*, or identification paper. Many people do not possess this document.[171] The figure here is little more than a guess. A license for canoe owners was also required in 1936; it is not included in the table because I do not recall how much it was. An item for fees paid lawyers (in Sololá) would also be in order, for in land matters the services of the lawyers in Sololá are sometimes bought; but I cannot estimate what the item might have amounted to in 1936.

[171] A poor woman said in 1937 that she had obtained her *cédula* 2 years before, grinding corn to earn the 10 cents for the stamp. When she had the money her husband suggested that she rather buy corn with it; what good would a *cédula* do her anyway?

Again in the matter of fines, perusal of official records might be of assistance in determining the amount. Offenders (usually intoxicated persons) are sentenced to a certain number of days in jail, the sentence commutable at so much per day in money. Such fines and jail sentences are levied even in cases of disputes of a "civil" nature, and when Indians quarrel and bring a case into the Indencia, the result most frequently is the fining of one or both parties. Indians stay in jail if they cannot pay the fine or if the money required is much more than their time is worth;[172] frequently they serve several days and then pay for the remainder. The amount of money included in table 72 is a rough guess, based on a number of cases noted.

The payment of interest on money borrowed is not as common as the pawning of land without set interest. The matter has been discussed above (pp. 80–81) and, again, the figure in table 72 is little more than a guess.

Summary.—Table 73 summarizes the expenditures for all purposes, both within and outside the community, of the Indians of Panajachel in 1936.

TABLE 73.—*Summary of expenditures in 1936*

Item	Expenditures		
	Total	Within the community	Bought outside
Housing: building and repairing	$263.33	¹ $183.33	$80.00
Clothing (including repairing)	4,640.02	574.40	4,065.62
Food	15,220.28	4,132.25	11,088.03
Supplies, furnishings, and tools	2,061.70	450.00	1,611.70
Ceremonies, fiestas, life crises, etc	² 2,080.40	178.60	1,901.80
Personal, legal, etc	958.00	267.00	691.00
Total	25,222.73	5,785.58	9,438.15

¹ See footnote 135, p. 147. Doubtless some of the labor on Panajachel Indian homes is done by Indians of other towns, but it is a negligible amount and is not subtracted from the total here.
² Leaving out the item "Food" of table 69, included with Food here. The unknown item of $3, not classified in table 69 either as locally produced or as purchased outside, is here considered as spent outside the community.

COMMUNITY WEALTH

Most of the wealth of the Indian community is in the land that it owns. Including standing coffee and fruit trees, the value of real estate in private hands amounts to over $20,000. The replacement value of houses owned by Indians has

[172] An Indian reported (1940) that a friend was in jail for having an unregistered rifle—fined $20 commutable to 20 days in jail. "Maybe it will be reduced to $10, but he will certainly serve time rather than pay. Who would ever pay a dollar a day when one can earn only 10 pesos or 20 cents a day?" In another case two young men were sentenced to 5 days in jail commutable at 20 cents daily (disorderly conduct while drunk); they stayed in jail 2 days, then borrowed money to pay for the remaining 3.

been calculated at a little less than $4,000. Thus real property amounts to a little less than $25,-000—about $158 per family and about $31 per capita. There is little profit in trying to calculate the value of community (public) property such as the church and public buildings and grounds, the roads, etc. These assets, not only solidly frozen but also not potentially usable by individuals, have only academic interest. Eight hundred dollars has been calculated to be the value of domestic animals owned, and $3,000 that of household goods and tools. The annual cost of clothing is $3,900, but the value of the clothing in the possession of the Indians at any point in time is probably closer to $3,500. To the resulting sum of $32,300 might be added, as part of the wealth of the community:

(1) The value at a point in time, or the average during the year, of crops standing in Indian fields and stored ready for sale. The value of standing coffee has already been partly included. Other produce on hand varies greatly with the season. Except in the cases of garlic and onion seed, they are very quickly turned into money. It seems more useful to treat this wealth as income balanced by expenditures rather than as a capital asset.

(2) The value of food and supplies on hand in the various kitchens of the community. Except in the case of corn in the months after the harvest, the Indians normally have only a few days' supply of food, and of many items even less. In both cases, the turnover in the course of a year is complete, and again such assets are treated only as items of expenditure.

(3) The amount of cash on hand. It differs with the season, but not as much as it would in a community where a cash crop is harvested at once. Corn, garlic, onion seed, and *pepinos* are harvested at particular times; but the much more important onions are harvested throughout the year, and various fruits ripen at different times. Most Indians balance expenditures against receipts with a short interval of time, and cash on hand is both a small and a temporary item. Sizable surpluses of cash can exist only in the case of very few families. A few wealthy families are known to have considerable cash on hand, kept in chests at home (banks are not used); in two or three cases it might amount, at times, to hundreds of dollars. But the rich seem generally to invest their funds in land, and are rich rather in the value of property

owned than in cash. I would be surprised to find more than $5,000 in loose cash in the community at any one time, including that which represents a lag between selling and buying, or more than about $2,000 in real savings.

Unless one includes the special knowledge of artisans and professionals, there are almost no intangible economic assets. The shamans occasionally teach others for a consideration; literacy is a recognized economic advantage—at least in the negative sense of making flagrant cheating by means of false receipts less likely—and persons who can write receive gifts when they assist others. The labor of persons with reputations for industry and skill in agriculture is in demand and perhaps commands better prices; but there is nothing formalized about this. Finally, there is a manuscript of the "conquest" dance owned by a local Indian, and he was at least once asked to teach the dance (for a consideration) in another town.

THE BALANCE OF PAYMENTS

The wealth and well-being of the community is better measured in its annual receipts and expenditures. Transactions within the community I shall not attempt to estimate. Most such transactions represent labor (for cash) which Indians do for one another. In contrast, there is very little commerce within the community, principally because most of the people produce about the same things. Merchants buy produce less from their neighbors than in the public market, where it is pooled and where its source in relation to its destination is difficult to analyze.

Table 74 summarizes the transactions between the Panajachel Indian community and the outside, comparing expenditures and receipts to strike what might be called the balance of payments. The total community expenditures outside the community ($19,544.18) come to $127 per family or $25 per person, receipts ($21,530.91) to $139 per family or $27.60 per person. The difference of over $2,000 between the two totals is such that each family, on the average, gains $12 a year in money or in what money will buy. Since there seems to be no possibility that this is either a paper balance, or represented by increased gold stocks, or anything of the sort, the wealth of the community and its standard of living would seem to be rising. The calculated balance of $2,000, although the result of countless smaller calculations of

TABLE 74.—*The balance of payments*

a. RECEIPTS

Item	Total	Consumed within community [1]	Sold outside
Plant gathering	[2] $40.50	$40.50	----------
Hunting, fishing, etc	56.00	46.00	$10.00
Net from agriculture	23,289.79	[3] 3,834.43	19,455.36
Net from animal husbandry	344.50	176.00	168.50
Net from arts and professions	777.05	----------	777.05
Labor for outsiders	[4] 1,060.00	----------	1,060.00
Net from merchandising nonlocal produce	60.00	----------	60.00
Total	25,627.84	4,096.93	21,530.91

b. EXPENDITURES

Item	Total	Produced within community [1]	Bought outside
Housing	$80.00	----------	$80.00
Clothing	4,065.62	----------	4,065.62
Food	15,220.28	$4,132.25	11,088.03
Supplies, furnishings, etc	1,394.93	----------	[5] 1,394.93
Ceremonies, fiestas, etc	1,901.80	----------	1,901.80
Personal and legal, etc	691.00	----------	691.00
Markets and travel	322.80	----------	[6] 322.80
Total	23,676.43	4,132.25	19,544.18

c. BALANCE

Balance received from outside the community in 1936 _____ $1,986.73

[1] The value of the labor of members of the community is not included; the totals should be the same in sections *a* and *b* of the table.

[2] This sum (the total of the herbs produced in the community—table 67, *c*) is chosen rather arbitrarily. Some of the herbs are not entirely wild, and other plants gathered—such as medicinal plants—are not included; but the total figure is still probably not far from the truth, and in any case the total of the table would not be affected by a shift of a few dollars from agriculture to plant gathering or vice versa.

[3] The difference between this figure and the total of $5,409.15 of table 38 is the value of the onion seed produced for planting. This seed is planted to produce onions, hence represents a cost as well as a receipt and does not figure in the net from agriculture.

[4] Including both agricultural labor (about $1,010) and domestic and other labor.

[5] Tools used mainly in agriculture have been subtracted from the total of table 68.

[6] Based on careful calculations made on the basis of data in the section on outside markets. (Market taxes, $110.80; bus fares, $112; launch and canoe fares to outsiders, $40; *posada* privileges, $10; and extra food and refreshment on the road and in markets, $50.)

greater or less difficulty and accuracy, cannot be very far from the truth. There is sufficient reason to believe, first, that the balance is in fact favorable rather than unfavorable; otherwise the Indians' lands would be lost or sold to outsiders at a greater rate than is the case, or the Indians would be leaving the community or working much more for outsiders, or the population would be decreasing rather than increasing. It seems unlikely, second, that the balance can be much more than about $2,000; for there is evidence neither of a great rise in the standard of living nor of the piling up of cash reserves.

THE STANDARD OF LIVING

The "average" wealth, or income or expenditures, in the community gives a very imperfect picture of what conditions among the Indians are. Discussion in Land Ownership and Practices (pp. 57–85) of the distribution of Indian land has already shown the inequalities of the wealth of the various families, and inclusion of other assets besides land makes very little difference in the conclusions drawn. A few families are, by local standards, very rich; and many more very poor. When two informants were asked, independently, to grade all 157 families' wealth on a scale of from 1 to 100, the dividing line between "rich" and "medium" was set at 70; one informant graded 12 families 70 or over and the other, 23 families. The line between "medium" and "poor" was set at 30; the first informant placed 96 families below that grade; the second, 76 families. Actually, there is quite a difference in wealth between the very richest family and the next, but after that differences are gradual; division into classes is arbitrary, and if proof of that were needed, differences in opinion between the two informants supplies it. The results of the informants' grading are shown in Appendix 3. Discussion of these differences are a main subject of the section on the Significance of Wealth Differences (pp. 191–204).

COMPARISONS

It seems to me unprofitable to say much in evaluation of the Panajachel standard of living. The fact appears to be that the average family consumes $160 worth of goods in a year, including the value of the labor required to produce some goods, but that does not mean that the standard of living is necessarily a fifth that of a community—say in the United States—where the average family consumes goods with a value of $800. Three other factors in the difference might be mentioned: First, there is a purely book-keeping matter. The cost of housing in Panajachel has been given as about $1.70 per family, the annual cost of building and repairing houses, including the value of labor. But the rental value of the houses of a family (if they were rented) would be closer to $10 a year and perhaps much more. Likewise the clothing costs have been calculated on the basis of actual cost to the Indians. Pursuing another method of bookkeeping, the value of goods consumed by the average family might rise from $160 to $200. Second, there is a difference of prices. A comparison of prices in Panajachel (Appendix 2) with those prevailing in the American community might well show that the $160 or $200 is the equivalent of two or three times that much. The Guatemalan *quetzal* and the American dollar are pegged in value in international exchange, but a *quetzal* buys much more in Panajachel than a dollar does anywhere in the United States. And, third, there are important cultural and social differences that make difficult, if not futile, any very broad comparisons. Indian houses are crude (and cheap) structures not necessarily because the people can afford nothing better but also because their culture requires that kind. They use no dairy products (which are expensive) partly, at least, because traditionally they do not like them. They pay little in taxes partly because they get little, but partly because their community is supported largely by their labor. Finally, of course, such wants as for automobiles, radios, motion pictures, electric appliances—while certainly beyond their means—are still quite beyond their culture.

Results of the food survey (table 75) show that the Indians are not grossly undernourished. Except for riboflavin (and lime?) they average at least the recommended quantity of every item analyzed, although this may well be because a minority have a better diet and a majority considerably worse. Certainly the poorest families fall far short of standard (table 65).

In comparison with neighboring towns, there is reason to believe that the standard of living in Panajachel is higher than in most.[173] Of the lake towns, only San Pedro probably has a definitely higher standard.[174] Probably Panajachel is also better off than such communities as Sololá and Chichicastenango. An indirect way of judging such differences is to note how the towns make their living. The Panajachel Indians rarely go to the plantations to work, or to other towns as day laborers. The people of such towns as Santa Catarina and Sololá work outside much more. On the seemingly sound assumption that people are forced by economic necessity to work outside, this is evidence that Panajachel is richer than most neighboring towns. Another way to judge is to examine the day-labor basic pay. In Panajachel it was 16½ cents in 1936, in Atitlán only 10 cents, and in Chichicastenango 12 or 13 cents (and down to 10 cents in 1935–38). I do not know of any place in the neighborhood where wages are higher than in Panajachel. If the Indians earn more in Panajachel, they probably spend more. Another point that may be made is that in the past years the Panajachel Indians have not been losing much land to outsiders while in neighboring Santa Catarina, at least, lands were being sold and lost at a high rate.

It is also probable that from 1936 to 1940, at least, the standard of living was improving in Panajachel. This was in part due to world economic conditions. In the late twenties Guatemala (with high coffee prices) was relatively prosperous, and every town got its share—Panajachel, certainly, because it grew coffee. When in

TABLE 75 [1].—*Comparison of average food intake in rural Guatemala per nutrition unit per day* [2]

Item	Food intake by groups in rural Guatemala						National Research Council's recommended allowances
	All (138) [3]	All Ladinos (47)	All Indians (91)	All "Poor" (56)	Panajachel Ladinos (3)	Panajachel Indians (6)	
Calories	3,008	3,093	2,965	2,725	3,076	3,004	3,000
Protein (mg.)	72	77	70	56	76	73	70
Calcium from food (mg.)	264	294	248	214	323	274	
Total calcium (mg.)	871	819	898	782	703	959	800
Iron (mg.)	23	22	23	21	24	24	12
Vitamin A, value (I. U.)	5,573	5,862	5,424	5,403	9,138	6,054	5,000
Ascorbic acid (mg.)	57	64	54	53	73	114	75
Thiamine (mg.)	3.3	3.2	3.4	3.2	2.7	3.3	1.5
Riboflavin (mg.)	1.0	1.2	.9	.8	1.5	.9	2.0
Niacin (mg.)	14.7	15.4	14.3	12.8	17.6	14.5	15

[1] From tabulations supplied by Miss Emma Reh, of Instituto de Nutrición de Centro America y Panamá.
[2] "Family units are expressed as nutrition unit equivalents of the moderately active male, according to the 1945 National Research Council's recommended allowances for specific nutrients by sex, age, and activity." (Quoted from note to table 2B in unpublished F. A. O. report by Emma Reh.)
[3] Numbers in parentheses indicate the number of people who partook of the family food during the week, subtracting fractions for meals missed and adding fractions for guests.

[173] Comparisons in table 75 indicate that the Panajachel diet is consistently richer than the average Indian diet in the several communities studied. Indeed, it falls very little short of the average Ladino diet, and of that of the Ladinos of Panajachel. The only two Indian communities (of 10) that had higher caloric intake were Santiago Chimaltenango and San Pedro la Laguna. By some coincidence the three "nutritionally best" towns are the only three in the sample for which we have general studies of the economy. Santiago Chimaltenango is the subject of Charles Wagley's monograph, The Economics of a Guatemalan Village, 1941. San Pedro was studied independently by Juan Rosales and by Benjamin Paul. A volume on the economy of San Pedro, prepared with the collaboration of Julio de la Frente, will soon be published (in Spanish).

[174] This is a judgment based on general observation. The nutritional data (for a sample of 14 families) bear it out. The results, following the order of table 75: 3,320; 81.3; 322; 1,134; 26; 5,702; 58; 3.8; 1; 16: superior to Panajachel in every item. Curiously, two poor families in San Pedro had a poorer diet than the averages of the poorest families in any other communities, with only 2,449 calories and 54.3 gms. protein.

the early thirties the coffee market collapsed, Panajachel along with other towns suffered depression: wages went down, people had to put away their flashlights and wear their clothes longer, and fiesta expenses were drastically cut. But by the time this study began, conditions in the world—and the coffee market—were improved, and times were better in Panajachel. However, Panajachel improved more rapidly than most other towns because of a new source of income—the increase of tourists, both native and foreign, the installation of new hotels and more "country homes" on the lake shore, and so on. The tourist business, was, during the period of study, steadily improving, resulting in the opening of new markets for the produce of the town, with better prices, and in a general increase of noncompeting population.

There was still another factor that tended to improve conditions in many towns, Panajachel among them. It was the mushroom growth of truck and bus lines. In 1936 there was one combination truck-bus plying between Guatemala City and Sololá (passing through Panajachel), making three trips each way every week. In 1937 there were three truck-busses each day in each direction besides others not so regular. Where Panajacheleños walked to Guatemala City and consumed a week to sell a load of onions, they then rode and spent 2 or 3 days to sell a larger load of onions. Competition cut the passenger and freight rates to a point where the saving in time easily made up for the fare. The total result for the region was that more time could be spent on the production of wealth than previously, with less required for distribution of goods. Since it is the Indian population of the country that takes care of distribution, as well as a good part of production, the Indians with the use of trucks are able to produce more and have more to consume. (In Panajachel that effect was but lightly felt, however, because with the use of trucks the price of onions in Guatemala City went down.) Panajachel has the difficulty of very limited land resources, and there is a limit to how much production can be increased simply with an increase of available time. With closer communications with the Capital and other towns, however, new crops can be raised and marketed. An example is strawberries, which are profitable only if large markets are quickly accessible; experience in 1937 and 1938 showed that dependence upon the local market alone simply brought down the price of the perishable berries when production was increased.

It is well to recall again, in any discussion of the relations of production and the standard of living that the Panajachel Indians are quick to learn and to take advantage of new economic opportunities.

FUNCTIONS OF WEALTH

METHOD

This section will tie together parts of the whole book, in terms of the associations of different degrees of wealth with (a) different ways of life and (b) families. It therefore represents a kind of summary of the book, selective as it is; but it adds considerable fact and interpretation. It also attempts to clarify the methods used in the field study. This is an example of a study in a very small society without written records and it may be used to illustrate how in such circumstances data are collected in relation to a problem.

In the Indian community of Panajachel, virtually only the landscape and the people, and what the people have done to the landscape, are available for study. Some problems are simply solved: for example, one collects folk tales by getting the Indians to tell stories, or one learns about the techniques of farming by observing and by asking questions. But the answers to many questions are not "in the heads" of the Indians themselves. For example, one cannot ask an Indian "What is your kinship system?" Instead, one collects a great variety of genealogical information, and facts about marriage, residence, the behavior of relatives, and the kinship terms in use, and "works out" the kinship system. Similarly, one cannot ask an Indian "What is the annual income in the community"; so he must collect records and draw his own conclusions.

These things are true about any community. One cannot in the United States, any more than in Panajachel, ask this sort of question except of the sociologist or economist who is willing to collect records on the basis of which to draw conclusions. The differences are that in the United States one depends upon written records, including information collected by other scholars. In Panajachel such do not exist, except for vital statistics data. Indeed, since the Indian community of Panajachel is not literate, one cannot even collect records by means of questionnaires and the like. There are no ways, no local censuses. One cannot ask school children to help. Every bit of raw data is personally set down in the hand of the ethnographer—or his wife or any local assistant he might be able to find and train. The compensating quality of the situation is of course that the community is small; it is *possible* to come to know personally many of its aspects.

Despite inherent difficulties, this study pretends to be *quantitative*, the quantities stated with reference to the *whole community*, and *complete*: It is quantitative in that at every point the effort is made to answer the question "How much?" as well as "What?," "Who?," and "How?" It has reference to the whole community in that the object is not to say only what and how much one or several individuals produce and consume, but what and how much the whole community produces and consumes in 1 year. It pretends to be complete insofar as it tries to report not some but all of the community expenditures, in time and money; it purports to inventory all of the time, the money, and the resources of the community.

What follows is far from a historical account of what I did in the field. Rather, it is an idealization; what I would like to have done—or, perhaps, what I like to pretend to have done. My actual fumbling is not worth committing to print; it is enough to have distributed it on microfilm. What follows distills some of what I learned through the experience of doing. Every individual item of method that I mention is honestly enough recounted. However the order is rationalized, the logical arrangement supplied by hindsight.

Suppose now that the reader comes to Panajachel (as I did) with some knowledge of the general area. Even a 2-week tourist will know from the regional differences and the money markets, and merchants—which are indeed part of the tourist attraction!—that the economy is something like ours. This is not Melville's island paradise to be approached as entirely novel. It might take a little longer to discover that there is a system of private ownership, economic rationality, and free enterprise, particularly since tourist guides frequently confuse issues. For example, one hears (and reads) that merchants will not sell on the road, but only in markets either because of taboos or because they enjoy the markets; or that the Indians become so used to the burdens that on return from market they substitute stones for the merchandise they have sold. Anybody willing to look will soon see, however, that there are simple economic motivations at work and that comparisons of this society with our own might be useful and valid. In this context it takes almost no time to note that Panajachel, specifically, specializes in growing vegetables, fruit and coffee and exchanges the produce for much of what is needed to live that is grown or manufactured in other towns similarly specialized.

Settled in Panajachel and making conversation with the Indians it is soon obvious that there are "rich" and "poor" people; they talk about this difference. Suppose one then asks how rich are the rich and how poor are the poor; how many are rich and how many are poor; whether differences sort out families or instead divide them; whether from generation to generation wealth remains within a family group; how much tendency there is for individuals to become rich during their lifetimes, or poor; and what the prerogatives of wealth are. Suppose further, that one is interested both in what people say or think about these questions and also what the objective facts are. Suppose, in sum, that without using the terms, one is interested in "class" aspects of differences in wealth.

This let us take as a problem area.

DEFINING THE COMMUNITY FOR STUDY

The first step then is to define the community of people about whom the questions are asked. It is apparent from the beginning—indeed from the census publications—that there are two kinds of people: Ladinos and Indians. Not only are they self-conscious groups, so that people will talk about themselves and others as Ladinos or Indians, but there are obvious signs. Ladinos speak Spanish as a mother tongue, Indians are those who are at home in an Indian language and who speak Spanish with an accent. Indians wear distinctive and rather colorful costumes; Ladinos, European-style clothes. Ladinos for the most part live in the "center" of town, where there are streets; the Indians are scattered among the gardens and coffee fields. Ladinos are more-or-less educated store-keepers and pharmacists (although some are illiterate and poor and in some ways "live like Indians") who live in houses with plastered walls and windows with shutters, and doors with hard-ware and floors covered with tiles, and stoves with chimneys in the kitchen, and so on. On each of these criteria borderline cases may be found, so that none of them can be taken too seriously. For example, for years I kept on my list of Indians several families of "Indians" who had Indian surnames and lived at least half like Indians; members of the family were married to Ladinos; and I finally decided they were best considered Ladinos because they participated socially with Ladinos rather than in the Indian community. When it could be seen that there are two *societies*, participation became the final test. The critical test of that came to be obligation to serve to the Indian politico-religious system. A family served in the system or it did not.

Having established the presence of two societies, the decision had to be made whether to ask our questions about one or the other or both. For purposes here, let us choose the Indians.[175] In large part we did in fact choose the Indians. One good reason is that the Ladino society is part of a generalized Ladino society that goes beyond local communities, and it would be difficult to answer our kind of questions by studying the Ladinos only of Panajachel.

It is almost equally apparent that there are "foreign" Indians to be distinguished from Pana-jacheleños. They are spoken of as Sololatecos, Totonicapeños, Catarinecos, etc.; they have differ-ent surnames; they wear different costumes (of their towns of origin) and speak dialects different from those of Indians whose families have long been resident in Panajachel. Again, however, the distinctions are not clear-cut. A few Indians of other towns change costume or marry Pana-jacheleños. Some households are "mixed." Some of the most typical Panajacheleño families

are descended from immigrant Indians of gener-ations ago. The useful test therefore becomes one, again, of participation. The concept is clari-fied not of a Panajachel Indian society but of a Panajacheleño Indian society; if a family fully participates in its organization and rituals, it is part of the more restricted society. For some purposes we shall be satisfied to study the "foreign" Indians less completely than the Panajacheleños.

Having now limited the community concerning which we shall ask the questions posed, the prob-lem becomes one of defining it. Who are the people, how many are they, where do they live, how are they interrelated, etc.?

Any pretense of working by simply checking casual impressions now ends. We must begin to collect records, systematically. The work may be divided into four parts:

(1) Taking a house-to-house census, with identi-fication of each of the inhabitants as to ethnic affiliation (Ladino, Sololateco, Panajacheleño, etc.), relationship within the household, approxi-mate age, and so on.

(2) Making a careful map on which are spotted all the households. The "spotting" is more difficult than it seems; the first time around, with a Ladino helper, I missed about a third of the Indian establishments hidden from the paths by coffee bushes. The object is to get all of the houses spotted and identified; then the possibility of omission is reduced to those within households. Map and census were made together. Although in another town the officials accompanied me on a tour to get a correct census (with attendant disadvantages), in Panajachel I depended upon Indian friends and a long period of time. After 2 years or more I was still correcting mistakes; but the time came when I never heard of a person I could not easily place and never came upon a house whose whole family I did not know; and although children's ages, and sometimes the sex of infants were occasionally left undetermined, we had a complete census.

(3) Collecting genealogical information which, when put together shows how everybody is (or is not) related to everybody else. The "foreign" Indians were included, as a check on their sepa-rateness. Genealogical information is obtained by asking one's friends for the names of their siblings and siblings' children, of their parents and parents' siblings' children, grandchildren, etc.; of their

<hr/>

[175] Anthropologists traditionally study Indians (i. e., people of very alien culture) but the tradition has rapidly broken down in recent years. Indeed, during our period of study an anthropologist (Isobel Sklow) joined us especial-ly to study the Ladino community of Panajachel. Recently the Committee on Latin American Anthropology of the National Research Council has out-lined a program for such studies (Amer. Anthrop., 1949).

great-grand-parents and *their* siblings, etc., etc., in ever widening circles until they no longer know anything. About each relative one discovers various things in passing (and for many purposes other than the problem under discussion). When one gets enough of these "ego" genealogies they are combined to show how all the people in the community are related. Again, it takes years to straighten this out, and perfection is never achieved; in 1941 I discovered (to me) amazing errors in notations on the families that had been closest to us since 1935! With this information added to that on the map, the community is defined: every individual accounted for and known in spatial, temporal, and biological (social) inter-relation.

(4) Learning enough about the social participation (among other matters) of every individual and family to know whether and how they fit into the local community; decisions (often somewhat arbitrary) are then made as to inclusions and exclusions from the Panajacheleño community. Thus a limited community at a point in time is fixed for study, a community with respect to which the problem now is as follows.

ESTABLISHING WEALTH DIFFERENCES

It is not difficult to make a decision as to the social unit to be used. Although it is quickly enough evident that individuals own property, talk about rich and poor *individuals* breaks down with the first question about whether a wife is richer or poorer than her husband, or whether a son in the family is rich. Those who form a household together are a single unit; wealth differences may be discussed usefully as between households, not individuals, the household defined as the family group sharing a single kitchen, and hence having at least partially a common budget.

Nor is it difficult to find a first approximate measure of wealth, for with farmers the obvious one of land owned suggests itself; since those who are said to be rich are also those who are said to own much land, and vice versa, one adopts the suggestion as a hypothesis with hardly a question. Then the first major task becomes to apply this measure:

What are the lands involved? The map which was made includes in addition to natural features and houses the boundaries of land ownership and the details of land use, since different lands prob-

ably have different value. What was done for the people is now done for the land. The object is to account for every bit of land, regardless of whether owned by Indians, Ladinos, or anybody else, and to understand its use. The areal limit to the community is easy to find because all the land owned by Panajacheleños is in the area immediately visible, on the delta and on the hills overlooking the delta, or said specifically to be in Santa Catarina or elsewhere. It is academic that the boundaries of the *municipio* of Panajachel extend far beyond the part mapped, since the community neither owns nor uses the remainder.

The problem now is to determine the land holdings of each Indian household. Wherever possible this was done, in course of making the map, by simple pacing. The map should have been accurate enough to enable measurements on it; eventually, it had to be redrawn to be made that accurate, and only after 5 years (the end of the study) could any measurable piece of land be compared with the map without too great shock. As with the people, it was necessary to keep for the map a base time, and through all vicissitudes keep track of who owned what land, and how it was used in May of 1936.

Independent of the map, which accounted for all the land, an inventory was made of lands owned by every family in Panajachel. Having made a 4 by 6 slip for each household, I simply ran through them with knowing friends who told me what lands were owned by each. This not only checked information taken the other way, but brought into the picture properties outside the area of the map. Land was the subject of many items of casual information, and again there came the time when most doubts and discrepancies were ironed out. In all hearsay information on lands owned, the vagueness of measures of land (*cuerdas* of different sizes) added to the usual difficulties.

The data on land ownership were never separated from those on land use, since it was evident that different kinds of land were differently valued. But the question of these differences of value required thorough understanding of:

(1) Agricultural practices, the technology and beliefs and practices concerning all aspects of agriculture and husbandry. Systematic inquiry, supplemented by observation, was required, and in addition we had the experience of managing the planting, care, and harvest of an experimental plot.

(2) Labor required to yield harvests. This requires general study of the value and use of time; the division of labor and differences in the use and value of the time of different age and sex groups. The problem of the time required for each task in the fields (for which we had the help of a document prepared for the President) involves the relative efficiency of paid and of family labor, of wages and other customary payments to hired help, and so on.

(3) Yields. The safest check on statements of informants is to sample and count, measure, or weigh. This is not difficult, once the investigator has friends willing to help. It is easy to count the harvest of onions, garlic, and the like (and correspondingly unnecessary to check informants, who are always counting them for sale!), much more difficult with corn which in Panajachel is harvested for home use and not really part of the commercial complex.

(4) Prices, which involve study of the whole market system, the variety of ways in which produce is disposed of, and so on. In a place like Panajachel where commerce is the breath of life, the investigator gets a good deal of this background simply by having to live, hence cope with it. So much so that I paid too little attention to recording prices; I should have kept a list of commodities on hand as a reminder to collect and systematically note prices at weekly intervals throughout the year, and in different places. Since I did not do this, I could check the knowledge of reliable Indians (which is excellent) only by the instances I happened to have noted, and the few published records available. It now becomes possible to make distinctions between (a) hill land, of relatively little value, in its subdivisions of valueless waste land, cornfield land, and fallow land usable for pasture; and (b) delta land, divided between (1) land that is not irrigable, on which rainy-season cornfield alone can be grown, though being nearly level it is better than hill cornfield; (2) land on which coffee stands; and (3) land on which truck farming is practiced all year. The validity of this classification depends upon all the information suggested above; for example, that the truck-farm land is equally valuable regardless of what happens to be growing on it is a conclusion based on knowledge of agricultural practices, yields, labor requirements, and prices.

At this point it is possible to tabulate the amount of land of *each significant class* that is owned by each household. Now in order to place a value on each kind of land, one returns to the data on yields and prices to see what is produced by the land; but data are also sought on the following: (1) Sale prices, when land is sold. This requires a collection and analysis of cases, with knowledge of the circumstances. One can even test conclusions "experimentally" by bargaining for land. (2) Rental values. This requires not only many cases, but a background of much information on rental practices, of which there are a variety. (3) Loan values. The practice of pawning land (the lender having the use of the land until the loan is repaid) is common; again, cases must have a background of a variety of kinds of general information for proper analysis.

Putting all this information together, a conclusion is reached as to the dollar value of each type of land and it is finally possible to tabulate the worth of the land of each family. But at this point it becomes clearly advisable to correct for pawned lands. Since income (and effective wealth) belongs not to the family that *owns* the land, but the one who is using it—often for so many years it might as well be transferred—it is necessary to make this correction by crediting pawned lands to the creditors.

We then have a tabulation of the wealth of all the households in terms of *land controlled*—the best that land can tell us about differences in wealth.

However, land is not the only thing in Panajachel culture. Among other things to consider are:

(1) Domestic animals. Investigation of family bookkeeping (a complicated process itself) discloses that fowl and pigs are—far from being a measure of wealth in the sense that land is—a liability in Panajachel (where corn to feed animals must be purchased). One gets into problems of psychology in studying cases where animals are kept (as well as where unprofitable crops are grown) and learns some interesting things—not relevant here—but the conclusion is clear that since the rich have more and the poor fewer animals, and since the value of the animals is small compared to that of the land, the order of wealth as determined by land ownership and control is little affected when one takes into the account the ownership of domestic animals.

(2) Fruit trees, a legitimate measure of wealth. A special census of trees has to be made, yields and prices, etc., calculated to determine their value. Fruit is especially valuable because the only labor required is in harvesting and marketing. But when all the data are collected, one knows that it will not upset the wealth scale as based upon land because trees grow on delta land, and the more trees owned the more delta land is apt to be owned. So, knowing this, elaborate calculations are avoided.

(3) Houses, utensils, furnishings, etc. These differ with different households, but a study of a sample of rich, medium, and poor (as measured by wealth in land) shows that the variation is not proportional to wealth. The same can be said of clothing, etc. These items check the land measure; they are too small to measure wealth, and of course they are not wealth producing.

(4) Nonagricultural occupations. There are artisans and professionals (shamans, etc.) as well as merchants in the community—all only part time. A careful census must be made of all of these, and a variety of information gathered to determine how economically important such occupations are. In a few cases they were sufficiently important to require consideration in setting up a wealth scale based on land alone.

A more significant independent check is found in the impressions of people. Informants who have been tested for carefulness as well as knowledge (preferably more than the two in number that were used in Panajachel) are asked to rate every household as to wealth on a scale from one to a hundred. The impressions of informants turn out to compare well enough, and well enough with the ordering according to land controlled. The problem is then to examine the discrepancies to see why the impressions might differ, or differ from what appears to be objective wealth as measured in land. For most flagrant differences between informants' impressions and wealth as measured there turn out to be explanations, and it is concluded that the land-controlled measure is a reliable one to measure wealth differences.

Using as an important basis of judgment the value of land controlled, the 134 Panajacheleño households could then be put in order of wealth (Appendix 3). The "Foreign" households were placed on the same scale, but in their case occupation and other criteria were often more impor-

tant than land in forming judgments. Then I added to the original numbering of the houses, which had been geographical, their wealth-order-number, and began to bring other data to bear on the following questions.

THE SIGNIFICANCE OF WEALTH DIFFERENCES

In order to test correlations of wealth and poverty, it seemed advisable to subdivide the 132 Panajacheleño households into wealth groups. Since 132 is divisible by four, I divided the families into quarters instead of the more usual thirds, the top wealth quarter consisting of numbers 1–33, the second quarter of 34–66, and so on.

LOCALIZATION OF WEALTH

When the house numbers become wealth-order numbers as well (map 3), careful examination of the economic positions of the various families as spotted geographically shows that there is a definable pattern of localization. The east part of the delta may be divided into a wealthy and a poor section. One can draw a line running from the river below houses 95 and 125, west about two-thirds of the way to the base of the hill, and then irregularly south so that houses 43, 56, 2, 11, 17, 51, and 37 are to the west of it, that will enclose 49 households of which

15 are in the first wealth-quarter,
17 are in the second wealth-quarter,
12 are in the third wealth-quarter, and
5 are in the fourth wealth-quarter.

Even if the north-south line were smoothed to include houses 73 and 119 in the area, and exclude house 2, the figures would still read 14, 17, 13, and 6 in each of the four quarters of the wealth scale, respectively, so that 31 of 50 families are in the richer half.

By contrast, in the remainder of the east side, comprising the whole of the north and east areas, of 29 households

2 are in the first wealth-quarter,
1 is in the second wealth-quarter,
11 are in the third wealth-quarter, and
15 are in the fourth wealth-quarter.

Or, with the line smoothed, the figures are 3, 1, 10, 14, respectively, with only 4 out of 28 families in the richer half of the population!

The west side of the delta does not present so

simple a picture, but it is noteworthy that here, too, the richest section is in the corner facing the river and the lake. In the whole southern portion of this side of the delta there are but five poorest-quarter families, and four of the second-poorest, out of a total of 26 or 28 families, depending upon where the line is drawn. The fact appears to be that if one should bring together the two sides of the delta, he would find the heavy concentration of rich families in the center of the wide portion facing the lake, with the poorer people (always recognizing exceptions) to the north and along the border of the hills.

Part of the explanation, certainly, is that the south-central part of the delta has the richest land, and the people whose homes are there have inherited enough of it to give them an advantage. It will be recalled that it is in this area only that Indians own most of the land (map 5). It is true also that this section, especially the east side of it, is the most Indian and the most Panajacheleño part of the delta, and the nuclei of the most stable old families are found here. It has been noted that land-losing Indians tend to keep their house sites longer than their other lands, and so obviously the place where most Indians live is the place where one would expect to find the greatest number owning at least a minimum of land; other things being equal, the Indians of that neighborhood are bound to be wealthier.

It must be pointed out that in native concept there is no suggestion of rich and poor neighborhoods. The Indians do not realize that more of the wealthy live in one section than another; nor did I until this study was virtually complete and I could enter the data on the map. I do not think that the rich tend to move into the central delta portion (if there is such a tendency—and I have no evidence for it) because it is preferred as a wealthy neighborhood. That sort of thing seems foreign to the thinking and the whole sociological set-up of the Indians of Panajachel. Neighborhoods are known only by landmarks and by the names of their most numerous families, and those recognized do not coincide with those that I have here distinguished.

LAND AND WEALTH

Since land is the important measure of wealth, it is significant to see how wealth relates to patterns of renting and pawning land. Table 76 compares the amount of land owned and controlled by all families involved in transfers of land by pawning.

Table 76.—*Wealth of Panajacheleño households involved in land pawnings*

Order of land wealth	Value of land	
	Owned	Controlled
Richest quarter:		
1	$952.95	$1,542.20
2	543.00	549.40
3	497.25	457.02
5	487.32	367.32
9 [1]	387.00	429.72
10	380.98	172.80
11 [1]	343.56	181.56
12	342.32	317.40
17	302.83	233.08
21	279.25	229.57
22 [1]	278.25	260.25
23	276.25	346.50
25	263.31	290.31
26	259.25	193.25
27	257.75	132.00
28	257.75	203.75
29	240.54	336.39
30	232.25	46.25
31	226.00	222.50
32	225.30	137.32
Medium-rich quarter:		
34 [1]	222.50	333.60
44	166.00	46.25
46 [1]	165.10	138.10
47	161.68	172.80
54	142.00	57.50
56	139.45	245.95
60	124.94	172.19
61	123.11	73.96
64 [1]	113.25	93.37
Medium-poor quarter:		
69	102.75	4.50
70	102.50	116.00
71	102.50	62.00
72	102.50	71.00
75	98.75	56.00
77	94.50	81.00
78 [1][2]	89.63	96.38
80	88.50	35.25
83 [1]	82.37	18.62
84	81.00	38.25
95	57.62	15.62
97	57.47	68.12
98	55.50	42.00
99	53.34	83.22
Poorest quarter:		
101	46.50	65.00
102	44.00	57.50
106	33.10	73.60
116	27.00	97.12
117	27.00	43.40

[1] Some land pawned to another; other land on pawn.
[2] Lands shared by 2 households; for some purposes I assume that each has half the land, but here the 2 are better treated as 1 case.

The poorest quarter includes the seven landless families, and others with small amounts of land with values up to only $48. Clearly, the reason no families of this group had borrowed money on their land is that most of them had no land or almost none, or only house sites without commercial value. In the medium-poor quarter the number that had pawned land was 10, in the medium-rich quarter 5, and in the highest 13. Eight families in all—two in the medium-poor group and three each in the medium-rich and the wealthiest—were in 1936 on both ends of pawning agreements. In three cases—one in each of the three top groups—land pawned out was worth less than that taken in, so the fact that they were debtor households is hidden in the table. Therefore the number of households with land pawned was really as follows:

Poorest quarter 0
Medium-poor quarter 11
Medium-rich quarter 6
Richest quarter 14

As one ascends the scale, the average value of the land given in pawn increases in each group, from $48 in the first to $63 to $98, presumably because there is increasingly more land to pawn.

In the same way, the number of households who controlled land on pawn in 1936 may be summarized as

Poorest quarter 5
Medium-poor quarter 5
Medium-rich quarter 6
Richest quarter 8

with the average value of the land $26, $18, $55, and $146 in the four groups respectively. Without one extraordinary household, the average value in the last group would be but $58.

It would appear that the poorest people who yet own a little land are becoming richer; that the medium-poor are going down rather than up; that there is considerable shifting of positions in the medium-rich group, so that as many are becoming richer as poorer; and that the richest families are tending to become poorer. It will also be noticed that most changes in amounts of land controlled are small, the families changing their relative positions but little. However one family (No. 69) dropped from the middle down to the very bottom of the landed families. Actually, in this case the household has since disintegrated—the widowed mother having died and her sons having left town to seek work. Another (No. 30) dropped from a medium-rich position to among the poorest; this family is well-known for having frittered away its inheritance. A similar case is that of No. 27; there is a story told that when his parents died, the boy who is now head of this household burned his heritage of paper money, thinking it was just paper. The down-sledding of the last extreme case (No. 5) began (I was told by a principal in the story) when the family lost the services of a debtor-relative whose labor had helped make it wealthy. Sickness and death were also involved,

and since 1936 the family has lost much more land. Extreme cases of improvement of position are not to be found.

Table 77 shows that most renters are in the middle economic groups. In the lowest quarter there are 11 renters, in the second, 13, in the third, 18, and in the highest only 6. If the rentals of bean land are omitted, the figures are 9, 13, 16, and 5, and the value of land rented is $336, $471, $753, and $164 respectively in the 4 groups. Apparently renting increases with land owned up to a certain point; but large landholders do not

TABLE 77.—*Wealth of households renting agricultural land*

Order of land wealth	Value of land			
	Owned	Controlled	Owned and controlled	Rented
Richest quarter:				
4			$496.00	$79.50
7			427.03	12.80
14			333.09	40.50
25	$263.31	$290.31		27.00
28	257.75	203.75		4.24
30	232.25	46.25		[1]9.00
Medium-rich quarter:				
35			217.56	38.36
36			210.41	54.00
37			206.87	31.24
38			191.25	7.12
40			177.50	[1]9.00
42			166.54	65.36
43			166.25	[1]18.00
44	166.00	46.25		54.00
46	165.10	138.10		8.56
47	161.68	172.80		120.00
51			146.29	17.04
53			143.00	54.00
55			139.50	82.38
57			138.25	7.12
59			137.50	5.68
60	124.94	172.19		199.50
61	123.11	73.96		{ [1]9.00 / 2.88
62			115.25	5.68
64	113.25	93.37		[2]54.00
Medium-poor quarter:				
67			107.25	27.00
70	102.50	116.00		{ [1]9.00 / 106.50
73			102.50	106.50
74			102.00	4.32
78	89.63	96.38		27.00
84	81.00	38.25		2.88
86			75.50	27.00
89			66.00	8.56
91			62.50	5.68
92			62.25	54.00
93			62.00	54.00
97	57.47	68.12		7.12
98	55.00	42.00		40.50
Poorest quarter:				
100			47.25	[2]27.00
104			42.75	[2]2.88
105			40.50	59.68
106	33.10	73.60		7.12
107			30.75	13.50
109			30.50	4.88
112			29.75	54.00
114			28.50	[1,2]4.50
115			28.25	[1]124.50
116	27.00	97.12		120.00
117	27.00	43.40		35.56
122			13.50	7.12
124			13.50	11.88
125			13.06	16.50
132				27.00

[1] The land as rented is not really worth this much because it is rented only for the growing of beans; but I have assigned it truck-land value.
[2] Land used without payment by permission of employer-owner.

rent land. The poorest people are laborers for others and do not have time for independent agriculture, hence do not rent land. The very wealthy have all the land they need. The renters are in between.

SPECIAL OCCUPATIONS AND WEALTH

Chart 19 indicates the economic level of specialists, both artisans and professionals. Several generalizations become evident.

(1) The immigrant Indians are set apart as a group of artisans, but among Panajacheleños there is no "class" of artisans. One mason has little land, the second is in the middle of the land scale; two of the women who prepare food for sale are of poor families, the third is of a family above the middle; most of the women who weave for others are of poor and medium-poor families, but one is of the near-wealthy group; the pig butchers are of the middle and wealthy groups.

(2) Nevertheless, it is clear that the land-wealthy engage in the arts less than do the poor. The land-rich pig butcher, for example, knows how to kill pigs but he hardly practices the art; the wealthier weavers work less at weaving for others than do the poor weavers.

(3) On the other hand, the professionals tend not to be of the poorest families, nor—as it happens—of the few wealthiest, but are distributed rather evenly through the middle group. It is likely that the practice of a profession improves one's economic position so that he can obtain

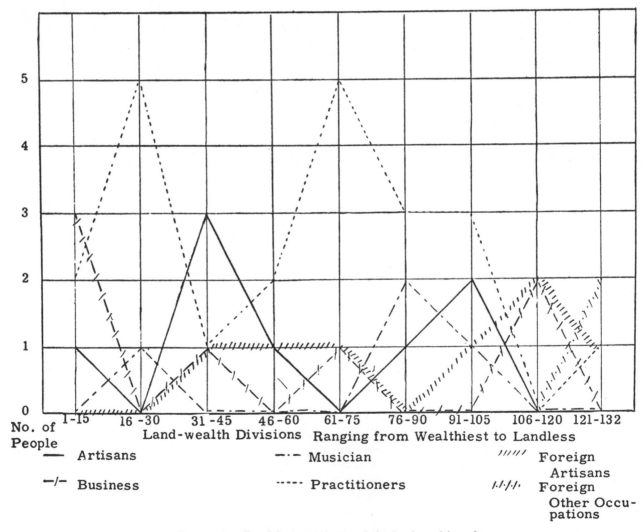

CHART 19.—Special occupations and the land-wealth scale.

more land and become wealthier (or so that he is not forced to sell land, hence to become poorer). That may be why professionals are not found (with one exception) among the poorest families as they are counted by land owned. It is also likely that in spite of the fact that shamans and midwives are said to be "called" to their profession (which they must then practice, lest they sicken and die), there is an important economic motive in the taking up of a profession. It may be true that a curer accidentally comes to know how to treat an illness and that then he is asked to assist, but it is likely that members of wealthy families who on the one hand have much land to take care of and on the other do not need special sources of income, resist gaining reputations as curers. It is difficult to escape the conclusion that shamans and midwives and curers and musicians become interested in learning partly for the income involved, that poorer people are attracted to such professions, and that they tend to become wealthier because of their profession.

Weavers are found at all levels of the population, but especially in the poorest half and, again, in the richest quarter (table 78). In addition to the 11 poorest-quarter families there are two whose women may weave (information lacking). It seems reasonable to suppose that the poor people weave because they cannot afford not to, and they also weave for others to earn money; that the very poorest weave less than the next-poorest because none of them are agricultural laborers; that the people of the second-richest quarter weave little because they can afford to pay others to do it while at the same time they have enough land to keep them busy in the fields. Why families of the richest quarter weave is explicable to me only on the grounds that they can afford to hire laborers in the fields so that the women can pursue the fine arts—but then I cannot explain why none of the wealthy women are able to put the designs into their *huipiles!* Evidence that in general these explanations are sound is found in the fact that in the poorest quarter 6 of the 11 weavers weave for others, for pay; only 4 of the 19 in the second quarter, only 2 of the 11 in the third quarter, and none of the 37 in the richest quarter weave for others. In the wealthy families also, all of the women and girls tend to weave. It is also interesting that the only recorded case of a woman who knows how to weave, but does

not do it, is found in the second richest quarter where I have supposed the women keep busiest in their fields.

LABOR AND WEALTH

It is evident that "laborers" are found only among the poor. But it may be well to ask what is the minimum land that a family may control to (1) permit its members to work exclusively on its own land and (2) to require it to hire outside labor. At first sight several complications would appear to make difficult, if not impossible, the resolution of these questions:

a. The size of the family, and its composition. A large family, especially with grown men, can work more land without outside assistance than can a small one, or one with few men. Family A with an acre of truck land might be able to work it without paid assistance and find that it consumes all of the time of the family; family B might be able to work the same land without assistance, but it might also have to seek work outside; family C might consume all of its time on the same acre and might require outside help besides; family D, with a shortage or absence of men, might require help on the land but in turn might have to work for others to fill in the time and make ends meet; and family E, with a shortage or absence of women, might find it economical to work outside and hire cheaper female labor for some agricultural processes.

TABLE 78.—*Distribution of Panajachel textile workers*

Economic level	Textile processes							
	All		Twisting and/or sewing		All except designs [1]		All processes	
	Number of households	Number of persons	Number of households	Number of persons	Number of households	Number of persons	Number of households	Number of persons
Poorest quarter [2]	11	14	2	3	8	10	1	1
Middle-poor quarter	15	22	2	3	9	15	4	4
Middle-rich quarter	11	11	1	1	9	9	1	1
Richest quarter	17	37	3	7	15	30	------	------
Total	[3] 58	84	8	14	41	64	6	6

[1] The woman who does no thread twisting is included here.
[2] On the scale of land controlled.
[3] The number of households in which textile arts are practiced is not the total of the numbers in which each process is practiced because in 1 household 2 persons only sew while a third also weaves.

b. The kind of land, and its use. Some crops require much more labor than others. A family with most of its land in coffee has both opportunity and need to hire out to others, while another family with the same land, but most of it truck, might be fully and profitably occupied only on its own land. Likewise, some truck crops require much more labor than others, and one family on an acre might have to hire labor, a second hire out, and a third—at different seasons—do both. Furthermore, whether for technical reasons or because of folk beliefs, cornfields are usually planted, cultivated, and harvested in as short a time as possible, so that regardless of the amount of land owned, Indians with cornfields frequently hire help and in turn—if they have little land—hire themselves out.

c. The "ambition" of the family, and its standard of living. One family may be satisfied to work its acre of land and do no more, while another with the same land might seek work outside in addition, while still another might hire help when, if its members preferred to exert themselves as do others, this would be unnecessary.

One must also take into consideration accidents and circumstances. Sickness may require the hiring of help when it would otherwise be unnecessary; or a period of municipal or religious service may make it impossible in a given year for a family to do all of its own work.

d. Other occupations, and occupational preferences. Important as farming is, it has been seen that some Indians devote time to other occupations, whether because they are more profitable or for social or mystic reasons (as when a shaman who does not answer a "call" becomes sick in consequence). Such persons of course must hire more labor on the same land than those who devote all of their time to farming.

In short, "other things" are rarely equal, and sound generalizations are exceedingly difficult to make. Yet an analysis of the available information, as shown chiefly in table 79, answers the two questions with surprising ease. Table 79 is based on incomplete information concerning employment of Indians by Indians except exclusively for milpa work. Using a wealth-scale based on the value of land controlled, both employers and employees are ranged in order of wealth and the original data entered. It is seen that 28 resident Indian families are known by me to have employed other Indians on their land. Two of these are foreign, 26 Panajacheleños. Of the latter no less than 18 are in the top quarter on the wealth scale, 7 are in the second quarter, and only 1 is as low as the very top of the second-poorest quarter. As one would expect, those owning most land hire labor. Likewise, 28 Panajachel Indian families

TABLE 79.—*Indians regularly employed by Indians in Panajachel* [1]

Employees, poor to rich	Distribution of Indian labor by employers, rich to poor																											
	1	2	3	4	6	7	8	9	10	11	12	15	18	22	25	26	28	31a	32	38	39	40	44	54	59	61	67	76a
127						f			f																			
124	m-f									m-m		f						f										
122	f-f																											
120									m																			
119																					m-m							
116		m																										
115	m																										f	
114	f		f									f											m					
113																						m						
112		m																										
107							f		f						f													
106	f																											
105	m		f									f					m						m-f					
102										m																		
100																				f		m						
99		m																										
97	m	m																										
96		m																										
92									m																			
83										m																		
80						m	m	m							m		m											
78	m-f	m																		m								
68																					m							
62							m																					
66									m																			
43	m																			m								
41						m													m									
25																					f							
Con			(m)	(m)			f			m-m		(m)	(m)f	(m)	(m)	m	(m)			m-m		(m)	(m)	m-m	(m)			
Sol																	(m)											
Jor																		(m)				(m)						(m)
Cat	m-m				(m)	m-m											(m)					(m)					(m)	
Tep											m-m																	

[1] Explanation of abbreviations:
  m=1 male of the household.
  f=1 female of the household.
  (m)=Unknown number of males.
  (f)=Unknown number of females.
  Con.=Indians of Concepción.
  Sol.=Indians of Sololá.
  Jor.=Indians of San Jorge.
  Cat.=Indians of Santa Catarina Palopó.
  Tep.=Indians of Tecpán.
  31a and 76a are Jorgeño Indians resident in Panajachel. They were not graded on the Panajachel wealth scale, but have been put in here because they hire other Indians to do agricultural labor. The number indicates where they fit in the Panajachel wealth scale if only their Panajachel lands are considered; this is inaccurate because both families probably own land in San Jorge as well, and on this I have no information.
  Numbers indicate employers and employees according to wealth scale.

regularly worked in the fields of other resident Indians, and 22 of these are in the bottom half on the wealth scale; 4 are in the second-richest quarter and one in the richest. Again, those who own little or no land are those who hire themselves out.

Information is not sufficient to explain all of the few exceptions to the rule. I suspect, for example, that the fourth richest man (No. 4 in table 79) hires men in his fields, since he cannot possibly do himself the six hundred and fifty-odd man-days of work usually done by men that is required in his fields, if my data about his fields are anywhere near correct. He is the only man in his household. Likewise, I have no information on men hired by the fifth-richest family, and although there are 3 women in the household, there is only one grown man. It is probable that again there is an omission in the data. On the other hand, the fact that No. 6 hired no men in 1936 is explicable by the fact that there were three grown men in the household. And, similarly, it is clear that the reason No. 10 hired so many is that he was too old to work and two young sons had to carry the burden. Also, the reason why No. 15 hired so many laborers, in spite of there being three grown men and four women in the house, is that the family grows an unusual amount of onions and onion seed. Were the basic data absolutely reliable, it would be worth while to analyze each instance in detail. As it is, I shall confine myself to discussion of the more striking exceptions. Numbers 38, 39, and 40 probably do not own enough land to justify their hiring labor. In the first case one of the two men of the household, however, was engaged in various enterprises aside from agriculture, and so could hire men; he also rented a sizable piece of truck land and worked his land more intensively than most. In the second case the head of the household is a shaman, and the three sons of the house were not full grown in 1936. In the third case, the head of the house, and his wife were past their prime, and only a daughter and her husband (and two babies) completed the household; the man cared for dairy cows and hired labor for the fields. No. 44 is an exception easy to explain; the head of the house was old and was an entrepreneur and a merchant— and the only other adults of the household were a school-teacher son and his Ladino wife. I cannot explain the case of No. 54, who had two grown sons and two grown daughters and—in addition—

two wives; it is true that most of his land was in onions, but the family should have been able to care for them, and whatever the reasons why they did not, there is no indication in my data of how he could support the family(ies) and still pay laborers. In the case of No. 59 the family consisted of a widow and her daughter and son-in-law (with two small children); according to my information, the land was not intensively planted, and I do not know why men were hired. No. 61, on the other hand, a family consisting of a couple with a young child, planted all of their land in onions, and doubtless required and could afford the female help. Even more easily is exceptional No. 67 explained, since in addition to the lands that the couple (of which the household consists) owned, they rented truck land and grew onions almost exclusively.

As far as employes are concerned, it may be emphasized that table 79 does not include mention of Indians who work for Ladinos. It has already been mentioned that the seven landless families (with one possible exception) are full-time laborers, but they work for the most part for Ladinos, hence do not appear in the table. The other land-poor Indian families shown as working for other Indians also work for Ladinos; the few exceptions are those who have part-time nonfarming occupations and/or who rent land. As they approach the middle of the land-wealth scale, however, the households of which persons work for others drop off sharply in number. Again, the exceptions are usually explicable. No. 68 was a household consisting of two grown men and a woman, and a nearly adult youth; although it controlled considerable land, and rented more, it doubtless had a surplus of labor to sell. On the other hand No. 62 and No. 66 were families with only one man, and even more land; but the men rented no land and had virtually all of their own planted in coffee, so in their cases they had at once little with which to occupy themselves, and the need to work outside. The case of No. 43 I can explain only on the basis of the man's being exceptionally industrious (which he is); he cultivated sufficient land intensively enough to keep himself very busy, and yet he occasionally worked for others. The same may be said of the woman of family No. 25, but here two other factors may enter: there are two men and three women in the household, and the balance is upset so that the family finds it necessary to hire a man, while one of the women can work elsewhere occasionally; and it may be recorded that doubtless a personal factor is important, for the woman who works is the widowed stepmother of the head of the house, and the family for which she works is that of her married daughter.

One may conclude, in answers to the questions put, that

(1) A family controlling at least $200 worth of land, normally distributed among cornfield, truck, and coffee, does not hire out its labor, and presumably does not need to. Two hundred dollars is the value of the land owned that divides 33 and 34 on the wealth scale, so it is seen that the only exception about which I know is that of No. 25 in table 79. That exception is not serious. A family controlling between $60 and $200 worth of land apparently hires (and needs to hire) out its labor only in unusual circumstances. ($60 is the amount of land dividing 90 and 91 on the scale.) Families owning less than $60 worth of land normally cannot live off of it and need some other source of income.

(2) A family controlling at least $335 worth of land hires (and presumably needs to hire) agricultural labor, assuming again that its crop distribution is normal. Three hundred and thirty-five dollars is the value of land owned that separates 12 from 13 in the wealth scale. Only one highly doubtful exception appears in my data. A family controlling between $170 and $335 worth of land ($170 being the amount of land separating 40 and 41 on the scale) almost as frequently as not hire hands and presumably (depending on circumstances) often finds this necessary. Families owning less than $170 worth of land usually do not find it necessary to hire hands, if indeed they can afford to.

It is because the factors involved in the hiring of labor for work in the cornfields are somewhat distinct that I have not included it in the above analysis. In 1936 there were 40 families growing at least 0.89 acre of milpa (5 *cuerdas*). Of these, I have specific information that seven hired help especially for the milpa, but others of course used their regular labor supply in the milpa as well as in the coffee groves and truck gardens. The seven families stood in places 84, 78, 67, 35, 32, 7, and 1 on the wealth (land-controlled) scale. For other years I also have notes showing that families

standing 95 and 44 hired labor in the milpa. On the other hand, I have specific information that members of 13 Indian families hired out to other Indians for milpa work. These stood 124, 121, 120, 114, 105, 97, 78, 77, 66, 58, 43, 38, and 36 on the wealth scale. The only coincidence in the two lists is No. 78, representing a family which hired labor for its milpa and in turn worked on the milpas of others. (This is not a case of work-exchange; the families do not work for each other.) The two lists also show that the very rich do not work in the milpas of others and that the very poor—in land ownership, of course—do not hire labor on their small or nonexistent milpas.

It is the general custom to plant, cultivate, and harvest a cornfield in as short a period of time as possible; and this of course explains why even a person with a small amount of corn tends to hire helpers. An informant in 1941 gave me a short list of persons who hire labor for the corn harvest and who give some sort of harvest festival. This shows that a family that in 1936 had 0.89 acre of corn hired 3 men; another with 0.98, also 3; one with 1.28, also 3; 1 with 1.95, 5; 1 with 2.95, 10; 1 with 4.63, 15; and 1 with 6.54, 8. The information is probably not accurate, but it gives some idea of the relations between the size of the cornfield and the number of laborers hired. One reason why the last-mentioned family hired (according to this information) relatively few men might be that his cornfield is in two lots and the work on each done at a different time. Two certainly reliable cases show clearly that labor is hired even on limited quantities of land. One is of the family of a widow, her grown son, and adolescent daughter (in 1940) which stood 95 on the wealth (land-controlled) scale. In 1940 it held on pawn 0.71 acre of cornfield in Santa Catarina; at the harvest three laborers were hired for cash: a cousin (of a family standing 43d) and two Catarinecos. The mother and daughter also helped, and the harvest was effected in one day. The other case (also 1940) is a family 78th on the scale consisting of a couple, a late-teen-aged daughter, and two young children. They had 1.42 acres of corn, and after half had been harvested the man went to hire "one or two" *mozos* to help him finish; the wife and daughter also helped. The men of both of these cases frequently are employed by others—Ladinos and Indians— as agricultural laborers; had they not been anxious to harvest quickly, they could easily have found time to do all of the work without assistance.

WEALTH AND DOMESTIC ANIMALS

Table 80 shows that the wealthy, naturally, have more than the poor of every kind of domestic animal, whether horses, dogs and cats, most obviously "consumption items"; or fowl and pigs, which also produce some return; or cattle, which presumably are kept for the income they produce.

TABLE 80.—*Distribution of domestic animals*

Kind	Total	Number of households owning specified animals				
		Panajacheleño				' Foreign"
		Richest	Medium rich	Medium poor	Poorest	
	(155)	(33)	(33)	(33)	(33)	(23)
Families_____	38	0	7	3	14	14
Animals_____	0	0	0	0	0	0
Families_____	61	24	13	13	10	1
Fowl (head)_____	846	439	164	157	82	4
Families_____	29	10	8	7	3	1
Pigs (head)_____	40	13	10	12	4	1
Families_____	10	3	2	4	1	0
Goats and sheep (head)_	27	6	8	12	1	0
Families_____	12	8	2	2	0	0
Cattle (head)_____	16	12	2	2	0	0
Families_____	3	1	0	2	0	0
Rabbits and guinea pigs (head)_	16	4	0	12	0	0
Families_____	6	4	2	0	0	0
Bees (hives)_____	18	12	6	0	0	0
Families_____	19	12	3	1	0	3
Horses and mules (head)_	20	13	3	1	0	3
Families_____	107	33	26	27	14	7
Dogs and cats (head)___	259	106	57	62	20	14

DIFFERENCES IN HOUSING

In the section entitled "The Level and Cost of Living" there is (pp. 154–158) a brief description of the houses in which 10 of the families live, designed to give not only some picture of the material differences in the goods of rich and poor but also an indication of what wealth does to the standard of living.

Table 81 lists these 10 sample households with the grade given each by the two informants above referred to (neither of whom is included among the 10) and the amount and value of land controlled by each in 1936. The 10 families vary in size from 3 to 10. As may be seen in the list of Appendix 3, the size of the family does not correlate with the wealth, but the four richest families happen to be among the largest, and none of the smallest families are among the richest. It is evident from table 81 that the amount of land owned increases roughly with the wealth; this is

natural, since land is the important determiner of wealth in Panajachel. The notable exception (the family No. 15, which has less land than that of No. 19) is explicable partly on the basis of family composition, partly on that of personalities. Family 15 had three men in 1936, including a deaf-mute who was a good worker; family 19 had but one man. At the same time, the head of family 15 was a young and progressive Indian who not only made the most of what land he had, but engaged in business in various ways.

A study of the descriptions of the 10 households makes two things clear: (1) that the rich live better than do the poor, and (2) that the differences are strictly limited—i. e., in degree not proportional to wealth and always within the bounds of the culture. Comparison of room space and the sleeping arrangements in the 10 houses (tables 82 and 83) shows this. In table 82 children from 4 to 15 are counted as half adults; those under 4 are not counted. Chicken houses, sweat baths, bake ovens, and granaries are not counted as "rooms," but their floor space is counted in the total. Although the poor have fewer houses and less floor space than the rich, regardless of family size, the

TABLE 81.—*Wealth of 10 households*

Order No.	Wealth grade		Land controlled		
	Informant 49	Informant 58	Acres		Total value
			Delta	Hill corn	
3_____	90	100	2.2	5.5	$411.51
5_____	84	90	2.0	8.5	367.32
15_____	50	80	1.2	_____	177.50
19_____	46	55	2.2	_____	346.50
28_____	46	53	.9	_____	139.50
37_____	42	41	.6	.5	83.82
94_____	8	19	.2	_____	28.50
95_____	6	35	.1	1.4	15.62
108_____	8	6	.1	_____	13.50
109_____	4	16	.1	1.1	13.06

TABLE 82.—*Rooms and living space of 10 households*

Family order No.	Number of "adults"	Number of rooms	Square feet of space				Square feet room space per "adult"
			Total	Yard	Porches	Rooms	
3_____	4.5	5	2,035	1,000	153	882	196
5_____	7	3	2,610	1,350	120	1,140	163
15_____	[1] 6	4	1,913	900	104	909	[1] 151
19_____	4	2	2,583	1,620	120	843	210
28_____	2.5	4	1,227	432	30	765	306
37_____	2.5	3	986	324	133	529	212
94_____	4	1	798	576	_____	222	55
95_____	8	1	1,182	900	_____	[2] 282	[2] 35
108_____	2.5	1	230	90	24	116	46
109_____	6.5	1	263	_____	_____	[3] 263	[3] 40

[1] Servant not counted.
[2] Projected house not included.
[3] House under construction included.

TABLE 83.—*Number and kinds of beds in 10 households*

Family order No.	Number of beds			Occupants of beds			
	Bought	Made	Floor	Bed 1	Bed 2	Bed 3	Bed 4
3	1	3		Couple and son	Daughter and her 2 sons	Daughter	Unused.
5		3	1	Couple and daughter	Son, wife, son and daughter	Son and wife	Sister.
15	3	1		Man and son	Wife and 2 daughters	2 sons.	Half-brother.
19		2		Couple and son	Sister and her nephew		
28		1		....do....			
37	1			....do....			
94		2		Widow, 3 sons, 1 daughter	Son		
95			3	Couple and daughter	2 sons	2 daughters	
108			1	....do....			
109		1	2	Couple and son	3 sons	Daughter	

family size is an influencing factor. Wealth equal, larger families need and have more space than smaller. But the size of the establishment does not increase proportionally with the number of persons, either among the rich or the poor.

The amount of doubling-up in sleeping is indicated in table 83, where the number and kinds of beds used are shown. Obviously, other factors besides wealth enter here, for custom with respect to the relations of the sexes limits the doubling up that can occur. Yet wealth is a factor. The poor family No. 94 would probably not sleep five in a bed if there were more money, hence more space. And wealth is certainly a limiting factor in the kinds of beds used. The poorer people tend to sleep on the floor; only the richer families have bought beds. Yet here again other factors enter.

The kind of houses used is evidently a function of wealth. Mass-adobe houses are cheaper to build than those of adobe brick. Tile is more expensive roofing than thatch, and corrugated iron by far the most expensive. Only families Nos. 3, 5, 15, 19, and 37 have adobe-brick houses; only the first has houses with tile and metal roofs. Such elements as formal porches, carpenter-made wooden doors, etc. also accompany greater wealth, as may be seen in the detailed descriptions of Appendix 3. The saint's house (even though never exclusively used for the purpose) is also to be found only in the wealthier compounds: only families Nos. 3, 5, 19, and 28 have one.

A reading of the description of the 10 house groups will help further to show how variations among rich and poor are held strictly within bounds. The richer families could certainly afford to plaster their adobe-brick houses; they do not. They could afford windows which they do not have. They could have lime-mortar or even brick floors, but they do not. They could have raised fireplaces (as the Government demands) and do not. And so on. They lack such things not because they are unfamiliar with them—for Ladino homes that they frequent have them—but because they do not want them. Why they do not want them is a question beyond the scope of this report; it is obvious that so-called "cultural factors," as opposed to economic, are involved.

DIFFERENCES IN FOOD

In the section headed The Level and Cost of Living there is some analysis of differences in diet among the middle to above-middle families (pp. 163–174) who constituted the sample used to estimate total consumption in the community and the very rich and the poor. The material collected independently in 1944 makes possible discussion in terms of food value, based on a slightly larger sample over a 7-day period. Table 84 shows the conversion of the net quantities of table 66 into chemical constituents.[176] It is evident that the

[176] The conversion was done by the Nutrition Division of the Food and Agricultural office of the United Nations, under supervision of Miss Emma Reh, from whose unpublished report I am permitted to quote:

"Dietary deficiency diseases were observed only in mild forms in Indian and *ladino* groups in a survey made in highland Guatemala in 1932. Pellagra was less severe and less frequent than among Mayan Indians of lowland Yucatan in Mexico. Scurvy and thiamine deficiency were not observed.

"Well marked anaemia (hemoglobin under 60 percent on the Tallquist scale) was found in only 3 percent of both Indians and *ladinos* in cases not associated with malaria or intestinal parasitosis. Goiter is common in certain highland areas but its exact distribution is not known.

"The Mayan Indians of Mexico and Guatemala are among the native people of America with the shortest stature. In recent measurements in the Guatemalan highlands, the average height of the adult male was found to be 155 cm., and that of the average adult female, 144 cm. The males weighed on the average 51 kilograms, and females, 45 kg. (T. Dale Stewart, 1948, U. S. Smithsonian Institution, Washington).

"The Mayan Indians of both Yucatan and Guatemala were reported to differ from whites in the United States in having higher basal metabolic rates and lower systolic blood pressures. In both measurements, people of mixed Indian and Spanish blood occupied positions intermediate between Indians and whites. The influence of many factors, racial or environmental, including diet, was considered in order to account for the difference, but definite conclusions were not reached.

"In calculating the nutritional value of the diets, all available analyses of Mexican and Guatemalan foods were used. These cover corn, beans, chile

table would appear more orderly if family 58 were placed between 13 and 15 and if the positions of families 37 and 49 were reversed. If the 1944 and 1936 data were collected at the same time, one might question either the wealth order or the conclusion that nutrition is correlated with wealth differences. I believe that the correlation is there, in general, and the discrepancy due in part to changed circumstances and in part to individual peculiarities. The fact is that from 1936 family 58 became much wealthier owing (may I believe?) to the fact that in 1937 I "staked" them to 5.5 acres of hill milpa land; that land would have brought them virtually equal in land wealth to family 15. Another reason why family 58 was becoming rapidly wealthy, even beyond the land it owned, was that its sons were maturing, but were still part of the household. Particularly, the eldest son had come back from military service with strong progressive ideas, literacy, and great ambition. For a year or two he successfully supervised the farm of a nearby plantation, and learned much. I would not be surprised to learn that by 1944 the family had become one of the wealthy. Both families 15 and 37 were probably slightly atypical in food habits because of personal peculiarities—for one thing the men liked business better than labor and probably did less physical work than any others of the sample. In some degree family 58 was also atypical, for the son was married to a somewhat Ladinoized woman. Since the last family in table 74 is "foreign" altogether (husband from Totonicapán, wife from San Antonio) it is evident that the sample is both too small and too peculiar to permit the drawing of statistical conclusions. Yet, if one moves family 58 to second position, it is evident enough that

wealthy families do get more calories, protein, iron, thiamine, riboflavin, and niacine than poorer families, and that the very poor (foreign) family gets a poorer share of about everything. The distribution of vitamin A is the most peculiar from this point of view.

TABLE 84.—*Seven-day food intake (1944) of 6 families [1] per nutrition unit per day [2]*

Item	Family (wealth order No.)					
	13	15	37	49	58	106a
Number in family [3]	3	10.9	3.9	6	5	6.3
Calories	3,552	2,766	2,569	2,920	3,532	2,686
Protein (mg.)	88.1	69.5	75.4	67.3	84.5	53.2
Calcium from food (mg.)	282	319	255	277	380	131
Total calcium (mg.)	1,289	826	735	956	1,257	692
Iron (mg.)	26	25	22	23	29	18
Vitamin A value I. U	9,513	5,162	2,599	11,223	1,544	6,268
Ascorbic acid (mg.)	102	366	74	96	21	28
Thiamine (mg.)	3.94	3.31	2.92	2.99	4.24	2.74
Riboflavin (mg.)	1.15	1.02	.86	.98	.97	.68
Niacin (mg.)	17.1	14.4	16.1	12.9	15.7	10.6

[1] From tabulations supplied by Miss Emma Reh of Instituto de Nutrición de Centro America y Panamá.
[2] "Family units are expressed as nutrition unit equivalents of the moderately active male, according to the 1945 National Research Council's recommended allowances for specific nutrients by sex, age, and activity," (quoted from note to table 2B in unpublished F. A. O. report by Emma Reh).
[3] This is *not* the number of nutrition units, but the number of people who partook of the family food during the week, subtracting fractions for meals missed and adding fractions for guests.

COSTUME AND WEALTH

The costumes worn by the Indian present a special case of the relations of material goods to wealth. As far as I know, only in matter of costume is there any suggestion of the material symbolization of wealth, class, or security that is so important in our society. Table 85 shows how the different styles of costumes are distributed in the various wealth levels of Panajacheleño society. The costumes differ in value (table 64), but other factors besides ability to pay enter into their distribution. These apparently are:

(1) *Loss of costume particularly with acculturation.*—It will be noticed that from 8 to 18 percent of the men and boys and from 1 to 10 percent of women and girls discarded Indian costume, for the male "city" attire or the female "Totonicapán" costume, both of which are nonregional Indian costumes. Virtually all these men have been in military service outside of Panajachel, and when soldiers return to Panajachel they rarely if ever revert to their old costume. Some boys grow up in trousers and never wear the local costume, and these, not called upon to serve in the Indian organization, are destined also for military service. The "sophisticates" who come from or have lived in other towns, speak Spanish, and so on. In cases of intermarriage this is frequently a clothing solution, for if the husband does not like the costume of his wife, she may change to Totonicapán clothes. Men's "city" costume and women's "Totonicapán" frequently go together in a family.

peppers, tomatoes, and many other common items. No deductions in nutrients were made for losses in cooking or in preparing food.

"The daily intake of calories and nutrients was computed on both a per person and a per consumption unit basis. Because the number of families in a diet survey is often small, differences in the age and sex distribution of the samples and the general population may be great. In the *ladino* group in this instance there were 69 males per 100 females, and in the Indian group, 111 males per 100 females. The *ladino* families were smaller, with an average of 5.4 persons, compared to 5.8 persons per Indian family.

"The consumption units employed for calories and nutrients were based on the 1945 'recommended allowances' of the National Research Council, Washington, U. S. A. On the basis of the field data, 5 percent of the adults were classed as very active, 76 percent as moderately active, 13 percent as sedentary. The remaining 6 percent were lactating women. The number of caloric consumption units per 100 persons in the Indian group was computed as 81, and in the *ladino* group, as 79.

"The smaller body size of Guatemalans was not taken into account. It was felt that, as regards energy expenditure, the strenuous life imposed by the environment would tend to offset the difference in size. The country is mountainous, trails to fields are long, burdens heavy and life unmechanized."

(2) *Conservatism.*—The expensive "old-fashioned" men's costume is worn by persons, some very poor, because (apparently) they are conservative. With rare exceptions, young men do not wear it. Most of the elders of the community wear it; these are the people who have performed their religious and political service for the community; they also tend to be rich, and could in general afford to wear any kind of costume. The women and girls of these conservative families, meanwhile, tend to wear the "simple" Panajachel costume. (I suppose that the use of silk must be, on this interpretation, relatively new.) It is significant that in the three wealthiest families and in 8 of the 11 wealthiest the women have no silk in their garments. The poor, evidently, wear conservative costumes when they are conservative and can afford it—the rich because they can always afford it.

TABLE 85.—*Panajacheleño costume distribution* [1]

Costume [2]	Percentage of persons in indicated quarter wearing various costumes			
	Poorest quarter [3]	Middle-poor quarter	Middle-rich quarter	Richest quarter
Male:				
"City"	9. 4	18. 3	10. 2	8. 0
"Modern"	47. 2	38. 8	35. 6	29. 3
"Newer"	1. 7	10. 2	6. 8	17. 3
"Old-fashioned"	3. 8	8. 2	6. 8	14. 7
"Fashionable"	37. 7	24. 5	40. 7	30. 7
Total	99. 8	100. 0	100. 1	100. 0
Female:				
"Totonicapán"	5. 7	6. 2	10. 0	1. 2
"San Andrés Variation"	9. 4	12. 5	8. 0	2. 5
"Simple Panajachel"	77. 4	62. 5	44. 0	60. 5
"Silk Panajachel"	0. 0	4. 2	4. 0	13. 6
"Elaborate Panajachel"	7. 5	14. 6	34. 0	22. 2
Total	100. 0	100. 0	100. 0	100. 0

[1] Only known cases of table 75, excluding "foreign" households, which are not rated on the wealth scale.
[2] On the scale of land controlled.
[3] In order of cost, least to most.

(3) *Comfort.*—The Panajachel climate (in my opinion) is too warm for the woolen *gabán,* and that is one possible reason why it is being discarded. The "new costume" is the conservative substitute. Many men also complain of the coarseness and the bulk of the *calzón,* and say they prefer the "modern" costume for that reason. Women meanwhile, argue that the Panajachel *huipil* is too warm and bulky and explain the use of the San Andrés *huipil* on that basis and on the grounds that, being white, it is cleaner. This *huipil* is also cheaper, however, and that may be the real reason for the change.

(4) *Fashion.*—The "fashionable" costume is certainly a young man's pride, and I am sure that these costumes are worn with particular pleasure. The fact that so many poor men wear this expensive costume may not indicate more than one of the reasons they are poor. Much the same can be said of the women's costumes with silk, although here the poor women would seem more self-denying, or conservative, than their men folk.

(5) *Competition.*—The fact that in the middle-rich quarter the most expensive costumes are worn may be evi-

dence of a *nouveau riche* complex of conspicuous consumption. Perhaps the richest families do not feel that they need this outward evidence.

(6) *Wealth* enters the costume picture in different ways, it is clear; but in the distribution of the "modern" costume it enters most simply. This is the cheapest local-Indian costume, and in a choice between it and the "fashionable" no factor is apparent other than the difference in economic ability or in individual values. It is clear, therefore, why the proportion of "modern" costumes decreases as wealth increases.

WEALTH MOBILITY

A comparison of the households as classified by wealth and their genealogical interrelations shows that there is no such thing as a "wealthy family" of two or more generations' standing. Cousins and siblings of the rich are likely to be found anywhere along the wealth scale. For examples, the man of the No. 1 family has four paternal uncles and aunts whose families in 1936 stood 36th, 57th, 119th, and 122d in the wealth scale. The man of the No. 2 family is the son of a woman who had two brothers whose descendants stand 49th and 130th in the scale. The only descendant of his father's brother stands 40th. These examples could be multiplied.

Of course the mere fact that there is inheritance of property indicates that there are wealthy families of one or two generations' standing. And there are. For example, the families standing 10th, 17th, 18th, 20th, 51st, and 52d are all of one originally rich household, and all tend to be rich. However, in the course of time, the children of a rich man tend to become widely differentiated in wealth. Thus the five grown children of the No. 3 man were, in 1936, Nos. 4, 11, 52, 75, and 103. One of the reasons for this is that with the division of land (not always evenly among the children) each child has but a fraction of what the parent had, and one or another may go up or down from there.

Marriages tend to cut across wealth lines, with a man of a richer family marrying a woman of a poorer family. In 36 cases (all later than 1936) on which I have information,

> The man and woman were in the same wealth-quarter in 9, with the man richer in 4, and the woman in 5;
> The man and woman were in consecutive quarters in 11, with the man richer in 8, and the woman in 3;
> The pair were in alternate quarters in 12, with the man richer in 7, and the woman in 5;
> The pair were in opposite quarters in 4, with the man richer in 3, and the woman in 1.

Put another way, the figures show that the families of bride and groom were separated by

> Less than 33 places in the wealth scale in 13 cases, between 34 and 66 places in 14 cases, between 67 and 99 places in 6 cases, and between 100 and 132 places in 3 cases,

which means that in only 13 of the 36 cases were the two families nearly at the same economic level.

Not only do men of richer families tend to marry girls of poorer families, as seen above, but the tendency in "mixed" marriages all along the line is for the difference to be greater when a richer man marries a poorer girl than when a richer girl marries a poorer man. Thus in marriages:

> Within the same wealth-quarter, the average number of places on the wealth scale separating the families where the man is richer is 14, and where the woman is richer, 11.4;
> In consecutive quarters, where the man is richer, it is 37.4, and where the woman is richer it is 25;
> In alternate quarters, where the man is richer, it is 63, and where the woman is richer, 63.8; and
> In opposite quarters, where the man is richer, it is 112.7, and where the woman is richer, 73.

Three questions arise: (1) Why do marriages cut across wealth lines? (2) Why do men marry girls poorer than themselves, and (3) what becomes of the daughters of the rich? The answers are all closely related. A wealthy man with a daughter to marry off is faced with the problem of having much land, with the prospect of losing a worker; if he marries the girl to a rich man, she surely leaves him, whereas he can sometimes obtain a poor son-in-law who will come to live with him. This is an exceptional, although not uncommon, marriage that cuts across wealth lines. It is a recognized "peculiar" marriage in a generally patrilocal culture; to arrange it, the girl's parents may even initiate the proposal—a rather abnormal procedure. This kind of marriage accounts for some of the recent cases in which the girl's family has been wealthier than the boy's. On the other hand, a family with a son prefers a relatively poor girl (all considerations of character, beauty, etc., constant) because she will more certainly come to live at the house and help with the work; she usually "knows how to work," and she will make a better daughter-in-law for the dependence she will feel and the advantages she will get.

The answer to the last question, insofar as I can answer it, is that the daughters of the rich tend to marry later for the reasons that (1) there is no economic pressure on her or her family to accept a husband, (2) suitors are apt to hesitate to ask for her hand for fear of a refusal and because of the expense involved in case of an acceptance, and (3) a man of a family as rich or almost as rich will prefer a poor girl for reasons mentioned above. In the richest family in the community there are two daughters who were, in 1936, about 31 and 16 years of age respectively; they were unmarried as late as 1941. The older girl might easily remain a maid; she is not unattractive, but of course there may be other factors involved. In the second richest family there were two girls of marriageable age in 1936. One has since married a poor man who was brought to the house to live; the other (about 17 in 1936) had an illegitimate child by a son of the richest family and was still unmarried in 1941. The two stepdaughters of the third richest family had had three illegitimate children by 1936 (two of them reportedly by the stepfather) and remained unwed. The only daughter of the fourth richest man was, again, married to a man who came to her father's house to live and work. And so on down the list of the very rich: late marriages, spinsters, unwed mothers, matrilocal residence are more common than among the poor.

I never heard expression either of envy or deprecation in connection with marriages between poor men and rich girls; I think that there is some loss of respect, however, if the girl's family takes the initiative and, in a sense, buys the man. Nor were there remarks about a girl's good fortune in marrying a rich man; in one case there was some pity for how hard the girl would have to work. There seems to be no notion of "marrying for money," perhaps because there are few romantic notions about marriage. That there is so little affect connected with cross-wealth-lines marriages doubtless makes them easier to contract. There also appears to be no strong deprecation of late marriage or feminine bachelorhood; it is true that few women remain unmarried, but comments about those who do are conspicuous by their absence. Thus, it is not as strange as it would otherwise be that the rich permit their daughters to go husbandless. Finally, the attitude toward illegitimacy is relatively mild; no great disgrace attaches itself to the girl or her family, and none to the child. (But the conduct of loose women is frowned upon, and illicit relations with Ladinos, especially, are taken seriously.)

From study of the genealogies, and the data on inheritance, it is evident that family wealth has a natural history that may be described as follows: A man attains wealth, partly through inheritance and/or marriage and partly through his own efforts. Unless he dissipates this wealth in his lifetime, it eventually comes to his children. The rich, probably because they are able to care for them better, tend to have more surviving children than do the poor. The original wealth, now divided, gives each child something of a start, and he probably gets a little—but less than his own—additional land through marriage. He may with industry and luck increase his fortune, or the contrary may occur. If he increases it, he becomes wealthy and the process is repeated. Frequently one son of a rich family increases his wealth and the others do not, and even become poorer; there is some tendency for the sons of the rich to become wastrels. If the son of a rich man becomes poor, his son may marry a wealthy girl and may get a start toward wealth; or, if residence in his case is matrilocal, his subsequent history parallels that of a son of a rich man. The daughter of a poor man, meanwhile, is apt to marry a richer man, and one or more of her children are given a start toward wealth. And of course any poor man—son or grandson of rich or poor—may himself have what it takes, including luck (for sickness and deaths in the family are important causes of disaster) and with the help of his children become rich.

So any family in Panajachel, in the course of two or three generations, has its important ups and downs, and the rich and poor are soon scrambled genealogically.

There is a special element in the society that tends to make the rich poor in Panajachel: the system of civil and religious services to the community. Every man (with his wife) is expected to climb the ladder of offices, but there are two factors that make the process absolutely more expensive for the rich than for the poor: (1) Where there is a choice, the more expensive positions are taken by rich men, and (2) the poor people, not being able to afford the offices, climb the ladder very slowly and occasionally skip a position altogether, and often never go through all of them before they die; while the rich cannot refuse and so make the ascent more quickly, becoming *principales* while still middle-aged. The result is that the rich not only spend more money and time

while young, but become habitual drinkers at an early age and spend even more money and time on liquor

Mobility in the economic scale is often very rapid. Given a little land and a few years of good fortune, a careful Indian has money with which to buy land, and if he continues industrious and his luck holds, he becomes richer almost by geometric progression. The No. 1 man in 1936 became rich in 20 years or less, and was rapidly increasing his fortune. He worked hard, had lost only two infants, and had five sons and two daughters grown to maturity. He taught them industry and the family lived conservatively. Money earned went to buy, or obtain on pawn, more land, and the greater earnings this produced brought still more land. On the other hand, it has been seen what happened to the Rosales family fortune—dissipated by most of those who inherited it, rapidly increased by one man, and then lost entirely in a few short years. The case of the man standing 16th despite the small amount of land he owned in 1936, is also instructive: he is not only industrious, but has four grown and industrious sons. The family was doing so well that in spite of its land shortage, informants placed them almost at the top in wealth. Since 1936, the family has acquired much more land and has ironed out some of the discrepancy between its land holdings and its presumed wealth.

MOTIVATIONS

It is frequently said of Indians in Guatemala, sometimes as a reason for not improving their work conditions and wages, that if they earn enough money for the week in 3 days, they will not work the rest of the week. I doubt if this is true on an important scale anywhere in the country, but as applied to Panajachel, nothing seems further from the truth than this dictum which implies that the Indians work for bare necessities alone and have no desire to improve their way of life, or attain the security that wealth (especially in land) gives, or accumulate something for their children. I think that enough evidence has been presented to make my assertion credible. The Indians already live above a subsistence level (by their standards); they are certainly working for the luxury of meat as well as for corn, for their church as well as for their food. I have never heard of a poor Indian ever refusing to work for another (when sober and capable of work) if he had nothing to do for himself and if the work and wage offered were reasonable by local standards. If a plantation owner should try to contract labor to go to the lowlands, he might get a contrary impression; but he would be in error because of ignorance of the fact that there *is* enough work in Panajachel where the climate and health conditions are more favorable and where the Indians have their families and friends. Furthermore, it has been seen that the Indians do strive for wealth and that there is strong motivation toward greater land holdings, a desire to have more for themselves and their children.

Without doubt, the first need that the Indians feel is for security. Wealth gives security, and a great deal of wealth is necessary for real security. When a sickness can take in a year what has been accumulated in a dozen or more, and when such catastrophes are ever on the horizon, it is not enough to be just a little ahead. Almost none of the Indians have enough to feel at all secure, and most of them have no security whatever. The need to keep as much as possible ahead, for the rainy day, keeps all Indians working. It must be remembered that there are in the community almost no mechanisms to alleviate the results of financial disaster. A man sells his assets, or borrows on them, when he has sudden need; and when his assets are gone, he has nothing to fall back on. There is no public and almost no private charity. There is the case of a poor Indian whose wife was ill, having given birth to a child. The midwife told him he needed to buy medicines, and he had no money. He spent at least 3 days unsuccessfully trying to borrow 25 cents, even offering his machete as security. I do not know what finally happened. In another case a very poor Indian whose wife had just given birth was called before the court for not having registered the child's birth and he was fined $2.00 for having no documents; in jail he could earn nothing for his sick wife, so a nephew (who happens to be Ladinoized) paid the fine "as an act of humanity."

In a large family, the number of persons is itself some insurance, for all are not apt to take sick at once. In a small family—say a man, his wife and a small child—if the man falls ill and there are no assets to pawn or sell, nor credit in the stores, I suppose that they live on what the wife can earn, and buy only what her earnings permit; if medi-

cines or the services of a shaman cannot be bought, the man presumably goes without, and perhaps dies. What happens if both the father and mother, in such a case, should become incapacitated, I do not know, for such a case was not noted; I suppose that neighbors or friends or relatives would assist. The picture is perhaps not as bleak as it appears, for really minimum needs are few: a roof over one's head costs nothing, for anybody will furnish that temporarily; a little firewood can always be collected; clothing may be in tatters, but the mildness of the climate makes that not too serious; and the food required, for a limited period of time, can be very little and very cheap—corn and a little lime, and water. In extremities of misfortune, the standard of life simply drops to that minimum.

Security from such contingencies is the first want, surely. But it is a negative want. The Indians also desire better living. That means, first, that they wish better food, clothing, and shelter than the minimum. It means, second, that they wish some real insurance against death. One Indian told me that the reason the rich have more children than the poor is that they can "defend" their children when they take ill. Recall also the poor girl who pointed out that the sons of a rich family could "sin" (in this case, work on Sunday) because they had the wherewithal to take care of the consequences (i. e., they could pay for curing). It means, third, that they want some degree of independence—to be able to choose their employers and the kind of work; not to have to ask favors and borrow money; and they want enough so that they can carry quarrels to legal conclusions and pay their fines no less than can their enemies.

Beyond that, even, the Indians want power to do favors and to give work to others. What they doubtless want, in the long run, is the respect of others in the community. Personal virtues, such as honesty, industry, and generosity, that are high in the values of the culture, are more or less independent of wealth. But there are at least two achievements of high value that are attained only through the accumulation of wealth. One is rapid ascent in the political-religious hierarchy of offices; a man with money is able to do his duty quickly and without stinting or complaining too much, and he becomes an honored *principal* at an early age, a respected power in the community. The second is the ability to provide well for one's children. Whether because of affection or a feeling of family duty, or because people speak ill of a man who wastes his substance and has nothing for his children, one of the strongest desires is to have land to divide. The fact that provision for children is one of the strong incentives for the accumulation of wealth, and especially land, is reflected also in the curious statement volunteered by an old Indian to Sr. Rosales. "We were born with nothing," he said, "and so we should die. Why should I save money (i. e., not spend it on liquor) if all my children are grown? Since we are now only two, I do not worry about anything."

CONCLUSIONS

Despite such motivations, the fact appears clear that on the whole wealth in Panajachel has not become attached to family lines. We have answered the questions put. But the answers, as they must, only lead to other questions, one of which may be interesting to try to answer. Is the fact that wealth-tied social classes have not developed in Panajachel accidental or passing, or is it in the nature of the community? I think the answer is that social classes have not developed, and are not likely to develop, in Panajachel, for three reasons:

The first is the low absolute wealth of the community. Although relatively rich, the wealthiest families are not far above the subsistence level. They have little margin of safety, and a series of bad times (sickness, drunkenness, etc.), may send them down. That is why there is so much mobility. Further, nobody is rich enough to establish his descendants; when lands are divided among the children, the margin of security is reduced for each and he is just as apt to become poorer as richer. In comparison with many a European community it is easy to see that family differentiation of wealth has little chance to crystallize.

The second and third reasons are instructive because they are suggested in part by comparison with other communities in Guatemala. Chichicastenango (a neighbor to the north) is unlike Panajachel in many ways. One of them is that the time of women in Chichicastenango has until recently not had cash value. (Increased weaving for the tourist trade may change this.) Therefore in Chichicastenango as opposed to Panajachel there is encouragement of marriage within the

same wealth class, and hence the tendency for wealth-tied social classes to develop. It is seen in contrast that the economic value of women in Panajachel militates against the development of such classes.

A major difference between the two communities is the size of the population, which has significant consequences for the problem at hand. In Chichicastenango there are some 25,000 Indians instead of 800. There is in general the same kind of social system, with its hierarchy of offices to be filled each year. But the number of offices is proportionally much smaller. In Panajachel 52 offices are divided among 132 families; in Chichicastenango about 350 are divided among some 5,000 families. The difference is one office for every 2 or 3 families versus one for every 14 or 15. But in Chichicastenango no less than in Panajachel a man is expected to rest only 2 or 3 years between offices; indeed were the periods of rest lengthened proportionally he would die long before getting up the ladder. The solution is, of course, that in Chichicastenango not all families participate fully in the system. Whereas in Panajachel every man can expect to become the *alcalde* eventually, in Chichicastenango only a relative few can pass up the ladder. The number is even more restricted than indicated, for in any town regardless of size *there is still only one first alcalde*. The fact is that in Chichicastenango, for every man of a given age level who serves as *alcalde* there are a hundred who do not. In consequence, there is in Chichicastenango need to select the relatively very few men who go up the political-religious hierarchy of offices. How is this selection determined? It will be recalled that in Panajachel the rate of progress differs; some men go up the ladder quickly and become elders in their early forties; others go much more slowly and do not achieve the office of *alcalde* until they are in their fifties, or later. The difference has been described as a matter almost entirely of wealth. Fundamentally the same process is always at work in Chichicastenango, but it is greatly exaggerated. The poor people neither can afford the expensive high offices, nor is it necessary that they serve. The higher officials are recruited from relatively few wealthy families. On the other hand, as a corollary, the *lower* officials —the messengers and street sweepers, and so on— are in practice recruited from among the poor people. The differences between theory and practice in Chichicastenango is therefore wide, for while in theory everybody passes up the fixed steps of the hierarchy of offices, in practice the masses of people serve in the lower offices and never get further, while a relatively few rich families monopolize the high offices without having passed through the low ones. The theory in both Chichicastenango and Panajachel is therefore much like the *practice* in Panajachel. Thus there is a tendency toward the formation of what approximate social classes in Chichicastenango. A relatively few families are not only wealthy, but have a monopoly of the respect that comes with the performance of ritual functions, and have as well a monopoly of political power. Furthermore, in Chichicastenango there is a strong tendency for these wealthy families to intermarry among themselves. As a result, they are not only more distinctly set apart as an elite class, but there is some tendency for the

wealth and power of the community to remain in the same families for generation after generation. There is a sort of aristocracy. The contrast between Chichicastenango and Panajachel is striking, and particularly interesting in that one sees operating a single cultural mechanism with such different effect. By the contrast one understands why Panajachel cannot have social classes.

It becomes evident that the full answer to the questions posed for Panajachel requires not only all of the variety of data presented in this volume, but insights gained as well through comparative study. At the same time, unique as conditions in Panajachel may be, it seems likely that understanding of its social and economic system, in terms of questions like these, will help us to understand mechanisms operative in other societies, including our own. That is the expectation, at least, on which anthropologists base their method.

APPENDIX 1

DOCUMENT RELATING TO LABOR

List of Tasks and Number of Man-days¹ Required for the Crops Grown in the Town of Panajachel, Dept. of Sololá

Milpa:

New land:

Clearing 1 *cuerda* of the stony land of the hills------------------------ 2 days.

Making a fire-lane around 5 *cuerdas*-- 1 day.

Burning 5 *cuerdas*------------------ Do.

Old land: Stubbling the field (*rastrojear*), 1 *cuerda* in------------------------- Do.

All land:

Cleaning the field (*chaporrear*), 1 *cuerda* in------------------------ Do.

Planting the maize, 2 *cuerdas* in----- Do.

Replanting ungerminated seeds, 10 *cuerdas* in---------------------- Do.

First cultivation (*limpio*) of 1 *cuerda* bad land in the delta------------- 2 days.

Second cultivation of 1 *cuerda* bad land in the delta------------------ Do.

Harvesting 2 *cuerdas* far from town-- 1 day.

Three trips carrying maize to the house in------------------------ Do.

Stacking 10 net-bags of maize in granary--------------------------- Do.

(General harvest per *cuerda*: 3-mesh bags, or loads)

Truck Farming:

Making *tablones* for growing vegetables (8 *tablones* each 3 *varas* wide by 32 *varas* long are made from 1 *cuerda* of land):

Scraping 1 *cuerda*-------------------- 2 days.

Watering 1 *cuerda* before making *tablones*-------------------------- 1 day.

Hoeing and preparing 1 *tablón*------- 2 days.

Onion Seedlings (in *tablones*):

Applying fertilizer to 1 *tablón*-------- Do.

Planting and covering with leaves, 1 *tablón*------------------------- Do.

First cultivation, 1 *tablón*----------- 4 days.

Second cultivation, 1 *tablón*--------- Do.

Pulling up seedlings of 1 *tablón* and preparing them for transplanting-- Do.

(Seedlings are watered every day for 45 days during the dry season; then for 15 days they are watered every 3 days.)

Truck Farming—Continued

Transplanting Onions:

Smoothing and planting 1 *tablón*----- 2 days.

Watering 2 *cuerdas* of onions-------- 1 day.

First cultivation of 1 *tablón*---------- 2 days.

Second cultivation of 1 *tablón*-------- Do.

Pulling up onions of 1 *tablón* and arranging in bunches-------------- Do.

(Onions remain 4 months in the *tablón* and are watered twice weekly.)

Garlic (in *tablones*):

Preparing the seed for 1 *cuerda*------ Do.

Planting 1 *tablón*-------------------- 1 day.

One (only) cultivation of 1 *tablón*---- 2 days.

Watering two *cuerdas*--------------- 1 day.

Pulling up and carrying home of garlic of 1 *tablón*----------------------- Do.

Before selling, braiding 15 bunches--- Do.

(1 *tablón* produces 40 bunches. Garlic is watered twice weekly, and always sunned 5 days before braiding.)

Black ground-beans (in *tablones*):

Planting 1 *cuerda* of beans---------- 2 days.

One (only) cultivation of 1 *cuerda*--- 3 days.

Watering 2 *cuerdas*------------------ 1 day.

Pulling up and carrying home dried beans of 1 *cuerda*----------------- Do.

Sunning and threshing beans of 1 *cuerda*-------------------------- 2 days.

(Black ground-beans remain in the *tablones* 3 months; they are watered twice weekly.)

Black pole-beans (in *tablones*):

(Same time as for ground-beans with the following additional.)

Finding and bringing poles for 1 *tablón*------------------------- Do.

Placing the poles in 1 *tablón*----- 1 day.

(Black pole-beans remain in the *tablones* 4 months; watered twice weekly.)

Cabbage, Beets, Turnips, Lettuce, Metabel, Swiss chard (in *tablones*): Require the same work as the growing of onion seedlings and their transplanting------

---

¹ The time is figured on the basis of what an industrious, full-grown man can do. The *cuerda* is always 32 *varas* square.

Truck Farming—Continued

Carrots (in *tablones*): Same as for growing onion seedlings, omitting the 2d cultivation; watered the same as onions; remain 4 months in the *tablones*.

Cucumbers (in *tablones*):
Planting and fertilizing 1 *tablón*_____ Do.
Cultivation (only one) of 1 *tablón*____ Do.
(Remain in *tablones* 3 months; watered twice weekly.)

Tomatoes (in *tablones*):
First seedlings are made just as with onions; transplanted in new *tablones* with same tasks as for planting sweet *pepinos*, below. Watered same as *pepinos*.
1 cultivation (only): 2 *tablones*, with ridges_____ Do.
(Tomatoes remain in *tablones* 3 months.)

Sweet *pepinos* (by *cuerdas*):
Scraping 1 *cuerda*_____ Do.
If land turned over, 1 *cuerda*_____ 4 days.
Digging the holes in 1 *cuerda*_____ 2 days.
Bringing and applying fertilizer, 1 *cuerda*_____ Do.
Planting 1 *cuerda*_____ 1 day.
Watering 1 *cuerda* (done twice weekly) Do.
Cultivating and ridging the mounds of each plant of 1 *cuerda*_____ 2 days.
(Cultivating done monthly; fruit harvested after 1 year).

When the plants bear, fences are made:
Finding posts for 1 *cuerda*_____ 1 day.
Planting posts for 1 *cuerda*_____ Do.
Finding reeds for tying poles and canes_____ Do.
Cutting and hauling cornstalks to fence 1 *cuerda*_____ 5 days.
Building the fence around one cuerda_____ 3 days.

Sweet cassava and sweetpotatoes: (in furrows 32 varas long):
Making 2 furrows_____ 1 day.
1st cultivation of 4 furrows_____ Do.
2d cultivation of 4 furrows_____ Do.
(Remain 6 months in ground; watered twice weekly).

Coffee:
Planting:
Opening 25 holes_____ Do.
Uprooting 50 plants with dirt_____ Do.
Carrying 100 plants a distance of 1 km_____ Do.
Planting 100 plants_____ Do.
(The shade trees require the same amount of work as the planting of the coffee itself.)

Coffee—Continued

Harvesting:
Cutting (picking) 1 50-pound sugar sackful of berries_____ Do.
Husking and picking-over 1 50-pound sackful_____ Do.
Washing 4 50-pound bags of husked coffee_____ Do.
(Washed coffee should be sunned for 5 days.)

Fruit trees always require a little work, such as removing the parasites from the branches and harvesting such fruits as Spanish plums, cross sapodillas, avocado, *limas*, oranges, etc. For the vegetable pear plants trellises must be made to raise the branches, etc.

The work in this town is not done in the same time as that in other pueblos because on every piece of land we have more than one thing planted, and we must do each task very slowly so as not to harm the things growing. Those things which require only three or four months to grow in the *tablones* are planted more than once a year:

Onions are planted three times a year.
Garlic is planted twice a year.
Black beans are planted twice a year.

It must be remembered that some tasks require more than one worker: cleaning the onions, clearing land in the hills, etc. Making up the accounts, it can be seen that only the *tablones* of one *cuerda* of onions give many man-days of work.

Every Friday, Tuesday, or other day of the week all must go to the markets of other towns to sell the products of our fields.

There are some who fatten animals such as steers, cows for milk, sheep, etc., and it takes part of their time to give the necessary care to the animals.

We make our houses in the form of ranchos, and for these we must go out some days to the country to find lumber, reed, cane, thatch, etc., and it takes time to build the houses.

Firewood is very important in our homes, especially in winter; we must prepare it on rather a large scale to save ourselves the worry when it rains much.

In the summer we must go to fix up the irrigation ditches of the town, sometimes farther than one kilometer; because we all use this water to water our fields, it often takes longer than listed above.

The onion seed which we harvest here is so delicate that it takes much time and patience to cut it, transport it, dry it, and clean it; it is so little that much is required to make up a pound. (This is aside from the time it has been in the *tablones*, its watering, fertilizing, and care given it against afflictions it may suffer.)

Dated, Panajachel, August, 1937.

[Signed by all the Indians]

APPENDIX 2

COMMODITY PRICES AND INDEX

The following alphabetical list of commodities is included for convenience in reference. Most items mentioned in the text are included in the list, and the page numbers refer to discussions in the text, both of prices and of consumption. These references are not repeated in the general index.

Prices of commodities in Guatemala City, where they are available, are listed. These have three sources, identified with asterisks, daggers, and double daggers, respectively:

* *Memorias de Hacienda y Crédito Público* for the years 1938, 1939, and 1940, tables 26, 38, and 57 on pages 597–598, 699–702, and 728–730, respectively. These tables give Guatemala City monthly prices of a few commodities over a period of years; among the three are given prices for the years 1935 to 1940, inclusive. In the following list minimum, maximum, and average prices are recorded for both the entire period of 6 years and

(**) For the 1 year, 1936.

(†) Tables 25, 37, and 56 on pages 596, 698, and 727 respectively, of the same *Memorias*, give monthly prices of "articles of first necessity" in Guatemala City for the year

of the *Memoria*. In cases where these data are used in the following list, the maximum, minimum, and average prices are given for the 3 years 1938, 1939, and 1940 combined.

(‡) The newspaper *El Imparcial*, Guatemala, at intervals, usually weekly, from April 3, 1937 to August 21, 1937, published current prices in the Central Market in Guatemala City. (The feature probably began before the initial date mentioned, but issues of the newspaper before then are not available to me; it was omitted after August 21, although it may have been resumed later.) Since I have records for only 5 months, obviously the "maximum" and "minimum" figures given in the table are not necessarily absolute for the year, and the average of the weekly figures are not necessarily averages for the year.

In the list are included some commodities without their prices either in Panajachel or in Guatemala City. This is done so that most commodities known to enter into the economy of Panajachel may be found listed in one place. Commodities that are not purchased, such as houses and the products of the women's looms, are not, however, included.

Price list and index

Commodity	Panajachel, 1936				Guatemala City				Pages in text
	Unit	Average normal	Minimum	Maximum	Unit	Average	Minimum	Maximum	
Alligator meat	Pound	$0.25	$0.25	$0.25					137, 172.
Amaranth	Pound bunch	.01	.00½	.01½	Bunch	‡$0.00¾	$0.00½	$0.01	173.
Anise	Ounce	.01½							130, 131, 135, 137, 171.
Anotta	do	.09			Pound	‡1.37	.90	1.60	135, 137, 171.
		Number	*Number*	*Number*					
Apples	For 1 cent	5	8	3					138, 143.
Avocados	do	3	5	2	1	‡.017	.01	.02	125, 127, 135, 138.
Axheads	Each	$1.15	$1.00	$1.25					27, 48, 90, 148.
Bags:									
Large mesh	do	.15	.10	.25					11, 49.
Small, Sololá type	do	.15	.10	.25					138.
		Number							
Balsamito seed	For 1 cent	3							135.
Bananas:									
"Apple type"	Stem	$0.03	$0.03	$0.04					
"Bird type"	do	.03	.03	0.04					
"Pig type"	do	.05	.04	.05					135.
Local	do	.07	.07	.08					56, 115, 122, 133 fn., 135, 136, 138, 143, 174.
		Number	*Number*	*Number*					
"Silk" coast	For 1 cent	4	8	2	100	‡.25	.20	.30	174.
Basins, tin:									
Large	Each	$0.20	$0.10	$0.30					
Small	do	.07	.05	.10					
Baskets:									
Large	do	.08	.06	.10					} 11, 134, 138.
Small	do	.01	.00½	.02					
Beans									12, 21, 25, 44, 46, 47–48, 52, 55, 82, 101 fn., 102, 122, 129, 134, 135, 138, 140, 141, 143, 169–170.
Dry, black	Pound	.016	.01¼	.02	Hundredweight	{ *2.03½ **1.72	1.17 1.17	3.81 2.57	
Dry, piloy	do	.01½							
Dry, red	do	.016	.01¼	.02	Hundredweight	†2.23	1.48	3.56¼	
Dry, white	do	.02	.01½	.02½	do	†2.23	1.48	3.56¼	
Beans, green	Pound measure	.01¼	.01	.01½	Pound	‡.05	.04	.10	52, 54, 92, 104, 109 fn, 110, 113–114, 121, 122, 127, 137, 143, 173.

Price list—Continued

Commodity	Price								Pages in text
	Panajachel, 1936				Guatemala City				
	Unit	Average normal	Mini-mum	Maxi-mum	Unit	Average	Mini-mum	Maxi-mum	
Beds	Each	$1.00	$0.75	$1.25					147.
Beef									22, 122, 134, 142, 172.
With bone	Pound	.05	.05	.05	Pound	‡$0.10	$0.06	$0.14	141.
Without bone	do	.08	.08	.08					
Beer	12-oz. bottle	.15	.12	.18					23.
Beeswax, black	1-inch ball				Pound	‡.50	.16	.20	
Beets									54, 114, 127, 130.
Large	Dozen	.01½	.01	.02					
Small	do	.00¾	.00½	.01		‡.12	.05	.15	
Belts, leather	Each	.25	.20	.30					150, 158.
Blankets, large (light)	do	1.25	.90	1.50					30, 175, 176.
Blanket (rodilleras)									11, 150, 158, 175, 176.
Coarse	Each	.70	.50	.85					
Fine	do	1.25	1.00	1.50					
Blouses, ready-made									
Girls'	Each		.30						
Women's	do		.50						26, 97, 151.
Bottles, empty, 24-ounce size.	do	.10							
Boxes, wood (gasoline)	do	.10							
Bread	1-ounce roll	.01	.01	.01					23, 96, 101, 102, 134, 135, 137, 138, 141, 171, 174.
Brooms, without handles	Each	.03½	03	.04					
Cabbage									44, 52, 54, 114, 122, 127, 130, 135, 138, 173.
Large	Each	.01½	.01	.02					
		Number	*Number*	*Number*					
Small	For 1 cent	3	3	2	1	‡.06	.04	.01	
Calzoncillo:									
Men's	} Each	{ $0.40	$0.38	$0.42					150, 151, 158.
Boys'		.25	.10	.32					
Calzones									153.
Men's									150, 151, 160, 202.
Boys'									158.
Candles									21, 27, 109, 116, 142, 176, 177, 178.
Paraffin	Pound	.30	.30	.30					
Tallow	25 pounds	.55	.50	.60					
Wax	Pound	.25	.25	.25					
Candy									135, 174.
Bocadillas (cocoanut)	Piece 2 by 1½ by ¼ inches.	.00½							
		Number	*Number*	*Number*					
Sugar	For 1 cent	5							
Carmelos panela	do	8							
Molasses (alfanique)	Ounce piece	$0.01							
Canes (bamboo lengths)	100	.40	.33	.45					144, 145, 146, 147–148.
		Number	*Number*	*Number*					
Carrots									44, 52, 54, 114, 130, 135, 138, 173.
Large	Dozen for 1 cent	1½	2	1					
Small	do	2½	3	2	Dozen	‡¾₁₀	.03	.12	
Carrying cloth					‡.04¾₁₀				153.
Totan., girls'	} Each	{ $0.35							
Totan., women's		.50							151, 153, 159.
Carrying frames (cacastes)	do	.16	$0.15	$0.20					
Chairs	do	.10	.05	.15					11, 147.
Chests, wooden		.50							147, 174.
Chichipate	Pound								137, 171.
Chickens	Each (2 pounds)	.20	.15	.30					14, 25, 93, 117–118, 122, 131, 134, 135, 136, 137, 138, 142, 171.
Chickpeas					Hundredweight	†2.90	2.62½	03.37½	
Chipilín	Pound bunch	.01	.01	.01					173.
Chocolate tablets	{ Ounce piece	01	01	01					134, 138, 141, 170–171, 181.
	{ Pound	.12	.12	.12	Pound	‡.16	.12	.20	
Cidras	Each	.01							138.
Cigarettes	Package of 12	.02	.02	.02					135, 136, 137, 181.
(Cheap)	Package of 27	.05	.05	.05					
Cigars	Each	.01	.01	.01					136, 137, 138, 176, 181.
Cinnamon (sticks)	Ounce	.02	.02	.02	Hundredweight	†72.60	55.00	90.00	135.
Cintula	Pound	.12	.10	.15					55, 127, 135, 137, 171.
Coconuts	Each	.05	.04	.06					138.
Coffee									12, 27, 40–44, 55–56, 60, 82, 84, 91, 93, 97, 99, 101, 102, 103, 104, 105, 107, 114–115, 122, 123, 128, 131, 134, 135, 141, 170, 185, 186.
Beans, in shell	Hundredweight	6.00							135, 136, 137.
Beans, shelled	Pound	.05	.04	.06	Hundredweight	{ *4.93	3.00	7.12	
						*4.69	4.50	5.00	
Beverage	8-ounce cup	.00½	.00½	.00½					
Ground	Ounce	.01½	.01½	.01½	Pound	†.11	.09	.12	135, 137, 141.
Seedlings	Each	.01¼	.01½	.01					
Coffins, full size		5.00	4.00	25.00					179.
Col	12-ounce bunch	.01	.01	.01					173.
Combs									135, 136.
Composition	Each	.07	.06	.08					
Wooden		.02							

Price list—Continued

Commodity	Panajachel, 1936				Guatemala City				Pages in text
	Unit	Average normal	Mini-mum	Maxi-mum	Unit	Average	Mini-mum	Maxi-mum	
Cookies (rosquitos)	Ounce	$0.00½	$0.00½	$0.00½					135, 136, 174.
Cordoncillo	Ounce bunch								
Coriander	Bunch of 5	.00½	.00½	.00½					55, 173.
Corn									11, 12, 16, 18, 21, 24, 25, 30, 37, 40, 44, 45, 46, 47, 48, 49–52, 56, 92, 101, 102, 104, 106, 109–110, 118, 119, 120, 121, 122, 128–129, 131, 133 fn., 134, 135, 136, 137, 138, 139–40, 141, 142, 144, 149 fn. and 149, 167, 169, 181, 183.
Gruel (atole)	8-ounce gourd	.00½	.00½	.00½					
Highland	Pound	.01¼	.00¾	.01½	Hundredweight	*$1.28 **1.09	$0.81¼ .79	$2.50 1.79	
Husks	Bunch of 50	.01	.01	.01	Pound	‡.15	.15	.15	
Cotton, seeded									11, 134, 152.
Coyoles	For 1 cent	*Number* 8							135, 138.
Crabs	Bunch of 4	$0.02	.02	.02					133, 136 fn., 138, 142, 172.
Cross-sapodillas	For 1 cent	*Number* 3	*Number* 5	*Number* 2					56, 115, 138, 143.
Cross-sapodilla seed									33, 135.
Cuajilotes									138.
Cuchinas									138.
Cucumbers	Each	$0.01							55, 138, 173.
Cups									134.
China	Each	.20	$0.15	$0.30					174.
Enamelware	do	.12	.04	.20					23.
Pottery	do	.02	.01½	.02½					
Custard-apples	For 1 cent	*Number* 3	*Number* 4	*Number* 2					173.
Dogs									21, 117, 121, 131, 164, 169.
Doors, wooden	Each	$1.50							144, 146.
Drawers:									
Boys'	Pair	.15							
Men's	do	.25							
Earrings		.10							
Eggs	Each	.01¼	$0.00¾	$0.02	Dozen	‡.17	.12	.28	118, 122, 135, 136, 138, 141, 172.
Fans									135.
Files (knife sharpeners)		.15							175.
Firewood	Load	.08							30, 33, 38, 57, 93, 101, 102, 103, 104, 105, 106, 133, 138, 148, 174, 176.
Fish									133, 136 fn.
Dried sea	Pound	.20	.20	.20		‡.24	.20	.35	135, 137, 138, 172.
Fresh lake Mojarra (large)	Each Pound	.07 .20	.02 .20	.12 .20		‡.19	.16	.20	142.
Fresh lake (medium)	Straw of 4	.00¾	.00¾	.00¾					135, 136 fn., 142, 172.
Fresh lake (small)	Measure								137, 138.
Flour, wheat (native)					Hundredweight	‡4.23½	3.62½	5.21¼	23.
Fodder grass									138.
Forks, table	Each	.07	.04	.10					134, 174, 175.
Garlic heads									12, 44, 45, 46, 52, 54, 55, 92, 104, 112, 113, 122, 126, 127, 129, 135, 143, 173, 183.
Medium	Bunch	.04	.02	.06					
Large	60 heads	.08	.04	.13	Bunch	.21	.15	.25	
Garlic, cloves (smallest)	12 pounds	.28	.25	.30					137.
Ginger	Ounce								135, 171.
Gourds									11, 138.
Jicaras	Each	.05	.03	.06					
Toles									
Grandillas	For 1 cent	*Number* 10							135, 174.
Grinding stones	Each	$0.90	0.30	1.50					11, 56, 133 fn., 138, 148, 174.
Guavas									138.
Gunpowder	Ounce	.10	.10	.10					
Hammocks	Each	.50	.40	.75					135, 136, 174.
Handkerchiefs	do	.10	.04	.25					136, 151, 158.
Hats, straw									11, 133, 135, 136, 151, 153.
Boys' (coarse)	Each	.10	.05	.15					151.
Coarse	do	.18	.15	.20					151.
Fine	do	.30	.22	.40					
Head bands									151.
"Panajachel"	Each	.10	.08	.12					151, 153, 158.
"Totonicapan"	do	.16	.12	.20					
Hoe blades	do	.50	.45	.70					23, 27, 48, 49, 53, 90, 102, 134, 148.
Honey	24-ounce bottle	.05	.05	.05	Bottle	.12	.12	.12	56, 120, 141, 171.
Horsebeans					Hundredweight	2.04	1.75	2.25	136.
Huipiles, Toton. type									18, 150, 151, 152, 153–154, 159, 160.
Girls'	Each	{ .75	}						151.
Women's		{ 1.75	}						
Huskcherries	Pound	.01½	.01						54, 133 fn., 135, 137, 143, 172.
Incense									109, 116, 137, 176, 177, 178, 179.
Copal	Ounce	.03	.03	.03					135.
Estoraque (1)	Pound	.33							
Estoraque (2)	Ounce	.00¾	.00¾	.00¾					

Price list—Continued

Commodity	Panajachel, 1936				Guatemala City				Pages in text
	Unit	Average normal	Minimum	Maximum	Unit	Average	Minimum	Maximum	
Indigo plant									138.
Ink	Bottle	$0.10							
Inner-tube bands									135.
Jabilla									
Jackets (coats)	Each	1.00	$0.90	$1.50					151, 160.
Kerosene	24-ounce bottle	.08	.08	.08					134, 174.
Knives									174, 176.
Kitchen	Each	.20							
Pocket	do	.25							
Table	do	.12	.08	.18					134, 174.
Kohlrabi									54, 135, 138.
Lamps, tin	Each	0.08	0.06	0.10					127, 174, 175.
Lard	Pound	.12	.08	.16	Hundredweight	{*$14.39 / *11.42	$8.00 / 8.00	$22.25 / 14.50	22, 27, 56, 96, 133, 134, 137, 141, 142, 172.
Lard cracklings									133, 137, 172, 174.
Loose	Ounce	.01							172.
Pinas	do	.06½							172.
Pressed	Pound								137, 172.
Large fish									
Lentils					Hundredweight	†3.73	2.50	5.50	
Lettuce					Dozen	‡.14	.08	.20	54, 130, 135.
Limas	For 1 cent	*Number* 6	*Number* 8	*Number* 4					56, 115, 122, 125, 127, 128, 136, 138, 143.
Lime	Pound	$0.00½	$0.00½	$0.00½					11, 14, 33, 56, 134, 135, 136 fn., 137, 138, 167.
Limes	For 1 cent	*Number* 10	*Number* 33	*Number* 1	100	‡.21	.02	.35	115, 135.
Linseed					Hundredweight	1 †6.65	1 5.75	8.00	135.
Liquor, *alumbique*	24-ounce bottle	$0.50	$0.50	$0.50					12, 23, 98, 134, 138, 177, 178–179, 180, 181.
Loom (strap, sticks)	Set	.40	.30	.50					152.
Lumber									33–34, 133, 145, 146.
Boards (8½' x 11" x 1")	Dozen	.90	.80	1.00					
"2 x 4" (8½' x 1½")	do	.60	.55	.65					
Planks (8½' x 11" x 1½")	do	1.80	1.60	2.00					
Other	Running foot (11 inches)	.01							
Calzentos	Dozen	.25	.25	.25					
Machetes	Each	.60	.40	1.00					23, 27, 48, 49, 90, 134, 136, 148, 175.
Maguey fiber	Dozen bunches	.10	.08	.12					145.
Maicenas									138.
Mangos	For 1 cent	*Number* 5	*Number* 8	*Number* 3					115, 138, 143.
Matches	Box of 45	$0.01½	$0.01½	$0.01½					135, 176.
Mats									11, 134, 133 fn., 135, 136 fn., 175.
Coarse type	Each	.10	.08	.15					
Fine type:									
Large	do	.60	.40	.75					
Small	do	.20	.15	.40					
Melocotones									135, 138.
Membrillos									138, 143.
Milk					Liter	‡.08	.08	.08	21, 23, 120, 131, 134, 164.
Miltomates (huskcherries)	Pound	.01½	.01	.02					138.
Mint									55.
Mirrors, small hand	Each	.12½	.10	.15					136.
"Mulberry" herb	Pound bunch	.00½	.00½	.00½					173.
Mushrooms									137.
Nances									137.
Napkins, small cloth	Each	.20	.15	.25					
Necklaces	do	.25							
Needles	do	.01	.00½	.01½					136.
Onions, green									12, 19, 29, 44–45, 52, 53–54, 55, 92, 99, 110–112, 114, 116, 122, 125, 126, 127, 129, 130, 135, 138, 142–143, 173, 183.
Large	}100	{ .11	.06	.15	}100	‡.39	.25	.60	54.
Medium		.05	.03	.08					
Small		.02	.01	.03					
Oranges		*Number*	*Number*	*Number*					56, 115, 122, 125, 127, 128, 135, 138, 143.
Sour	For 1 cent	11	15	7					115.
Sweet	do	4	10	2	1	‡.01½	.01	.02	115.
Orégano									135.
Padlocks	Each	$0.08							
Papayas									56, 115, 135, 173.
Local	Each	.01	$0.00½	$0.02					
Coast		.04	.02	.08	1	‡.08	.05	.10	
Paper:									
Tissue	Sheet	.00½	.00½	.00½					176.
Writing tablets	Each	.25	.25	.25					
Pataxtes									135, 138.
Paxtes, prepared									

1 2 years only.

INSTITUTE OF SOCIAL ANTHROPOLOGY PUBLICATION NO. 16

Price list—Continued

Commodity	Panajachel, 1936				Guatemala City				Pages in text
	Unit	Average normal	Minimum	Maximum	Unit	Average	Minimum	Maximum	
Peaches, season	For 1 cent	*Number* 8	*Number* 12	*Number* 4					56, 115, 138, 143, 173.
Peanuts, roasted	Ounce	$0.00½	$0.00½	$0.00½		‡$0.04	$0.03	$0.04	135, 136, 137, 174.
Pears									138, 143.
Peas (in pod)					Hundredweight	†7.68	4.00	16.75	54, 55, 130, 137.
Pencils	Each	.04	.04	.04					
Pen points	do	.05							
Pepinos									44, 45, 46, 52, 53, 55, 92, 114, 122, 127, 129, 130, 135, 138, 183.
Large	}100	{ .40	.30	.50	}				
Medium		.15	.10	.20					
Small		.08	.05	.10					
Pepitoria					Pound	‡.29	.28	.30	135.
Pepper de castillo	Ounce	.02	.02	.02	Hundredweight	†22.17	22.00	24.25	
Peppers									114, 136, 137, 141, 170.
Piquant	Ounce	0.00½	0.00½	0.00½	Hundredweight	5.57	6.00	43.75	
Piquant green ("7 broth")	2-ounce measure	.02			Pound	.04	.03	.05	135, 138, 170.
Piquant, "horse"									
Piquant, "chocolate"									
Piquant, "pico sanak"									
Piquant, "zambo"									
Piquant, "pasa"									
Piquant, "gobanero"									
Piquant, "chiltope"					Pound	‡.13	.07	.25	
Sweet, "guaque"									
Petaxte seed									
Photographs									181.
Pickax heads	Each	85.	.75	1.00					48, 53, 55, 102.
Pigs									14, 22, 93, 96, 117.
Grown									199.
Young									
Pimienta gorda									135.
Pineapples					1	‡.07	.03	.10	138.
Pinole									137.
Pitchers, china									135.
Pitchwood									133 ftn., 134, 135, 136, 138.
Plantains	Each	.00¾	.00½	.01	100	‡.83	.80	.90	135, 138, 173.
Plates, enamelware	do	.11	.10	.20					134, 135.
Pork	Pound	.08	.08	.08		‡.12½	.08	.20	122 fn., 133 ftn., 134, 136, 142, 172.
Pork ribs (cooked)									137.
Pork sausage (chorize)	½ ounce	.01	.01	.01					138.
Pork sausage (longaniza)									172.
Pork-blood sausage	½ pound	.03	.03	.03					135, 172.
Potatoes									135, 136, 137, 143, 173.
First grade	Pound	.04	.02	.08	Hundredweight	{ *2.59	1.94	3.75	
						**2.40	1.94	3.40	
Second grade	do	.03	.02	.06	do	†1.69	1.50	2.25	
Third grade	do	.02½	.01½	.04	do	†1.16	1.00	1.50	
Potato shoots									
Pots:									
Perforated									
Pitchers	Each	.05							
Water jars	do	.15	.08	.25					148–149.
Pots, bowls	do	.08							11, 25–26, 138, 174, 175.
Pots, cooking									11, 136, 138.
Largest	Each	1.00	.75	1.10					
Large apastes	do	.50	.40	.60					
Medium apastes	do	.15	.10	.25					
Small apastes	do	.05	.02	.08					
Prickly pears	For 1 cent	*Number* 4	*Number*	*Number*					138, 173.
Radishes									44, 52, 54, 114, 130, 135, 138.
Large	do	14	15	12					
Small	do	18	20	16	Dozen	‡.01½	.01	.02	
Raincoats	Each	$4.00							
Raw cotton									136, 137.
Brown									
White									
Rice					Hundredweight	{ *4.07	2.56¼	5.60	}21, 135, 137.
						**3.75	3.37	3.95	
Rice-and-milk beverage	8-ounce glass	.01							122, 135, 136, 174.
Rings, finger		.10							
Rockets, quality	Dozen	.80	$0.60	$1.00					177.
Rodilleras									160.
Coarse:									
Boys'	Each	.75							158.
Men's	do	1.00							150, 158.
Fine:									
Boys'	do	1.40	1.20	1.60					
Men's	do	1.75	1.50	2.00					150.
Rope, heavy		.04							34, 135, 138.
Rope measuring cord	Each	.15							
Rose-apples									138.
Rubber bands (of inner tube)									135.

Price list—Continued

Commodity	Panajachel, 1936				Guatemala City				Pages in text
	Unit	Average normal	Minimum	Maximum	Unit	Average	Minimum	Maximum	
Rue									55, 138, 173.
Salt	Pound	$0.01½	$0.01½	$0.02	Hundredweight	*$1.59 / **1.39	$0.88¾ / 1.25	$2.40 / 1.46	11, 134, 135, 136, 137, 138, 170, 173.
Saltwort									138.
Sandals, high	Pair	.60							24, 30.
Sandals (caites)	____do	.20	.10	.40					11, 135, 136, 151, 158, 159.
		Number	*Number*	*Number*					
Sapodillas	For 1 cent	2	3	1					115, 135.
Sashes, Chichi, type:									
Boys'	Each	$0.08							
Men's	____do	.20							150, 153, 158.
Sashes, women's Totonicapan type	____do	.37½	$0.25	$0.40					151, 153, 159, 160.
Scissors	Pair	.20	.20	.20					
Sesame seed					Hundredweight	†$4.09	$3.00	$7.00	135.
"Seven shirts" herb	Pound bunch	.00½	.00½	.00½					173.
Shells (shotgun)	Box	.25							
Shirts									136, 158.
Boys'	Each	.16	.15	.20					153.
Men's ready-made									150–151, 160.
Fine	Each	.40	.30	.50					
Coarse	____do	.24	.20	.28					
San Pédro	____do	1.25	1.00	1.50					
Men's Sololá	____do	2.00	1.75	2.25					
Shot	Pound	.08							
Shotguns	Each	1.00							32, 133 ftn., 174.
Shrimp, dry	Pound	.25	.25	.25	Hundredweight	†19.23	15.00	25.00	135, 136, 137.
Sickles	Each	.15	.10	.25					
Skirt material									26, 94, 151, 154, 159.
Sololá Pédro	Varas	.37½	.33	.40					11.
Tie-dyed type	Piece	2.00	1.50	3.00					151.
Soap, black	1½-inch ball / 3-inch ball	.01 / .03	}		Pound	‡.13½	.13½	.13½	21, 22, 27, 137, 142, 176.
Soft drinks:									
Carbonated	8-ounce bottle	.06	.05	.07					
Pineapple	8-ounce glass	.01	.01	.01					
Iced	____do	.02	.02	.02					
		Number	*Number*	*Number*					
Spanish plums									56, 57, 115, 122, 137.
De corona	For 1 cent	15	20	10					
De chicha	____do	25	35	15					
De petapa	____do	20	27	12					
De panchey	____do	20	27	12					
De tamalito	____do	50	40	60					
De mico	Measure for 1 cent	50	40	60					
Spindles	Each	$0.01½	$0.01	$0.02					152.
Spoons	____do	.07	.04	.10					134.
Squash									21, 47, 49, 52, 110, 121, 130, 135, 138, 173.
Ayote	Each	.01½			1	‡.08	.03	.10	48, 52, 173.
Chilacayote	____do	.03							
Guicoy	____do	.01½			1	‡.10	.05	.20	48, 52, 173.
Seed									137.
Ayote	}Measure								
Chilacayote									
Starch (yuquilla)					Hundredweight	†2.62	2.18½	4.50	135.
Steels	Each	.05	.03	.10					
Sugar									134, 135, 137, 138.
Low refined (panela)	Tapa of 3 pounds	.08	.07	.09	350 pounds	*8.22 / **6.39	4.87 / 4.87	11.87 / 8.25	134, 135, 136, 138, 141, 170. 170.
White	Pound	.05	.05	.05	Hundredweight	*3.76 / **3.75	3.65 / 3.75	4.00 / 3.75	
Sugarcane	Foot / Section	.00¾	.00½	.01					107, 135, 136, 138.
Sweet cassava	Pound	.01¾	.01	.02	1	‡.02⁷⁄₁₀	.02	.05	44, 52, 55, 114, 130, 137, 173.
Sweetpotatoes	____do	.01	.00¾	.01½	1	‡.03	.02	.06	44, 52, 55, 114, 129, 130, 135, 137, 173.
Swiss chard	Bunch of 8	.01	.01	.01					54, 135, 173, 175.
Tables, large	Each	.22	.20	.25					11, 137 ftn., 147, 174.
Tamales									
Tamales									24, 106, 122, 133 ftn., 135, 136, 167, 172.
With beans									24, 138.
With pork									138.
Thatch	100 bunches	.80							133, 144, 145, 146, 200.
Tiles, roof	1,000	8.00	6.00	10.00					134, 145, 147, 200.
Tin pitchers									
		Number	*Number*	*Number*					
Tins (5-gallon gas)	Each	12	10	15					134.
Tomatoes	Pound	$0.01	$0.00½	$0.14	Pound	†.08	.03	.15	14, 53, 55, 129, 130, 135, 137, 139, 143, 172.
Toronjas									138.

Price list—Continued

Commodity	Price								Pages in text
	Panajachel, 1936				Guatemala City				
	Unit	Average normal	Mini-mum	Maxi-mum	Unit	Average	Mini-mum	Maxi-mum	
Tortillas_____		*Number*	*Number*	*Number*		*Number*	*Number*	*Number*	12, 24, 95, 97, 106, 138, 153, 167, 170, 174.
Dry corn_____	For 1 cent_____	8	6	10	For 1 cent_____	‡6	6	6	
Fresh corn_____									
Totoposte_____									138.
Towels_____	Each_____	$0.20							175.
Troughs for grinding stone___	Set_____	.10							174, 175.
Tump straps_____	Each_____	.13	$0.08	$0.17					94, 174, 175.
Turkeys_____	Each (6 pounds)___	.75	.60	1.10					21, 22, 118, 131, 142, 171–172.
Turnips_____									52, 54, 114, 130, 135, 136, 138, 173.
Large_____	Dozen_____	.00½	.00½	.01					208.
Small_____	___do_____	.004	.003	.005	Dozen_____	$0.08	$0.02	$0.15	
Vegetables_____		*Number*	*Number*	*Number*					27, 41, 54, 55, 114, 122, 123, 126, 127, 128, 129, 134, 142–143.
Vegetable pears_____	For 1 cent_____	3	5	1	100_____	‡.54	.30	.90	
Vegetable pear root_____	Pound_____	$0.01½	$0.01	$0.02		‡.16	.06	.30	
Vegetable pear shoots_____									57, 93, 135, 173.
Vinegar_____	24-ounce bottle___	.06							56.
Warping boards_____	Each_____	.33							152, 175.
White sapodilla_____	For 1 cent_____	5	8	3					93, 115, 136, 138, 143.
Woolen cloth (for gabán)____	Vara_____	.33	.33	.33					22, 23, 93, 138, 150, 154, 158, 160, 202.
Yard goods_____									135, 136.
For woman's blouse_____	Blouse_____	.41½	.40	.43					
For drawers_____	Vara_____	.13	.13	.13					11, 134, 151, 153.
Yarn, cotton, red, green, yellow, lavender.	{Ounce_____	.04							
	{Pound_____	.67							
Yarn:									
Cotton, thread, black No. 10.	Spool_____	.08	.06	.10					11, 26, 134, 135, 136.
Cotton, tie-dyed_____	Pound_____	.67							
Cotton, white_____	___do_____	.33							
Silk_____	Ounce_____	.20							134.
Zacatinta (dye plant)_____									138.

APPENDIX 3
HOUSEHOLDS IN ORDER OF WEALTH

The following list of Panajachel Indian households includes all that were in the community studied in 1936. The families are ordered according to wealth (rich to poor) as judged by the following:

(1) The opinions of two Indians, labeled SY and BC, who are themselves found in places 49 and 58, respectively, in the list. Independently they graded each of the families on a scale of from 1 to 100, whereupon the households could be put in order of wealth. The results are seen in columns 2 and 3 of the final list, where the numbers represent the order of wealth (according to the two who gave judgment) and not the grades given.

(2) Their standing in the scales of the value of land owned and of land controlled, as shown in columns 3 and 4.

(3) Other indications of wealth, such as houses and stock and sources of income other than agriculture. The number and kinds of houses, of domestic animals, and of fruit trees cannot be shown in the list because so much data would make it even more unwieldy than it is.

Whenever there was doubt, I trusted the informants' judgment—where it was clear. Obviously, neither they nor I can tell how accurate the judgments are, but clearly the extremes are well defined and families are not far out of place.

Data concerning the number of persons (men, women, boys, girls, and infants) are included in the list because they help to explain in many cases why families are richer or poorer than their land-holdings would indicate. For the same reason, special occupations are noted.

The numbers of Panajacheleño households run from 1 to 132; it will be noted that the two polygynous cases are each treated by bracketing the households in spite of the fact that informants judged each separately. The foreign-Indian households are included in the list in their places on the wealth scale, but they are given intermediate numbers preceded by "F." Foreign Indians or foreign Indian families attached as "servants" to Panajacheleño (and in one case a foreign) households are not numbered separately.

The order number (column 1) is the key to the numbering of Indian houses on map 3.

Order No.	Judgment of—		Land		Number in family						Special occupations
	SY	BC	Owned	Controlled	Total	M	W	B	G	I	
1	1	1	1	1	9	4	3	2	------	1	
2	3	3	2	2	10	2	3	2	2	1	
3	2	1	8	9	7	1	3	1	------	2	
4	6	5	4	3	6	2	2	1	------	1	
5	4	5	5	10	10	3	4	------	------	3	Dairying business.
6	7	4	60	40	6	2	2	------	------	2	Shaman.
7	10	7	14	15	11	3	4	------	------	4	Pig butcher.
8	13	9	7	8	5	4	1	------	------	------	Small dairying business.
9	11	14	3	6	6	3	2	------	------	1	
10	9	17	10	4	4	1	1	------	1	1	Shaman, bleeder.
11	14	10	11	36	10	3	5	------	1	1	Marimba player.
12	17	14	9	7	6	2	4	------	------	------	
13	20	8	29	12	4	1	1	1	1	------	
14	14	25	34	14	8	3	2	------	1	2	
					1	1					
(1) 15	24	10	40	38	8	3	1	2	2		Canoe business.
					1		1				
(1) 16	7	4	106	79	9	5	3	1	------	------	Midwife, curer.
17	24	10	15	17	8	4	3	1	------	------	Caponizer, bleeder, masseur.
18	5	16	17	26	8	2	3	------	2	1	
19	30	30	23	11	5	1	2	2	------	------	
20	12	40	16	18	2	1	1	------	------	------	
21	63	25	6	5	7	1	3	2	------	1	Curer.
22	16	17	37	32	6	2	2	1	------	1	
23	21	17	20	22	5	1	2	1	1	------	
24	23	18	22	24	5	3	1	------	1		Bleeder.
					1	1					
(1) 25	28	17	33	28	5	2	2	1	------	------	
26	19	23	73	65	6	3	3	------	------	------	
27	28	34	19	20	8	3	4	1	------	------	Marimba player.
28	30	34	55	51	3	1	1	1	------	------	Shaman.
29	39	29	25	21	5	2	1	1	------	1	

See footnotes at end of table, p. 219.

Order No.	Judgment of—		Land		Number in family						Special occupations
	SY	BC	Owned	Controlled	Total	M	W	B	G	I	
30	17	51	56	25	6	2	3	1			
31	61	23	28	33	6	1	2	1	1	1	
32	92	25	36	31	7	1	2		1	3	
33	24	36	65	61	3	1	1			1	
34	30	37	21	27	3	1	1		1		
35	30	66	35	30	11	4	3	1		3	
36	36	30	78	69	2	1	1				
37	36	51	99	74	3	1	1	1			Canoe business, marimba, baker, netter.
38	39	30	117	99	4	3	1				Shaman, bleeder.
39	39	37	119	116	6	2	1	2		1	Mason.
F39a	82	10	0	0	3	1	1				Full-time butcher.
40	99	40	12	16	5	1	2		1	2	
41	68	49	31	29	4	1	2		1		
42	39	53	49	46	8	3	3		2		
43	22	65	51	48	9	4	2	1		2	
44	30	66	52	49	7	2	2		1	2	Mason, carpenter.
45	58	25	67	63	3	2	1				Full-time butcher.
F45a	82	14	0	0	2	1	1				
46	39	66	26	34	5	2	1			2	
47	39	66	38	35	7	2	2		1	2	
48	24 / 78	40 / 40	58	54	11	1½ / 1½	2 / 2	1		2	Caponizer.
49	63	39	61	78	4	1	2		1		
50	39	66	97	82	3		1		2		
51	39	76	13	13	5	1	2	2			
52	39	76	24	23	3	1	1			1	
53	55	53	62	59	5	1	2			2	
[1]	---	---			3	1	1	1		1	
54	55	62	18	19	5	2	2			1	
55	88	30	45	44	7	2	1	1	1	2	Ladinoized teacher.
56	35	76	76	67	3	1	1				
57	36	82	43	43	4	1	1	2			
58	39	53	63	60	9	3	2	2		2	Pig butcher.
59	68	40	48	45	4	1	2	1			Mason; restaurateur
60	62	49	110	109	4	1	2			1	
61	63	53	41	41	4	1	1	1		1	
62	63	82	39	37	1		1				Curer, weaver.
63	68	53	42	42	6	1	2		1	2	Shaman.
64	68	63	53	50	5	3	1			1	
65	68	64	47	39	6	4	1	1			Shaman, bleeder.
66	74	40	96	93	7	4	1	2			Shaman.
67	92	40	46	53	3	1	1	1			
68	92	40	92	88	3	1	1	1			
F68a	82	53	[2]	[2]	4	1	1			2	Full-time mason.
69	88	53	54	92	4	2	2				
70	99	53	91	87	9	3	4		1	1	
71	68	66	84	105	6	3	2		1		Weaver.
72	98	75	27	56	3	1	1			1	
F72a	99	75	0	0	2	1	1				
73	39	76	112	111	6	1	1	1		2	
74	74	76	74	66	5	2	1			2	
75	74	76	86	77	6	4	2				Curer.
76	39	85	116	68	4	3	1				
F76a	39	93	[3]	[3]	5	1	1	1	1	1	
77	39	93	98	102	3	1	1		1		
78	57	93	57	52	3	1	1			1	
79	78	85	68	64	2	1	1				Flutist.
80	78	87	85	76	3	1	1	1			Do.
81	99 / 151	53 / 140	89	84	9	½ / ½	3 / 1	2	1	1	Midwife, weaver. / Barber, adobe maker
82	78	87	105	103	5	1	1	2		1	
83	63	93	44	98	2	1	1				
84	82	93	59	55	5	1	1	1	1	1	Shaman.
85	92	93	70	58	5	1	1	2		1	Weaver.
F85a	96	84	[4]	[4]	8	2	3	2			
86	99	87	77	75	6	2	2	2		1	Midwife, weaver, bleeder
87	39	103	102	94	8	1	3	1	3		
F87a	39	110	[5]	[5]	4	1	1			2	
88	74	103	64	71	4	1	1			1	
89	58	110	82	73	4	1	1		1	1	
90	60	110	81	72	4	1	2			1	
F90a	82	110	0	0	5	2	1		1	1	Carpenter.
91	88	108	101	85	4	1	1		1	1	
92	88	121	32	57	8	2	5		1		Shaman.
93	99	99	30	97	6	3	1		1	1	Weaver.
94	99	99	114	113	6	2	1	1	1	1	
95	133	66	95	119	8	3	5				Shaman, bleeder.
96	133	73	71	89	7	1	3		1	2	
97	135	87	90	86	7	3	2	1	1		
98	135	87	104	101	3	1	1			1	
99	99	101	122	121	4	1	3				
100	99	103	109	108	3	1	2				Marimba player.
101	99	103	113	112	6	2	1	1	1	1	
102	99	107	88	83	6	2	2		1	1	
103	99	108	103	100	8	2	4	2			
104	99	115	111	110	3	2	1				Curer, weaver.
105	99	116	93	90	6	3	2			1	Ex-butcher.
106	99	116	100	96	3	2	1				Bleeder.
F106a	99	116	0	0	4	2	1		1		
107	135	114	76	62	4	1	1		1	1	
108	99	119	123	122	3	1	1				Messenger-carrier.
109	138	102	125	124	7	4	2	1			
110	96	121	50	47	3	1	1			1	
111	99	119	68	125	2	1	1				

See footnotes at end of table, p. 219.

Order No.	Judgment of—		Land		Number in family						Special occupations
	SY	BC	Owned	Con-trolled	Total	M	W	B	G	I	
112	99	121	79	70	3	1	1			1	
113	99	121	80	104	3		1	1	1		
114	99	121	115	114	6	1	4			1	
115	99	121	120	117	5	2	1	1	1		Restaurateur.
116	99	121	83	118	6	1	1			4	
117	99	121	121	120	4	1	1	1	1		
118	138	121	72	80	6	1	1	2		2	
F118a	138	121	0	0	5	1	1		1	2	Farm foreman.
119	99	131	75	95	3	1	1		1		
F119a	99	131	0	0	2		1		1		
F119b	138	131	0	0	3	1	1		1		Full-time mason.
120	138	131	87	81	2		2				
121	138	131	94	91	4	1	3				
122	138	131	107	106	2		2				Curer.
123	138	131	108	107	5		4	1			
124	138	131	118	115	4	1	1	1	1		
F124a	82	151	0	0	3	1	1			1	Pig butcher.
F124b	99	140	0	0	6	2	2			2	Full-time restaurateur.
125	99	140	124	123	7	1	2	2	1	1	Shaman.
126	99	140	0	0	5	2	2		1		
127	99	140	0	0	3	1	1			1	Drummer.
F127a	99	140	0	0	4	1	2			1	
F127b	99	140	0	0	2	1	1				
F127c	99	140	0	0	3	1	1			1	
128	147	121	0	0	3	1	1		1		
129	99	149	0	0	3	1	1	1			
F129a	147	140	0	0	5	1	2		2		
130	149	149	0	0	3	1	1			1	
131	151	131	0	0	2		1		1		
F131a	149	151	0	0	4	1	1		1	1	
F131b	151	151	0	0	2		1		1		
(1)					1		1				
F131c	151	154	0	0	2	1	1				
F131d	155	154	0	0	2	1	1				
132	155	154	0	0	3	1	1	1			Weaver.
F132a	155	154	0	0	5	1	2	1	1		

[1] Foreign servant(s).   [2] Land value: $13.50.   [3] Land value: $214.50.   [4] Land value: $19.50.   [5] Land value: $79.50.

GLOSSARY

The glossary is divided into three parts: the "General" glossary gives the meanings in Panajachel of Spanish terms used in the text. The glossaries of plants and animals include in alphabetical order all but the most common ones mentioned in the text, whether in English, Spanish, or Indian. Following each term is (1) the Panajachel Spanish equivalent of the English name used, if there is a Spanish equivalent; or (2) the Indian equivalent in the International Phonetic Alphabet if the term used is a translation or corruption, and (3) the scientific term. The botanical and zoological identifications are taken from Villacorta, 1926—indicated by (V); Mejiá, 1927 (M); Rojas, 1936 (R); Wisdom, 1940, unpublished addenda, (W), who credits identifications of plants in the Chorti region to Dr. Paul Standley of the Field Museum; and McBryde, 1940 (Mc), most of whose identifications are credited to literary sources, especially Standley, and a few to the University of California herbarium to which he brought specimens. Some animal identifications were taken from signs in the Zoological Park in Guatemala City.

GENERAL

Alambique, an *aguardiente* (hard liquor primarily of sugar) distilled in copper kettles.

Alcalde, mayor; a civil office, now legally nonexistent in Guatemala, whose functions, administrative and judicial, are now performed by the *intendente;* in Panajachel, the highest annually changing civil office in the Indian hierarchy.

Alquacil, constable; a civil officer with functions, in a small town like Panajachel, of messenger, laborer, janitor, and policeman.

Almul (or almud), dry weight measure for grains ranging from 8 to 17 pounds. In Panajachel 12 or 12.5 pounds.

Arroba, a unit of weight equal to 25 pounds.

Auxiliar, probably short for *regidor auxiliar,* auxiliary *regidor;* an office in the municipal government.

Ayudante, or **regidor ayundante,** assistant to a *regidor;* an office in the municipal government.

Banda, woven sash-belt; in Panajachel usually the kind made elsewhere and bought.

Barril, a liquid measure equal to 2 demijohns or 22 bottles.

Caballería, land measure equal to 64 *manzanas* or 110.464 acres.

Caites, sandals, usually made of a single sole with attached leather thongs which are passed between the first two toes and around the heel.

Calzón, drawers; in Panajachel usually the home-woven and sewed variety.

Calzoncillo, drawers; in Panajachel a long white variety that approaches trousers in appearance.

Cédula de vecindad, personal identification pocket booklet, required by law for every adult and issued by the *intendencia.*

Chica, a fermented drink made of *panela* and a variety of Spanish plums.

Cinta, ribbon; specifically the long strip worn in the woman's hairdress.

Cofrade, the highest official of a *cofradiá,* and an office in the politico-religious hierarchy.

Cofradía, confraternity; a group of men, consisting of a *cofrade* and two or three *mayordomos,* who have the stewardship of a saint for a year; also, the house of the *cofrade* where the saint is kept.

Colono, a laborer living permanently on a plantation.

Copal, a kind of incense that comes in small disks.

Corredor, porch of a house, consisting of the space formed by extension of the eave of one side of the house supported by posts.

Corte, a wrap-around shirt; also, a length of cloth.

Cuerda, land measure; in Panajachel usually 32 *varas* square (0.178 acre).

Culata, annex of a house consisting of an extension using a wall of the original house as one of its walls.

Faja, woven sash-belt; in Panajachel, usually the home-woven variety.

Fiscal, treasurer; an office of the religious hierarchy of the Indians.

Gabán, in Panajachel, a woolen cloak worn by some of the men.

Galera, a wall-less house structure consisting of a roof supported by posts.

Habilitador, a labor contractor.

Huipil, blouse, usually without tailored sleeves.

Intendente, the highest authority of a *municipio,* appointed by the President of the Republic.

Jefe politico, the administrative head of a Department, appointed by the President of the Republic.

Jefetura, the administrative building or office of the Department; office of the *jefe politico.*

Juzgado, court of law; town hall, now officially called *intendencia* instead.

Ladino, a non-Indian; a class of persons who speak Spanish, dress in European-type clothes and in general are representatives of the Spanish cultural tradition rather than the Indian.

Machete, a cutting tool; in Panajachel a factory-made knife with a short handle and a long blade.

Mancuerna, a package of 2 balls, or 4 *tapas* of *panela.*

Mandamientos, a system of enforced labor whereby employers sought and were given quotas of laborers.

Manzana, land measure, 100 *varas* square, equal to 1.736 acres.

Mayor, or **alquacil mayor,** an office in the municipal government and in the Indian hierarchy.

Mayordomo, majordomo, an official of a *cofradia*, and the politico-religious organization.

Milpa, cornfield, in which is grown principally corn, beans, and squash.

Monte, the territory outside of town; rural, whether wooded or not.

Mozo, common laborer, field hand.

Municipio, township, the smallest political unit into which Guatemala is divided.

Olla, an *aguardiente* (distilled liquor primarily of sugar) often flavored with fruit, in which earthenware vessels are utilized in the making.

Ornato, a head tax, the proceeds of which are spent on public works.

Panela, brown, noncrystallized sugar, usually sold in Panajachel in large balls, two of which form a *mancuerna*, half of each a *tapa.*

Patrón, an employer, usually for a long period of time.

Peso, in the old currency, a unit of money now equal to 1⅔ cents, in terms of which negotiations are still carried on.

Pinole, a beverage made, in Panajachel, of toasted and ground dry kernels of corn.

Principal, an elder of the community; a man who has passed through most of the offices of the politico-religious hierarchy.

Pueblo, town; the smallest category—followed by *villa* and *ciudad*—of community that is the seat of government of a municipio; in Panajachel applied to the whole delta portion as opposed to the *monte* districts.

Pulique, a meat dish; especially a sauce with which meat or fowl is served.

Quintal, a unit of weight equal to 100 pounds avoirdupois.

Recomendado, checked; an article left with somebody until called for.

Red, a mesh bag open at both ends, used to pack loads for transport and storage.

Regidor, councilman; an office in the municipal government and in the Panajachel legal and extralegal hierarchy.

Rodillera, a small woolen blanket worn by men—in Panajachel, wrapped around the waist and extending to the knees.

Rosquito, a kind of doughnut-shaped cookie of wheat flour.

Sacristán, sacristan; an official of the church and of the Panajachel religious hierarchy.

Sandalia, a sandal built more like a shoe than a *caite.*

Sute or **tzute,** a cloth worn as a headpiece.

Tablón, a garden bed; a rectangular raised bed, separated from others by gutters into which water for irrigation is admitted.

Tamal, a dumpling made of boiled and ground corn and often other ingredients, wrapped in leaves and steamed or boiled.

Tapa, half of a ball of *panela.*

Tarea, stint, a unit of work, usually the amount that a man can do in one day, but varying widely with the type of work.

Tortilla, a griddle cake of boiled and ground corn.

Totoposte, a large, much toasted tortilla carried on journeys

Vara, a Spanish linear measure of 36 Spanish inches or about 33 English inches.

Zarabanda, a public dance in a tavern or *cofradia*

PLANTS

Alusema. Not identified.

Amaranth (bledo). *Amaranthus paniculatus* L.? (Mc); *A. p.* (R); *A. retoplexus* L. (M).

Amate. *Ficus* sp. (W, M); *F. pluribus* (V); *F. tecolutensis*? (R).

Avocado (aguacate). *Persea americana* Mill. (W, Mc); *P. gratisima* Gatum (V); *P. gratisima* Gaerth (M).

Ayote. *Cucurbita pepo* L. (W, M, V).

Balsamito seed. Not identified.

Barrej'on. Not identified.

"Bird's claw" vine (šk'yeɋɟ'ikin). Not identified.

"Bitter sunflower" (girasol amargo). Not identified.

"Buzzard tree" (palo de zope). *Derris grandifolia* (R).

Cajete. *Achioma lagopas* (M).

Capulin. *Trema micrantha* (R, W); *Tila argentia* (M).

Castor tree (higuerillo). *Ricinus communis* L. (V, W, M).

Cayu. Not identified.

Chichicaste. *Urera baccifera* (L.) Graudichaud (W, Mc); *Urtica* sp. (M); *U. dioitica* (V).

Chichipate. *Sweetia panamensis* Bentham (W).

Chilacayote. *Cucurbita ficifolia* Bouché (W); *C. citrulus* (V).

Chilca. *Thevitia nerifolia* (M. V.).

Chipilín. *Crotalaria vitellina* (R); *C. guatimalensis* (V); *C. striata* (M); *C. longirostrata* (Mc); *C. l.* Hook & Arn. (W).

Chipoc. Not identified.

Choreque. Not identified.

Cidra. *Citrus medica* L. (Mc, M, V).

Cintula. Not identified.

Col. Some kind of cabbage called "salt cabbage" in the Indian language, not identified.

Coral tree (*palo de pito*). *Erythrina corallodendrum* L. (M, V, Mc); *E. rubrinervia* H. B. K. (W, Mc); *E. cristagallis* (V).

Cordoncillo. *Piper* sp. (W); *P. angustipolium* Ruiz y Pav. (M); *P.* Rus & Paw (V); *P. longium* (V).

Coriander (culantro). *Coriandrum sativum* L. (W, M).

Coyol, *Acrocomia vinifera* Oersted (Mc, W, M); *A. mexicana* (R); *A. scherocarpa* (V).

Cross-sapodilla (injerto). *Calocarpum viride* Pittier (Mc).

Cuajilote. *Parmentiera adulis* (R); *P. adulis* D. C. (M).

Cuchín. Not identified.

Custard-apple (anona). *Annona cherimola* (Mc); *A. diversifolia* Safford (W); *A. reticulata* (M, V); *A. squamosa* (R).

"Deer's tongue" (lengua de venado). *Scolopendrium officinalis* (R).

Easter flower (flor de pascua). *Euphorbia pulcherrima* (V).

Elder tree (sanco). Several varieties known by this name locally.

"Flower of death" (flor de muerte). *Tajetes erecta* L. (M); *T. patula doble* (V).

Granadilla. *Passiflora ligularis* (Mc, M, W); *P. edulis* (V); *Brya specialis* (M, V).

Guachipilín. *Pithecolobrium albicans* (M); *Dyphysa bobinoides* (M).

Guave (guayaba). *Psidium guajava* L. (Mc, M); *P. pomiferum* (V); *P. cerstedianum* Berg (W).

Huis. *Solanum capense* (V).

Huskcherry (miltomate). *Physalis* sp. (W, Mc); McBryde calls the species found in Guatemala uncertain, but suggests *pubescens* L.

Ilamo. *Almus acuminata* (R).

Indigo (jiquilite). *Indigofera suffruticosa* Miller (W,Mc); *I. añil* L. (M): *Jacobina tintoria* (V).

Jabillo. *Hura polyandra* Baillon (W); *H. Crepitans* L. (M,V).

Laurel (Laurel). *Litsea glaucense* (R); *Nectandria* sp. (M).

Lima. *Citrus limetta* Risso (Mc).

"Lime tea" (té de limón). *Andropogan citratus* (V,M); *Cymbogogan c.* (DC) Stamf (W); *C. nardus* (L) Rendle (Mc).

"Little broom" (escobilla). *Sida rhombifolia* (M,V).

Madrone (palo de jiote). *Busera mexicana* (V); *B. simaruba* (L.) Sarg. (W).

Maguey (maguey). *Furcraea* sp. (M,Mc,R); *agave* sp. (Mc). McBryde mentions several species of *Agave*.

Maicena. Not identified.

Melocoton. *Sicana odorifera* (Vell.) Naudin (Mc,W).

Membrillo. *Cydonia oblonga* Miller (W); *C. vulgaris* Pers. (M).

Metabel. Not identified.

Mint (hierba buena). *Mentha citrata* Ehrhart (W); *M. virides* L. (M,V).

"Mother of Maize" (madre de maiz). *Ustilago maydis?* (R).

"Mouse ear" vine (račikinčoy). Not identified.

"Mouth of the dragon" (boca de dragón). *Lamourouxia visciosa* (V).

"Mulberry herb" (hierba mora). *Solanum nigrum* (M,V).

Nance. *Brysonima crassifolia* L. (Mc,W): *B. c.* HB & K (M); *B. cantifolia* HB & K (M,V).

Nogal. *Jugland pyriformis* Liebermann (W); *J. regia* (V,M); *J. ṇigra* (V,M).

Oak (encino, roble). A number of species.

Orégano. *Origanum vulgare* L. (M,W).

Pacaya. *Chamaedorea* sp. (W,V); *C. graminifolia* Wendland (Mc); *C. g.* Wendalandia & Schiedeana (Mc); *C. bifurcata* (M).

Pataxte. *Theobromo bicolor* (M); *T. b.* Hum. & Boupl. (W).

Paterna. *Inga* sp. (W): *I. spectabilis* (V).

Pega pega. *Turenthia lappacea; Desmodium incinatum* (M).

Pepino. *Solanum muricatum* Aiton (Mc). This is the Spanish word for cucumber, but it is not the cucumber.

Pepitoria. *Cucurbita pepo* L. (W).

Pimienta gorda. *Pimenta officinalis* Lindley (W).

Prickly pear (tuna). *Opuntia* sp. (Mc); *O. dejecta* (V); *O. Monocantha* (V); *Platyopuntia* (Mc).

Purslane (verdolaga). *Portulaca campestre* (R); *P.* sp. (M); *P. parviflora* (V).

Pus (p'us). Not identified.

Queché. q'etʃe'. Not identified.

"Rose-apple" (manzana rosa). *Eugenia jambos* L. Sp. Pl. (Mc,V); *Jambosa vulgaris* (M).

Rosemary (romero). *Rosmarinus officinales* L. (W,M,V).

Rue (ruda). *Ruta chalepensis* L. (W); *R. graveolens* L. (V,M).

Sabagasta. *Aristida scabra* (R).

Sajoc (saxok). Not identified.

Sapodilla (zapote). *Achras zapote* (M); *Lacuma mammosa* (V); *L. m.* Gaertn. (M); *Calocarpum mammosum* (L.) Pierre (W).

Sedge (tule). *Typha latifolia* (R); *Cyperus canus* Preal (W).

Silk oak (gravilea). *Gravillea robusta* (V); *G. r.* Cunn (Mc).

"Skunk plant" (hierba de zorro). *Croton dioicus* (R).

Soapseed tree (jaboncillo). *Sapindus saponaria* L. (M, V,W).

Spanish plum (jocote). *Spondias purpurea* L. Sp. Pl. (Mc, W, M, V).

"Sunflower of the rocks" (giransol de la piedra). Not identified.

"Sweatbath plant" (hierba de temazcal). *Rhus terebinthifolia* (R).

Sweet cassava (yuca). *Manihot esculenta* Crantz (W); *M. dulcis* (Crmel.) Pax (Mc).

Sweetpotato (camote). *Ipomea batatas* (Mc).

Tamarisk shrub (taray). *Eysenhareitia adenostylis* (R); *Mimosa* sp. (M); *Caesalpina bonducella* (M).

Taxisco. *Perymenium turckheimu* (V); *P. t.* Vatke (M).

Toronja. *Citrus decumina* (R).

Tziquinay (ǧ'ikinay). Not identified.

Vegetable pear (güisquil). *Sechium edule* Swartz (W, M, V).

White sapodilla (matasano). *Casimiroa edulis* (Mc).

"White soap" (saqčupaq). Not identified.

Willow (sauce). *Salix* sp. (M); *S. alba* (M).

Yucca tree (izote). *Yucca guatemalensis* (R); *Y. elephantipes* Regel (W); *Y. gloriosa* (V, M).

Zacatinta. *Fuchsia parviflora* (R); *Jacobina tinctoria* Hemls. (M).

ANIMALS

Armadillo (Armado). *Tatusian novencienta* (M, V).

Buzzard (zopilote.) *Catharista atrata,* Lawr. (M, V).

Coati (pizote). *Nasia nasica* L. (M, V); *Nasua narica* (Zoo).

Coxpin (koʃpin). An unidentified bee or wasp.

Coyote (coyote). *Canis letrans,* Say (M, V).

Deer (venado). *Cariacus virginianus* Brok (M, V).

Grackle (sanate). *Quiscalus macrurus,* Scl (P, M, V).

"Honey-bear" (oso colmenero). *Myrmecophaga jubata M. tetradactyla* Sim.

Hummingbird (gorrión). Many species.

"Lazy bird" (pájaro haragán). Not identified.

Mojarra. *Cichlasoma guttulatum,* Gunther (Mc, P).

Opossum (tecuacín.) *Didelphys virginiana,* Kn. (M, V, P).

Porcupine (puerco espín). *Syntherés puntacta* (M, V).

Rabbit (conejo). *Lepus palustris* (M, V).

Raccoon (mapache). *Procyon lotor* (P, zoo); *P. l.* Allen (M, V).

Skunk (zorillo). *Mephitis mephítica,* Baird (M, V); *M. putorius,* Cones (V); *Conepatus mapurito,* Cones (V).

Taltuza. *Geomys hispidus* (M, V, P); *G. mexicanus* (P).

Tepescuintle. *Caelogenys paca,* Sim (M, V); *C. p.* (zoo); *Geomys p.* (P).

Weasel (comadreja). *Mustela brasiliensis,* Sew. (M, W).

Widgeon (gallareta). *Mareca americana,* Scl. (M, V).

Wildcat (gato de monte). *Vulpes virginianus,* Baird (M, V, zoo).

LITERATURE CITED

BUNZEL, RUTH L.
n. d. Chichicastenango. MS. (1938).

CARNEGIE INSTITUTION OF WASHINGTON.
1940. Maize cultivation in northwestern Guatemala. Compiled . . . from data collected in the field by Raymond Stadelman. Publ. No. 523, Contr. 33, pp. 83–266.
1944. Yearbook No. 43 (1943–44).

EL IMPARCIAL.
1937. Guatemala.

GOUBAUD CARRERA, ANTONIO.
1946. Estudio de la alimentación de Guatemala. Bol. Inst. Indigenista Nacional, I, Nos. 2–3, pp. 31–45. Guatemala.

GUATEMALA.
n. d. Constitution of Guatemala. Guatemala.
1924. 4° Censo de la Republica de Guatemala (1921). Guatemala.
1927. Leyes vigentes. Guatemala
1937. Memoria de las labores del ejecutivo en el ramo de agricultura (1936). Guatemala.
1938. Memoria de las labores del ejecutivo en el ramo de agricultura (1937). Guatemala.
1939. Memoria de las labores del ejecutivo en el ramo de agricultura (1938). Guatemala.
1939 a. Memoria de las labores del ejecutivo en el ramo de hacienda y crédito público (1938). Guatemala.
1940. Memoria de las labores del ejecutivo en el ramo de hacienda y crédito público (1939). Guatemala.
1941. Memoria de las del ejecutivo en el ramo de hacienda y crédito pública (1940). Guatemala.
1942. 5° Censo de la República de Guatemala (1940).

JONES, CHESTER LLOYD.
1940. Guatemala past and present. Minneapolis.

KNIGHT, F. H.
1941. Anthropology and economics. Journ. Political Economy, vol. 49, pp. 247–268. Chicago.

LANGE, OSCAR.
1945–46. The scope and method of economics. Rev. Economic Studies, vol. 13 (1), No. 33. London.

MAUDSLAY, MRS. ANNE CARRY (MORRIS), and MAUDSLAY, ALFRED PERCIVAL.
1899. A glimpse at Guatemala, and some notes on the ancient monuments of Central America. London.

MCBRYDE, FELIX WEBSTER.
1933. Sololá: A Guatemalan town and Cakchiquel market-center . . . Tulane Univ., Middle Amer. Res. Ser., Publ. No. 5, pp. 45–152. New Orleans.
1936. Map of Lake Atitlán region of Guatemala.

1947. Cultural and historical geography of Southwest Guatemala. Smithsonian Inst., Inst. Soc. Anthrop. Publ. No. 4.

MEJIA, J. V.
1927. Geografía de la República de Guatemala. 2d ed. Guatemala.

MÉNDEZ, ROSENDO P.
1927. Leyes vigentes. Guatemala.

NATIONAL RESEARCH COUNCIL. COMMITTEE ON LATIN AMERICAN ANTHROPOLOGY.
1949. Research needs in the field of modern Latin American culture. Amer. Anthrop., vol. 51, No. 1, pp. 149–154.

O'NEALE, LILA M.
1945. Textiles of Highland Guatemala. Carnegie Inst. Wash. Publ. No. 567.

REDFIELD, ROBERT, and VILLA R., ALFONSO.
1934. Chan Kom, a Maya village. Carnegie Inst. Wash. Publ. No. 448.
1939. Notes on the ethnography of Tzeltal communities of Chiapas. I. Carnegie Inst. Washington Publ. No. 509, pp. [105]–119.

ROSALES, JUAN DE DIOS.
1949. Notes on San Pedro la Laguna. Microfilm Collection of Manuscripts on Middle American Cultural Anthropology, No. 25. Chicago.

SMITH, ADAM.
1937. Inquiry into the nature and causes of the wealth of nations. New York, Modern Library.

STADELMAN, RAYMOND. See CARNEGIE INSTITUTION OF WASHINGTON.

STIEBELING, HAZEL KATHERINE, and PHIPARD, ESTHER F.
1939. Diets of families of employed wage earners and clerical workers in cities. U. S. Dept. Agric., Circ. 507.

TAX, SOL.
1937. The municipios of the midwestern highlands of Guatemala. Amer. Anthrop., vol. 39, pp. 423–444.
1941. World view and social relations in Guatemala. Amer. Anthrop. vol. 43, pp. 27–42.
1942. Ethnic relations in Guatemala. América Indígena, vol. 2, No. 4, pp. 43–48. Mexico.
1950. Panajachel: Field notes. Microfilm Collection of Manuscripts on Middle American Cultural Anthropology, No. 29. Chicago.

VÁZQUEZ, FRANCISCO.
1937. Crónica de la provincia del santísimo nombre de Jesús de Guatemala. 2d ed. Guatemala.

VILLACORTA, CALDERON JOSÉ ANTONIO.
  1926. Monografía del Departamento de Guatemala. Guatemala.

WAGLEY, CHARLES.
  1941. The economics of a Guatemalan village. American Anthropological Association, Mem. 58.

WAUCHOPE, ROBERT.
  1938. Modern Maya houses, a study of their archaeological significance. Carnegie Inst. Washington Publ. No. 502.

WEBER, MAX.
  1947. The theory of social and economic organization. London.

WISDOM, CHARLES.
  1940. The Chorti Indians of Guatemala. (Addenda not published.) Chicago.

GENERAL INDEX [1]

Adobe making, 93, 96, 134, 145, 147
Agriculture, temperate, 2
    tropical, 1–2
    See also Crops.
Agua Escondida, 62, 139
Alta Vera Paz, 144 fn.
Animals, *see* Domesticated animals; Fauna, wild.
Artisans, 96, 97, 121, 134, 183, 191, 194
    See also Adobe-maker; Carpenter; Mason.
Atiteco, 31, 96, 122, 128
    Atitecos, 6 fn., 135, 136 fn., 140, 152
Atitlán, 1, 2, 6 fn., 11, 14, 30, 31, 96, 106, 119, 123, 126, 127, 151, 159, 160, 185

Baker, 96, 134, 164, 175
Balance of payments, 183–184
Baptism, 178
Barbering, 96, 181
Bargaining, 136, 136 fn.
Beliefs, about animals, 32
    as distinct from "foreign" Indians, ill omens, 32
    impeding economic judgment, 16
    on electricity, 20
    toward nature, 29
    toward supernatural, 29, 130
Births, 87, 98, 178
    rate of, 6
Blacksmith, 23, 27, 134
Bloodletter, 95, 98
Bunzel, Ruth, 137
Butcher, 22–23, 96, 119, 122 fn., 123 fn., 134, 142, 164, 175, 191
Buying for consumption, 133–136

Cabrera, Manuel Estrada, President, 106
Canoe, manufacture of, 31
    renting, 96, 97
    transportation, 126, 127
    use in hunting, 32
Cantel, 20, 26
Capitalism, ix, 13 fn.
Caponizer, 95, 98, 164
Carnegie Institution of Washington, x, 163
Carpenter, 27, 95, 96, 134, 145, 146, 175
Ceremonies, 177–181
    governmental, 86, 177
    religious, 86
    See also Fiestas; Births; Funerals; Harvesting rites.
Cerro de Oro, 105, 133 fn., 136, 139
Chiapas, 8
Chicacao, 2, 123, 127
Chichicastenango, 6 fn., 11, 14, 35, 100 fn., 107, 119 fn., 122, 123, 133, 135, 136, 144 fn., 145, 150, 151, 158, 160, 185, 206–207
    Maxeño, 6 fn., 133 fn., 135, 136
Children, providing for, 206
    See also Labor, division of.
Chimente, 25 fn., 26
Church, 57, 83, 85, 103, 178, 204
Classes, economic, 181, 184, 190
    social, 7, 206–207
    See also Wealth groups.
Climate, 4, 29–30

Clothing, 30, 136, 205
    cost, 153–154, 184
        See also table 63, 161–163.
    manufacture, 93–94, 133, 151–154
    men's, 150–151
    women's, 151
    See also Costumes.
Community service, 86, 103, 181
    See also Political-religious hierarchy; Officials.
Comparison with neighboring communities, 11
Competition, ix, 15, 19, 27–28
    effect on prices, 137, 186
    in clothing, 202
    in selling, 133 fn.
Concepción, 99, 107, 123, 127, 133, 145, 152, 159, 160, 163, 186
    Concepcioñeros, 133 fn., 145, 163
Consumer goods, 133–154
    See also Commodity index, Appendix 2, 210–216.
Contractors, 96
    See also Adobe-making; Carpenter; Mason.
Costs, agricultural, 109–117
    animal husbandry, 117–121
    clothing 153–154, 160–163
    food, 168–169, 174
    houses, 146–147
Costumes, distinction from Ladinos and "foreign" Indians, 8
    foreign, 160
    men's and boys', 158–159
    wealth differences, 187–188
    women's and girls', 159
Credit, ix, 13–14
    See also Land, pawned.
Crops, combinations, 46–47
    determination of choice, 128, 129
    innovations, 128, 130–131, 186
    value, 184
    yield, beans, squash, 52, 113
        coffee, 56, 131
        corn, 49–52, 108–110
        garlic, 54, 113
        herbs, 55
        measuring, 190
        onions, 53–54, 110–112, 130
        pepinos, 114, 131
        possibilities of increasing, 128
        tablón, 110–116
            fruit, 56, 115
            vegetables, 114
        tubers, 55, 114
Cubulco, 135
Cult of the Saints, 177
Curers, 95, 96, 98, 180, 195
    curing ritual, 177

Dances, 163, 177, 183
Death, 178–180, 193
    mortality rates, 6, 28, 30
Diet, 9 fn., 24, 28, 129, 163–174, 185, 200–201
Domestic production, *see* Houses, building; Furniture; Clothing, manufacture.
Domestic servants, 99, 101 fn.
Domesticated animals, pre-Conquest, 22
    animal husbandry, 93, 117–121
    value of produce, 108, 131, 142, 190–191
        See also Commodity index, Appendix 2, 210–216.
    for fertilizer, 128

[1] The final manuscript was prepared, proof read, and index made with the excellent assistance of Mrs. June Nash, whose intelligence, patience, care, and industry are here gratefully acknowledged.